GANGLAND

London's Underworld

D1331715

GANGLAND

London's Underworld

James Morton

WARNER BOOKS

A *Warner* Book

First published in the United Kingdom
in 1992 by Little, Brown and Company

This edition published by Warner in 1993
Reprinted 1993 (twice),1994 (three times), 1995 (twice), 1996,
1997, 1998, 1999, 2000, 2001

A CIP catalogue record for this book is
available from the British Library.

ISBN 0 7515 0393 2

Printed in England by Clays Ltd, St Ives plc

Warner Books
A Division of
Little, Brown and Company (UK)
Brettenham House
Lancaster Place
London WC2E 7EN

www.littlebrown.co.uk

Contents

Introduction		ix
1	The Early Years	1
2	After the War	33
3	The Years Between	69
4	The Richardson Brothers	95
5	The Rise and Fall of the Firm	131
6	The Dixons and the Tibbses	169
7	Prostitution and Pornography	185
8	Robbers and Robberies	229
9	Supergrasses	271
10	Helpers and Hinderers	291
11	The Killers and the Killed	325
12	The Last Decade	375
And then . . . ?		427
Bibliography		433
Index		439

Photograph Credits

For Dock Bateson with love

Introduction

On 8 March 1882 C. Vincent at Scotland Yard wrote in beautiful copperplate to the Clerk of Arraigns at the Old Bailey:

> I have to request that you will have the goodness to furnish me with copies of Mr Justice Hawkins' observations as to the prevalency of organized bands of roughs in the metropolis, as expressed by him at the trial of Galliers and Casey for manslaughter at the Central Criminal Court on the 4th inst and Kennedy and others for riot at Hackney.
>
> The Commander of the Metropolitan Police is particularly desirous of having that portion of the learned judge's remarks relating to the existence of 'gangs' on the streets and the alleged general lawlessness of the roughs. He would also like to have a copy of the evidence adduced in support of the statements that such bands do exist, and that on a certain occasion through the absence of police some roughs scoured the neighbourhood of Hoxton for three hours stabbing persons as they went.

The reply indicated that the Clerk of the Court had been present during the evidence and he confirmed the existence of two gangs, the Dover Road Fighting Gang and the Green Gate Gang. Thomas Galliers and James Casey together with some twenty others had encountered Frederick Williams and Arthur Thompson from the Dover Road boys and had asked where they came from. On being told, they said 'we pay [meaning hit] the Lambeth chaps' and 'trashed them with square brass-buckled belts'. Williams died from his injuries.

Nearly 110 years later, on 23 October 1991, the Kray twins' birthday, the Labour MP turned television presenter, Robert Kilroy-Silk, hosted a programme devoted to crime and posed the question whether things were better, for the public, when the so called gangs or firms of the 1960s ran various parts of London as their own small empires.

This book is an informal history of what happened between those two events. It is intended only as that and not as a sociological explanation of how gangs rise and fall, or of their effects on the community.

But were things better in the days of the gangs? The answer would be no so far as the Dover Road Gang was concerned. There is, however, some evidence that throughout the century, alongside their other less attractive habits, powerful families both north and south of the Thames have provided rudimentary community policing in their areas with the consensus of the public.

Anyway what is a gang? 'I don't act for gangs,' one North London solicitor told me recently, 'I act for families.' And if those families find they need the help of friends and acquaintances, does that make them a gang? Surely gangs are for little boys giving secret passwords and meeting in the same shed every Thursday? Gangs are for American television films, says Reggie Kray. They are not for London and the rest of the country.

I think that is a matter of semantics. A gang does not

necessarily maintain the paid-up subscription requirement and list of members that the Garrick does. It is nevertheless a clearly recognizable if floating body with the equivalent of a chairman, members of the board, officers of the club and ordinary members who come and go for a variety of reasons. Some are in prison, some die, some go to another club as Garrick members might move to the Savile. But for a period of time they are members in one form or another.

'Gangsters', from the turn-of-the-century East End villain Arthur Harding onwards, have been keen to paint the picture of a loose association of helpful friends rather than a gang. It may be that the word itself and its connotations of organization brought heavier punishment from the judge. Nearly half a century later Eddie Richardson supported that contention. The friends of the Haward brothers who fought with him one fateful night in Mr Smith's Club were not a gang. They were a 'group'. 'In the villain business they are not called gangs,' wrote Maurice O'Mahoney. On another occasion, 'Arrangements were made to meet a south London team.'[1]

In the first part of the book I have tried to present a more or less chronological history of the various families and their friends who have exerted both a benevolent and malevolent presence in their communities. Although some of the gangs have indulged in pimping and trafficking in women, this is more of a sideline than anything else. These activities have never been a British sport; it is said that we, as a nation, lack the temperament. Accordingly prostitution and pornography are dealt with as separate if integral subjects in a chapter on Soho. Armed robbers too earn a separate chapter: although they have generally drawn their teams from one

---

[1] O'Mahoney, M (1978) *King Squealer*, p. 27. London, W. H. Allen.

area of London or the country, since the mid-1960s they have been a more amorphous body and many have operated independently of the families. The helpers and hinderers, wives, friends, go-betweens, solicitors and, of course, the police who regularly play a most ambiguous role are all also given a separate chapter. At the end there is an account of the current state of play and of the players who are still left in the game, those who have been sent off the field and, in some cases, those who have been buried under the grandstands.

Some people, I suspect, and many, I certainly hope, will buy the book in the anticipation that their names will appear. Several, I am afraid, will be disappointed. I have not dealt in detail with the question of art robberies or forgeries, except for the fatal shooting in 1986 at the Sir John Soane's Museum in London.

Some things and some people have had to be left out. For example, I have not given a chapter to those perennial criminal sports of horse- and dog-doping. With few exceptions there has been no hard evidence that the dopers have been more than fringe members of the underworld, although one did have the distinction of being sentenced in a horse-doping trial before appearing in a dog-doping case two years later. Perhaps he was weaning himself from the heroin of horses by way of the methadone of greyhounds.

Over the years there have, of course, been great scandals, such as cutting the blower at Bath and ringing, doping and fixing cases. Eleven racehorse trainers were disqualified in the years 1948–50 and in 1955, and being stood down as a trainer at a dog track is even today an occupational hazard. Everyone has heard stories of dogs not exercised the night before the race or who have run with elastic bands round their paws, but these have been small-time operations.

Early in my career as a criminal lawyer I was involved in the defence of a greyhound trainer. His weekly earnings and outgoings were totted up and showed a horrible deficit. 'How do you survive?' he was asked. 'Well sir, once a fortnight, one of them dogs runs just for me,' he replied.

In the first of the major horse-doping cases of the 1960s, the police interviewed Bertie 'Bandy' Rogers at stables in Oxfordshire. He shot himself that night and so missed the trial at Gloucester Assizes when a former jockey was found guilty of attempting to dope a horse and, despite the pleas of Sir Gordon Richards, received an eighteen-month sentence.

Three years later in 1963, at Lewes Assizes, in what was perhaps the last of the great horse-doping trials, William Roper, as ringleader, received three years for conspiracy to dope horses. A pretty Swiss girl had toured stables on the pretext of buying a horse and of the twenty-one stables she had visited, twelve favourites had been got at. She received a sentence of twelve months' imprisonment but her punishment was doubtless more tolerable since she had taken the precaution of selling her story to a Sunday newspaper to be published on her conviction. Another defendant, Edward Smith, known as the Witch Doctor because of the potions he carried with him, had unfortunately fallen to his death from a landing in Lewes Prison on the eve of the trial and so missed the proceedings. Can his name have had any possible connection with the Catford club where the Richardsons had their shoot-out with the Haywards and Hennesseys, or is it sheer coincidence?

In more recent years a number of betting coups and ringers have been run, one of the more celebrated being when the three-year-old Flockton Grey had run in a two-year-old race at Stockton and, not unsurprisingly, won by a considerable margin. These enterprises, however, have in general been the work of individuals, such as the Irish gentlemen who on their arrest in a betting coup said, 'We were just out for some Saturday afternoon's crack.'

So far as dog-doping is concerned there has been a steady stream of cases, including one in 1954 when a Harley Street doctor received fifteen months for his part in a conspiracy. His mitigation was that he only functioned at flapping, or unlicensed, tracks rather than at the real thing. In 1965 Peter Hubbard was named by the *People* as King of the Dog Dopers – in fact over the years, depending on which newspaper printed the article, there have been several claimants holding that title concurrently. Hubbard later went into pirate videoing and pornography as a career, along with one of his co-defendants, although he always maintained his interest in racing. At the time of his death in the late 1980s he was a close friend of a prominent Newmarket trainer.

As for boxing, that arena beloved by the fraternity, again there is no evidence of systematic interference. There have been suggestions over the years that the Sabinis and Jack Spot took a particularly close and unhealthy interest in some contests, whilst Buller Ward recounts the sad tale of Tony Mella who was being groomed for stardom with the assistance of his opponents. He also tells of a couple of title fights in which Dai Dower and John L. Gardner faced men who, unbeknownst to the champions, had been paid to take an early shower. But certainly there have never been any underworld figures taking any kind of control of the sport.

An informal history of this nature is bound to be selective, particularly in the field of armed robbery and drug smuggling, where some former and current participants will, perhaps rightly, believe that their efforts were financially or technically superior to the ones I have recorded. I can only apologize to them. If they care to send me details of their exploits I will carefully consider them for any future edition. Nor have I tried to deal with crimes which went to finance politics in any shape or form. Therefore the accounts of money obtained through bank robberies and protection of bookmakers at dog tracks, to be channelled back to the IRA, go unrecorded. Profit and not politics has been the keyword.

Of course much of this book is oral history and the narrators of the tales may not be wholly reliable. Quite genuinely their memories will have faded but also there are axes to grind, scores to be settled, no longer with knives but in print, proving yet again that the pen is mightier than the sword. It has also to be said that some of the reporting in the old days, as since, was not aimed at a sociological study but at the number of copies of the newspapers or magazines to be sold. In their time Hill and Spot were just as much sought after for quotations, gossip pieces and their accounts of life as the Krays and, to a lesser extent, the Richardsons. One of the major causes of the break-up of the Spot–Hill partnership was their rivalry over the publication of their respective memoirs. Wearing one of his less attractive hats, the newspaper reporter Duncan Webb was used by Hill, whose autobiography he ghosted, to discredit and embarrass Spot. Nevertheless, I have tried to check one recollection against another before setting it down.

Many books have been written on specific cases, some of which are more accurate than others. Indeed most police officers who published their memoirs have been keen, no doubt at the insistence of their publishers, to emphasize their involvement in cases in which they had only a peripheral part. A good example appears in *Fabian of the Yard*, where Robert Fabian ends his account of the murder of Berthier with his return to his wife and the news that he had solved his first murder case. A perusal of the committal papers shows that his part was confined to producing a plan of the club where the murder took place.

I have relied in particular on some of the seminal accounts of the London gangs, such as Piers Paul Read's *The Train Robbers*, John Pearson's *The Profession of Violence* and Robert Parker's *Rough Justice*, for, respectively, aspects of the Great Train Robbery, the lives of the Kray twins and of the Richardson family and friends. I have, of course, consulted the memoirs of Charles Richardson and all those of the Kray brothers. In respect of the supergrass era, *Scotland Yard's Cocaine Connection* by Andrew Jennings, Paul Lashmar and Vyv Simpson, as well as *Lundy* by Martin Short, have been invaluable.

My thanks go in strictly alphabetical order to Michael Beckman, Dave Brady, Carl Chinn, for his introduction to the world of betting and the Sabini family, Peter Donnelly, Tony Edwards, Jeremy Fordham for allowing me to use his aunt Peta Fordham's papers, John Frost, Jeffrey Gordon, Dominique Harvie, Mrs G. Houghton-Jones, Bill Ilsley, Ralph Haeems, Frances Hegarty, Brian Hilliard, John Kay, Peter Kelly, Cal McCrystal, Bernard Perkoff, Sid Rae, Nipper and Pat Read, Robert Roscoe, Linda Silverman for the picture research, Harry Stevens, Etta Tasiemka for endless patience in letting me use her cuttings service, Richard Whittington-Egan, and the staff of the Lord Chancellor's department, Public Records Office, Hendon Public Library and the Law Society's library, plus the many others who have made a contribution but who, for various reasons, did not wish to be acknowledged personally. Obviously without them this book would have been even more imperfect. Such errors as there are are mine alone.

Finally, I could not possibly have written this book without the unfailing help and support of Dock Bateson.

1

The Early
Years

Nowadays, the consensus of opinion among lawyers, police and those of the villains' friends who are still alive and able to think straight is that in the 1940s and 1950s Billy Hill and Jack Spot between them were the first to control the twentieth-century London underworld to any great extent. They were not. They were only following in the long, if not honourable, line of more disorganized protection men, minders, bully-boys and racketeers, thieves, hitmen and hardmen, who went before them in such districts of London as Clerkenwell, Elephant and Castle, Hoxton, the Angel and Notting Hill, and who eventually gravitated in the 1920s to Soho and Mayfair where the pickings were that much bigger. Nor seemingly were Spot and Hill any more violent than their predecessors.

In his autobiography *Detective Days*, published in 1931, Frederick Wensley, former Commander of Scotland Yard who arrested the Clapham Common murderer, Steinie Morrison, wrote:

> Any reader of the daily papers these days might come to the conclusion that Chicago is the only place in which organized bands of desperate criminals ever existed. The public have a short

memory. It is not so very long ago that we, in the East End and some other districts of London, were engaged in stamping out groups of criminals, many of whom carried arms, and who waged a sort of warfare among themselves and against the public.

In the early part of the century there was one gang of this class who had established a real reign of terror among certain people in the East End.

The victims were those same people who are always the victims.

In the main, however, the victims were persons who for some reason or another were a little shy of bringing their troubles to the notice of the police. Keepers of shady restaurants, runners of gambling dens, landlords of houses of resort, street bookmakers and other people on the fringe of the underworld were among those peculiarly open to trouble.

And of the others:

Sometimes small tradesmen were offered 'protection' against other gangs at a price. If they did not take kindly to this blackmail all sorts of unpleasant things were liable to happen to them. . . . Persons who had resisted their extortions had been brutally assaulted, their premises wrecked – in one case an attempt to burn down a building had been made – and any portable property stolen.

The East End gang which operated around the turn of the century was the forty-strong pack, the Bessarabians, from the predominantly Russian–Jewish Whitechapel quarter.

The Russian Jews with their ingrained terror of the police would, in practically every case, rather put up with the gangs than risk the consequences of complaining to the police. . . . we were continually having to let cases drop through lack of evidence.

They levied a protection toll on timid alien shopkeepers, proprietors of coffee-stalls and so on. The faintest shadow of protest on their part at this blackmail and the gang descended on them in force armed with guns, knives and such weapons as broken bottles.[1]

In *Lost London* former Detective Sergeant B. Leeson gave another example of their methods:

Lists of people to be blackmailed were drawn up by the gangsters, and amongst these, prospective brides provided the happiest and most productive results. A few days before the wedding ceremony a gangster would approach the bride's parents and threaten to expose all sorts of imaginary indiscretions of which their daughter had been guilty if their silence was not bought. The victims, fearful of the scandal that might ensue, invariably paid up.[2]

The chief rivals of the Bessarabians were the Odessians, so called because the proprietor of a restaurant called the Odessa took the gang on. Weinstein, also known as Kikal, refused to pay protection money and according to Leeson fought them off with an iron bar when they came to demand their wages. The rival gang, which did not include Weinstein, took his restaurant's

---

[1] G.W. Cornish, *Cornish of the Yard*, p. 4.
[2] B. Leeson, *Lost London*, p. 147.

name as a tribute to his courage.

For the next year or so there were the usual gang skirmishes. The Odessians threatened to cut off the ears of a leading Bessarabian named Perkoff. He was lured into an alley and one ear was removed before the local police arrived. In return a coffee-stall under the protection of the Odessians was attacked.

The end of the Bessarabians came in October 1902 following an attack by them on a sing-song in the York Minster, a public house in Philpot Street off the Commercial Road where a number of Odessians were thought to be. The Bessarabians attacked indiscriminately, slashing and stabbing. One man, sometimes called Brodovich but also known as Kaufmann, was stabbed to death.

In the ensuing confusion the public was less discreet than usual and names were named. As a result a Bessarabian leader, Max Moses, who boxed as Kid McCoy and who had fought at the old Wonderland Arena in Whitechapel, was sentenced to ten years' penal servitude following a conviction for manslaughter. He had been thought to have had championship potential.

With the leaders in custody the local population began to name more names. Members of both gangs were arrested and convicted on a variety of charges, including another of the leaders, Samuel Oreman, who received five years' penal servitude. With their leaders in prison the gang disintegrated. Meanwhile the police chipped away at the Odessians. Many went to America, where they joined forces with the local crooks. One known as 'Tilly the burglar' is said to have become a Chicago policeman.[3] It is interesting to note that one of the current terrors of New York is the so-called Russian Mafia.

[3] According to Leeson, McCoy also went to America on his release and became a successful businessman.

After the convictions following the York Minster affray remnants of both the Odessians and the Bessarabians lingered on. Even before them, however, the Blind Beggar gang, a team of skilled pickpockets who were not averse to roughing up their victims if they complained, had flourished. They took their name from the Blind Beggar public house, later to become famous as the scene of the Cornell shooting by Ronnie Kray. One story about them concerns an attack on a travelling salesman by a man named Wallis who, acquitted of murder, is said to have been driven back from the Old Bailey in triumph in a phaeton drawn by a pair of bays. This whole story, like so many stories of the gangs, is probably apocryphal and seems based on the true story of Paul Vaughan, who went under the name of Ellis. He was charged with manslaughter following the death in 1891 of Frederick Klein, a perfectly respectable man who with his wife had been subjected to a series of racial taunts. There is no record of Vaughan's acquittal and the gang broke up.[4]

Another team, the Strutton Ground Mob from Westminster, which ran protection rackets there, endeavoured unsuccessfully to move on the stall-holders in Petticoat Lane, a manoeuvre regarded by local villains as requiring swift and violent reprisals. But it seems that after the rule of the Odessians and the Bessarabians, for a short time at any rate, properly organized crime in the East End died away.

An early trick was coining, regarded by the police as a particularly despicable crime because, once again, it was the small shopkeeper who suffered. A coiner would make dud coins from plaster of paris moulds filled with heavy metal, which was poured through a hole in the mould called a 'git'. They were then sold in loads to

---

[4] In some accounts the Wallis story is attributed to a Tottenham-based gang.

'smashers' – men and, more often, women who would make a purchase requiring change from a half crown in a small shop. There would be a back-up man to keep a look-out for emergencies and only one half crown would be carried at a time. The reason for this was simple. To be in possession of one coined half crown was a misfortune which could happen to anyone. To have two or more was almost inexplicable to even the doziest of police officers and magistrates. It is interesting to note that many of the stolen credit cards and cheques about in the country today are proffered by women.

The gangs of the early years of the century seem to have been informal associations, something which has continued throughout the century. One, led by the engagingly named One-Eyed Charlie, hung out around Clark's coffee-shop near a railway arch in Brick Lane. According to Arthur Harding, a major villain of the time and later a chronicler of the East End, they do not seem to have acted much in concert. The leader, Charlie Walker, had tuberculosis and, true to his name, had lost an eye. Another of the gang, Edward Spencer, seems to have been the only 'complete all round criminal'. A well-built man who took a great pride in his appearance and was known as 'the Count', he was a thief and robber. Most of the others were pickpockets and tappers (beggars), van draggers (those who stole from vans), watch-chain or handbag snatchers, or petty blackmailers. The Walker team flourished, if that is the right word, until about 1904, when Charlie Walker died in a prison hospital, and re-formed some years later with younger men, among them Arthur Harding who became the leader. Although he did not regard his loose 'connection of youngsters' as a gang, it was a much more cohesive organization: 'We were a collection of small-time thieves ripe for any mischief. . . . We were ready to steal anything. Sometimes we went in couples, sometimes alone – it was only when there was a big fight on that we went as a gang.'[5]

It was their activities as a gang that earned them the name the Vendetta Mob. Associations were formed and broken. For example, the 'top man of the Jews', Edward Emmanuel, at one time had a liaison with Harding, then broke with him and joined up in the 1920s with the Sabinis, broke with them and later in the 1920s worked almost as an independent, being regarded as a great fixer with the police.

A more organized gang which came from the very rough area of Nile Street, a market street off Shepherdess Walk near the City Road police station, was the Titanic Mob, so called (in tribute to the liner) because they were always well dressed. Their specialities were robbery and pickpocketing at race meetings, railway stations and at the theatre, although they do not seem to have been averse to burglary either. They were highly regarded in the trade, partly because they only robbed men. Harding recalls that in 1908 his gang fought the Titanics following an argument over the protection of a coffee-stall in Brick Lane. The Titanics seem to have been the smarter of the teams.

What they done was crafty. They set a trap for us. They was well in with the police and directly the fight started the police were there. They got hold of us – including Cooper who had a loaded gun on him. It wasn't an offence to carry a gun, but we got a week's remand for causing an affray. I always had it in for them afterwards. I thought, 'You twisters – you always have the bogies on your side.'

Guns were easy to come by. Harding bought his first

[5] R. Samuel, *East End Underworld*, quoting Arthur Harding, p. 148.

in about 1904. A Royal Irish Constabulary revolver cost half a crown in Brick Lane, others four or five shillings. Harding and the Vendettas made a speciality of holding up spielers (illegal gambling clubs) and stealing the cash-box.

The Titanics, whose operational strength totalled around fifty, received a severe set-back in January 1922 when they were swooped on by the Flying Squad after a football match. A further raid took place a few days later when other members were found to be working the underground at Baker Street. Although only short sentences were handed out to members, from then on it would seem the team splintered and broke up.[6]

A succession of gangs from around Hoxton Street, with the generic name of the Hoxton Mob, operated over some forty years. One of the early versions had its headquarters at the Spread Eagle public house and, amongst other interests, they were into the protection of the local clubs and spielers such as Sunshine's, a card and billiard club in an alley off Shoreditch High Street. Harding is dismissive of them: 'They weren't such good-class thieves as the Titanics. They were more hooligans than thieves. . . . They worked ten- or twelve-handed. . . . They all finished up on the poor law, or cadging. Their leader died a pauper, whereas the leader of the Titanics ended up owning a dog-track.'

Another local gang leader of the time was Isaac Bogard, known as Darky the Coon. Although he was Jewish he was so dark-skinned that some references to him are as a black man. His mob was accordingly known as the Coons. Although when giving evidence he described himself as an actor, Bogard had a long criminal record which included a sentence of flogging for living off immoral earnings. He was certainly functioning

---

[6] S. Felstead, *The Underworld of London*, p. 41.

from the early years of the century until the 1920s, when he was then what was euphemistically described as the 'governor' of the market stall-holders in Petticoat Lane and Wentworth Street.

On 10 September 1911 about 8.30 in the evening he was set upon by Harding and the Vendetta Mob in the Blue Coat Boy in Bishopsgate. Bogard and his team ran a string of prostitutes in Whitechapel High Street and the quarrel had been about their ownership and the protection of a stall in Walthamstow Street market. Harding describes the fight: 'We did a lot of damage. The Coon had a face like the map of England. He was knocked about terrible. I hit him with a broken glass, made a terrible mess of his face. I knew I'd hurt him a lot, but not anything that could be serious.'[7]

Bogard, who in evidence at the subsequent trial said his throat had been cut, was taken to the London Hospital where after he had been stitched he discharged himself. But the next weekend there was more of the same for him. He was attacked once again by Harding and friends on the Sunday evening.

The outcome was dramatic. The police arrived and arrested Bogard and a man called George King on charges of disorderly conduct, for which they were to appear at Old Street Magistrates' Court on the Monday. Meanwhile Harding – then known as Tresidern – and his Vendettas met at Clark's the coffee-shop in Brick Lane to rally support against the Coons, who were about to commit the one really unforgivable crime: ask for police protection.

Accounts vary as to exactly what happened, as they do to the exact lead up to the battle and the arrest of Bogard. This is not surprising. Wensley, the police officer in the case, did not write his memoirs for another

---

[7] R. Samuel, *East End Underworld*, p. 154.

twenty years and Harding did not give his oral account of his life for another forty. Sir Charles Biron, the magistrate that day, wrote:

One morning two men were charged before me with disorderly conduct. It was a confusing case. The only thing clear was that there had been a disturbance in the street in which they had been involved. In the end I bound them both over to keep the peace. One of them applied to me for police protection on the ground that there was an armed body of men waiting outside the court to murder them. I told the man to sit down and affected to doubt the story, which indeed seemed incredible, but I had a very shrewd suspicion there was something in it. If there were, I felt it would be a mistake to do anything that would put the gang on its guard; accordingly I gave instructions to the police not to let either of the men leave the building and then sent for the Inspector of Police and saw him in my private room.

'Is this true?' I asked.

'Yes,' he said, 'it is. These two men used to belong to the Tresidern [Harding] gang. They turned respectable and left them. The gang regarded them as deserters and attacked them this morning in the street, which led to them being arrested for their own safety.'

It was an amazing story and seemed incredible.

'Do you mean to tell me,' I said, 'that a mob armed with revolvers is waiting outside this court to murder these two men?'

'Yes,' he said, 'that is so.'

Then I saw a great opportunity.

'Telephone at once to Scotland Yard,' I said, 'mention my name and state the facts. Tell them on my authority to send down an overwhelming force of armed police as soon as possible to deal with the situation and,' I added, 'impress upon them above everything not to make the mistake of failing to send a sufficiently strong force.'

This was done and Scotland Yard adopted my suggestion. I finished my work for the day and sat in my room awaiting the result. Just after five o'clock my Inspector came to me and said 'It's alright sir.' The police force had arrived.

Leading from the Old Street Police Court there were two not very wide roads. These the police had blocked with two hooded vans, filled with a force armed with revolvers. 'Now,' I said, 'let the two men out.' In a second, firing began and the police surrounded the gang.

There were five, all armed, and they were five of the most desperate characters in Hoxton led by their chief, Tresidern. In a few minutes they were all arrested and that day's work was the beginning of the end of what is hardly an exaggeration to call a reign of terror. Tresidern conducted the defence, which he did with considerable spirit. After his arrest his rooms were searched and Stones' *Justices Manual* was found carefully underlined and noted up. They were all committed for trial and in due course sentenced. The result was salutary. The Tresidern gang was finished, and the rival gang was a very inferior combination; the ordinary police methods together with firm administration of the law soon put them out of action, and after a few months the police had the criminal element fairly in hand.[8]

[8] Sir Charles Biron, *Without Prejudice*, p. 267.

According to the depositions taken on committal Wensley arrived at Old Street Court early in the afternoon and kept observation from an unmarked horse-drawn van, turning the horse from time to time to avoid suspicion. Bogard and King were taken to the entrance of the court at infrequent intervals and each time the crowd, led by Harding, rushed the steps. Harding had a revolver which he displayed quite openly. Eventually Wensley made his move on the crowd.

Both Wensley and Harding agree there were more arrests. Harding was taken at the court but the police foraged down Brick Lane and arrested another three people. The defendants were on remand for fourteen weeks and the police had trouble keeping a hold on their witnesses. Bogard thought better of giving evidence and a witness summons had to be issued.

Money was found from somewhere because Harding and the others were defended privately; Harding by the well-known barrister Eustace Fulton. It did him little good. In December 1911 the team appeared at the Old Bailey in front of Mr Justice Avory, who when passing sentence gave this little homily:

This riot was one of the most serious riots which can be dealt with by law, for it was a riot in which some, at least, of the accused were armed with revolvers, and it took place within the precincts of a court of justice.

I wish to say that the condition of things disclosed by the evidence – that a portion of London should be infested by a number of criminal ruffians, armed with loaded revolvers – ought not to be tolerated further, and if the existing law is not strong enough to put a stop to it some remedial legislation is necessary.

Harding received twenty-one months' hard labour to be followed by three years' penal servitude. His career was sketched by Wensley when giving the antecedents of the convicted men before sentence:

> When he was fourteen – he is now only twenty-five – he was bound over for disorderly conduct and being in possession of a revolver.
>
> At the age of seventeen he became a terror to Bethnal Green, and captained a band of desperadoes. In all he has been convicted fourteen times, yet he was one of the complaining witnesses before the Police Commission.
>
> He has developed into a cunning and plausible criminal of a dangerous type. I have never known him do any work.[9]

Wensley records that after Harding's sentence, peace returned to the East End – for a little while anyway.

But Harding and his Vendetta Boys were children compared to the well-organized and long-lived Sabinis, a gang which flourished for something like three decades. There is a tendency nowadays to dismiss them as 'only working the race-tracks' but there was very much more to them than that. Horse racing was certainly a major way into the protection business and organized crime. The Sabini brothers, of whom Charles (known as Darby, and said to be connected to the Mafia), Harryboy, Joseph, Fred and George can be counted as the leaders of the London underworld from the 1920s, are best remembered for that but they had other activities. They came from the Clerkenwell area of London near King's Cross, and they provided what was euphemistically called protection and what, in reality, was demanding money with menaces from the bookmakers.

---

[9] *Illustrated Police News*, 23 December 1911.

Darby Sabini was born in 1889 in Saffron Hill, known as Little Italy. Although the leader of the Sabinis, he was one of the youngest of the six brothers. His Italian father died when he was two and the family was raised by their Irish mother. He left school at the age of thirteen and joined Dan Sullivan, a boxing promoter and bookmaker. At one time it was thought he could, in the words of Marlon Brando, 'have been a contender'. Whilst still in his teens he had knocked out the fancied middleweight Fred Sutton in the first round. Unfortunately he did not like the training required and instead became a strong-arm man for Sullivan's promotions at the Hoxton baths.

The race-track protection worked in a number of ways. First there was the question of the pitches themselves. The Sabinis and their rivals simply bullied the hapless bookmakers away from their spots and then sold or let them to their cronies. Much later, in 1947, Jack Spot took over the £2-a-day pitches provided at point-to-points and charged the bookmakers £7. One way of preventing a bookmaker attracting any business was to surround his stand with thugs so the punters could not get to it to place their bets.

Then there was the bucket drop. If a bookmaker wished to avoid this trouble he would drop half a crown in a bucket containing water and a sponge. The bucket was carried up and down the line between races and the sponge used to wipe out the odds next to the printed sheet of runners on the board. If the tribute was not paid then the odds would be wiped at inappropriate and totally inconvenient times. The sheets of runners had themselves to be purchased; costing about a farthing to produce, they were retailed by the Sabinis to the bookmakers for another half a crown. Chalk had to be purchased and a stool cost ten shillings to hire for the day. Other manoeuvres included starting fights near a bookmaker's pitch, claiming a non-existent winning bet, and having other pitches put so close to the non-paying bookmaker that he physically could not operate. Quite apart from that there was a straightforward demand for a non-repayable loan of £5 or £10.

The sums may seem small but, added up, came to big money. 'The race-course business was a profitable one. When a gang went to a race-course like Brighton they could clear £4000 or £5000 easy. At Epsom on Derby Day, it could be £15,000 to £20,000.'[10]

There was not much subtlety in their operations. 'Darby Sabini and his thugs used to stand sideways on to let the bookmakers see their hammers in their pockets,' wrote Detective Chief Superintendent Edward Greeno in his autobiography.[11]

The Sabinis cannot be given the credit for thinking up the idea of race-course protection. It was well established in the nineteenth century. In 1848, for example, there was considerable trouble with a Glasgow gang, known as the Redskins because of their scarred faces, at Paisley Races, and from the 1870s onwards the bookmakers themselves had protection – often in the form of active and retired prize-fighters – paying out only when they had done well and using bully-boys to dissuade punters from claiming their winning bets. After the First World War the bookmakers themselves became the victims.

There were, of course, a number of well-organized gangs outside the Smoke. One of the first originated in Birmingham. Run by bookmaker William Kimber, it was known as the Brummagen Boys despite the fact that most of the members came from the Elephant and Castle area of London. They had a fearsome reputation, being said to be willing and able to kill rats by biting them.

[10] R. Samuel, *East End Underworld*, p. 184.
[11] E. Greeno, *War on the Underworld*, p. 12.

Their organized race-course protection began in around 1910 and for a time Kimber's mob had control of the race-courses down south such as Newbury, Epsom, Earls Park and Kempton. There were also other gangs operating from Leeds and Uttoxeter. Later Kimber's men had a loose alliance with one of the metamorphoses of the Hoxton mob known as the 'Lunies' (not to be confused with a small independent marauding team, the 'Looneys'). The southern bookmakers accepted the imposition fairly philosophically.

Around the same time the Sabini brothers, known as the Italian Mob, began to put together their organization; it became a mixed Italian and Jewish alliance which was said to import gangsters from Sicily. The fact that 'there wasn't an Englishman among them'[12] did not mean they spoke anything but English. Once when Mr Justice Darling, who fancied himself as a linguist, addressed one of them in Italian the man stared in amazement.[13]

The Sabinis may have had no command of Italian but they had command of the police:

Darby Sabini got in with the Flying Squad which had been formed about 1908 or 1909; they got in with the race-course police, the special police, and so they had the police on their side protecting them. Directly there was any fighting it was always the Birmingham mob who got pinched. They was always getting time, five-year sentences and that.[14]

[12] R. Samuel, *East End Underworld*, p. 182.
[13] Apparently until this moment Darling had been taking a close interest in the case. After that he confined his remarks to the jury to the effect that the witness must be descended from the Sabines and went on to tell the story of the Sabine women.
[14] R. Samuel, *East End Underworld*, p. 183.

With the arrival of the Sabinis and their superi
relationship with the police, Billy Kimber and his ga
retreated to the Midlands. For some time the factio
lived in an uneasy relationship. Kimber and Co. work·
the Midlands and northern tracks; the Sabinis, alo
with a gang called the East End Jews, the London a
southern ones.[15]

The favourite weapons were razors but these we
subject to changing fashion and regional preference
Ex-Superintendent Fred Narborough recalls:

The safety razors embedded in the peak of the pull-
down cloth cap, which would gouge out a man's
cheek with one swipe, originated in Glasgow.

The same kind of blades, preferably rusty to set
up infection, stuck into a big potato with only a
quarter of an inch of metal showing, came from the
Midlands. In the eyes of the owner this possessed
the merit of leaving warning weals once the wounds
had healed, without risking a murder charge.

The flick knife was unknown at the time and
even recently I have heard this backwardness on
the part of the manufacturers deplored in certain
circles.

Coshes came in infinite variety, many weighted
with lead to give the gangster the right 'feel' – like
a golfer with his set of clubs. Then there were
bayonets with serrated blades, the metal shavings
from workshop lathes enclosed in old cotton
stockings, jemmies, carefully chosen lead piping
which would go down a trouser leg, tyre levers

---

[15] There were numerous tracks in the south many of which, such
as Gatwick, Lewes, Alexandra Park and Hurst Park, have now
closed down. In addition trotting was popular, with courses at
such places as Greenford and Hendon.

fitted with non-slip rubber grips, the hair-splitting stilettos of the Sabini gang from Clerkenwell, bottles of vitriol and other acids.[16]

In some versions of the legend the meteoric rise of Darby Sabini can be traced back to a fight he had in 1920 with 'Monkey' Benneyworth, the enforcer for the Elephant Gang, when Benneyworth deliberately tore the dress of an Italian girl serving behind the bar of the Griffin public house in Saffron Hill. Benneyworth was knocked out and humiliated by Sabini and when his broken jaw had mended he returned with members of the Elephant Gang. They were driven out of Little Italy by Sabini with the help of young Italians who looked on him as their leader. Now, with them behind him, he saw the opportunity to muscle in on some of the smaller gangs who were operating protection around the race-tracks. Although the big gangs such as the Broad Mob from Camden Town, the mainly Jewish Aldgate Mob and the Hoxton Mob could boast a membership of up to sixty they could be spread thinly because they were obliged to operate several tracks a day. Darby and the rest of the Sabinis moved in in force.[17]

It is curious how throughout the history of organized crime the victims align themselves with their oppressors who, in turn, through that alliance somehow gain a quasi-respectability. After bookmakers at Salisbury races had been forced, at gun point, to pay a levy for the privilege of having a pitch, in 1921 they formed themselves into the Racecourse Bookmakers and Backers Protection Association, today a highly respected

[16] F. Narborough, *Murder on my Mind*, p. 36.
[17] For a full account of the early days of bookmaking and the involvement of the Sabinis, see Carl Chinn's *Better betting with a decent feller*.

organization. Eight stewards were appointed at a wage
of £6 per week. The stewards were the Sabini family and
their friends, including Philip Emmanuel, son of
Edward. It is said that at the time Darby was earning
£20,000 a year. This may be an exaggeration but taken
at the lowest level sixty runners' sheets sold at 2s 6d
amounted to a working man's wage for the week, and
there is no doubt Darby did better than that.

Kimber's Birmingham or Brummagen Boys did not
give in easily and the fighting continued throughout the
year. A bookmaker under the Sabinis' protection was
threatened at Sandown Park and was beaten up when he
refused to pay a £25 pitch fee. Darby Sabini sent a
retaliatory force to Hoxton. He himself was caught at
Greenford trotting track on 25 March 1921 and seems to
have escaped a bad beating by the Birmingham Mob by
shooting his way out of trouble. It was one of the
occasions when he was arrested but he was acquitted
after arguing self-defence and bound over to keep the
peace.

From time to time offers of reconciliation, genuine or
not, were made and spurned. Kimber went to Darby
Sabini's home at King's Cross. He was found two hours
later shot in the side but was quite unable to identify his
assailant. He was, after all, only obeying the underworld
tradition of silence. A Jewish bookmaker, Solomons,
from Sandown Park gave himself up to the police over
the shooting but the case was stopped. 'If that's all the
evidence you can produce it's useless to go on,' said the
trial judge. Solomons remained a Sabini friend for the
next fifteen years, eventually paying for that friendship
at Lewes race-course.

Reprisals came quickly. On 4 April at the 'Ascot of
North London', Alexandra Park, a small track known as
Ally-Pally which closed in the 1960s, the police were
informed of a showdown. By one o'clock all they had

found were two Birmingham bookmakers' touts who had been beaten up. Later, however, two Jewish taxi-drivers, chauffeurs to the Sabinis, were caught in the silver ring by the Birmingham men. One was shot twice as he lay on the ground. He too could not identify his shooter. A further reprisal came at Bath when Billy Kimber and his men attacked the East End Jews found in the two-shilling ring.

Not all the attacks were well directed. A fight on Derby Day 1921 appears to have been engineered by Reuben Bigland, the Birmingham tycoon, following a complaint by the publisher and later convicted swindler Horatio Bottomley. He complained that it was wrong that Italians such as the Sabinis should be depriving 'our boys' of a living, particularly after their gallant fight in the First World War. The outcome was a punitive expedition by the Brummagen Boys, the Mancinis and the Vendetta Boys. After the Derby itself, won by Steve Donoghue on Humorist, the Birmingham Boys left the course and blocked the road with their charabanc, lying in wait for Sabini and his friends. Unfortunately for them the Sabinis had already left the scene and the victims were their allies.

Violence spread away from the race-courses. In April 1922 four 'racing men' were stabbed in and near Coventry Street and another was beaten up in nearby Jermyn Street.

The Derby meeting that year, when Captain Cuttle won after spreading a plate on the way to the start, passed off quietly but, two months later, the Sabinis were back in the dock, charged after a fight in Camden Town during which shots were fired. A Birmingham man had been out walking with his wife and some friends when he was ambushed. For once the Birmingham men were able to give the names of their attackers to the police but by the time the case was heard they had forgotten them.

Things did not stop there and the Jockey Club seriously considered shutting down the courses on which there was trouble. A Sabini boy was stabbed to death in a club off the Strand, another was thrown on a fire. Cardiff bookmakers were beaten up in their offices, a man was killed in a Tottenham Court Road fight. The Sabinis and their rivals fought for supremacy on street corners, on trains, on the roads and at the race-courses.

At the Doncaster St Leger meeting the Brummagen team sent word that no bookmakers or their employees would be allowed to attend Town Moor. As a result, in open defiance, Sabini and his men 'protected' the London bookie Walter Beresford, putting him safely on the train to Doncaster where it was met by Kimber's men, who then allowed only him and his staff to go to the race-course.

The next trouble spot was at the autumn meeting in Yarmouth, a course claimed by the Sabinis as theirs. They arrived the day before to search the public houses in the town to see if the Brummagen men had arrived. They had not. Instead they were met by Tom Divall, an ex-Chief Inspector of the CID now working for the Jockey Club, and something of a supporter of the Midland team. He calmed things down.

Divall wrote of Kimber that he 'was one of the best' and of another incident: 'Just to show what generous and brave fellows the aforesaid Sage and Kimber were, they would not give any evidence or information against their antagonists, and stated that they would sooner die than send those men to prison.'[18]

It is difficult to comprehend Divall's attitude without alleging corruption. Describing another incident when the Leeds organization had tried to take control of

[18] T. Divall, *Scoundrels and Scallywags*, p. 200.

Hawthorn Hill in the south and Divall was attacked by them, he wrote:

> One of them swore with a terrible oath he would kill me. He made for me and was just about to carry out his intention, but Darby Sabini rushed up to my aid and knocked the other chap down with a heavy blow in the mouth. The others seeing 'the red light', got hold of the wounded warrior and hurried him away. I have often wondered what would have been my fate if such a good ally as Darby had not popped up at that critical moment.[19]

Whatever Divall's position, one explanation of the Sabinis' success and longevity comes from Billy Hill:

> There were more crooked policemen about than there are today. The Sabinis received protection from certain elements of the law. If a thief or pickpocket was seen on a course a Sabini man would whiten the palm of his hand with chalk and greet the thief with a supposed-to-be 'Hello'. In doing so he would slap the thief on the shoulder, just like a long lost friend. The whitened hand-mark would identify him to the law. Then they knew without doubt that this man was safe to be nicked for being a suspected person . . .[20]

According to Divall, however, it was Beresford who 'brought the two sides together, he is still continuing in the good work, and I am very pleased to see the two crews are associating together, and, in addition, to have their principals assuring me that no such troubles will ever occur again.'

[19] Ibid, p. 209.
[20] B. Hill, *Boss of Britain's Underworld*, p. 4.

Divall had it only partly correct. The Sabinis and Kimber did agree to divide the race-courses between them and certainly the race-course wars did die down, but not before the Jockey Club had threatened to close down courses such as Bath and Salisbury where the worst troubles were taking place. In 1925 the Jockey Club set up a team under Major Wymer to drive out the undesirable elements from the official enclosures. By 1929 the bookmakers' pitch committees were firmly in control and a strict pecking order amongst bookmakers had been established. The pitches were personal to the occupant. They could not be sold or leased out. When a bookmaker retired or died the next in seniority took his pitch and a vacancy occurred at the end of the line.

There were still, however, the independents and in 1927, when one Dai Lewis tried to muscle in on the Rowlands Gang who controlled Cardiff, his throat was cut.

But if by the 1930s Darby Sabini had made his peace with that fine fellow Billy Kimber, in the 1920s he had been under threat from other sources inside his own organization. Some of the troops decided to seek a higher percentage of the takings. The four Cortesi brothers, also known as the Frenchies (Augustus, George, Paul and Enrico), were deputed to act as shop stewards to put the case. Almost immediately afterwards part of the Jewish element in the gang, to become known as the Yiddishers, also formed a breakaway group. In true business fashion the Sabinis negotiated. The Cortesis would be given a greater percentage. The Yiddishers were given permission to lean on one, but only one, of the bookmakers under protection.[21]

Peace did not last long. The Yiddishers began to side with the Cortesis and defections amongst the troops to

[21] A. Tietjen, *Soho*.

23

the Frenchies substantially weakened the Sabini position. In the autumn of 1922 the new team effectively hijacked the Sabini protection money from the bookmakers at Kempton Park. Retribution was swift. As a result of the reprisals, Harry Sabini was convicted at Marylebone Magistrates' Court of an assault on George Cortesi. More seriously, one of the other leaders of the breakaway group was attacked, for which five of the Sabini troops were sentenced to terms of imprisonment for attempted murder.

On 19 November 1922, just before midnight, Darby and Harry Sabini were trapped in the Fratellanza Club in Great Bath Street, Clerkenwell. Darby was punched and hit with bottles whilst Harry was shot by Augustus and Enrico (Harry) Cortesi. Darby suffered a greater indignity. As he told the magistrates' court, his false teeth were broken as a result of the blows from the bottles. He was also able to confirm his respectability.

'I am a quiet peaceable man,' he asserted. 'I never begin a fight. I've only once been attacked. I've never attacked anyone. . . . I do a little bit of work as a commission agent sometimes for myself and sometimes for someone else. I'm always honest. The last day's work I did was two years ago. I live by my brains.' He had only once carried a revolver and that was when he was attacked at Greenford Park. Indeed he turned out his pockets in confirmation that he was not carrying a gun.

The Cortesi brothers, who lived only five doors away from the Fratellanza Club, had been arrested the same night and at the Old Bailey on 18 January 1923 each received a sentence of three years' penal servitude. A recommendation by the Grand Jury that the Cortesi brothers should be deported was not followed by Mr Justice Darling:

I look upon this as part of a faction fight which has

raged between you and other Italians in consequence of some difference which the police do not entirely understand. You appear to be two lawless bands – the Sabinis and the Cortesis. Sometimes you are employed against the Birmingham people, and sometimes you are employed against each other. On this occasion you were carrying out a feud between you and the Sabinis. . . . I have the power to recommend an order for your deportation. I am not going to do it. I can see no reason to suppose that you two men are worse than others who have been convicted in these feuds and have not been recommended for deportation. But the whole Italian colony should know of the Grand Jury's recommendation, and I wish to say to you all if this kind of lawless conduct goes on, those who get convicted in future will be turned out of this country with their wives and children.

Without their leaders the Cortesi faction folded. The rebellion had been short-lived and it was not until the 1930s, when the Sabinis had expanded their territory into greyhound racing, that the Sabinis again came under serious threat from another team. This time they came from Islington and were the White family. They had been getting stronger over the years and were now set to challenge the Sabinis. There was also the small matter of the pitches on the open courses at Epsom and Brighton which were outside the control of the racecourse stewards, as well as bookmaking at point-to-points, let alone the dog-tracks where 'they terrorized the bookmakers' according to the son of a man who ran a pitch.

On 1 September 1936 Massimino Monte Columbo was stabbed to death at Wandsworth Greyhound Racing Track, which had been opened some four years earlier. A fight broke out in the 2s 6d ring, witnessed by Jim

Wicks, who thirty years later was to be a manager of boxers who included Henry Cooper. At the time Massimino, described as the idol of the girls in Little Italy, worked for Bert Marsh, the *nom de ring* of boxer Pasqualino Papa. Marsh, a popular bantamweight, had fought at Lime Grove Baths and Shepherd's Bush. He was described by the officer in the case as 'quick-tempered, excitable and easily provoked'. Once Marsh was appointed to a job at the stadium he got the Columbo brothers work there and at his request Wicks employed Camillo. The quarrel was allegedly over a bookmaker called Samuels employing Bert Wilkins rather than another Monte Columbo brother, Nestor, who along with Marsh and Wilkins came from Little Italy. The Columbo family objected. They were also looking for more money from Marsh. Fighting broke out and Massimino was stabbed in the neck.

Marsh had undoubtedly suffered kicks and punches in the fight and when he and Wilkins were surrendered by their solicitor, J.A. Davies, to the police, Marsh sensibly asked that the fingerprints on a 'life preserver' or cosh were checked. 'It'll show they weren't mine. I was nearly killed,' he told Divisional Detective Inspector John Henry.

At the Old Bailey Marsh and Wilkins were defended by eight barristers including three silks led by Norman Birkett KC. The funds for their defence were said to have been subscribed by racing men and the 'pretty young Mrs Marsh, mother of eight', who had pawned her jewellery and drawn out her savings to retain Birkett. It was money well spent. Newspapers noted that many bookmakers and even film stars were in court for the verdict.

Whilst on remand in Brixton Prison, on 28 October Marsh and Wilkins had assisted Prison Officer Payne during exercise when, according to reports, he had been attacked by a powerfully built man and bitten and kicked. It was something which stood them in good stead throughout the trial.

The murder charge was dismissed and Marsh, as the older man with a criminal record of assaults and unlawful wounding, received twelve months for manslaughter; Wilkins got three months less. The judge specially took into account the part they had played in assisting the prison warder, who 'might have been killed'. Later it was alleged that friends had organized the 'attack' so that Marsh could step in and obtain credit for his efforts. This sort of 'put up attack' was by no means new, nor was it the last time it was used. In a later incident Billy Hill 'pulled' Jackie Rosa, one of a number of brothers from the Elephant, off a screw, thereby gaining both kudos and a loyal member of his organization.

Both the Berts were to become major figures in Soho in the 1950s, Marsh as a street bookmaker, supporter of Albert Dimes and friend of George Dawson, the Cockney businessman later imprisoned following a commercial fraud. Bert Wilkins owned the Nightingale Club which was later to become Aspinalls.

Meanwhile, from the 1920s onwards, the Sabinis had been branching out, taking interests in the West End drinking and gambling clubs, and installing and running slot-machines. They were also extending their protection to criminals. If a burglary took place the Sabinis would send round for their share.

Burglars and thieves had no chance. If they wandered up West they had to go mob-handed. And they had to be prepared to pay out if they were met by any of the Sabinis. If they went into a club it was drinks all round. The prices were usually especially doubled for their benefit. If they did go into a spieler they never won. They knew better than to try to leave while they were showing even a margin of profit. If one word was spoken out of place, it was all off. The Sabinis, who could rustle up twenty or thirty tearaways at a moment's notice anywhere up West, stood for no liberties, although they were always taking them.[22]

But the Sabinis and the Whites were not without rivals. In 1937 the crime writer and novelist Peter Cheyney wrote in the *Sunday Dispatch* that there were five major London gang districts: Hackney, Hoxton, North-East London, North London and the West End, this last being 'worked over' by a loose alliance of the Hoxton Mob, the Elephant and Castle Boys and the Hackney Gang as well as the 'West End Boys'. Until 1927, wrote Cheyney, 'the Hackney Gang was supreme in the West End. Then came the battle of Ham Yard when the gang suffered a severe reversal in terms both of blood spilled and prestige lost.'

Apart from the gangs which ran their areas, splinter teams such as the squad of pickpockets from Aldgate worked the nearby City. Additionally there were teams of smash-and-grab raiders, one of which was led by the future self-styled 'Boss of the Underworld' Billy Hill. Also flexing his young muscles was his rival for the title, Jack Comer, known as Jack Spot. He had interests in the pitches on the open courses at Epsom and Brighton.

There are in the London District quite a number of shops and cafes which are either actually owned or controlled by gangs. The merchandise, provisions, cigarettes, hosiery or fancy goods sold at these places are invariably stolen property, the result of burglaries effected by crooks who work in

[22] B. Hill, *Boss of Britain's Underworld*, p. 5.

close co-operation with, or under definite orders from, gangs.[23]

Cheyney considered that the activities of the London gangs – excluding greyhound and race-course affairs – included working on the smaller and more subversive night clubs, arranging the pickpocketing of what he called 'Good time Charlies' – men looking for 'a bit of fun', organization and protection of street prostitutes, selling lines of stolen goods, organizing the beating (paying) of individuals who have upset members or friends, and protecting and organizing independent sneak thiefs whose work was now often contracted (laid-out) for them and from whom a cut was taken.

As for the race-courses, the last major pre-war fight took place at Lewes race-course on 8 June 1936 when the Hoxton Mob ran riot. In retaliation for an incident at Liverpool Street when a member of the Whites had had his throat cut, thirty members of that gang went to the races with the specific intention of injuring two of the Sabinis. They did not find them and instead set upon the bookmaker Arthur Solomons (who nearly two decades earlier had been acquitted of the attempted murder of Billy Kimber) and his clerk, Mark Frater, who were known to be friendly towards the Sabinis. After a running battle sixteen men were arrested. They were defended privately at Lewes Assizes by the very fashionable J. D. Cassels KC and G. L. Hardy. On pleas of guilty, the ringleaders drew five years' penal servitude from Mr Justice Hilbery, who imposed a total of fifty-three and a half years on the defendants.

After that an accommodation was reached. The Sabinis would have the West End, the Whites the King's

23 P. Cheyney, *Making Crime Pay*, pp. 65–6.

Cross area. The latter became known as the King's Cross
Gang and Alf White would hold court in the Bell public
house or Hennekeys in the Pentonville Road, exercising
strict discipline amongst his followers. 'No bad language
was allowed,' says John Vaughan, a police officer from
King's Cross. 'First time you were warned. The next
time – out.' It had been the same with Darby Sabini:
women were to be treated properly; Italian youths could
not drink before they were twenty. It was a reasonably
benevolent dictatorship.

Darby Sabini lost another battle when, following a
series of unfavourable articles, he sued the offending
newspaper for libel. On the day of the action he failed
to appear and costs of £775 were awarded against him.
He did not pay and bankruptcy proceedings were com-
menced. It was put to him by the counsel appearing for the
petitioning creditor that he was the king of the Sabini gang.

'I do not admit that,' he replied.

'And that you make twenty- to thirty-thousand pounds
a year?'

'No.'

Thirty years later his successor Jack Spot was to fare no
better in the civil courts when he battled with the *People*.

The Sabini empire was effectively destroyed by the
outbreak of the Second World War. Darby Sabini had
moved to Brighton, where his daughters were educated
locally – Saffron Hill legend said it was Roedean but
there are no records of the girls there – and where he
had a penthouse flat in the Grand Hotel. With the
beginning of the war in 1939, they were regarded as
enemy aliens and were interned on the Isle of Man. The
one brother who escaped internment was sentenced in
1942 to nine months' imprisonment for attempting to
prevent that fate. Their business empire was up for
grabs. For a time their West End interests were shared
by the Whites, 'Benny the Kid' from the East End (the

nom de guerre of Jack Spot) and the Elephant Gang, with the Whites increasingly the dominant force.

Just what were Darby Sabini and his brothers like? A picture taken of the Cortesis and the Sabinis before the Fratellanza shooting shows Enrico Cortesi in a straw hat sitting in the centre of the group like the captain of a cricket team. To his left is Darby, less than middle height, wearing his customary flat cap and a shirt with no collar. His dark brown suit with a high buttoned waistcoat, black silk stock and light-checked cap was the outfit he had selected when he was twenty and he wore it for the rest of his life, indoors, outdoors and, so it is said, sometimes in bed. To Cortesi's right and in the background is handsome Harryboy Sabini, who wore highly polished spring-sided boots. Brother Joe liked cherry checks whilst George wore a grey fedora.

Over the years Darby became a folk hero to the Italians of Saffron Hill. Tradition there has it that he was one of the three people to whom to turn when the rent was due. A white five-pound note – no interest asked – would be produced and the debt repaid because the borrower knew he could ask again in times of trouble. He may not have had to pay interest but he incurred a debt of loyalty. Sabini, in turn, defended the locals against the depredations of the Hoxton Mob when in the late twenties they invaded the quarter demanding protection money. The Sabinis placed minders in the shops to repel boarders. The culmination was the battle of Ham Yard in 1927, which resulted in the defeat of the Hoxton boys and their allies, the Hackney Gang, and the emergence of Darby as the controller of the West End.

'I called him Uncle Bob,' says the son of one of the men who worked for Darby Sabini. 'Every time I saw him he gave me a shilling.'

After the war Harry joined his brother in Brighton, to which Darby had retired with, according to Saffron Hill legend, two sacks of gold. In the late 1940s Darby functioned as a small-time bookmaker with a pitch on the free course at Ascot. When he died in Hove in 1950 his family and friends were surprised that he apparently had little money. Yet the man who had been his clerk, Jimmy Napoletano, was stopped leaving the country on his way to Italy with £36,000. The racing tradition is kept up. A member of the family still runs a book in the silver ring at London race-courses. Another, outside the racing fraternity, had a newspaper pitch in Holborn.

But Darby and his brothers' names lived on in the courts as an example of gangster stardom. 'Don't go thinking you are the Sabini brothers,' said a judge, discharging the Krays through lack of evidence. Darby also lives on in fiction and film as the Brighton gang leader, Colleoni, in Graham Greene's *Brighton Rock*. One of the key scenes in both book and film is the meeting between him and Pinky in a Brighton hotel. The slashing of Pinky at the race meeting is based on the Lewes battle in 1936.

'Darby had a purist dislike of razor-slashing and though he was to send razor teams in pursuit of his enemies he always walked away when the cutting began,' recalled George Sewell, his one-time lieutenant. It resembles the story of the Bishop of Chicago who when the first snow fell each winter left for Miami because 'he couldn't bear to see the poor suffer in the cold'. But, on the greyer side, 'In company with most of his top men, he toted a gun, a loaded, flat black Webley and Scott automatic pistol in his back pocket. Like his cap, that gun stayed with him twenty-four hours a day.'

The family 'kept in touch'. One member, Johnny Sabini, 'though now an older man, comes to see me in Broadmoor,' wrote Ronnie Kray nostalgically.[24]

[24] R. and R. Kray, *Our Story*, p. 19.

2

After
the War

With the internment of the Sabinis, the Whites, according to both Jack Spot and Billy Hill, took over the West End (although Hill called them the Blacks).

> They were a gang of hoodlums run by five brothers named Black. Some of them had been in their time thieves and burglars, but they had neither the guts nor the brains to do any good at it. They looked at the Sabinis and came to the conclusion that there was room for two at that game. They nearly got away with it. At least, they made room for one and a half. The war was a godsend to them.
>
> They took over the horse-race tracks and the dog-tracks concessions. They continued the blackmail of club owners, cafe proprietors and publicans. They even ran some of the brasses on the streets and used them to steer the mugs into the spielers and drinking-clubs.
>
> All through the war years they had it all their own way. No one could open a drinking-club or spieler in the West End without the Blacks' permission. And their permission usually meant the payment of a dollar-in-the-pound out of the takings.[1]

[1] B. Hill, *Boss of Britain's Underworld*, p. 6.

On the night of the declaration of war against Italy there had been rioting in Soho. Shop premises owned by Italians had been stoned and there had been fighting amongst the rival patriotic factions. The round-up of the Sabinis had left the area open to the Whites and to the Yiddishers, who now aligned themselves with the new masters. One of the Italian Gang, Antonio 'Baby Face' or 'Babe' Mancini, remained, however, to lead the group protecting the old order's interests.

Over the years protection of clubs has worked in a tried and tested way: a suggestion of a weekly payment, a refusal, the entry into the club by two or more men whilst the public is present, a fight, bottles and glasses smashed, a foot through the drummer's kit, furniture overturned, staff molested, and the next day a reminder that for a smallish weekly sum this sort of behaviour which frightens off the punters and costs very much more to repair can be prevented. But for a time, at the beginning of 1941, protection was a very different game. The rule seems to have been to inflict the maximum amount of damage so that the rival's club could be closed for good, leaving one less competitor.

On 20 April Eddie Fletcher, also known as Eddie Fleicher and Joseph Franks, became involved in a fight with Bert Connelly, the doorman at Palm Beach Bottle Parties, a club in the basement of 37 Wardour Street. The worse for drink, Fletcher not only received a beating but was banned from the club for his pains by Joe Leon, the manager. Two more clubs were housed at 37 Wardour Street, the Cosmo on the ground floor and the West End Bridge and Billiards Club on the first floor. On the night of 30 April a Sam Ledderman – who many years later would give evidence in the first of the Kray trials – came to the Palm Beach to tell Mancini, the catering manager and doorman for the night there, 'They're smashing up the [Bridge and Billiards] club.'

According to the statement made by Mancini to the police, he replied that it was no real business of his but a friend was upstairs. Leon told Mancini to go on the door of the Palm Beach and let no one in.

'I went and stood inside the door and then went and changed out of evening clothes,' he told Detective Inspector Arthur Thorp, adding, 'I went up to see the damage. As I was going upstairs I heard someone say, "There's Babe, let's knife him."' The voice resembled Fletcher's. Mancini sensed someone was behind him and went into the club. He was followed by Fletcher, Harry 'Little Hubby' or 'Scarface' Distleman, whom Mancini had known for some fifteen years, and another man. Distleman had managed the Nest Club in Kingly Street for four years until 1938. Since then he had not worked but, so his brother said, he had won a good deal of money on horses and greyhounds. His brother, 'Big Hubby', ran a string of small brothels in the West End. He died in the 1980s leaving £4 million in safety deposit boxes.

According to Mancini, Fletcher started fighting and came at him with a raised chair. Mancini saw a knife on the floor and picked it up to defend himself. Distleman, stabbed five inches deep in the chest, called out, 'Baby's stabbed me in the heart, I'm dying.' He was right. Half-carried out to the street by his friends, he fell down in the doorway of another club and died later in Charing Cross Hospital. Mancini then left the club and threw the dagger away. Later he changed his story to say that he had carried the dagger to protect himself from gangs from Hoxton and King's Cross.

At Mancini's trial for murder the evidence emerged that Eddie Fletcher and other members of the Yiddisher Gang had earlier been playing pool in the club when in walked part of the Italian Gang led by Albert Dimes. Fighting broke out and the unlucky Fletcher was badly beaten again. He went to hospital and returned an hour later 'to get his coat'. This was when Mancini, quite by chance, came up the stairs to survey the damage. According to such witnesses who were prepared to speak at the committal proceedings, Albert Dimes, along with Joseph Collette and Harry Capocci, were still there, with Albert being held back by his brother Victor. As usual in these matters the prosecution had difficulty in persuading any of the forty people present at the affray to give evidence. Few had seen anything happen at all.

Mancini was unlucky. At his trial it was argued that a death in a gang fight was at worst manslaughter. Indeed, the closing words in the brief to prosecuting counsel read that if Mancini was prepared to plead guilty to wounding Fletcher and to the manslaughter of Distleman, 'Counsel will no doubt consider it, as the witnesses of the assault on Distleman are vague and shaky.'

Despite a summing up to that effect by the trial judge, Mr Justice McNaughten, Mancini was convicted and sentenced to death. In September his appeal was rejected by the Court of Appeal. The summing up had been 'favourable to the defence, perhaps too favourable in some respects', said the Lord Chief Justice. And the House of Lords also found against him. On 31 October 1941 Mancini became the first London gangster to be hanged for over twenty years.

Afterwards Dimes, Collette and Capocci were arraigned for the unlawful wounding of Fletcher. One by one the witnesses declined to identify any of them and as the prosecution's case collapsed the Recorder of London, Sir Gerald Dodson, asked whether it was worth going on with the trial. Capocci was acquitted and Collette was bound over in the sum of £5 to come up for judgment if called on to do so within three years. 'You were probably expecting prison,' the Recorder told them, 'and no doubt you deserve it, but I am going to bind you over.'

Dimes was also convicted and he too was bound over to come up for sentence. A deserter from the RAF, he was returned to the force. Over the next thirty years he was to become a major figure in the control of the London underworld, best known for his 'fight which never was' with Jack Spot in Frith Street on 11 August 1955, an event which threw that control into turmoil.

'Italian' Albert Dimes was born of a Scots mother and Italian father who came from Scotland to Saffron Hill in the 1930s. His father first opened a fish shop and, when that failed, a cafe club, La Venezia. Nor did that succeed. In those days Little Italy was a square of four streets in which the whole community lived and worked cheek by jowl and Dimes, along with many others who knew the Sabinis and their friends, drifted into their company. Until the 1950s he operated as a bookmaker, strongman and owner of small spielers principally for the Italian community. Apart from his troubles with Babe Mancini he received only one further sentence, on a conviction for larceny in 1943 at Marlborough Street Magistrates' Court.

Jacob, sometimes John, Colmore, also known as Jacob Comacho, also known as Jack Comer and best known as Jack Spot, was around a long time – not as long as the Sabinis, but getting on for twenty years – as one of the kings of the underworld. In fact that title was a contributing factor which led to the violence which ended his reign.

One of four children, Spot – so called because he liked to say he was on it if help was needed (or more prosaically because he had a mole on his cheek) – was born on 12 April 1912 in Myrdle Street, Whitechapel, the son of Polish immigrants. His brother was a tailor, his sister a court dressmaker. At fifteen he became a bookie's runner and the next year joined forces with a leading figure of East End protection rackets. Strictly small-time, together they protected the Sunday morning stall-holders in Petticoat Lane. He fell out with the man and they fought, leaving Spot the winner. He then called himself the King of Aldgate.

After a short spell as a partner with Dutch Barney, an East End bookmaker, he joined forces with a house-breaker, acting as his look-out and minder. This ended with an appearance at Middlesex Quarter Sessions when amazingly, since he admitted to around forty offences, he was bound over. He returned to bookmaking and the race-courses.

For a time he ran a typical fairground scam called 'Take a Pick' at the major race meetings. The mug punters paid 6d to pull a straw with a winning number from a cup. If they were extremely fortunate they won a cheap prize whilst Spot cleared between £30 and £40 a day. Later the enterprise was extended to Petticoat Lane where 'Take a Pick' earned him another £50 a morning. He was also an active bookmaker on the free course. On a bad day he welshed, leaving before paying out on the last race. The old-time jockey Jack Leach may well have had Spot in mind when he advised racegoers, 'Never bet with a bookmaker if you see him knocking spikes in his shoes'.

In 1935 Spot became a local folk hero by leading a Jewish team against Oswald Mosley's Blackshirts when they marched down Cable Street in the East End. According to Spot he approached Mosley's leading bodyguard, a six-foot-six all-in wrestler, 'Roughneck', and felled him with a chair leg filled with lead. It was a story on which he traded for the remainder of his working life.

The rest of his pre-war career was not as heroic.

Certainly he protected the Jewish shopkeepers against Mosley's Blackshirts but they were obliged to pay up to £10 to ensure their premises were not damaged in the demonstrations. In 1937 he was sentenced to six months' imprisonment for causing grievous bodily harm to a Blackshirt during one of the marches through the East End. It was to be the only prison sentence he received in his career. When he was released from prison he became an enforcer, collecting subscriptions for an East End stall traders' fund run by Larry Sooper. 'This was a private association formed by stall owners who kept the depression at bay by refusing to let any other new trader break in and set up a stall.'[2]

During the war he served for a short time in the Royal Artillery stationed in Cornwall but was given a medical discharge in 1943. It is impossible to trace the accuracy of some of Spot's stories but, according to him, after his discharge he returned to London and gravitated to the West End where he became involved in a fight in a club in the Edgware Road. The man, Edgware Sam – in all Spot's stories the men are Manchester Mike, Newcastle Ned and so forth – ran out of the club, some said to get a gun. Whether Spot believed this or thought that Sam had gone to the police, he feared a prison sentence and fled north to a land where the black market and organized crime were rampant. Goods were being stolen from the ships at Hull docks and the cash had to be spent somewhere. Where illegal gaming and drinking clubs are established, protection is sure to follow. Spot helped a club owner, Milky, of the Regal Gaming Club in Chapeltown, Leeds, clear out a Polish protection racketeer from his club, became the owner's bodyguard and, as a reward, was given a pitch at the local greyhound-track.

He worked as what he described as a 'troubleshooter'

[2] H. Jansen, *Jack Spot, Man of a Thousand Cuts.*

for various northern clubs until he heard Edgware Sam
had been gaoled for fraud. Perhaps fraud is too grand a
word. It seems to have been for 'working the tweedle',
a short-time con trick of taking a ring into a jewellers for
valuation and then declining to sell it. At the last
moment the grifter changes his or her mind and offers
the ring once more. This time, however, the ring
appraised by the jeweller has been switched and he is
now offered a fake in the hope he will not bother to
examine it a second time. In any event Spot returned to
London, pleaded self-defence and was acquitted.

Now he was in great demand. He was called to help
club owners in the major northern cities, which was
when he earned his nickname. According to his
accounts, which appeared not only in book form but in
numerous articles in Sunday newspapers, he assisted in
establishing the proper allocation of pitches at northern
bookmaking tracks, having to deal with 'Fred, leader of
a big mob in Newcastle' along the way.

> Newcastle Fred was not only a gangster but a race-
> course operator as well. He thought he had the
> say-so on flogging out bookmakers' pitches, but he
> made a mistake when he tried to get nasty with me
> and a few of my pals at Pontefract races. There was
> a battle . . . a proper free for all, and we had
> settled it before the police and race-course officials
> got wise to it. We'd settled Newcastle Fred's
> business too.[3]

There were other accounts of the story, including one
from an eyewitness. One bookmaker recorded, 'What
Spot doesn't tell is that old Fred celebrated his sixty-fifth
birthday a few days before Spot bravely kicked him with

[3] *Daily Sketch*, 29 September 1958.

his pointed shoes into the race-course dirt covered in blood. That's how courageous Spot was.'[4] Again it is difficult to assess the accuracy of the story. It could be said the bookmaker, who had 'scars tearing across the top of his scalp – relics of the days when he had to fight the slashing gangs who terrorized Britain's race-tracks between the wars', was not wholly disinterested. The bookmaker was Harry White, the son of Alf White who had challenged the Sabinis during the 1930s.

Shortly after the end of the Second World War Spot ran the Botolph Club, a spieler in Aldgate, reputedly taking £3000 a week tax free from illegal gambling. The figure may be accurate; large sums of money changed hands there. A solicitor's elderly managing clerk remembers:

> There was a burglar known as Taters, best screwsman in London. He once went out and did a job, pulled in £7000 and then went and did it all in a night playing chemmy with a Jewish bookmaker in Spot's club in Aldgate. It was a straight game but mugs always want to beat the finest and they never succeed. Tragedy really.

'We didn't serve drinks,' said Spot, 'drinks interfere with business and they can lead to people taking liberties or starting a battle.' Spot saw himself as a Jewish Godfather in the East End. He left an account of how his version of protection worked:

> I didn't have to buy nothing. Every Jewish businessman in London made me clothes, give me money, food, drink, everything. Because I was a legend. I was what they call a legend to the Jews.

---

[4] *Daily Herald*, 8 October 1955.

Anywhere they had anti-semitic trouble – I was sent for: Manchester, Glasgow, anywhere. Some crook go into a Jewish shop, says gimme clothes and a few quid, the local rabbi says Go down London and find Jack Spot. Get Jack, he'll know what to do.

So they did and I'd go up and chin a few bastards. The Robin Hood of the East End, a couple of taxi drivers told me once. 'You helped everyone', they said.[5]

But Spot was still interested in race-course bookmaking. The White family had control of the pitches on the free courses at Ascot, Epsom and Brighton and at the point-to-point races not yet under the control of the Jockey Club and the National Hunt Committee. It was an arrangement which had been going for more than thirty years.

[H]arry White's father, Alfred, had been collecting about £2 from every bookmaker working at the Points meetings.

It all went as a voluntary contribution to the Hunt Committees which organized the meetings.

Harry himself eventually became responsible for organizing bookmakers' pitches; he kept off welshers and pickpockets.

Everybody – including County police forces – was pleased with the arrangements.

Now Spot took over. Exactly how it happened depends upon the version preferred. This is Harry White's account as related to Sidney Williams in the *Daily Herald*.

[5] *London Standard* (Michael Ewing), 6 January 1986.

His fear of Spot began in January 1947 in a club in Sackville Street, off Piccadilly. He was drinking with racehorse trainer Tim O'Sullivan and a third man.

Spot walked in with ten thugs, went straight up to Harry and said 'You're Yiddified' – meaning he was anti-Jewish.

White denied it. He said: 'I have Jewish people among my best friends.' Spot wouldn't listen, and hit him with a bottle.

As White collapsed in a pool of blood, the rest of Spot's men attacked O'Sullivan and the third man who was employed by White.

O'Sullivan was beaten unconscious and pushed into a fire in the corner of the club. The other man was slashed with razors and stabbed in the stomach.

It is not totally surprising that Spot's version of events is a different one. His account in the *Daily Sketch* reads:

But the biggest, toughest and most ruthless mob was the King's Cross gang, led by a bookmaker named Harry who had taken over the race-course protection racket from the Sabini Boys.

Their word was law, not only on the race-courses but in the clubs and pubs – even in the fashionable night clubs of the West End.

He goes on to record that in a 'Mayfair Club' a challenge was thrown down and the King's Cross Mob 'partly wrecked' the place. A few nights later the 'same crowd' returned and were told that Jack Spot was a friend of the Guv'nor.

'F— Jack Spot,' came the answer. 'He doesn't work for us – when we want him we'll call him.'

There were other encounters until 'We finally ran them down at a place in Sackville Street off Piccadilly.'

> Harry had seven of the toughest of his boys with him when I led my pals into the room. There wasn't any politeness this time. They knew what I'd come for. And I sailed right in.
>
> At the first smack I took at them Harry scarpered. You couldn't see the seat of his trousers for dust.[6]

Clearly they are both talking about the same incident.

If one accepts White's version there was another fight, this time at the point-to-point races at Bletchley in February 1947. With little difficulty Spot cleared the decks: the £2 pitch fee became £7. For the next eight years he exercised such strict control over point-to-point bookmaking that, for example, at the Puckeridge Hunt meeting in 1955 he refused to let betting take place on the Grand National; the announcement was broadcast to the meeting over loudspeakers. Meanwhile Harry White paid him twenty-five per cent of his winnings.

According to both Hill and Spot (whom Hill calls Benny the Kid in his memoirs) the Whites were finally routed in the week of 9 July 1947 when Hill and Spot united to clear them out of their interests. There had been a previously scheduled meeting, the Baksi–Woodcock fight at Harringay Arena on 8 April that year, but the police had wind of this and had warned both sides to stay out of trouble. According to both Spot and Hill huge armies were summoned and searched for the Whites. In Spot's tale Harry simply vanished and the gang faded away. Hill has a rather more colourful version which included roasting one White over the fire.

[6] *Daily Herald*, 3 October 1955.

Each tells the story in almost identical terms with the emphasis placed on the teller's organizational qualities. This is not surprising; after all, each was writing for a different publication. It was this vanity which was to tell against Spot.

According to Hill it was he who was giving the orders. '"It's alright," I said to Benny the Kid, "we won't need shooters in this town anymore. Get 'em off the boys and get rid of them." They collected the shooters and the bombs and the machine gun and destroyed them. They were actually thrown down a manhole.'[7]

But according to Spot he had had a compulsory chat with Chief Superintendent Peter Beveridge, who had explained that the police were not going to have gang warfare in London:

> When I got back to Aldgate I called the heavy mob together at once.
>
> 'We've got to pack it up,' I said. 'Get rid of the ironmongery.'
>
> So we collected all the Stens, the grenades, revolvers, pistols and ammunition, loaded them into a lorry and dumped the whole lot into the Thames.[8]

Whoever was in charge, the West End had new owners for nearly a decade, each keen to emphasize how order and safety were restored to the streets. Both Hill and Spot were essentially businessmen. Accommodations could be reached with anyone and since neither had any real interest in vice it was easy to continue the *laissez-faire* arrangement with the prostitute-running Messina brothers.

[7] B. Hill, *Boss of Britain's Underworld*, p. 7.

[8] *Daily Sketch*, 3 October 1955.

They were peaceful and highly profitable years in 1950 and 1951. Visitors and strangers must have found the West End a rather dull place with no running gang-fights and feuds. . . . The truth was that we cleared all the cheap racketeers out. There was no longer any blacking of club owners and restaurant keepers. In fact so peaceful did it all become that there was no gravy left for the small timers.[9]

'Hill reigned almost with the blessing of the police,' says a solicitor's managing clerk from the period. 'He was a very likeable bloke, always paid his bills. If you overlooked his reputation you'd never have dreamed who he was. Whilst he was in control there was a peaceful scene. He kept discipline.'

Others believe the peaceful reign was simply that Spot and Hill paid off the police and an even less charitable view comes from one of Hill's friends. 'He kept control with the razor. People were paid a pound a stitch, so if you put twenty stitches in a man you got a score. You used to look in the evening papers next day to see how much you'd earned.'

Support for that opinion comes from a West End solicitor of the era. 'If no one tried to muscle in it was because they didn't dare to.'

One of those who did dare and who failed was Tommy Smithson, an ex-fairground boxer with a penchant for silk shirts and underwear, a man of immense courage and little stability or ability who was known as Mr Loser. Born in Liverpool in 1920 and brought to the East End two years later, he had served in the Merchant Navy until his discharge in the 1950s. Back in Shoreditch he found things to be different. The Maltese coming to

[9] B. Hill, *Boss of Britain's Underworld*, p. 155.

England on subsidized passages which had, in some cases, cost as little as three pounds, had moved in and had themselves established a network of their own gambling and drinking clubs and stables of prostitutes. Smithson decided to set up his own protection racket devoted to these Maltese businessmen, as well as working a spinner[10] with a Tony Mella around the dog-tracks.

Initially he worked as a croupier for George Caruana, whose gambling clubs included one in Batty Street, Stepney. At the time Caruana and the other Maltese were keen to avoid trouble and Smithson soon extended his interest to a share of the takings in the clubs. Smithson took a shilling in the pound from the dice games, earning up to £100 an evening. He also obtained backing and opened up a one-room club in Maidenhead Passage near Wardour Street.

But police raids followed and Smithson moved to nearby D'Arblay Street where he opened the Publishers' Club 'for authors'. Nobody was fooled and it was back to Berwick Street. Raided again, he could not raise the fine and in default of paying it went to Brixton, from which he was rescued with a whip-round by his friends. He moved to yet another address in Berwick Street and set up as a bookmaker. But now he had moved into competition with the Hill–Spot interests. He was involved in a fight with Frederick 'Slip' Sullivan and threw him out of French Henry's club, cutting his throat in the process. Sullivan, who was later stabbed to death by his girlfriend, was the brother of a member of the Hill–Spot firm and reprisals were swift.

A week later Smithson was betrayed by the Maltese he had been protecting. Told there was a peace offer on the table, he was asked to attend a meeting and was

---

[10] A crooked roulette wheel.

collected in a shooting-brake. On the dramatic signal of a cigar butt tossed on to the pavement Smithson was dragged from the car and slashed over his face, arms, legs and chest. He was then thrown over a wall in Regent's Park and left to die. The slashes on his face were in the form of the letter V, cut down each cheek to meet at his chin. Smithson had not been wholly naive; two loaded revolvers had been taken from him before his slashing. Somehow he survived and forty-seven stitches were put in his face.

His reward for honouring the code of silence was a party, the soubriquet 'Scarface' and £500, with which he bought a share in a club in Old Compton Street, and then another for illegal gaming. This too was closed down by the police and Smithson took up fencing as an occupation. For a time he was successful but then word began to spread that he was a police informer. This time he received twenty-seven stitches.

It signalled his retreat from what he had seen as the big time and he went back to the East End to provide protection for the Maltese. But yet again he miscalculated. The new generation of Maltese were becoming more powerful. They may not have wished to have trouble but they were themselves preparing for a move into the recently vacated Messina territory and were not prepared to tolerate the likes of Smithson.

Poor Tommy had other problems. At the time he was involved with a former prostitute, Fay Richardson, on remand in Holloway Prison on forged cheque allegations. Originally from Stockport where she had been a mill girl, she was what could be described both as a gangster's moll and a *femme fatale*. Three of her lovers were murdered and others suffered bad beatings. According to Commander Bert Wickstead she was

a blonde lady of many secrets, very preoccupied

and very hard . . . She couldn't have been described as a beautiful woman by any stretch of the
imagination. When she spoke there was no out-
ward sign of any great wit, warmth, intelligence or
charm. Yet she did have the most devastating
effect upon the men in her life – so there must have
been something special about the lady.[11]

Pictures of her at the time show a mousey-haired,
rather plain, thin-lipped woman. She had met Smithson
in an all-night cafe in Baker Street and it was something
approaching love at first sight. At least from the time she
met him her convictions for soliciting ceased, although
at the time of her arrest she was working as a prostitute's
maid. She said of the handsome Smithson, '[He was] a
dapper dresser, very fussy about having a clean shirt
every day. He was a big gambler. He could have £400
on the nose.'

On the cheque charges she was being defended at
Inner London Quarter Sessions by William Hemming, a
former detective who was one of the first police officers
to become a barrister and who modelled his speech
patterns on Winston Churchill whom he admired
greatly. Much of his work came from recommendations
by former officers and he was not known for accepting
legal aid work. Money had to be raised for Fay's
defence. Smithson collected £50 from his former
employer, George Caruana, and complained bitterly it
was not a hundred. On 13 June 1956 Smithson, together
with Walter Downs and Christopher Thomas, went to a
cafe in Berner Street, Stepney, and confronted Caruana
and Philip Ellul, a Maltese who ran a second or third
division string of prostitutes. Smithson said he wanted
more than £50 from Caruana and in the ensuing fight

[11] B. Wickstead, *Gangbuster*, p. 26.

Caruana's fingers were slashed as he protected his face from a flick knife. Other Maltese in the cafe were held off at gunpoint by Thomas. Thirty more pounds were produced. In accordance with standard gangland practice Ellul was told to start a collection for Fay and provided with a book to record the contributions.

On 25 June Smithson was found dying in the gutter outside Caruana's house in Carlton Vale. He had been shot in the arm and neck. His last words were said to be 'Good morning, I'm dying.' The full story of his death did not emerge for almost another twenty years. Its solution was to have considerable repercussions for the next generation of criminals and the police alike.

With Smithson's killing as her mitigation and given that she had no prior criminal convictions – for the purposes prostitution does not count – Fay Richardson was placed on probation with a condition she returned to Lancashire and did not visit London for three years. Whilst on remand, she had applied for leave to attend Smithson's funeral and had been refused. Instead a wreath was sent in her name: 'Till we meet again, Fay.' Other tributes at the funeral, attended not by the bosses but by almost everyone else from the milieu, included pairs of dice, an anchor in recognition of the fact he was a naval man and, from his mother, a chair. It was a classic example of a major gangland funeral with the cortege half a mile long.

Some time after that, Tommy's old mum, a wonderful old girl, had a life-size statue of an angel made to place over Tommy's grave. It's still there in St Patrick's Cemetery, Langthorne Road, Leytonstone. When she had it made, she showed me a photo of it, and out of respect I couldn't laugh at the time, but I had to have a good laugh as I walked away – a villain like Tommy Smithson to have an angel over his grave.[12]

Fay Richardson headed back north, pausing only to visit Tommy's grave in Leytonstone – an act of piety faithfully recorded by the press. Later she returned to London and took up with Jackie Rosa, Billy Hill's team mate and Elephant and Castle hardman. Some time later Rosa was killed in a car crash. He was disqualified from driving at the time and his last words to the police are said to have been, 'It wasn't me who was driving.'

'Her men never did have any luck,' said one of Rosa's friends cynically.

Of course from time to time there were other troubles to disturb the Hill–Spot-induced calm. One arose when Francis Fraser from the Elephant and Castle, who had had interests in the West End for over a decade and was to continue to do so for another, re-emerged. According to Hill, Fraser and his team quarrelled in Soho with the Carters from South London and Hill stepped in to quieten things down after a man was glassed. Alliances were formed and broken and as the relationship between Spot and Hill deteriorated so Fraser became a running mate of Hill.

Just how much control Spot did exercise is debatable. He claimed to have united the gangs from as far apart as Upton Park and Aldgate in the east, Forest Hill and the Elephant and Castle in the south, through to Islington, Shepherd's Bush and Clerkenwell. Possibly he never even aspired to 'running' Soho which was, at the time, synonymous with the 'underworld', although he had a club there and took a cut of £200 a week from another. He held court in the Galahad Club off the Tottenham Court Road. He was a family man living at Hyde Park Mansions in Bayswater with a beautiful wife,

[12] H. Ward, *Buller*.

Rita, whom he had met at Haydock Park races and who had stood by him for years through the troubles which came his way. Perhaps, as has been said, he was too happily married to be a proper gang leader. Yet at his peak he maintained a style reminiscent of the American gangsters of the 1930s.

The crime reporter Michael Jacobson thought little of him. 'I knew Spotty well and he was never more than just a thug. He had no initiative of his own. He was never a gang leader. Hill was.'

On the other hand, Leonard 'Nipper' Read, who as a young officer at Paddington knew Spot and later arrested the Krays, thought quite well of him.

> By the 1950s he . . . was something of a grand old man. He had mellowed since his early days and was now well groomed with well tailored, usually brown suits, a brown fedora hat and hand-made shoes. He would leave his flat, walk across the road to his barbers and then down to the Cumberland Hotel where at a table in the corner of the Bear Garden he would hold court offering advice and wisdom to anyone who sought it. He looked like a successful businessman. He seemed to have modelled himself on the American mafioso, Frank Costello, but had neither that man's intellect, power or political connections.[13]

Read had not much time for Billy Hill, whom he described as 'short, slim, and with his hair greased and pasted back [and] looked every inch a spiv of the 1950s'.[14] Hill had been born in Seven Dials, near Leicester Square, in 1911. For years, indeed up until the gentrification

[13] L. Read and J. Morton, *Nipper*.
[14] Ibid.

of Covent Garden in the last twenty years, it was one of the rookeries of London crime. He was one of twenty-one children and his one-eyed sister, Maggie, was a famous shoplifter known in the trade as 'Baby Face, the Queen of Forty Elephants'. The nickname came from the shape she acquired after hiding the merchandise in her hoister's bloomers and coats.

According to his version of events, Hill did his first chivving (slashing or stabbing) at the age of fourteen. 'Suddenly he took a liberty with me. Without the slightest qualm I got hold of a pair of scissors and drove them into his back. And it came quite natural to me. It was as easy as that.'[15]

Even earlier he was a fully fledged burglar. According to Narborough, his arrest of Hill was to lead to his first gaol sentence. It was for being a suspected person and Hill seems to have been most co-operative. 'No one was quite sure where we were, so Billy Hill volunteered to direct us to the nearest police station.'[16] From there he continued a life of burglaries for which he received a string of prison sentences, at the same time moving ever upwards in the hierarchy of the underworld. He was popular with his lawyers. 'Send in a bill and it was paid on the nail,' says one managing clerk who acted for him.

The consensus is that despite their totally different personalities Hill and Spot got along well. For years they maintained a low profile and were always prepared to enter an accommodation with, say, the Maltese who ran prostitution. 'It was as if the police gave them a licence to keep things under control,' says a solicitor's managing clerk.

Spot's troubles when they came were mainly in the form of Duncan Webb, the crime writer for the *People*

---

[15] B. Hill, *Boss of Britain's Underworld*, p. 19.

[16] F. Narborough, *Murder on My Mind*, p. 38.

and ghost writer for the other boss of the underworld, Billy Hill. Spot became jealous at the publicity being handed out and which was not rubbing off on to him. Spot wrote in his book: 'Billy Hill was a friend of mine. But he had his own way of working. His own personal ambitions and his own ideas and plans; ambitions and ideas can sometimes clash.' And on another occasion: 'I made Billy Hill. He wrote to me when he was in gaol, wanted me to help him. . . . Then he got to be top over me. If it wasn't for me he'd never have got there. I should've shot Billy Hill. I really should.'[17]

Hill had this to say of the deterioration in their relationship: 'Jack was becoming insecure and a bit jealous of me. He was an older man, you see, and once he got this persecution complex he was impossible to work with anymore.'[18] 'The worst thing I ever did,' he told an acquaintance, 'was to give Jack £14,000 from the Eastcastle Street job.'

There is no doubt that by the summer of 1955 Spot's career as a gang leader was just about in ruins. Things had deteriorated so much that he feared for his pitches on the course at the Epsom spring meeting. Fraser and another hardman, Billy Blythe, were now more closely aligned with Hill than he was. They would be at the meeting. So he called on the Kray brothers in their billiard hall in the East End to seek help. The Krays were never keen on Spot, nor, it seems, he on them. They had their day at the races, their first outing into the upper echelons of underworld society. There was no trouble. At the end of the meeting they took their money and drove off.

It wasn't that we liked him. We despised him

---

[17] *Sunday Times* magazine, 8 August 1965.

[18] J. Pearson, *The Profession of Violence*, p. 85. (1977 Ed.).

really. We just turned out with Spotty to show everyone that *we* was the up-and-coming firm and didn't give a fuck for anyone. Old Spotty understood. Whatever else he may have been he wasn't stupid. He knew quite well that though we were there in theory as his friends, we meant to end up taking over from him.[19]

According to Pearson, after the spring meeting Fraser and Blythe wished to meet the Krays at a pub in Islington to sort things out. The Krays spent time arming themselves and assembling a team but Hill, having got word of the challenge issued by Fraser and Blythe, was strong enough to have the meeting called off. 'The last thing he wanted was to have bloodshed,' says Pearson. The Krays waited around the pub and then drove home, no doubt satisfied that Fraser did not dare to enter their manor.

As for Spot, he lamented:

At first little things went wrong. When a raid was carefully planned and schemed, something would go wrong at the last minute. The man detailed to steal the getaway car wouldn't be able to steal it or a bunch of skeleton keys that should have opened a door failed to do so at the crucial moment.

The men who'd been responsible for these slipups had been bawled out. But they hadn't cried. Instead they'd walked straight out on me and got themselves a job with another organization.[20]

Slowly he lost both his gang and his reputation. The word was out in the underworld that he was a grass. 'We'd had his sheet pulled from the Yard,' says one of

[19] Ibid, p. 87.
[20] H. Jansen, *Jack Spot*, pp. 117–18.

Hill's close friends, 'and there it was for all to see.'

On the other hand Hill's friends and allies remained staunch. They included the daredevil safe-breaker, Eddie Chapman, who had been released from prison during the war for work in German territory, and ex-boxer George Walker, brother of Billy, who was to go on to found the Brent Walker group of companies and whose daughter married into the aristocracy.

Spot was also being pursued by Duncan Webb and on 21 October 1954 he assaulted his tormentor, breaking his arm. On 18 November at Clerkenwell Magistrates' Court he was fined £50 for inflicting grievous bodily harm. More seriously, the incident led to a civil action in the High Court and to Spot's eventual bankruptcy.

Once splits occur in underworld factions even the slightest quarrel or perceived insult can trigger a string of repercussions. One such incident occurred in Manzi's restaurant off Leicester Square when one of Spot's men, Bill Diamond, gave Johnny Jackson, a man more aligned to Hill, a backhander. Such a public display caused both a loss of face and loss of patience.

The effective end of Spot's reign came on 11 August 1955 when he was told in the drinking club, the Galahad, that 'Big Albert' Dimes wanted to see him. This must have been the crowning insult. His temper up, he went to find Dimes and caught up with him on the corner of Frith Street in Soho, where they fought amongst the barrows with a large lady fruiterer trying to stop them by banging Spot with a brass weighing-pan.

'If she hadn't intervened Spot would have done him,' says a bystander who never gave evidence. 'Once she hit him Albert got the knife away and did him.' Both men were badly injured. Dimes got away in a taxi. Spot picked himself off the pavement, staggered into a nearby barber's shop, said 'Fix me up' and fainted. Both went to hospital and were arrested as they left their respective hospital beds. When questioned Spot had said, 'It is between me and Albert Dimes – between us, and nothing to do with you.' When asked who had attacked him Dimes replied, 'You know as well as I do. It was Jackie Spot. I'm not prossing.' When he was asked to make a formal statement he said he had been attacked by 'a tall man. . . . I don't know his name.' Another version of the story is that Spot went after Dimes because he was not paying his tribute. A third is that the Italian Mob led by Bert Marsh had put Dimes up to aggravate Spot because he was losing control and was ripe to be taken.

Spot had been stabbed over the left eye and in the left cheek as well as the neck and ear. He had four stab wounds in the left arm and two in the chest, one of which had penetrated the lung. Dimes had his forehead cut to the bone, requiring twenty stitches, a wound in the thigh and one in the stomach which, the prosecutor later said, 'mercifully just failed to penetrate the abdominal cavity'.

But, almost miraculously, their wounds had sufficiently healed eleven days later for their appearance before Marlborough Street Magistrates' Court charged with wounding with intent to commit grievous bodily harm and affray. Clearly the tradition of the underworld that one member should not give evidence against another did not apply to their defending lawyers. Counsel for Dimes said his client had acted completely in self-defence after being attacked by 'this other murderous, treacherous rascal'. Bert Marsh, who just happened to have been in Frith Street at the time and who could not now abide his former friend Spot, loyally gave evidence favouring Dimes and was roundly attacked for his pains. There was clearly a case to answer, said the magistrate. Spot and Dimes were committed for trial at the Old Bailey where they were prosecuted by Reggie Seaton, later to become chairman of the Inner London Quarter Sessions.

The way Seaton put the case for the Crown was that Spot had started the attack and that Dimes had at some time in the struggle wrested the knife from him and struck back, going far beyond the limits of self-defence.

The trials which followed were genuinely sensational. At first Mr Justice Glyn-Jones refused an application for separate trials. This, on the face of it, was reasonable. The defendants were charged with making an affray. Unfortunately he had what would be described, in the world of Spot and Dimes, as a touch of the seconds. The next day he asked the counsel for Spot, Rose Heilbron (who was later to become the second woman High Court judge), and that for Dimes, G. D. 'Khaki' Roberts, a doyen of the Bar, what they had to say about making an affray in a public place.

Roberts argued that the reactions of a man fighting for his life could never be described as making an affray. Reggie Seaton for the Crown, accepting that view, then tried to take the affray into the greengrocery shop itself where the fight had ended. If, he argued, it was a public place then Dimes' conduct after he had wrested the knife from Spot was capable of being an affray. It was not a view accepted by the judge, who withdrew the charge of affray against both Spot and Dimes from the jury and told the jury that, if they wished, they could acquit Dimes on the charge of wounding Spot.

'It is not for Dimes to prove that he was acting in self-defence. It is for the prosecution to prove that he was not.' The jury were not convinced and in the circumstances Glyn-Jones discharged them, saying that 'a joint trial without the first charge would not be lawful'. He then directed that Dimes be acquitted of possessing an offensive weapon, gave him bail and remanded Spot in custody. The separate trial of Spot was fixed to take place forty-eight hours later.

On 22 September Spot went into the witness box to say that he had gone to Frith Street to meet Dimes following a telephone call which warned him off race-courses. He told the jury that he paid £300 for the pitches and, keeping one for himself, let the rest out at a fee. Dimes had told him: 'This is your final warning! I don't want you to go racing any more'; adding that he had been going on long enough and it was time someone else had his pitches.

As for the fight, 'We started pushing each other. All of a sudden he pulls a knife out and makes stabs at me. I put my arm up, and it goes through my arm. I fight my way back to the door of the greengrocer's shop. He goes at me again and gets me in the face.' So far as he was concerned Dimes received his injuries in the struggle.

There was a witness to corroborate this version of events: Christopher Glinski, then an interpreter, who a decade later would feature in the Richardson torture trials and a number of other criminal cases both for and against the prosecution. Spot was right, he said. 'I saw Spot push the other man. Then the other man charged him. The other man took a knife out of his pocket. The man in the dock lifted his arms to defend himself. I saw the knife cut into his arm. Then I saw another blow cut his face.' Glinski had got in touch with Peters & Peters, Spot's solicitors, after reading the reports of the magistrates' court committal proceedings and realizing they did not tally with what he had seen.

But there was more, and better, to come. The Reverend Basil Claude Andrews, eighty-eight years old, came to court to say exactly the same thing. He was sure the darker man (Dimes) had attacked the fairer one (Spot). On the face of it here was an unimpeachable eyewitness. In scenes of triumph and jubilation Spot was acquitted. Immediately afterwards in a separate trial Dimes too was acquitted.

But retribution was to follow. The police were informed by disgruntled bookmakers and friends of Dimes that, far from being a saintly old man, the Reverend Basil was an old rascal who welshed on his bets. His only course of action was to go to a newspaper, the *Daily Sketch*, longtime supporters of Spot, to publish his side of the story.

> I am fully aware that cowardly people who dare not come forward into the light of day are suggesting that I am a fraudulent witness and that I hoodwinked Mr Comer's [Spot's] legal advisers.
>
> I would recall to you that when I gave my evidence last week I gave it on my solemn oath, and I need not remind you that I am a Clerk in Holy Orders.

He went on to deny he had committed perjury, adding:

> Any financial difficulties due to my changes of address and my harmless flutters in the sporting world are only temporary, due to my age and inexperience.
>
> Those who are dunning me will soon be repaid if they have patience – some debts have been settled already.
>
> My innocent walk in Frith Street, Soho, that day has made me finish up in a nest of trouble, with enemies in an underworld I never dreamed existed.

And for good measure, he finished: 'I would like to bring about a reconciliation between the parties in the strife who seem to have forgotten that, by what they have done, they are debasing the sacred Brotherhood of Man.'

By the end of the year the Reverend Basil was back in the Old Bailey giving evidence, this time on behalf of the prosecution. The police, unhappy about the collapse of the Spot–Dimes case, had been busying themselves and had now brought a prosecution for conspiracy to pervert the course of justice. Andrews admitted that he had given his evidence following a meeting with Bernard Schack, known as 'Sonny the Yank', and Morris Goldstein, 'Moisha Blue Boy', in the Cumberland Hotel at Marble Arch. His reward had been £25. The Reverend Basil was again believed. Goldstein was sent to prison for three years, Schack for two, whilst Rita Comer, Spot's wife, was fined £50. No one seems to have thought twice about Glinski.

After the trial Spot announced he was quitting Soho and the race-courses. He would, he said, open a small cafe. He would have been fortunate if he had done so. Soho was up for grabs once more. Dimes does not appear to have been too interested. He took over Spot's point-to-point interests. Newspapers reported that there were five major gangs each seeking to put their top man into the position vacated by Spot. Francis Fraser, along with Robert Warren, the elder cousin of boxing promoter Frank, was re-establishing his business of putting gaming machines into Soho clubs. Billy Hill now returned from Australia. He had decided to emigrate there but was refused entry when he turned up with a young woman who certainly was not Aggie, the lawful Mrs Hill. Curiously, however, the outbreak of gang violence, anticipated with some relish by the press, never quite reached all-out war.

There were, however, to be further reprisals against Spot, who knew from rumours in the underworld that he was due for punishment and repeatedly went to Paddington police station seeking protection. Read recalls:

He started by talking to Peter Beveridge, the Detective Chief Superintendent of the District, and worked his way down through the Detective Inspector and various sergeants until he ended up with me. He told me on numerous occasions that the other mob was going to do him and he often pleaded with me to do something about it but as I pointed out, unless there was more direct evidence there was nothing we could do. As a betting man Jack must have known that it was 6/4 on that he would become a victim eventually but it would have been impossible to offer him any sort of protection against a situation he had manufactured himself.

When the police could not help, Spot rented himself a personal bodyguard, Joe Cannon, the minder at the Miramar Club where he drank, paying him £50 a week.

Spot had thought seriously about buying a pub in Paddington and on 2 May 1956 he and Rita had been to look at the Little Weston off Praed Street when at about 9 p.m. they were attacked by a number of armed men. Spot was knocked to the ground with a shillelagh (recognized by his wife as one which, in happier days, he had given Billy Hill), kicked and slashed. At first he made a statement giving the names of his attackers but later retracted it. Rita was made of sterner stuff. She named Frank Fraser and Bobby Warren as leaders of the attack. Both Hill and Dimes were arrested and questioned but never charged.

But where was Spot's minder, Joe Cannon, a man who had been in Portland Borstal, although rather later in time than another former pupil, Billy Hill? Spot had told him that he was taking Rita out for a meal in the Edgware Road and to meet him back at the flat. Cannon had taken his girlfriend Ellen out for the night and had forgotten the time.

. . . when I looked at my watch it was one o'clock
in the morning, long past the time when I was due
to meet Jack and Rita. Still, there was no use
crying over spilt milk, so I spent the rest of the
night with Ellen.

In a way I was lucky. If I had been with Jack
when he made his way home I would have been
dead or, at best, seriously injured.[21]

After the attack, and once it was realized it was a
police matter, there were the usual out of court
negotiations. It was arranged that Cannon should go to
Hill's office at Warren Street, just off Tottenham
Court Road. According to his memoirs Cannon took
the precaution of taking a .45 revolver with him to the
rendezvous, where he met Hill and Albert Dimes. The
message he was to convey was that Spot knew Rita
was set on going to court but that he, Jack, would talk
her out of it. The quid pro quo was that Hill should
stop the escalating aggravation between them. Hill was
not pleased, telling Cannon that Spot was a wrong 'un
and that he would get the same treatment if he
remained his man. Indeed, it was only the kindly
intervention of Frankie Fraser, who had put in a
good word for Cannon, which had kept him unmarked
so far.

Dimes appears to have been the peacemaker. All that
mattered now was that no one was nicked. Could
Cannon fix it so that a couple of the Hill boys could get
in to Spot's bedside so things could be agreed in person?
One problem was the police sitting by the bedside. The
negotiator, a man called Jimmy Woods, went with
Cannon to the hospital and in whispers it was agreed that
there was no point in nicking Fraser and the rest. Jack

[21] J. Cannon, *Tough Guys Don't Cry*.

said he would persuade Rita not to go ahead. So far as Spot knew it was a genuine settlement negotiated by interested but not involved parties. As he was leaving Woods was asked by the ever percipient Spot whether he had seen Hill recently. 'Haven't seen him for months,' was the reply. Unfortunately, instead of waiting for Cannon and Woods at the Fifty One club as arranged, Hill had come to the hospital, where he was photographed with Woods and Cannon. Cannon and Spot realized they had been set up.

Fraser went to Ireland until matters had, so he thought, died down. He was only lured back when the police let it be known the matter was closed and was arrested at London Airport on his return.

Nevertheless, once the trial began Spot tried to do his best for his attackers. 'I do not recognize these men,' he told the court. 'I know that these men did not attack me.'

But Rita was quite prepared to go through with it. She was cross-examined vigorously by Patrick Marrinan on behalf of Warren, who put to her that she was giving evidence to get rid of Hill, Dimes and friends to re-establish her husband as 'King of the Underworld'.

'I don't care about the other people. I just want to be left alone with my husband and children,' she replied, after earlier saying, 'I would be very happy if they let my husband and me alone. I'd like him to get just a small job.'

Marrinan asked her whether it was right that on the day after the attack she had telephoned a Mrs Harry White and said, 'I'm going to get your husband ten years. I saw him with a knife in his hand stab my husband last night.'

'No,' she replied, she had said, 'I suppose you and your husband are pleased now.'

Harry White certainly must have been.[22] After the Spot–Dimes fight he had given an interview to his old friend Sidney Williams, spitting on the floor as he said, 'That's how frightened we are of Jack Spot and his men now. He hasn't got five men he can rely on to stand at his back.'[23]

Frankie Fraser, who by then had fifteen convictions and had twice been certified 'insane', had, said his counsel John Ritchie, been made use of by other persons for a foul purpose. Warren, with no convictions for violence, received the same seven-year sentence as Fraser.

A week later the same judge, Mr Justice Donovan, sentenced two others, Richard 'Dicky Dido' Frett and David Rosa, for a separate attack. The victim, Johnny Carter of the Carter family and friend of Spot, was connected with the Elephant and Castle Boys who were now flexing their muscles to establish control over Soho and to clear out once and for all any remnants of the King's Cross gang who might be thinking of returning to the West End. An effort by Patrick Marrinan, appearing now for the defendants, to establish that Carter was a member of the Elephant Boys was ruled inadmissible.

'It sounds like the worst days of Prohibition in Chicago rather than London in 1956,' said the judge when imposing seven-year sentences.

On 11 July two more men, 'Billy Boy' Blythe and

[22] Harry White's actress daughter was killed while filming *Ocean's 11* with Frank Sinatra and the Ratpack in America. White had close links with Sinatra and provides an early connection with transatlantic interests. A devout Catholic, he discovered whilst providing the betting for a Church Donkey Derby that the animal a boy was riding was a heavy favourite. 'If it looks like fucking winning make sure you fall off,' he told the child, who duly obliged.

[23] *Daily Herald*, 8 October 1955.

Robert 'Battles' Rossi, were to appear to answer for the attack on Spot, and later another man, William Dennis, joined them at the Old Bailey. Blythe received five years and the others four apiece.

But by now Jack Spot was himself back in the dock at the Old Bailey. He was accused of attacking 'Big Tommy', Thomas Falco, a driver for Dimes – 'I work for Albert Dimes when we go to the races. . . . When he wins, I get wages' – outside the Astor Club on 20 June 1956. He had required forty-seven stitches as a result of this attack and maintained that as Spot had slashed him he had said, 'This is one for Albert . . .'

A witness, ex-boxer Johnny Rice, who gave his occupation as a steel merchant but who was photographed within a few days on a bookmaker's stand at Brighton races along with Tommy Falco and Harry White, remembered the words as 'This is one for Albert Dimes . . .'

At the committal proceedings, James Dunlop for Spot said of the allegation that 'it is a complete and utter fabrication from start to finish'. He would, he said, be calling a witness who had volunteered first-hand information.

The whole story came out at Spot's trial at the Central Criminal Court when that witness, Victor 'Scarface Jock' Russo, came to give evidence. He had, he said, been offered £500 by Albert Dimes to allow himself to be slashed so that Spot could be framed. The offer had come in a car in Frith Street. He had gone there and met Dimes, Hill, Frannie Daniels and Johnny Rice after a back-room meeting at Peter Mario's restaurant in Gerrard Street, Soho. There Hill had said to Duncan Webb, the crime reporter, 'I want you to have a go at Spot this week', and Webb had agreed to write something to Spot's detriment in the *People*. How would they know that Spot did not have a cast-iron aiibi? 'I will get Kye-Kye [Sid Kiki, a bookmaker] to find out,' said Hill. Russo had thought it over and then declined. Later he had heard of the slashing of Falco. When Spot had been arrested he had both gone to the police and telephoned Billy Hill telling him what he had done.

Hill gave evidence denying Russo's allegation. Almost all he would admit to was being boss of the underworld. Afterwards he held a press conference saying that Fraser and Warren were his boys and complaining that the police watched him day and night.

Would he make peace with Spot? 'I am a powerful man,' he said, 'and I don't have to make peace with anyone.'[24]

Billy Hill retired to his villa in Spain saying he had had enough. He had become a minor celebrity. The launch of his book had been attended by Lord and Lady Docker and he had organized the return of her Ladyship's jewels when they were stolen. A picture taken at the book launch shows Frankie Fraser draped artistically over the piano.

'His bottle went,' said one of his former friends, 'he'd lived by violence and now was afraid of getting it.'

Spot went downhill. On his bankruptcy examination he maintained that his memory had gone through too many bangs on the head. He had liabilities of £12,321 and assets of £125. He and Rita were evicted from their Hyde Park Mansions flat. He obtained his discharge from bankruptcy in January 1957 and later that year, with her earnings from newspapers – shortly after the attack she had been paid £300 by the *Daily Express* for posing with her husband – she opened the Highball Club in Bayswater. On 21 July it was wrecked by a gang. Whilst still under police guard it was set ablaze on 13

[24] There are numerous accounts of the series of trials. One of the more entertaining is by Laurence Wilkinson, *Behind the Face of Crime*.

August. It was not reopened.

According to Cannon he expected some reprisals from Hill but in turn he was offered the then enormous sum of £2000 to shoot him. He waited outside the Modernaires Club and shot at Hill and Dimes as they left in the early hours.

> I reckon Hill knew that I was the culprit. So did the Old Bill, but there was no reaction from either, maybe Billy felt that it was beneath his dignity to declare war on a nineteen-year-old. . . . It all came right in the end. Dimes contacted me and offered me a drink if I would have nothing more to do with Spotty. I took it, and there the whole thing finished.[25]

Spot drifted into employment as a meat packer and some years later was fined for stealing from his employer. He became estranged from Rita and changed his name to Comacho. Over the years he could be seen at small-hall boxing tournaments in London as perky and ebullient as in his prime.

[25] J. Cannon, *Tough Guys Don't Cry*, p. 45.

3

The Years Between

By the late 1950s control of Soho and the West End was seemingly wide open. Curiously enough none of the likely candidates appeared either to want it or to be capable of taking it. Although he retained interests in the West End, Hill was living in Spain in semi-retirement. Such families as the Carter brothers from Peckham still remained loyal to Jack Spot, but he was effectively disgraced and exiled to Notting Hill. Immediately after the Dimes–Spot fight in August 1955 there had been reports of meetings to discuss the Soho scene but nothing had really come of them. Frankie Fraser, who had had interests in the Soho clubs for some time and whom the newspapers considered a natural successor, was in prison serving seven years for the second Spot stabbing. For the time being it seemed there was no one with the necessary charisma and will to take over.

A number of small-timers popped their heads over the parapet to see what was about, but no real hardman, capable of dominating the scene, emerged. This was probably for a number of reasons apart from the fact that there was no one person or family about with the interest or, if they had the interest, the strength and ability to convert it into action. Although he does not seem to have wanted Soho for himself, the now middle-aged 'Big

Albert' Dimes, as Hill's right-hand man, almost certainly exerted a calming influence. Questions of territory and ownership were referred to him for a solution.

But as for ownership, 'he couldn't fight for fuck,' says one contemporary. Albert Donaghue, later on with the Kray firm, puts it more diplomatically. 'He didn't have the backing necessary,' he says. 'What he was, though, was King of the Point-to-Points.'

Certainly Dimes was now in control of the best pitches at the tracks, and he remained so, granting the concessions and making sure that the odds chalked up suited him. 'If he had the favourite at say 7/4 and took a load on it then he would wipe it to 6/4 and Bobby Warren or one of his men would walk down the line telling us it was the same price for the rest of us,' says Donaghue.

It is a curious fact about the English gang leaders of the period that they never seemed to aspire to the trappings of wealth sported by their admittedly grander-scale American counterparts. True, Hill had a boat, but that was used for business purposes – for the smuggling of cigarettes. He lived in a modest flat in Moscow Road. Spot was a seemingly devoted family man living in Hyde Park Mansions. 'If they went to the Astor Club a couple of nights a week that was a big deal,' says Nipper Read.

Dimes seems to have been in that mould. Read says:

Of course he never had to pay for a meal anywhere, never had to spend any real money. He held court in the Italian Cafe in Frith Street and would have his suits made for free, free haircuts, and tributes like chickens and meat brought to him. But he was never a man who, whilst he was always well dressed, ever threw money about.

At the time the earnings of a gang leader were in the five-figure mark annually. Lesser fry would receive £20 a week, said *The Times* in 1956.

Dimes remained the almost unseen Godfather, keeping out of the public eye and surfacing only on rare but sometimes quite spectacular occasions. In 1956 he was awarded £666 for a back injury sustained when the cab in which he was travelling was involved in an accident with a van. He was, he said, working as a commission agent, earning about £10 a week. He was fortunate enough not to have paid tax since 1951. A little later in a separate case he agreed to pay arrears of National Insurance Contributions of £135.

In 1956 he was named in the House of Commons by Anthony Greenwood, who called him a 'squalid, cowardly, small-time hoodlum'. He went to see Mr Greenwood for an explanation of the adjectives but the Conservative MP refused to see him. Dimes admitted to a short stretch in Borstal in 1931 and a four-month sentence 'years ago' but surely, he complained, that did not qualify him for Mr Greenwood's attack.

Then in November 1959 he fell out with the National Hunt Committee over the collection of bookmakers' voluntary contributions at the East Essex point-to-point. He had been the only one capable of collecting these illegal payments and had taken on the job out of the goodness of his heart when Harry White, showing even more public spiritedness, had refused to make the collections because 'they [the NHC] wanted too much. I thought it was a liberty asking £10 each for a pitch when they might not take that much from the punters. Albert took over just to keep the peace.'

A year later his name came up in the trial of a former apprentice jockey charged with conspiracy to dope racehorses. The jockey said he had made £1200 from bookmakers and backers when Faultless Speech won the William Hill Gold Cup at Redcar earlier that year. Dimes was alleged to have contributed £100 to the jockey's earnings.

In 1961 he was said to have received £8000 from the swindling of a Bradford chinchilla dealer who had been persuaded to part with £35,900 to finance the purchase of a fleet of ships. The con man, a Charles de Silva, received only £4100 from the deal, and later six years' imprisonment.[1] Dimes obtained the services of Dai Tudor Price, later a High Court judge, to make a statement in open court denying his involvement in the scam.

Two years later Brighton club owner Harvey Holford, accused of the murder of his wife Christine and convicted of her manslaughter, explained his possession of a gun by saying it was to protect himself against Hill, Dimes and their cohorts. Holford had been having difficulties over the installation of 'Legalite' gaming machines in his Blue Gardenia Club.

Dimes last swam into public view in early 1968 when he was at the Tavistock Hotel in Bloomsbury to discuss money owed by a Max Fine to a Mr Corallo, described in a subsequent libel hearing as an 'American gangster'. He also met Angelo Bruno of the Philadelphian family, of whom it was said he was the secret and trusted representative. Bruno came to London between 27 November and 3 December 1966 in a gambling junket organized by a New York gambling club. Another of the card players on that junket was the celebrated Meyer

[1] Ceylonese-born de Silva, described as looking like Omar Sharif, had been a long-time friend of Billy Hill. He was supposed to be the black sheep of a wealthy family and lived well off the art of the con man. He is one of the few examples of a Hill man who was linked with the Krays but at one time he was under their protection. He had been paying over a share of his profits to Charlie Mitchell. The sale of the fishing fleet was the last of his great scams. Later he took a drug overdose rather than face another substantial term of imprisonment.

Lansky, now accepted as one of the great Mafia financiers. Dimes visited Bruno in Philadelphia the next year to discuss the installation of gaming machines in various clubs.[2]

In November 1972 Dimes died of cancer. The Krays sent a wreath costing £20 with the inscription 'To a fine gentleman', a message destroyed by friends on the grounds that it brought shame to the family. The funeral in Kent was attended by over 200 mourners, among them Stanley Baker to whom he had given technical advice on films, including *Robbery*, based on the Great Train Robbery. On his deathbed Dimes is said to have ordered that the police be told the truth about the killing of 'Scotch Jack' Buggy at a gambling club in Mayfair. At his funeral the priest spoke of how proud Dimes had been that he could recite the Creed in Latin.

So ended an unbroken forty-year involvement with Soho, its clubs and frequenters.

But was Dimes the true Godfather or was there someone else standing behind, and over, him? The suggestion in some quarters is that there was. It was the redoubtable Pasqualino Papa – Bert Marsh, who had been acquitted of the murder of a Columbo brother at Wandsworth Greyhound Track. He seems to have been noted by the press only once, when at the Spot–Dimes trial he was accused by Spot's barrister of trying to provide false witnesses for Albert Dimes. But, even today, some major underworld figures speak very highly of him:

---

[2] On 21 March 1980 Angelo Bruno left the Cous restaurant in Philadelphia and was shot behind the right ear when in his car, along with his bodyguard John Stanfa. Bruno died instantly. It was advanced that the reason for his death was his refusal to enter into the lucrative narcotics trade.

Bert ran a betting shop in Frith Street and had an off-licence in Old Compton Street and an interest in at least six books. He was a quiet man, a very very dapper man. He was the Guv'nor all right. He died a very rich man.

Another says:

He was something of a mystery. I met him in the early sixties in Clerkenwell when I was going out with an Italian girl. He was a very pleasant man, very courteous. People respected him, something I didn't understand then. I was later told that he was the Mafia's top man in this country and a man to be friends with.

Meanwhile, fairly unobtrusively, the Maltese had strengthened their grip on the Soho entertainment industry into a stranglehold. Although from time to time the press did what it could to generate some interest in the Soho protection scene, there was little mention of the Maltese involvement until 1971.

On the domestic front, however, in August 1957, with little else going on in the journalists' silly season, the *Daily Sketch* reported that Robert Padgett from West Hartlepool had his sights on the big time. 'I reckon things are soft in London so I'm taking my Pink Domino Gang (named after the tattoos on his left hand) down there. . . . Jack Spot and all that don't frighten me. They don't know what street fighting is.' He was rapidly exposed as a fake a few days later by the same paper, which called in a psychiatrist to evaluate the lad's boasts.

Nearly two years later, in June 1959, a rather more genuine claimant, Joseph Francis Oliva, a Gibraltarian by birth but now from the Bourne Estate in Clerkenwell, London, emerged to give an interview also in the *Daily*

Sketch. He was known, he said, as King Oliva and ran protection rackets and could call up a gang of 400 men. He had been shot a couple of days previously in retaliation, so he claimed, for a fight in a dice spieler in a Camden Town club three weeks before when he and five others had cleaned up all the money, amounting to some £80.

I am going to be boss of the night clubs – and run the night clubs around the West End. I have got to shift one or two big gang leaders to do it. But I have got a man behind me financing me. I already work for him. We have got to have cars to get around in and 'clobber' to look the part.

We already get a nice little living from East End clubs and some in the West End. And we look after about twelve clubs. We see no one takes liberties with the juke-boxes and we make sure there is no trouble in the clubs. The club owners pay us for this and we give the money to the 'Governor'. He is a London businessman who owns property and lives in a big house on the outskirts of town.

I command about 400 people. I can get them all at twenty-four hours' notice just by fifteen to twenty phone calls to individual top men in each gang. Then I am the governor of them all. They are different gangs from all North and South London but mostly in the Theobalds Road area.

All the 400 do not get paid. They do it for kicks. They are all teenagers. They worship me – King Oliva.

We last called the 400 up six months ago for a big fight at the Memorial Hall, Camden Town. But the other side backed out.

I have two lieutenants. I split equally with them. I am drawing about £30 a week at the moment.

He stalwartly maintained that he was no menace to the general public. 'We don't want to have a go at the public. Only gang governors like us in the underworld. I am going to be boss because there are some rich pickings. All a fellow needs is guts and backing – and I've got both.'[3]

It was a statement he largely denied when five years later he was called to give evidence at an enquiry into the behaviour of Detective Sergeant Harold Gordon Challenor and how it was possible for that officer to continue on duty at a time when he appeared to have been affected by the onset of mental illness. Both James Fraser, a relation of the better known Frankie, and Oliva had received sentences following a brush with Challenor. Oliva had received six years' imprisonment for conspiracy to demand money with menaces in relation to the Geisha Club in Moor Street and the Phoenix in Old Compton Street, Soho, and related offences; Fraser had been given fifteen months for possessing an offensive weapon in a public place. Both convictions had been quashed by the Court of Appeal in July 1964.

In their turn some club owners became fairly blasé about violence, regarding it as part of life's rich tapestry. On 11 February 1961 a home-made cocoa-tin bomb was thrown into the Gardenia Club in Wardour Mews, blowing a hole in the door, after Harry Bidney, the manager, had refused admission. On the previous Friday the owner of a nearby club had been slashed when he refused admission. 'A gang of young men are trying to terrorize club owners, but I'm not afraid,' said Bidney.

By then one family had emerged as a force with which

---

[3] Report of Inquiry by Mr A. E. James QC, p. 127, Cmnd 2735. Whilst £30 a week now seems less than pocket money it should be remembered that in 1959 a newly qualified solicitor would be earning less than £20 a week.

to be reckoned. They were the Nash family from Islington, 'the wickedest brothers in England' said one newspaper happily.[4] There were six brothers, from Billy (the fixer and the eldest, in his late twenties) ranging through Johnny (five years younger), Jimmy, Ronnie and George to Roy, the youngest, who had been convicted of manslaughter at the age of sixteen following the knifing of a youth in a dance hall fight. They were friends of the Krays and also of the Richardsons, so establishing a loose cross-London alliance.

Starting out in the 1950s in the traditional way of minding Cypriot cafes at £2 a week, the enterprise had grown until in the early 1960s Johnny Nash, who liked to be called the Peacemaker, was believed to have twenty clubs, including the Embassy in the West End, under his protection. He was said to have escalated the art of the gang fight so that fist was fought with knife, knife with axe and axe with gun. He maintained he was now King of the Underworld. In an interview on 5 March 1961 Billy Nash, who blamed the Street Offences Act of 1959 for much of the troubles in the West End, said there were ten to a dozen families in the club game, running prostitutes, protection, gambling and one-armed-bandits.[5] 'A back-street club was taking £30 to £50 a week and then the birds came in and it became a goldmine.'

Operational methods hadn't changed much, nor had payments. One of the Nash minders reported that he and friends had broken up the Little Londoner Club on Christmas morning 1959. 'I was paid £10 for the smash-up and £5 expenses.' Life was more expensive in London

---

[4] *Sunday Pictorial*, 19 February 1961.

[5] Following the Wolfenden report, the Street Offences Act of 1959 had effectively eliminated street prostitution. The girls had moved into clubs or taken rooms in Soho from which to work.

than in Liverpool, from where it was reported that a slashing could be organized for eighteen shillings.

The Nashes had a considerable North London following. After the dance hall fight at Highbury Corner in December 1959, when Ronald Marwood stabbed a policeman to death, he was hidden out for nearly a month by Johnny Nash. 'I had Big Ronnie stashed away. I had him in a flat in Holloway. He never left the place except after dark and even then he did not go far.'

Underworld legend has it that when the police net was closing in Marwood gave himself up rather than cause trouble for his protector and in return Johnny and another brother tried to help Marwood escape from Pentonville. Later the brothers sent wreaths on the anniversary of his execution.[6]

Although the Nashes held sway for some years, their power was never really the same after a seemingly unimportant occurrence – a minor road accident – blew up into a major gangland incident.

Selwyn Keith Cooney, manager of the Billy Hill-owned New Cabinet Club in Gerrard Street, and no friend of the Nashes, was in a relatively minor car accident involving another car driven by prostitute Vicky James, known as Blonde Vicky, who was a friend of Ronnie Nash. Cooney, a huge personable man from a middle-class Leeds family, known both as Jimmy Neill and, despite his size, Little Jimmy, instead of doing the more sensible thing and forgetting about the matter, sent the bill for 54s 9d damages to Vicky James. She was not insured and the bill remained unpaid. Quite by chance Cooney met Ronnie Nash in a Notting Hill drinking club. Words were exchanged and each suffered a black

---

[6] The Krays also claim to have hidden Marwood. For a full account of the Marwood story and the Krays' version of their involvement see chapter 5.

eye in the subsequent fight. Reports were that Ronnie Nash came off the worse. Two days later Cooney went to the Pen Club in Duval Street near Spitalfields Market.

The Pen Club, said to have been bought with the proceeds from a robbery at the Parker Pen Company and named as an underworld joke, was managed by none other than Tommy Smithson's nemesis Fay Richardson, now renamed Fay Sadler after her marriage to a gambling man. At the time, however, the club was owned by former boxer Billy Ambrose and Jeremiah Callaghan, a member of another leading family from Walworth and a figure who was to reappear time and again over the next two decades. Both were serving ten-year prison sentences but came home on parole at the weekends. The club was frequently raided by the police and, almost as frequently, it changed hands.

Reports of the background to the incident on 7 February 1960 vary. One version is that Jimmy 'Trunky' Nash, who worked as a minder at the Astor Club in which the family had an interest, set out to avenge his brother's beating. Another is that Jimmy, the mildest of the brothers, was sucked into the incident. Bert Wickstead, later a Commander of the Flying Squad but then a Detective Sergeant, believed that, no matter what was on the surface, the real reason behind the incident was that it was part of the West End power struggle with the chance accident providing an opportunity to establish a new pecking order.

Jimmy Nash, together with his red-headed girlfriend, a hostess named Doreen Masters, and two other former professional boxers arrived at the Pen Club a little while after Cooney. According to witnesses Cooney was pointed out to Nash by Doreen Masters and, together with the boxers, he went straight over, broke Cooney's nose with one blow and proceeded to give him a severe beating. 'That will teach you to give little girls a spanking,' he said. Cooney, protesting he had done nothing of the kind, fought back and there was a cry, 'He's got a gun.' Two witnesses were adamant that Nash then shot Billy Ambrose in the stomach and Cooney in the head at point-blank range.

Others in the club attacked Nash and another man, who was hit over the head with a bottle. They ran out of the club and Nash was driven away. Billy Ambrose, although badly hurt, still managed with some help to carry Cooney's body from the club and put it on a pavement some distance away. He then drove himself to hospital, reporting that he had been shot outside a club in Paddington. He could not remember its name.

With a death on the pavement and the wounds Billy Ambrose had suffered it was clear the police would be notified by somebody sooner or later, and they were – by the hospitals which received the body of Cooney and the injured Ambrose. Jeremiah Callaghan couldn't resist going back to the club to find out what was happening and was seen in Duval Street by the police. The bloodstains on his clothing came from a brawl outside a pub in Walworth, he said. Fay Sadler was seen leaving the London Hospital. Giving her name as Mrs Patrick Callaghan, she said she had simply called to see her friend Billy Ambrose. Then two others in the club were brought in for questioning. The first was Cooney's girlfriend, a nineteen-year-old barmaid from the New Cabinet, Joan Bending. The second was Johnny Simons, who had hit the man over the head with a bottle. Both were to point the finger at Jimmy Nash and the boxers. Fay Sadler was brought in for questioning and she too confirmed the picture. Jimmy Nash's flat in the Charing Cross Road was searched and a mackintosh stained with blood of the same type as Cooney's was found. Of Nash himself there was no trace. Meanwhile Joan Bending had picked out both the boxers at an identification parade.

Two days later James Nash surrendered himself at City Road police station. He was accompanied by Manny Fryde, a solicitor's managing clerk from Sampson & Co. Fryde, said by some to have qualified as a solicitor in South Africa but never in England, was one of the doyens of criminal work in post-war London. In those days, well before the Police and Criminal Evidence Act of 1984 with its built-in safeguards for suspects, the arrangement for Nash's surrender had been negotiated on the basis that there would be no pressure on him to make a verbal or written statement.

Bert Wickstead recalls him as a negative person.

> He had a very quiet voice for such a violent man, but I don't recall him saying anything that seemed worth remembering. He was a man of negative values – a non-smoker, non-drinker, who ate a pound of boiled sweets every day. He would sit in his cell, chewing them endlessly. Judging by the expression on his face he could have been on another planet.[7]

He, the boxers and Doreen Masters were charged with the capital murder of Selwyn Cooney. What followed was one of the worst examples of post-war witness interference and jury intimidation.

It began on 16 March with a razor attack on Johnny Simons in a Paddington cafe. His face needed twenty-seven stitches to repair it. The assault was followed by two on his girlfriend, a twenty-three-year-old model, Barbara Ibbotson. On the first occasion she was snatched in broad daylight in Soho and thrown into a car

---

[7] B. Wickstead, *Gangbuster*.

where her face was slashed four times. Three weeks later she was the victim of another attack when three men broke into her flat whilst she was taking a bath, held her under water and slashed her again. This time she received wounds requiring twenty-seven stitches. Now Bending and Simons accepted the police protection offered them. Joan Bending went to the Edgwarebury Country Club at Elstree.

On 20 February the officers in the case had heard that Fay Sadler had disappeared and the police went to considerable efforts to persuade her to contact them. There was a report that she would come out of hiding if she was guaranteed protection for five years. 'Our message is – come forward at once . . . we will guarantee you full and complete protection at all times.' She did not.

The trial began on 21 April with the public gallery filled with 'faces', including members of the Billy Hill organization, the Callaghan family and the Kray twins as well as the Nash family in force. Now only Nash and the boxers stood trial. The charges against Doreen Masters had been dismissed.

Of the ten male jurors one who was later found to have a conviction for dishonesty as a juvenile had appeared to nod towards Billy Nash in the public gallery. The police overheard a remark that one of the jury was to be nobbled and a watch was kept on this particular juror. One day after court he was followed by officers who had seen a young man run away from his car. 'You won't catch me putting a foot wrong now,' he said with the emphasis on *now*. Meanwhile, it seems that one of the two women on the jury had a husband on remand in Brixton. He is alleged to have told Nash and the boxers that his wife had made up her mind that Nash was guilty of capital murder.

The facts were reported to the judge by both the

prosecution and defence and on 25 April Mr Justice Gorman discharged the first jury.

In the second trial both Simons and Bending stood up under considerable fire from the defending lawyers. This time the defence case was reached and a surprise witness, David Sammons, was called to say that at the time Cooney had been shot Johnny Simons had been drinking in another bar and that Joan Bending was so drunk she had had to be helped out of the bar before the fight. The boxers were acquitted on 2 May and the next day James Nash gave evidence that he had never had a gun but that he had hit Cooney 'twice on the nose with my fist because of the things he was saying'. He had hidden out at his brother William's flat in Old Street for four days before surrendering. 'I didn't want to get involved. I was waiting for the police to arrest the shooter.'

Wickstead believes the real turning point was Victor Durand QC's final address to the jury. '[It] surpassed anything I have ever heard before or since. It was brilliant, spell-binding stuff.' But there is little doubt that Durand's brilliance was helped by the forgetfulness of many of the witnesses.

The all-male jury took ninety-eight minutes to acquit Nash of Cooney's murder, but at a second trial which began an hour later he was found guilty of causing grievous bodily harm and was sentenced to five years' imprisonment. 'You have been found guilty on abundant evidence of a brutal assault upon a man who is now dead, in a drinking club frequented by crooks. . . . An example must be made of you and people like you,' said Mr Justice Diplock.

'My son's death won't go unavenged,' shouted Cooney's father from the public gallery. Cooney's body was taken back to Leeds for burial. 'I have read somewhere that a Mr Billy Hill was giving Selwyn a funeral, but this is not a circus. He will have a funeral with dignity,' said Cooney's mother.

Simons, under police protection, was put on an aeroplane for Majorca where he hoped to work for a Spanish bookmaker. Three months later he was back saying he was broke and he could not get a job. He went to stay with Cooney's parents in Leeds and three months later was attacked outside the city's bus station. He was cut three times on the face and once on his arm.[8]

Fay Sadler did turn up again on 12 May but only to allow herself to be photographed by a *Daily Express* reporter in the Anchor public house in Clink Street, Southwark, and to give a short interview.[9] The reporter, Victor Davis, paid a fee for the privilege to her minder, who gave his name as Ted. Fay had been ill and this had given her another chance to rethink her lifestyle.

'I was just being faithful to the code by which I have lived,' she said, adding, 'I am waving goodbye to the drinking clubs, the dog-tracks, the mad parties, and all the boloney that I thought was the essence of life when I was a kid.' Would she go somewhere ducky like Cheltenham? speculated the *Express*.

That was the effective end of the Nashes, but lurking in the background and gaining in strength were Ronnie and Reggie Kray, the twins. There were also small, independent and often not very successful teams operating. In May 1963 John Maguire of Kentish Town received four years and six other members of the firm lesser terms for operating a protection racket on the Chinese community in Soho. They had been convicted of demanding money with menaces and robbery and assault. Maguire had worked on the principle that the

[8] N. Lucas, *Britain's Gangland*.

[9] Clink Street had been the site of a prison in the nineteenth century, giving rise to the expression 'in the clink'.

Chinese had difficulty in distinguishing one European from another. They may have had but they did have clothes sense. He was caught after one Chinese business-man had identified a girl member of the team by the dress she wore when posing as a prostitute and working the Murphy game.[10]

Out of the immediate central London area the Mussies, from Muswell Hill in North London, led by Ronald Gordon Fletcher, enjoyed a reputation as tearaways. Their three-year reign of terror ended at the Old Bailey in July 1962 after a fight at a youth club dance in Finchley. Mr Justice Melford Stevenson gaoled Fletcher for five years.

Another singular influence in Soho at the time was the very odd Detective Sergeant Harold Challenor, feared by villains everywhere. He had spent several years in the Flying Squad when, in 1962, he was sent to West End Central police station (Savile Row) as a second-class sergeant. In the 1960s, when the time between arrest and trial by jury at the Old Bailey or the Inner London Sessions was only a matter of a few weeks, he soon made a great impact on the community and the courts.

Soho sounded like Chicago when Challenor des-cribed it. The courts were obviously impressed, although magistrates, judges and members of juries all knew that perfectly respectable people – like magistrates, judges and members of juries – could spend a pleasant evening in Soho without indulging in crime or coming to any harm. London's West End has the best theatres, restaurants, cinemas, clubs and pubs in the country, and they

---

[10] The Murphy game is the robbing of a prostitute's client by her pimp. It is also a confidence trick and gets its name from the alleged simplicity of the Irish.

are frequented by regular customers and provincial visitors who never once catch a glimpse of a drug-orgy or a gun-fight. Yet the detective-sergeant was not only believed when he brought his conspiracy and offensive weapon charges; he was increasingly admired for his skill and courage in tackling the bandits.[11]

His finest hour came in September 1962 with his smashing of the protection racket being run by Riccardo Pedrini, Oliva, John Ford, Alan Cheeseman and James Fraser. That, at least, was the evidence of Wilfred Gardiner, a man with a conviction for living off immoral earnings, who ran the two strip-tease clubs, the Phoenix and the Geisha. Gardiner gave evidence of threats, damage to his car, demands to be 'looked after' and 'If you try nicking us I shall shoot you. You're a dead man anyway. You won't live the rest of the year.' He also spoke of another occasion when he saw Oliva cutting the hood of his car. 'That's how we're going to cut your face,' he was told.

On 21 September Riccardo Pedrini and Alan Cheeseman were arrested outside the Phoenix Club by two of Challenor's aides to CID. They were taken to Savile Row police station and told to put their belongings on a table. Cheeseman was slapped and, so he said at the trial, Pedrini was taken into a cell and beaten. Both he and Cheeseman had weapons planted on them. Ford, who had been involved in a longstanding quarrel with Gardiner, lived in the next block of flats to Pedrini. There is no doubt there had been trouble on a fairly regular basis between them. He was arrested on 22 September and charged with demanding money with menaces. On 24 September Joseph Oliva was arrested

[11] M. Grigg, *The Challenor Case.*

driving along Berwick Street. Challenor and two younger officers dragged him from his car. He was found to have a bottle of turpentine with a piece of torn-up towel in the neck and a knife in his pocket. At the trial Challenor said he had information that Oliva intended to attack the Phoenix Club and Oliva was said to have remarked, 'If I don't burn him someone else will.' Fraser was arrested on 26 September when he was pointed out to police officers by Gardiner. He was found to have a knife. It seems that the only connection between him and the others was that he had once been in a van with Oliva when there had been a near accident with Gardiner in his open car. On that occasion both had called the police.

On 6 December, charged with conspiracy to demand money with menaces, demanding money with menaces and possessing offensive weapons, they appeared at the Old Bailey. After a retirement of two and a half hours Fraser was acquitted of conspiracy and the others found guilty. Their convictions were quashed by the Court of Appeal in 1964.

By this time, Challenor, the former scourge of Soho, was in disgrace. His war on Soho characters had been perfectly successful whilst he stuck to the louche element who had a few convictions in their background, and even their associates with no convictions but on whom the tar would stick. They were not likely to be believed by a jury when they flatly contradicted the evidence of a detective sergeant who, in addition to being a rising star in the Met, was a deservedly well-decorated war hero from the Tank Corps. Unfortunately for Challenor and the police he lighted upon political demonstrators rather than underworld figures, which was to prove his undoing.

On 11 July 1963 a demonstration took place around Claridge's hotel to protest against a state visit by Queen

Frederika of Greece.[12] One of the demonstrators carrying a banner was Donald Rooum who, fortunately for him, happened to be a member of the National Council for Civil Liberties. He was arrested by four plainclothes policemen, one of whom was described by Rooum as 'a big, stocky, flat-nosed man with a dark suit, boots and a very short back and sides'.

'You're fucking nicked, my old beauty,' said the policeman. At West End Central police station Rooum was pushed upstairs to a detention room by Challenor who repeatedly hit him on the ear.

'Boo the Queen would you?' he asked.

'No, not at all,' replied Rooum and was rewarded with another blow.

'There you are, my old darling,' said Challenor, 'have that with me. And just to make sure we haven't forgotten it . . . there you are, my old beauty. Carrying an offensive weapon. You can get two years for that.' And with that, said Rooum, Challenor produced from his own pocket a piece of brick wrapped in paper. That evening six other men and a juvenile were arrested. Each was given a piece of brick by Challenor or his subordinates. Each refused to sign for their property, denying the bricks had been in their possession.

When it came to it Rooum was doubly fortunate. He had been refused bail by the police and he was represented by Stanley Clinton Davis, a well-known criminal lawyer. Rooum's case was adjourned for trial until 19 July. The basis of his defence was that he could not have been carrying a brick because there was no brickdust found in his pocket. An independent expert was found who confirmed this. Here was Rooum's good

---

[12] The origins of the protest, now almost forgotten, had arisen following the death of a Greek political activist, Lambrakis. A banner carried by Donald Rooum read 'Lambrakis RIP'.

fortune, for since he had been refused bail he had had no chance to change his clothes before handing them over to Clinton Davis after the initial remand hearing.

At the hearing Rooum was defended by Michael Sherrard, who would later defend Hanratty. A forensic scientist gave evidence that there could have been no brick because not only was there no dust but a broken brick, the size of the one produced, would inevitably have scratched the lining. Edward Robey, son of the comedian Sir George, was the magistrate sitting at Marlborough Street when the case was heard. After he had handled the brick and found how easily it crumbled he expressed his doubts and acquitted Rooum, refusing an application for his costs to cover his expenses.

Another of the defendants, John Apostolou, was not so fortunate. With the same solicitor, barrister, forensic scientist and the same story Robey found him guilty and fined him £10. Two juveniles, Ronald Ede and Gregory Hill, were due to appear at Chelsea Juvenile Court. The case was first adjourned because Challenor was ill and then on 9 October the prosecution offered no evidence. Apostolou appealed against his conviction and on 22 October the prosecution indicated they would not seek to support it. Later Rooum was awarded £500 and Apostolou £400. There had been a number of convictions of other defendants who had been fined £5 and in one case given a conditional discharge.

Challenor, who had had a distinguished war record winning the Military Medal, now found himself at the Old Bailey on 4 June 1964 on a charge of corruption. Defended by Manny Fryde, of Sampson & Co, solicitors for the Krays, he was committed to a mental hospital having been found unfit to plead. Three other officers were found guilty, receiving sentences of four and three years.

At the end of the trial Mr Justice Lawton called for John du Rose, known as Four Day Johnny because of the speed with which he solved his cases.

> Chief Superintendent du Rose, I would be very grateful if you would bring to the attention of the Commissioner my grave disturbance at the fact that Detective Sergeant Challenor was on duty at all on 11th July 1963. On the evidence which I heard from the doctors when he was arraigned, it seems likely that he had been mentally unbalanced for some time, and the evidence which I heard from Superintendent Burdett in the case has worried me a great deal. It seems to me the matter ought to be looked into further.

At the enquiry which followed, Arthur James QC, later to preside over the Great Train Robbery trial, reported on the circumstances in which it was possible for Challenor to have continued on duty at a time when he appeared to have been affected by the onset of mental illness. The report was a whitewash. Mr James found that Challenor was allowed to continue because of the extreme difficulty in diagnosing paranoid schizophrenia and it was no fault of his fellow officers that they had failed to notice his unsocial behaviour. If there was a clash of evidence between witnesses to the enquiry and police officers, then the evidence of the latter was invariably preferred. Allegations that Challenor had taken bribes were dismissed almost out of hand. 'Such allegations form part of the armoury of the criminal and are directed at any target which it wished to destroy.'

In the Pedrini case, Fay Sadler's defender, William Hemming, along with his long-time companion Margaret Laville, a solicitor's clerk through whom he obtained much of his work, gave evidence. Not only was Hemming a member of the Bar, he was also a longtime member of a louche Soho drinking club, the Premier, as was Miss Laville. Evidence that Cheeseman had met Challenor in the club in her presence could not be accurate, she said, and Mr James unhesitatingly accepted it. Hemming gave evidence that he had held Challenor in high regard as an officer. The allegation that Challenor had received a £50 bribe was dismissed.[13]

Later Challenor found work as a solicitor's clerk, taking instructions in criminal cases. He was certainly not able to accept the acquittal of Rooum with good grace. In his own memoirs he wrote:

> . . . soon afterwards Rooum heard me repeating details of his arrest and stating that I had found the brick in his pocket.
>
> Whether Mr Rooum had prepared himself for such an eventuality I do not know, but he certainly had his wits about him for his mind went back to a book he had read entitled *Science in the Detection of Crime*, by a former Scotland Yard officer, and he realized that if he could prevent the brick being placed in his pocket he could prove his innocence because there would be no trace of dust in his pocket and no fingerprints on the brick. This would make nonsense of my evidence.
>
> To achieve this, however, it was essential for him to remain in custody over night in order to prove that he was wearing the same clothing when he was examined by an independent forensic expert. For that reason he did not seek bail, but refused to sign for his property which included the brick.[14]

[13] It was always said that the Bar never forgave Hemming over the evidence he gave at the Challenor enquiry and that it was a major reason he was never made a QC.

[14] H. Challenor with A. Draper, *Tanky Challenor*, pp. 13–14.

Whatever the truth behind the Challenor illness there is no doubt he presented a formidable figure to the Soho villains, and was undoubtedly feared by them. He knew the gang leaders and believed that 'fighting crime in Soho was like trying to swim against a tide of sewage; you made two strokes forward and were swept back three. For every villain you put behind bars there were always two more to take their place.'[15]

Once Challenor was out of the way there were reports that:

London's West End is bracing itself for an outbreak of violence between rival gangs running the 'protection' rackets in strip clubs, gambling casinos and betting shops. The power struggle created largely by the recent release from prison of notorious mob leaders and by a more inhibited police approach to the job of tackling criminals is expected to lead to a vicious internecine gang war.

Recent petrol bomb attacks on betting shops in Shepherd's Bush are believed to be the work of a South London combination of five gangs determined to take over the territory of established gangsters. A Soho strip club set alight; a member of a powerful East End gang beaten up.

By securing the services of a dangerous psychopath who gained underworld prestige during the violent gang warfare in the fifties the South London family has managed to merge five small gangs, drawn from an area embracing Southwark, Camberwell, Balham and Tooting.

Already the new syndicate has installed its own fruit machines in some West End clubs and the leader is said to be collecting a modest £50 a week

---

[15] Ibid, p. 154.

for 'looking after' at least one gambling casino.

The new boys can't win. They don't have the money behind them and their stooges only get about £20 for a petrol bomb attack. The men behind the established mobs are rich and almost respectable. They have had it good in the West End for years and they are greedy. They won't give it up easily.[16]

Whilst it was right that Frankie Fraser was now out of prison, the petrol bomb attacks on betting shops in Shepherd's Bush were something of a red herring. They were nothing to do with Billy Hill or his successors. Rather they were the work of a small independent firm headed by Patrick Ball, who went under the name of the Professor because of his neat appearance. He had approached one of the leading bookmakers in the area, James Burge, asking for the princely sum of £5 a week. When Burge turned him down his shop was bombed a fortnight later. Nathan Mercado, who traded as Sid Kiki and who was a police informer, was also threatened and he turned to the police for help. Nipper Read, then a sergeant at Paddington, was sent to Kiki's shop to work as a clerk one Saturday afternoon in June and arrested Ball and his colleagues when they came into the shop after the last race to collect their share of the winnings.

In his autobiography Read tells both of the traumas of the afternoon when there were meetings all over the country and he pulled the ticker-tape from the machine and broke it, as well as those when Kiki, enraged at the approach by Ball, forgot the prepared script. It had been agreed he should ask such questions as 'How much will it cost?' and 'What will I have to do?' Instead he started shouting, 'You can fuck off, I'm not having any of this,'

[16] Cal McCrystal in the *Sunday Times*, 1964.

and Read had to step in to make something of a premature arrest. Ball received a six-year sentence and his companions three years each.

But by now the twins – 'It's unlucky to call them by their names' – were moving westwards.

4

The Richardson Brothers

Just as history at large is constantly in the process of being rewritten and revised, so is the history of the London underworld. In 1967 the Richardson brothers' empire was described in suitably shocked terms by Mr Justice Lawton and the press as 'built on fear', 'built on thuggery', 'terror', 'torture'. Now with the passage of time Charles Richardson at least is seen in more pastel colours. Was he really anything more than an over-enthusiastic businessman struggling to protect his companies against the ravages and predatory overtures of con men and crooks?

Until recently the East End villains have always had a much greater press coverage than their South London counterparts, but informed observers have always regarded the latter as the more dangerous, perhaps because they have displayed a greater ability to keep their heads below the parapet. One good example is Kimber's Brummagen boys, many of whom really came from the Elephant and Castle.

Sometimes, of course, things happened almost by accident and lives became more public. In May 1961 George Porritt killed his stepfather and was nearly hanged for it. Porritt had become involved with Florence 'Fluffy' Copeland, the former girlfriend of Edwin

Copley, also known as Cadillac Johnny, who had been killed when his car crashed at 75 mph in a chase over Tower Bridge. He had been given a traditional gangland funeral. Fluffy had subsequently defected to a rival family, the Porritts. It was not an arrangement which pleased the remainder of the Copleys and a quarrel broke out in the Manor House Club near Wrotham in Kent between Mrs Copley and Fluffy. Later that night six armed men came to the Porritt home and George, who had amassed a complete arsenal of guns, seeing two men attacking his stepfather, fired a shotgun, hardly damaging the men but killing his stepfather. He was charged with capital murder.

On 5 July 1961 the jury convicted him and recommended mercy. Porritt was sentenced to be hanged at Wandsworth Prison on 27 July. Now began a period of intense activity. George had to be saved and Fluffy began collecting signatures to present in a petition to the Home Secretary. The Copleys joined in. 'We think the dead man was the real villain in the piece, inciting Georgie to violence against us,' said one of the family.

His appeal was allowed on the day before he was due to hang. Even though the defence had not raised the question of manslaughter the judge should have done so on his own volition, said the Court of Appeal. A sentence of ten years' imprisonment was substituted. Although she told newspaper reporters she did not drink Fluffy celebrated with whisky and gin. 'We owe it to George.' As part of the triumph she had changed her platinum-coloured hair to gold.

It would be pleasant to record that things went well for George and Fluffy after this near miss but it would be inaccurate. Fluffy faded from the scene. On 17 February 1963, whilst he was in Dartmoor, George married a Manchester girl, Sheila, a former heroin addict ('H', as addicts call it, she told a newspaper on her wedding day). Nor was that marriage a conspicuous success. She was later convicted as the driver in a wages snatch back in her home town. She had apparently taken along her child from a former relationship because she could not find a child minder. Later she did find a minder for an evening and paid her £2 with some of the stolen money. She received five years whilst others in the team drew up to fifteen. One of them, Albert Reddans, collected ten years but this was made consecutive to another ten-year sentence he had received the previous month.

There were rumours and press stories of South London villainy, of course. The so called Elephant and Castle Gang of the immediate post-war years were said to have a language of their own – it turned out to be the usual Cockney and underworld backslang. Unusually for the period they were said to include women in their teams, behaviour unheard of at the time. Members were certainly involved in the shooting of Alec De Antiquis in Tottenham Court Road in 1947. Even so the history is littered with names – the Hawards, the Hennesseys, the Callaghans, the Copleys, the Porritts, and the Frenches, as well as those of two of the great South London families, the Brindles and the Frasers.

Tommy 'Tom Thumb' Brindle was originally a small-time crook who dealt in the black market during the war, disposing of cigarettes, stockings and razor blades. 'But he was a gentleman,' says one solicitor's managing clerk who remembers him.

After the war he decided crime was no fun and so he started as a street bookmaker taking about £50 a week. Later he formed the Street Bookmakers' Federation and when the Betting and Gaming Act came into force in 1960 he applied for a licence and was granted one. From then on he was totally respectable.

'Tommy didn't care for Frankie Fraser. He regarded him as you would an obnoxious neighbour,' says one long-time observer of the South London scene, whilst another comments, 'There wasn't much outside violence. The Brindles were too occupied feuding with the Frasers and the reverse.'

Tommy's brother Jimmy had married Frankie Fraser's sister Eva. It is Frankie Fraser, now in his late sixties and said to be partly of Red Indian blood, who, along with Albert Dimes half a generation before him, has provided one of the great continuing professional criminal links of the century. And it is Fraser, one of a number of brothers from South London, who was a stalwart of the Richardson family's empire.

Fraser is described by Charles Richardson as 'one of the most polite mild-mannered men I've met but he has a bad temper on him sometimes'.[1]

> He was quite small – a stocky bloke of about five foot two – but he was game, he was hard to handle, he was not afraid to speak out for his rights, and he was more than capable of doing what he threatened. His word was his bond. People knew they should never say to Frank, 'I want to chin a screw,' unless they meant it because he would expect them to do it, and rightly so.[2]

Since the age of thirteen when he was sent to an approved school for stealing forty cigarettes, he has racked up thirty-two years in prison or detention sentences. Seemingly impervious to pain during his years inside, he was switched from prison to prison on over a hundred occasions as one governor after another found

[1] C. Richardson, *My Manor*, p. 62.

[2] T. Lambrianou, *Inside the Firm*, p. 148.

him almost impossible to control. In November 1959 he was sentenced to be birched for his attack on one prison governor. He was due to receive eighteen strokes. Jimmy Andrews, whom Georgie Cornell had visited shortly before his death, was due for fifteen, and Jack 'the Hat' McVitie a mere twelve. The Home Secretary remitted the punishment, much to the indignation of the Prison Officers' Association.

On two occasions he was certified insane, something of which his defence would make use. 'He had not been the willing tool that a man in full possession of his faculties would have been,' said John Ritchie ingenuously during the Fraser–Rossi trial for the slashing of Jack Spot.

Certainly during the 1970s and 1980s, after his involvement in the Parkhurst Prison riot of 1969 in which he was designated the leader, he was regularly tormented by prison officers.

> Nothing ever got to Frankie. He was a rock. Once when he was in prison, he was in solitary for months – not unusual for Frank. Every day a group of screws would deliver his food but just before the plate was handed to him a screw would spit in it. Frank would throw the plate at him. There would be a fight, Frank would get a terrible beating and the screws would leave him to nurse his bruises for another day. This went on for months.[3]

One prison officer stole his medical records and sent threatening letters to Fraser's sister Eva Brindle. The warder slipped under the door of his cell the part of Fraser's record which said he would serve at least twenty years, to 'blow him up to kick up trouble so the

[3] C. Richardson, *My Manor*, p. 83.

authorities would have him moved'. On conviction the prison officer received a conditional discharge.

In June 1959 Fraser had brought an unsuccessful libel action against the now defunct Sunday newspaper the *Empire News*. He complained that the article implied that he knew about the false allegation that Spot had attacked Falco, but the judge would have none of it.[4]

After his release from prison, on 17 May 1985, when he was driven away in some style in a Rolls-Royce, Fraser found himself in more trouble. He was convicted of dishonestly handling coins amounting to £35,000. He was sentenced to three years' imprisonment, reduced in November 1987 to two years when Canon David Diamond told the Court of Appeal he believed Fraser had reformed and had been doing good work in the community. It was his twenty-sixth conviction.

Fraser goes back to the days of Spot and Hill. Apart from the picture of him draped on the piano at the launch of Billy Hill's book, another shows him with the actor Stanley Baker, the boxing promoter Burt McCarthy, and a train robber or two, as part of the Soho Rangers football side. In the front row is his friend and business partner Eddie Richardson.

Eddie Richardson and his more celebrated brother Charlie were born in 1936 and 1934 respectively, Charlie in Twickenham, Eddie in Camberwell. Four years later a third brother, Alan, was born.[5] The elder two boys

---

[4] After the beating he received following the Parkhurst Riot he brought an action for assault. Tickets for a benefit were sold at £4 a head to raise sufficient money to pay the lawyers as he had been refused legal aid. Later he was offered, and reportedly rejected, £750 for his injuries.

[5] Alan drowned in a motorboat accident near Waterloo Bridge. The boat driven by Charlie ran into the wash of a larger boat and overturned. Charlie and his girlfriend, Jean Goodman, survived. Alan did not.

were evacuated during the war and on their return went to Avenue Secondary Modern School in Camberwell. Their first excursions into crime were the so called jump-ups, thefts from the backs of lorries. It was then that Charlie began to acquire the nucleus of friends who would later stand trial with him. Brian Mottram, an expert fraudsman, said of the time: 'It marked Charlie out, even at this age, as an organizer. We all looked up to him.'

Run-ins with the police were common. After a spell on probation, the remand home, Stamford House, was followed shortly afterwards by three years in an approved school. It was not a success. Charlie escaped and was sent to another school where he finished his sentence.

Charles Richardson from the start was a businessman. Born in another world, in another generation, he might have ended up with a company quoted on the stock market. He began selling his mother's ice-cream and soon moved into the scrap metal business. Even from the start, however, he was not too worried if his sponsors got their money back. His first coup was the purchase of two aeroplanes as scrap. He and his Uncle Jim borrowed money from a local businessman and started cutting up the craft. Unfortunately they neglected to repay the investor, who called in the Fraud Squad. Here Richardson learned an early lesson. Many policemen had their price. For £150 they were prepared to drop the investigation and put a frightener into old Uncle Jim as a joke for Charlie.

At the age of nineteen he heard of a scrapyard for sale in Addington Square. His mother was persuaded to stop work and look after the books. Eddie was cajoled into joining the family firm. With a combination of hard work and an astute eye for bent goods, the scrapyard prospered. Then tragedy struck. He was accused and convicted of receiving stolen scrap. The two-year probation order was nothing compared to the revelation that he had not registered for National Service. Like the Krays he developed an instant allergy to military life. Like the Krays he engineered his own court martial. Like the Krays he ended up in the military prison at Shepton Mallet, where he met up with his future rivals as well as Johnny Nash. It took him all of eight months before he could return to South London.

Back in Peckham he began to consolidate his business. One of the first to join him was Roy Hall, whom he found stealing copper wire from his yard and then trying to resell it to him. Hall's father had been killed while working on the railway at Waterloo Station and his mother had been left with no pension. After bawling him out Richardson employed him. He could have asked for no more loyal helpmate.

By 1956 Richardson had some £20,000 saved up and a business of five scrapyards in and around South London. Hall was now allowed to run his own yard at Waterloo, at a wage of £25 a week. A year later Richardson reckoned that he personally was worth £250,000. Some of the money came from the purchase of stolen metal but much came from sheer hard work.

Richardson was not satisfied. Many of his enterprises were at least a percentage legitimate. He had, in his words,

to swim hard upstream and feel the current on my gills. Like any good entrepreneur I had to feel I was growing and diversifying all the time. I opened up yards and drinking clubs all over the place. The breweries had the pubs sewn up so I started clubs where drinking was twenty-four hours. They were a bit illegal, given the licensing laws, but the police were on the payroll. When a big raid was planned they gave us the nod and the target club would be closed when the vice squad turned up.[6]

But acceptance as the King of the Manor was what he craved and the opportunity came to establish his credentials once and for all when Jimmy Brindle, Frankie Fraser's brother-in-law, was involved in a fight with one of the Rosa brothers. They were of Turkish extraction and were a force to be reckoned with in the Elephant and Castle area. It was Jack Rosa who had had the fake fight in Borstal, which helped Billy Hill and who later became associated with the Black Widow, Fay Sadler. Now a Rosa-led gang had beaten up Jimmy Brindle and another friend, Reggie Jones, in the Good Intent. Despite his relationship with the Frasers, Brindle was not really a Richardson man. He was a street bookie carrying on his brother's business. At the time he believed the police fancied to pull him if they saw him driving in the neighbourhood. Rosa asked him for a lift to the West End. Jimmy Brindle, who saw himself at risk of a prison sentence if he was caught driving, declined and so earned himself a beating.

Jones escaped and went round to one of the Richardson clubs, the Casbah, for help. According to Richardson he and his friends went in search of the Rosa brother, finding him in the ineptly named Reform Club at the Elephant.

> He was much taller than me so I got good momentum when I leaned up and nutted him on the bridge of his nose which I felt crumble under my head . . . Meanwhile Eddie and Roy and the others jumped on Rosa's friends. We worked together like a well-practised team until they lay unconscious at our feet in pools of blood and

[6] C. Richardson, *My Manor*, p. 106.

broken teeth. We sat and had a drink. Everybody
else in the bar watched as we calmly stepped on the
broken bodies on the way out. The deed was
registered and guaranteed for entry in local folk-
lore. It was not the first time we had sorted
somebody out but Rosa was big PR and our soaring
reputation would protect us from challenges from
ambitious competitors.[7]

They were certainly not prepared to venture much
across the river and into Kray territory. After a fight in
an East End pub in which a man had his jaw broken, the
Kray firm turned up at the New Church Road yard. It
took considerable negotiating to calm things down. The
Krays returned across the water, leaving Richardson
'heading the biggest firm on the manor and my manor
was South-East London. To outsiders it might have
looked like a gang, but gangs are what kids have – or big
kids in American films. I was a businessman who had to
protect his interests.'[8]

But in his own manor Richardson behaved like the
Sabinis of old. There was help for those who needed it
with turkeys at Christmas and a few quid here and there.

We reduced local crime to a dribble. I was pissed
off with all the thefts from my yard and I would be
enraged when local people would come to tell me
of burglaries to their houses. While the police filed
incident reports and complaints in their dusty
drawers we would know within hours who had
done the job, give them a smack and tell them to
fuck off to the West End to steal from rich people
who could afford an insurance policy. The sad

[7] C. Richardson, *My Manor*, p. 108.
[8] Ibid, p. 110.

battered radios and half crowns from the tin in the kitchen would be returned with our compliments.[9]

There was also a sinister side. Whilst the Sabinis and the Whites had held court in clubs and pubs, the Richardsons held trials of their acquaintances and former friends who had in some way offended or even cheated them. It did not seem to alter the relationship too much. John Bradbury, supplier of much of the stolen merchandise which was sold in Richardson's long firm markets, seemed to regard a beating he took over a £10 debt as an occupational hazard.[10]

And if there were difficulties with the police, witnesses were there to be straightened. A man had an argument with his wife, who took off with the family furniture and another man. The man was beaten and the furniture liberated. His wife went to live in Albany Road, Camberwell. Later she told police her husband and Eddie Richardson had hit her with the butt of a gun. At Tower Bridge Magistrates' Court she changed her story.

There had also been a shooting incident outside her house, following which Johnny Nash, Charlie Richardson and John Lawrence were charged. It was alleged they had been trying to persuade the Roff brothers, another local family, not to give evidence in an assault case. There were witnesses, including Mrs Lawrence, and the police were no doubt confident of a successful prosecution, but at the committal proceedings Mrs Lawrence, although she had been with the men when the shots were fired, could not identify anyone.

Charlie's luck was to run out soon. In 1959 he was charged with receiving sides of bacon. He was sentenced to six months' imprisonment. Almost immediately, in

[9] Ibid, p. 111.
[10] R. Parker, *Rough Justice*, p. 88.

May 1960, he was charged again, this time with receiving stolen metals. Now the matter was more serious and Charlie did not stay around to try to deal with witnesses. He left for Canada together with his mistress, Jean Goodman, whom he had met at the Astor Club. He left behind his wife Margaret and their five children. Two sureties forfeited £500 each but were repaid by Eddie, who now took control of the businesses.

In Canada he and Jean Goodman put together a scrap metal business but, tiring of Toronto, sold it and slipped back into England. It was inevitable he would be arrested but once more the witnesses went his way and he was acquitted.

Now it was time to restructure his empire. The Addington Club was burned in a fire which destroyed its contents but not the fabric of the building. With the insurance money it was completely refurbished as a wholesale business complete with a small menagerie. John Bradbury ran Richardson's Shirley Anne drinking club in Peckham and supplied goods for Richardson's East Lane market. Much of the merchandise sold there had been hijacked. It was through Bradbury and his friend Tommy Costello that Richardson learned how a long firm fraud could really be profitably operated.

Long firm frauds are simple swindles to run. A warehouse or shop is taken by a front man, preferably someone who has no previous convictions. Goods are bought on credit and then sold perfectly properly through the shop. The supplier receives his or her money. More business is done with more and more suppliers until there is one big bang, a massive amount of goods are obtained on credit, knocked out at prices often below the purchase price in a great 'liquidation sale', and the premises are closed. The scam is not a new one. In the 1920s it was estimated that several million pounds a year were being made through long firm frauds. In the 1960s a properly run small LF could expect to realize a profit of between £100,000 and £150,000.

One variant on the long firm was used for Richardson's initial foray into the art form. A warehouse in Mitre Street in Aldgate was filled with silk stockings. In the late autumn of 1962 the stock was taken out and sold before the premises were torched. The idea was for the front men in the LF to tell the manufacturers that there had been a fire and that unfortunately the stock was uninsured. There would, however, be a perfectly good insurance claim. In this way the profits would be doubled.

The torching was a greater success than anyone could have hoped for. Petrol was poured inside the building one Saturday afternoon and the arsonist, a friend of Charlie's, went to have dinner. When he came back there was a courting couple in the doorway so he had to wait until they left, by which time the fumes had spread. A Guy Fawkes' rocket in a milk bottle was aimed at the semi-basement window, the site of the petrol spillage, and because of the build-up of the fumes the blast was far greater than had been anticipated. Much of the street was effectively wrecked, including the building of a spice merchants opposite.

When the facts were reported and the dishevelled arsonist and his assistant returned to report, Richardson was initially furious. 'I was mad with them but the picture of Tommy and Mike trying to aim this rocket in a milk bottle at the window was too much for me and I exploded in a fit of laughter that had me doubled up with tears streaming down my face. The others joined in and after a change of clothes for Tommy and Mike we all went out to a club.'[11] Charlie made around £250,000 from the explosion.

[11] C. Richardson, *My Manor*, p. 128.

Gradually he learned how a simple long firm fraud could be turned into a complex structure with interlocking companies. His mentor was his old friend, Brian Mottram, who had had a share in the Mitre Street business and had counselled against the fire. Although he had known him from childhood, initially it was not a relationship without problems. Mottram, a man to be reckoned with, had taken some of the Richardson men from the Catford end of the business and opened up his own long firm near the Charlton Athletic football ground. Richardson believed one of Mottram's men had turned him over and he, Eddie and a third man arrived at Mottram's premises to give him a whack. They were told by Mottram, a hulking great man who ignored his longstanding heart condition, to go away. They disregarded the request and Mottram, defending his employee, had dealt satisfactorily with the third man and was giving Eddie a seeing to when he was hit over the head from behind by Charlie. When he recovered he threatened he would shoot Charlie.

Quite apart from being a physically huge and handsome man, Mottram was connected to a team from the Surrey Docks. Charlie deemed the best way to deal with things was to send down some tame policemen to speak with his by now wholly alienated friend. If Mottram did not co-operate he could expect a spot of prison. They in turn were given their marching orders and Mottram began to carry out a guerrilla war, putting canisters of gas up the exhaust pipes of Richardson cars. A meeting was arranged at the Army and Navy pub in South London. Richardson grudgingly apologized and paid Mottram £3000 as compensation, additionally giving him another long firm to run.

It was shortly after this that, through Tommy Costello, Richardson met his nemesis, Jack Duval, an extremely talented con man who had been operating untroubled on

Richardson territory for the past few years. A Russian-born Jew, Duval had in turn lived in France, joined the Foreign Legion, deserted from it, served in the RAF, owned a club in Great Marlborough Street, run an airline ticket fraud, and been involved with George Dawson in the great Orange Juice swindle which had ended the career of one of the earliest post-war tycoons. He also managed to acquire the ownership of the Bank of Valetta. He arranged to supply Richardson with yet more stockings.

It was when his empire began to fold in March 1963 that Duval slipped away to Milan. He had been declared bankrupt over a Camberwell car company, there was an enquiry into a fraud at the bank and the major airlines were just discovering how they had been swindled out of up to £500,000-worth of airline tickets. From Italy he sent over some of the stockings but when the supply dried it was discovered he had been using the age-old trick of paying off past debts with present monies. Nevertheless he sent over airline tickets and Eddie Richardson went to sort things out. The supply of stockings recommenced.

With Charlie trying to expand his horizons he began to encounter men who were much smarter than himself. Duval may not have had any muscle behind him but he was mega-smart as well as being mega-crooked.[12] Eddie, who was more old-fashioned in his thinking, began to worry about Duval and his equally astute and dishonest friends, such as Benny Wajcenburg and Lucien Harris who ran offices in Cannon Street. For a time the brothers split, with Eddie – disenchanted with life in general and Jean Goodman in particular – striking off

---

[12] Other deals of his at the time included trying to sell fake Old Masters to the Krays and the swindling of a Lugano jeweller to the tune of £50,000.

back to his roots and working the race-courses. In time he set up his own wholesale business, a large walk-around supermarket in Deptford High Street.

Gradually things improved between the brothers and Roy Hall returned to work with Charlie. John Bradbury was brought back to work Bradbury Trading in the Addington Square premises, running a scam involving the purchase tax on radios.[13] A company with its own purchase tax number was a valuable commodity in those days. The Krays too had been sniffing around Harris, whose Cannon Street company was wrongly believed to have such an item.

And then from Duval's friend and helpmate, Bunny Bridges, Richardson heard the con man was back, if not in town, at least in Brighton. He was summoned to talk about a bit of business. On his arrival Duval found that Charlie was too busy to see him immediately and was sent round to Bradbury Trading in Addington Square where he was set upon by Eddie Richardson and Bradbury. Afterwards he was taken to see Charlie, who appears to have behaved with kindliness. If Eddie might be PC Dirty, then Charlie was DS Clean. Duval was given a cup of tea and then sent off with Wajcenburg to buy a new shirt and to the local chemist to be patched up. On his return it was all sweetness and light again. He was given some money and sent away to consider new business propositions. Duval was back in the fold but now surely he knew who was the master and who the dog.

The business proposition was a major long firm

---

[13] If a company had a purchase tax number it did not need to pay the then twenty-five per cent tax to the manufacturers. It was supposed to, but did not, pay the tax itself. This allowed a crooked company to undercut its rivals – another variant on the long firm. For a full account of these and other deals see R. Parker, *Rough Justice*.

working out of the Cannon Street offices and called Common Market Merchants. Duval was to change his name to Longman and be the buyer in Germany. Wajcenburg was invited in. Apart from his own proven abilities he had that invaluable asset, his own purchase tax number. A local magistrate added respectability to the board of directors. But things did not go well. Shortly before Christmas 1963 Wajcenburg wanted commission on the old radio transactions. Charlie did not wish to pay him and said in reality it was he who was owed – £5000 to be exact. Wajcenburg did not agree. The books were checked by Duval and a local businessman, Ken Nicholson, who had been brought into work at Peckfords. Wajcenburg was right. No money was owing. Richardson, believing he was being taken by the smart boys, lost his temper and began to shake the Pole. Later that evening Wajcenburg borrowed £1000, sent it round to Richardson and fled the country. It was only after the intercession of Duval that, a year later, he agreed to return to Common Market Merchants.

On Christmas Day Richardson quarrelled with Tommy Costello, whom he visited along with his brother, Roy Hall and Johnny Longman at the Rabbit Club in Catford, over Tommy's refusal to have anything to do with Common Market Merchants. Perhaps it was Christmas, perhaps old friendship, but Costello escaped a beating, warning Richardson against the rapacious Duval.

Charlie didn't listen. Nor apparently did he see anything wrong when the magistrate resigned from Common Market Merchants early in January 1964, seeing it as a clash of temperament between the magistrate and Jack Duval, who was spinning the con man's web of greed. The loss of the magistrate did not matter, a man called Phil Wilson would take his place. Duval had found four or five others to make similar investments. In a few years' time there would be enough money to open a merchant bank. One company would lead to the next. Despite the advice of the doubting Thomas Costello, Wilson invested £1400, Charlie £4000, and Jimmy Bloor (or Blore) and Harry Waterman also became investors. One company which did lead to the next was Twelve Estates, which arose phoenix-like from the ashes of Bradbury Trading. Bradbury himself and Jimmy Bloor were in charge whilst Duval and a friend set up Exmosdale to provide the references essential for a successful long firm. At the same time the more or less legitimate scrap side of the Richardson business was going well, with contracts from the Ministry of Works.

The year 1964 was a turning point for the Richardsons. Back into the fold came George Cornell, aka Georgie Myers, a former member of the Watney Street mob on transfer, so to speak, from the Krays. He had fallen out with them after an association over the years and had teamed up with none other than Frankie Fraser, now released from prison for his part in the Spot slashing. Back also came Brian Mottram, everything forgiven and forgotten, to join in another long firm with Cornell and Charlie.

Poor Wilson lost all his investment in Common Market Merchants. Most of the time he was just dazzled by Duval's sleight of speech. Cheques were shoved at him 'for wages', 'for purchasing samples' and he signed them. He did, however, find out that the office manager, a Mr Wade, was an undischarged bankrupt. Duval was unrepentant and replaced him with a Len Rugg whose company was then facing charges of receiving stolen material. There was worse to come. Wilson answered the telephone and heard an irate bank manager demanding £2500 to meet cheques that afternoon. Other calls followed. Wilson went to see Richardson to complain that Duval had been emptying the kitty but, once more,

Duval talked his way out of trouble. Later a solicitous Duval went to see Wilson and offered to buy him out for £2500. Wilson completed the transfer of his shares; Duval did not complete the cheque.

There followed the first of the main incidents which were to lead to the Old Bailey. On 12 June 1964, along with Jimmy Bloor, Duval was summoned to Peckfords. Fat Jack Duval was knocked to the ground. When he came to he was sitting in a chair, his wallet and watch together with his wig on the desk in front of him. Bloor's problem was that he was inextricably linked in Richardson's mind with Duval. Richardson picked a knife from a canteen of cutlery and threw it at his arm. Then he did the same again. However angry Richardson was he had the sense to realize that with the collapse of Common Market Merchants there were serious problems. Wilson had already told the Fraud Squad in Holborn of his fears. In any event another English creditor had complained. The banks would certainly have followed. After all they could not be fobbed off in the medium term like German manufacturing companies. By his actions, Duval had jeopardized a number of people.

Once I defended a man charged with a long firm fraud. According to the evidence he had been taken to see a solicitor in North-West London whose first question was 'Is it too late to have a fire?' After Mitre Street another fire was out of the question for Common Market Merchants, but a robbery was the next best thing. Cornell and Bradbury were sent round to clear the premises. They did – of stock and paper work. Next they cleaned out Duval's flat off the Edgware Road. Cornell and Bradbury were seen at the Cannon Street offices and the police were called. It cost Richardson £1500 to shut down the police investigation.

While Bradbury and Cornell were office cleaning, Duval was explaining how the money could be recovered. Bloor was sent to be cleaned up at the chemists and on his return he and Duval were ordered to be back the next morning. Duval took the opportunity of cashing three cheques, one with Johnnie Longman and two with Charlie's friend Alfie Berman. All would be dishonoured but he had no intention of being there when that happened. He went to ground in a hotel in Russell Square, telling only Lucien Harris, another man and his girlfriend where he was. Next day he left for Brussels and on to Israel. There were to be no further beatings for him.

The relatively innocent Lucien Harris was not so fortunate. Johnnie Longman turned up at Inter City, Harris' firm in Great Portland Street. Where, Charlie wanted to know, was Jack Duval? Harris knew that Duval was by now abroad but he certainly was not going to say so. Next day Harris went to see Richardson. He wanted to collect some money owed. Richardson wanted to collect information. At first things were calm. Harris was, after all, not the toe-rag Duval was. He had a degree. It is also possible that he sneered at Richardson about his ill-fated dealings with Duval. Richardson kicked Harris in the hand and threatened him with a knife. 'Is this going to take long?' asked Eddie Richardson. 'There's something I want to watch on the telly.'

According to Harris' evidence, it was now that the infamous wooden box was brought out by Roy Hall. One of the men was sent out to buy scampi. On his return Charlie Richardson shoved some into Harris' eye. His shoes and socks were taken off and the box was fixed to his toes. Hall turned the handle. Harris crashed to the floor. He was stripped and the handle turned again. Nothing much happened and a bottle of orange squash was tipped over him to increase the conduction. Harris was now tied and gagged. One lead was attached to his penis, the other inserted into his anus. The handle was turned again and again.

And then suddenly it was all over. He was untied and ordered to put his clothes back on. While he was doing so Bradbury stabbed him in the foot. Then, according to Harris, Charlie changed again. Harris had done well and stood up to things bravely. Now, asked Charlie, how would you go about finding Jack? Harris replied he would use the phone and he did so. It did not really matter. Duval was long gone. A bottle of scotch was sent for and Harris had a couple of drinks. Charlie gave him £150 and sent him on his way.

The next to receive the treatment was Bunny Bridges, Jack's longtime friend. He was attacked from behind by Cornell and then kicked as he lay on the ground. The box was again produced, with little effect. Bridges did not know where Duval could be found except possibly with his ex-wife in Manchester. He was ordered to drive there to find out. In the meantime some papers he had with him regarding a heavy plant deal were confiscated.

Eddie Richardson was increasingly distancing himself from his brother. He had teamed up with Frankie Fraser in the fruit machine operation. Through Albert Dimes, Fraser had long had an entree into Soho, where some of the most profitable sites could be found. Sir Noel Dryden was recruited to be the respectable front man for Atlantic Machines, the Fraser–Richardson company.[14]

From the beginning Billy Nash, one of the most enterprising of the Nash brothers, had been one of the first to see the benefits of the machines and others were quick to follow him. A machine, costing £400, could, when placed in a good site, bring in £100 a week. The usual percentage split was 65–35 in favour of the

---

[14] On 29 March 1970 the *News of the World* reported the death of Sir Noel Dryden of an overdose of drugs and alcohol. It was said that people had traded on his naivety.

operator. As an inducement to take their machines Atlantic would offer club proprietors forty per cent. There were small problems. If their machine went into a club, someone else's had to go. But both Eddie and Frank were more than capable of dealing with a problem such as this. They employed good mechanics and good machines. In addition they were well connected. It did no harm to a club owner for them to be seen drinking in his premises.

But it was Atlantic Machines which was to provide another link in the chain which would lead to the downfall of the Richardsons. In the summer of 1964 Eddie and Frank were invited to Southport to the Horseshoe Club where the proprietor was having trouble with staff dishonesty. Late in the evening they told Peter Joannides, a Greek who was operating the gaming tables, that they were running the club from now on and invited him outside. Sensibly, he declined. The ensuing fight was stopped by the stewards and Joannides went to the bar. Eddie pushed a broken glass in his face and in turn was set upon by the locals. He and Frank were chased ignominiously from the club. The next day they were charged with grievous bodily harm.

Eddie was allowed bail of £15,000 and went to work. By the time the case was heard in July it was the familiar story. If anything, Joannides had been the aggressor. The Greek personally could not remember much about the incident. He had been drinking heavily. There was no case to answer. Atlantic Machines went into the club and some fifty other clubs countrywide. And then two years later the proprietor of the Horseshoe opened Mr Smith and the Witchdoctor Club in South London.

Charlie Richardson's businesses expanded independently of his brother's. Eddie was content to work primarily in London and certainly within England.

Charles had his eyes on wider horizons. He toyed with the idea of a coal tip in Wales, discarded that and then met Major Herbert Nicholson. The Major, an alderman in Bedford and well connected in the Conservative party, was to be to Charles what Sir Noel Dryden was to Eddie, but on a much greater scale. Through a Welsh contact Charles had heard of the opportunity to obtain the mining rights on four million acres in Namaqualand, South Africa. The group who had the rights needed finance. Nicholson was the man to help Charles along the road.

Once in South Africa, Richardson found a number of opportunities available, including the chance to smuggle diamonds in frozen fish.[15] He learned this from a business friend of Thomas Waldeck, the geologist involved in the Namaqualand mining rights scheme. Gradually Waldeck persuaded Richardson of the benefits of the mining rather than the illicit diamond smuggling. He would sell Richardson half his stake in Concordia. Richardson was hooked, not least because he had fallen in love with Jean La Grange, the stunningly good-looking wife of a South African journalist.

The South African venture deteriorated steadily. First Waldeck and Richardson agreed to turn over the remaining partners in the mining venture and stake a claim for themselves alone. Then over the months the relationship Waldeck had with Richardson cooled. Each came to believe the other was trying to swindle him. John Bradbury had come to South Africa and for a time soldiered as a mercenary. To complicate matters he let it be known that he was Charlie Wilson, one of the Great Train Robbers who had escaped from prison. On 29 June 1965 Waldeck was shot dead on the porch of his

---

[15] The idea was not really new. It formed the basis of an early Raymond Chandler story, 'Moors', when he was writing for the pulp magazines. It was none the worse for that.

home. Bradbury was picked up and questioned for a period of three weeks but the police investigation got nowhere.

There were still business matters to be attended to in England. Richardson had to raise money for the machines to work the mining rights. Berman, who had invested over £30,000, did not want to invest any more. He pleaded poverty, blaming a man called James Taggart for owing him money. Taggart received a major beating from Fraser and Charlie Clark, a new man on the firm.

Similar treatment was dished out to a man involved in a swindle being run by the National Car Park attendants at Heathrow Airport, well known as Fiddle City. The men were taking £1000 a week by altering time clocks to show that customers – who paid the full price – were staying for shorter periods. One of the attendants was kidnapped, stripped naked and beaten with a knotted wet towel. He had already agreed to pay the £500 and the beating was, said Richardson, to show who was the guv'nor.

Things finally fell apart almost by accident. Richardson had heard of a bank being opened in Wigmore Street. Frankie Fraser and Frank Prater were sent to check it out. Quite by chance they ran almost point-blank into Taggart. He tried to ignore them and was followed along Oxford Street. As he walked towards a policeman Richardson appeared in front of him. He managed to hail a passing cab and escaped. The next morning he went to see Gerald McArthur, then the Chief Constable of Hertfordshire.[16] Taggart, Harris and the others felt that they could not go to the Flying Squad

---

[16] McArthur had been the officer in charge of the investigations into the Great Train Robbery. He had never really been given the credit he deserved and had left the Met.

with their stories, fearing that it would only be a matter of time before a corrupt detective would pass the information back to Richardson. Prater was soon to defect as well.

Back in South Africa it looked as though all Charlie's efforts were going to come to a successful conclusion. He had interested yet another businessman in providing finance; he was buying out or dismissing staff and former partners who stood in his way. His affair with Jean La Grange was going well.

But John Bradbury had started to drink and he told his wife that he and another man had shot the Waldecks' dog, Rex. They left South Africa and crossed to Zambia to find work. He drank more, began to pick fights in hotels and was eventually deported back to South Africa. Sheila Bradbury decided to return to England while her husband stayed behind to try to earn some more money. Instead he drank more and began talking to one of his drinking companions about the killing. His chanced-on buddy was an investigator looking into the insurance aspects of Waldeck's death. On the second night of drinking the police were tipped off. Bradbury made a full confession, naming Charlie Richardson.

When the story of Bradbury's confession appeared in the *News of the World* Richardson had his solicitors send a letter before commencing a libel action. Undeterred, the newspaper began its own investigation. On the home front Frankie Fraser quarrelled with the old-time con man Christopher Glinski, a former witness in the Spot–Dimes case, beating him with an umbrella. Glinski joined the team telling all to McArthur.[17] The South

[17] Glinski was a perennial thorn in the side of both the police and the villains. On one occasion he was awarded £250 damages for wrongful arrest. He had been prosecuted for fraud but the trial judge stopped the case against him.

African proceedings rumbled on.

On the night of 7 March 1966 came the incident in Mr Smith's which finally broke the Richardsons' hold on South London. Richard Hart, a Kray associate, was killed, whilst Eddie Richardson and Frankie Fraser, described initially in newspaper reports as businessmen having a drink on their way home, were badly injured.[18]

The club was popular; it had a dance floor, gaming table, a bar and a decent restaurant. It also had minders. A South London team led by the Haward brothers, Billy and Flash Harry, described variously as 'a League Division Two team' and 'amateurs but reckless amateurs', had originally dealt with trouble in the club in exchange for free drinks. The Hawards themselves had clubs and were well known to the Richardsons. Indeed, in the previous few weeks, there had been what euphemistically could be called some discussions between Frank Fraser, on behalf of Charlie Richardson, and Billy Haward over a possible partnership in one of Haward's clubs. For the moment that had come to nothing.

But now there were signs that the Hawards were beginning to make Mr Smith's their unofficial headquarters, using it as an answering service, something which did not appeal at all to the management. Eddie Richardson was approached to see if he could help. It was something he was good at. In return for clearing out the Haward team he could expect to have his and Frankie Fraser's gaming machines installed in Mr Smith's.

In the first week of March 1966 Eddie and some

---

[18] Hart, a firm friend of the Krays, was not a run-of-the-mill gangster. He had attended a grammar school and had several 'O' levels. He had then left school and drifted into selling cars and bricklaying. A gambler by nature, he was gaoled for hijacking a lorry and later held a club licence.

friends had visited Mr Smith's. He and Frankie Fraser returned on the Monday afternoon. Security was discussed. 'I wanted to get hold of some employees with good local knowledge who would keep better order than I thought was being kept,' said one of the witnesses in the subsequent court case. Eddie now regarded himself as having an unwritten contract to police the club. All that remained was for the position to be explained to the Hawards.

Richardson and Fraser stayed in the club the rest of the evening. Eddie spoke with the barmaid, then Billy Haward had a word with her. Seemingly the Richardson team mixed sociably with the Hawards. But as the evening progressed the staff noticed not only signs of tension but also a .410 shotgun strapped inside Billy Haward's jacket. 'We'll be alright, don't worry,' he said as he took a telephone call. It was noticed that Dickie Hart had a .45 automatic pistol.

As another friend of Eddie Richardson's, Jimmy Moody, joined the party, the manager sent home as many of the staff as possible and breathed a sigh of relief when about 2 a.m. the men seemed to be chatting happily, pulling tables together and drinking with each other.

The trouble came an hour later.

'Right, drink up, that's your lot,' said Eddie. Haward protested, saying he and his friends were just getting the taste. 'No more,' replied Richardson. 'I'm running the club.'

Dickie Hart told the barmaid to get into the kitchen. 'Let her stay here,' said Haward, 'there's nothing to bother us.' It cannot be that he wanted a witness. Perhaps he genuinely thought the situation was under control. She sat down alone, well away from the men. Peter Hennessey, one of the family, called out to Richardson, 'Who do you fuckin' well think you are?'

Adding, 'I'll take you any day, you half-baked fuckin' ponce.'

Eddie said that from now on he was the only one who could order drinks. Hennessey was not best pleased. 'Ah, fuck you, you cunt, I'll help myself.' He grabbed at the bottle. Richardson smashed his glass on the table and dragged him to the dance floor. It was then, as the newspapers say, fighting broke out.

Hart fired his gun, Eddie continued to hammer Peter Hennessey and the remaining thirteen men started to fight. Harry Rawlins was shot in the left arm. Haward was hit on the head with a rod and collapsed. Then somehow, Hart lost his gun. He ran through the back entrance into Farley Road chased by Frank Fraser and some others. Ronnie Jeffrey, a Richardson man, seems to have tried to stop the fighting in Farley Road. He was right to. The neighbourhood was awake; 999 calls were being made. It was only a matter of time before the police arrived. 'Turn it up,' he screamed and started to walk away. His name was called. He turned and was shot in the groin.

Now Henry Botton, a Haward man, saw Fraser kicking the prostrate Hart on the pavement. 'You're fucking mad, Frank,' he yelled.

When the police arrived all that was left of the fight was the body of Dickie Hart lying under a lilac tree in the garden of Number 48. He had been shot in the face and his face was smashed in. Initially he was mistaken for a sack. Fraser had escaped; he had been shot and his thigh bone shattered. Haward was gone; he had taken himself off to a friend's where his head had been stitched. Jimmy Moody had scooped up Eddie Richardson, who had also been shot in the thigh and the backside, driving both him and the wounded Henry Rawlins off in his Jaguar. Rawlins was in a poor state and Moody, with Eddie, who was discomforted rather than badly injured, and another man laid him over a children's cot in the casualty department of Dulwich Hospital. Once done, Moody raced off into the dawn.

The hospital reported the gunshot wounds and Chief Superintendent John Cummins, head of the Catford police, went to see just who was there. Rawlins was unconscious and he spoke to Richardson, who had first given his name as Smith and then George Ward. 'Well,' said Cummins, when he saw who was in the cubicle, 'if it isn't Eddie Richardson. And how did you get this little lot?'

Two days later George Cornell went to visit Jimmy Andrews, who had been shot in the leg, in hospital across the water. Despite the fears of his friends, he stopped off in the Blind Beggar for a drink. He was shot at point-blank range by Ronnie Kray, incensed that an enemy should be found on his territory.

The next weekend the *Sunday Times* believed that 'crime syndicates hired gunmen to carry out killings'. They had been told that the men who had killed Richard Hart had received some £50 each, while the killer of George Cornell 'is thought to have received £1000'.

Eddie Richardson and Francis Fraser were arrested. Fraser was charged with the murder of Hart; the rest of those rounded up after the fight with an affray. On 28 June Greenwich Magistrates committed them all in custody for trial. There was solidarity amongst the Richardsons and their friends in prison but there were still enemies about. Ray Rosa was one of them. Somehow he had managed to obtain an iron bar to attack Richardson and avenge the battle at the Reform Club. A bystander reported, 'Ray's eyes are very bad. He hit Bobby Cannon as he came down the stairs.' Bobby Cannon was not a man to report such a mishap. He had, he said, fallen and hurt himself.

Charlie Richardson was now back in London and

doing what he could for his younger brother. Initially he tackled the witnesses and the management of Mr Smith's Club. He had some success with the witnesses, whose recollections of events became vague and imperfect, but the latter were fearful of losing the valuable drinks licence. He decided the best bet was the jury.

When the trial opened at the Old Bailey on 1 July 1966 Charlie, together with his friend Johnny Longman, was in the public gallery looking for likely helpers. A unanimous verdict was still required in 1966 and so it would only require one juror to obtain the necessary disagreement. A very strong bent juror might even sway the rest, as Henry Fonda had done in the film *Twelve Angry Men*, and so produce an acquittal.

By the fifth day of the trial the judge, Mervyn Griffiths Jones (who as Treasury Counsel had asked the jury in the Lady Chatterley case, 'Would you allow your wife or maid-servant to read this book?'), said he had been told that 'two attempts have been made since Thursday to "nobble" an Old Bailey juror hearing the trial of seven men accused of offences connected with a gang fight at Mr Smith's gambling club, Catford.' He went on: 'Unhappily there are often people who are ill intentioned or misguided enough to think they can help their friends or relatives by acting in this kind of way.'

Charlie's second effort had been to have a bottle thrown through the juror's window. The bottle contained a note, intended to confuse things, reading '. . . bring them in guilty or else. A lot more where this came from. You're not alone amongst twelve.'

After long deliberations the jury returned mixed verdicts. Frankie Fraser, tried separately, had been found not guilty of Hart's murder on the judge's direction. There was no evidence he had fired the fatal shots, but he was found guilty of affray and sentenced to five years' imprisonment. Now Billy Haward was convicted of an affray, as was Henry Botton,[19] but Ronnie Jeffrey and Harry Rawlins, two of the Richardson team, were found not guilty. The jury failed to agree on the cases of Eddie, Jimmy Moody and Billy Stayton. Next day Haward received a total of eight years and Botton five.

At the retrial Richardson gave evidence that he had been the victim of an unprovoked attack. He was found guilty and sentenced to five years' imprisonment. Stayton and Moody were found not guilty.

Charlie had already issued a writ against the *News of the World*, but his solicitors had lodged no statement of claim – the detailed account of just what is complained about. The action was struck out with costs.

When Bradbury's trial began he pinned his defence on long-range duress, saying he feared reprisals by the London gang against his family. In support of his story that he was the driver forced to go to the scene, he told the judge of the mock trials held in London by Charlie.

Along with Brian Mottram, Roy Hall, Tommy Clark, Alf Berman, Jean Goodman and some others, Richardson was arrested on 30 July 1966.[20] McArthur had conducted his enquiry with great secrecy, taking a

---

[19] In common with the others Botton received five years for his part in the affray. On 17 July 1983 he was shot dead on the doorstep of his house in Shooter's Hill Road, Greenwich. It was said he had been having troubles over 'some recent deals'. The recent deals turned out to be giving evidence against a powerful South London operator. On 16 October 1984 Billy Clarkson was convicted of Botton's murder. He had given nineteen-year-old Colin Burke a shotgun with which to kill the sixty-three-year-old Botton, saying 'Go out and shoot him for me.' Burke, dressed as a policeman, shot Botton as he opened his door. Burke, sentenced to life youth custody, had told the police, 'I wanted to refuse the favour, but it was like being under hypnosis.' Clarkson was recommended to serve a minimum of twenty-five years.

well publicized holiday in Austria shortly before the arrests.

Richardson was not to go down without a fight. Bunny Bridges was offered £3000 to tone down his evidence, and Frank Prater's wife was similarly approached. Frankie Fraser's loyal sister Eva Brindle, along with Albert Wood and Josephine Shaer, was later charged with attempting to bribe Benny Coulson. Today she still insists she had merely been trying to assist her brother. Miss Shaer, who was Charlie Richardson's secretary, had been to ten firms of solicitors and finally to the National Council for Civil Liberties to get an affidavit drawn up in which Coulson withdrew his allegations. All except the NCCL had thrown her out or threatened to call the police. Clifford Smythe from the NCCL came to court to confirm the evidence. One curious incident occurred in the trial. Much was made of the point that she had the exact amount of £2000 in her wardrobe, the specific sum Coulson said he had been promised. When the money was counted so that the defence solicitors could have their fees paid it came to several hundred pounds over the sum. All three were convicted.

Shortly after that, on 14 March, Mr Smith's Club lost its licence. With true advocate's rhetoric Richard Du Cann told the licensing committee that the club was a 'canker that has gone too deep'. The club was now called the Savoy Social Club but in a police raid the officers had found there were some 300 people present and the guest book in a poor state, full of scribbles and blanks. On 29 June 1967 at a creditors' meeting of Wellreed Ltd, the owners of Mr Smith's, creditors were told there was a deficiency of £38,450. The directors blamed the club's downfall on that single night of violence. One of them

---

[20] No evidence was offered against Jean Goodman and shortly before the trial she married Peter Colson, a window cleaner.

1920: the 'racing fraternity' of Saffron Hill. Darby Sabini and Paesani. From the left standing: Joe Sabini; Micky Papa; Paul Cortesi; Angelo Giannicoli. Sitting: Harry Cortesi; Darby Sabini; Gus Cortesi; Harry Boy Sabini; George Cortesi; Saca Alzapiedi.

1952: warming up for their career. Ronnie (right) and Reggie work out for the camera.

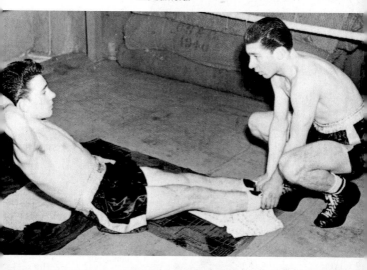

above: Francis 'Split' Waterman in his days as the idol of the speedway fans.

1955: A happy Albert Dimes and his wife leave the Old Bailey after his acquittal in the Battle of Frith Street with Jack Spot.

Bert 'Battles' Rossi.

Fay Sadler; the woman who captivated Tommy Smithson.

1954: Jack and Rita Spot leave the Old Bailey after her conviction for perverting the course of justice in the Spot-Dimes trial.

1964: solicitor's clerk Manny Fryde (in hat), and colleague Ralph Haeems (in glasses) with former Kray adviser Leslie Payne, leave the Old Bailey during the Hideaway Club trial.

July 1956: Victor 'Scarface' Russo leaves the Old Bailey after giving evidence which led to Jack Spot's acquittal.

below: A happy day when Reggie Kray marries Frances Shea. Ronnie smiles on the left.

Seventeen years on, Reggie Kray (left) is escorted to his
mother's funeral.

Ronnie Kray peeps out at the camera at the memorial service for
Red Hot Mama Sophie Tucker.

Connie Whitehead and George Dixon (left and third from the left) with friends.

1967: the interior of the Blind Beggar, Mile End Road, the home of the turn-of-the-century Blind Beggar gang and the scene of the end of Georgie Cornell.

above: Esmeralda's Barn, Knightsbridge; despite appearances for a short time perhaps the smartest of the Kray nightclubs.

George Cornell (aka Myers).

spoke of his dream smashed by London gangsters. 'We did not know about the gangsters. If we had, we would never have come.'

Brian Mottram never stood trial in the main case. He had a heart condition which, it was said, could be fatal under stress. Shortly before the remand hearings he would be found in his cell in a state of collapse. Eventually, the day before the Richardson case began, he was given bail and finally no evidence was offered. It was said informally and unkindly that he was able to produce his heart condition by masturbating. He lived another fourteen years with the help of a pacemaker. Part of the time was spent in custody for his part in a substantial long firm fraud which he worked with Jack Duval. Duval received nine years for his part and on his release ran a dress shop in North London. He had earlier been acquitted of stealing a car. The judge at the Inner London Sessions in July 1967 ruled he had no case to answer.

The 'Torture' trial, which lasted ten weeks, began on 4 April 1967 before Mr Justice Lawton. There were fifty challenges by the defence to potential jurors and a further thirty-five were stood by for the Crown, its equivalent of a challenge. The trial had only been going a short while when Frankie Fraser, through his counsel, objected to the trial judge on the basis of an incident at Victoria Station when he had abused the judge after he and Richardson had had a night out at the Astor. The application was rejected.

Charles Richardson received twenty-five years' imprisonment. Eddie got ten, as did Roy Hall and Frankie Fraser. Tommy Clark was sentenced to eight.

In December 1967 twelve men were convicted of the parking fraud at Heathrow. They were said to have netted £200,000 in four years.

Fraser did his time the hard way. He was given a

further five years as leader of the 1969 Parkhurst Prison riot. Losing nearly all his remission he served most of his total of twenty years. Charlie Richardson escaped from an open prison in May 1980 and spent some weeks on the run in London and Paris complaining bitterly that he had unjustifiably been refused parole. Whilst on the run he conducted part of his campaign from a porn shop near Earls Court station.[21] He became careless and was arrested after giving the name Roy Hall. Unfortunately for him the real Roy Hall, who had been chauffeuring him earlier in the day, had also been stopped and had given his correct name.

Eddie Richardson was released from prison in 1976 and returned to work at his scrap business. Charlie was finally released in 1984.

In October 1990 at Winchester Crown Court Eddie Richardson was sentenced to twenty-five years' imprisonment for his involvement in a drug smuggling operation. Along with Donald Fredwin from Crystal

---

[21] On 8 October 1984 Johnnie Maile, known as Johnny the Flower, who ran a flower-stall at Earls Court tube station, was found shot dead in a lock-up garage in Redfield Lane, Earls Court. He had been killed with two shots to the head from a small-calibre weapon. The killer had cut the garage's padlock with bolt cutters and then lain in wait. A substantial sum of money, thought to be the takings of his business, was found in Maile's pockets.

He had witnessed Richardson's arrest and had given a graphic account to the newspapers. At the inquest held the following March Detective Chief Inspector Michael Anderson was at pains to emphasize that Maile was not a police informer. He went on to say that 'Mr Richardson is fully aware of how he came to be arrested and he knows that it is not attributed to John Maile.' Anderson, who said, 'This was professional work, a contract killing', added after the inquest that the police had also investigated the possibility that Maile had been mistaken for another man who was having an affair with a prisoner's wife.

Palace he had been the central figure in the importation of cocaine from Ecuador. In March 1990 153 kg of cocaine, nearly one third of the total seized by Customs, plus two tonnes of cannabis had been confiscated at Portsmouth, hidden in a consignment of balsa wood on a ferry from Le Havre. Richardson had bought the cocaine from South America at between £12,000 and £13,000 a kilo, selling it on in the UK for £26,000 a kilo. By the time it had reached the streets suitably cut, the price was an astounding £240,000.

Richardson had been seen in his Peckham scrapyard with Fredwin and had been watched when he visited three South Americans in a Bayswater hotel. He was also seen with them at his daughter's home at the Surrey Docks. The drugs were shipped, addressed to Globe Overseas Ltd, from Ecuador on the appropriately named *Silver Happiness*, and then transferred on to the *Viking Valiant* where they were intercepted by customs officers.[22]

During his time in prison Eddie Richardson has developed into a considerable artist.

[22] *Daily Telegraph*, 21 July 1990.

5

The Rise and Fall of the Firm

Legend has it that Ronnie and Reggie, the Kray twins, had their first proper outing in polite society at the spring bank holiday meeting at Epsom Races in 1955. Spot and Hill were feuding – a quarrel which would come to a head in August of that year – and Spot was afraid that his now tenuous hold on the bookmakers' pitches on the Downs, the free course, would be taken from him. He had, according to his rank, the No 1 pitch and he collected rent from the others. But now Billy Hill had with him Frankie Fraser and another wildman, Billy Blythe. Spot needed help from somewhere and he went down to the twins' billiard hall, the Regal in Eric Street at Mile End. He found them a good bookmaker to mind. No hard work unless Fraser and the others made a move. All they had to do was to stand by his pitch and take their percentage at the end of the day.

According to John Pearson the Krays did not take their work that day too seriously. When one of the Saffron Hill Italian Mob offered them the advice that they were stark raving mad to show up as Spot's minders they laughed and offered him a drink.

For the rest of that day the twins kept up their show of insolent indifference against the best-known gangsters in the country. They drank, they entertained their friends, they roared with laughter, they ignored the racing and the betting. Finally Ronnie yawned and rolled off to sleep. When the day ended they collected what was owed them, and without bothering to thank Spot drove off in their van.[1]

The day's exercise had gone well. They had seen and been seen, although they were not to make any substantial move on the West End for nearly another decade. With the impetuosity of youth they dismissed Spot and the others as tired old men. 'We never liked Spotty. Never thought much of him,' said Ronnie.[2] Years later Spot bemoaned the fact that the twins had not listened to him and his advice. 'I could have taught them everything,' he explained.

In fact legend is wrong about that Epsom outing being a first. The twins had been out of their area and about for some time, working as minders first for Jack Spot in his spieler, the Aldgate Fruit Exchange, confusingly located in Covent Garden, and then making a book with Teddy Machin, at Marks Tey races. At that time meetings about pitches and how they should be allocated were run by Albert Dimes at the Central Club in Clerkenwell. At one meeting a shot was fired at bookmaker Tommy Falco and from then on the Krays had five shillings in the pound from the pitch takings. The twins also had a foothold in the West End, minding the Stragglers Club at Cambridge Circus for a half share with Billy Jones and a former boxer, Bobby Ramsey.

The Kray twins – Ronnie was the elder – were born in 1933 in Stean Street, London E8. They had an older and loyal brother, Charles, a grandfather, Cannonball Lee,

[1] J. Pearson, *The Profession of Violence*, p. 96.

[2] Ibid, p. 93 et seq.

who was once a well-known flyweight boxer, and a father, Charles senior, who spent much of their early years either totting or ducking and diving his way out of the army. They also had a devoted mother, Violet.

Much has been made of the brothers' boxing abilities but their ring records, kept by the British Boxing Board of Control, show that of the three only Reggie, a lightweight, had much promise. Ronnie, as a welterweight, won four of his six bouts between July and December 1951, ending his career with a disqualification against Doug Sherlock at the National Sporting Club and finally a points defeat by Bill Sliney at the Royal Albert Hall on 11 December. It was a night when all three brothers boxed on the same bill. Reggie, who had one more bout, had boxed Sliney twice, beating him both times on points. He began and ended his career with a points win over Bobby Manito. Charlie Kray's sporadic career lasted nearly two years. He lost all three of his contests, finally being counted out in the third round that night at the Albert Hall, in a bout against the up and coming Lew Lazar.

The twins' much more successful career as club owners began with the Regal in Eric Street, which they simply commandeered. From there they acquired the Green Dragon and later Reggie opened their showpiece, the Double R Club, financed in part by their profits and in part by poncing from local villains. Poncing in this context takes the form of demanding a share of proceeds from a burglary or robbery in a given area. 'On an occasion when two youngsters did Attenboroughs the jewellers in Bethnal Green Road the twins copped £2000 from the proceeds of the job,' says one former colleague.

The twins had their ears to the ground. It was often not a complete secret when a good job was to take place, partly because others, not involved, wanted to be able to put up an alibi. The twins' information service put them in a position to know when good jobs such as major breakings, hijackings of lorries and sometimes, but not usually, bank raids were to take place. After a job members of the Firm, as the Krays' organization had become known, were sent to see the perpetrators and to invite them out for a drink. The twins would chat about the job and assess its overall value and then ask for a substantial part of the take. Even members of the Firm were not immune. If they conducted a piece of business out of hours, so to speak, they were still expected to pay up. For thefts, the going rate paid by a receiver was one third of the value of the goods. The Krays would ask for a third of a third.

But they were despised by the real heavy bank robbers.

> There really is a load of shit talked about them. They ran the East End but they never ran the West End. If they'd come near us they'd have been seen to. Of course they protected clubs. There's a lot of weak people in this world. They never had the arsehole to rob for themselves. Are they nice people? Well, tell me if this is nice. You get a young boy come into the club with his girlfriend. He's got a load of cigarettes to sell. They take the cigarettes, never pay him and he ends up getting shagged.

'Is that nice?' asks a former bank robber.

The twins also knew villains who were stealing cheque books by office creeping and then flew kites[3] to get equipment to set up a gymnasium over the Regal club, itself just a drinker. It was at the Regal that the Firm

3 In criminal slang office creeping is burglary and to fly a kite is to proffer a stolen or forged cheque.

was born, helped by the loyalty of former prisoners whose families had been looked after by the Krays while they themselves were away.

The twins also had the controlling interest in the Regency, a Stoke Newington club run by the Barry brothers, one of whom, Tony, was to be instrumental in bringing down their empire. Once the brothers had opened up the club and paid the expenses the Krays started 'nipping' – demanding up to a pony (£25) or a few bottles of spirits at a time – until they simply moved in, took over a room for their private drinking and required a pension. On to the door went their helpmate and bouncer 'Big' Pat Donnelly, a twenty-stone ex-boxer.

But even had they wanted, they were not in a position to challenge their friends the Nashes for the title of Emperors of the Underworld. One of the reasons was that Ronnie was about to get three years' imprisonment.

The trouble arose from the twins' connection with Bobbie Ramsey, part-owner of the Stragglers, as well as from a long-running feud with a mainly Irish fighting gang, the Watney Streeters. The Watney Street Mob were mainly dockers who, apart from their fighting qualities, stole from the docks. They were led by Jimmy Fuller and many of them were related. The gang's decline in strength paralleled the decline of the London Docks. Other East London gangs of the time included the Trocksy Mob from Pitsea Street. 'They were all thieves and good drinkers, but as they grew up and got married the gang broke up in the 1950s and 1960s,' says a contemporary. Another team of the 1950s was the Butlers. 'A lot of these families had a brother who was a bit divvy, sort of backward, fearless and violent.'

One of the Streeters, Charlie, had a small scam going with local post office drivers, who would readdress parcels to places where he could collect them. Ronnie, hearing of the potential, demanded fifty per cent of the profits. Charlie was dilatory with payments and was listed by Ronnie as someone with whom he would soon have to deal severely. The opportunity came when Charlie had a fight with Billy Jones, another part-owner of the Stragglers. The next night Bobby Ramsey, as Jones' partner, sought out Charlie and beat him up. Two nights later Charlie, this time with a complement from the Watney Street Gang, beat Ramsey unconscious outside the Artichoke pub in the East End.

Although strictly not involved, Ronnie apparently wanted to make an example of Charlie and shoot him but both Ramsey and Jones argued against this. Instead it was agreed that a severe beating would be handed out to the Watney Streeters in the Britannia public house on Watney Street territory. Ramsey and Jones went with Ronnie, backed by a dozen others. They found the Britannia empty except for a boy, Terry Martin, who was playing gin rummy. The Watney Street Gang had escaped through the back entrance. Martin was made to suffer for their display of cowardliness. He was dragged out of the pub, slashed with a bayonet and kicked about the head.

Instead of going home Ronnie decided to look for the Watney Streeters. Driven by Ramsey, he was found with a revolver when the police stopped the car in Stepney around midnight. In the car there was a crowbar and a machete. Ronnie explained the bloodstains on his shirt by saying he had had a nose bleed. Efforts to buy off Terry Martin failed and Reggie was also charged, but was acquitted after the jury accepted that bloodstains on his jacket might have come from boxers in the gym.

On 5 November 1956 the Recorder of London sentenced Ronnie to three years' imprisonment. Ramsey received five years and Jones three. The Stragglers was shut down shortly afterwards. Reggie said, 'But it didn't really matter. . . . I bought an empty shop in the Bow Road and turned it into a club. I called it the Double R – a sort of tribute to Ron. Above the club we built a very snazzy gym and I got Henry Cooper to open it.'[4]

The Double R may have been the jewel in the crown but even then there were numerous other interests, each paying money – a drinking club in Stratford, second-hand car businesses, and the celebrated illegal drinking club next door to Bow Road police station.

Reggie claims that one of the great problems he had with the law was over police killer Ronnie Marwood, of whom he maintains, 'I owed Marwood nothing and I knew he was going to cause me nothing but trouble. But, despite what they say, there is some kind of honour among thieves, a sort of code of conduct. Right or wrong, I took Marwood in and hid him in a safe place until he was ready to make a run for it.'[5]

It is interesting how this story corresponds and contrasts with the Nash version. The run for it in Reggie's tale never took place in the Nash account, in which Marwood surrendered himself to a police station. On the whole the Nash version is the one to be preferred. There are, for example, no pictures of Reggie

---

[4] R. and R. Kray, *Our Story*, p. 34.

[5] R. and R. Kray, *Our Story*, p. 35. On 14 December 1958, his first wedding anniversary, Ronald Marwood went drinking in various pubs and ended up outside a dance hall in the Seven Sisters Road, involved in a fight between the Essex Road and the Angel gangs. A twenty-three-year-old police constable, Raymond Summers, tried to break up the fight and was fatally stabbed by Marwood, who, believing to the last that he would be reprieved, was hanged at Pentonville Prison on 8 May 1959. The jury had recommended mercy. A demonstration outside the prison had been broken up by the police and booing took place in cinemas when newsreels of the incident were shown. Marwood's was one of the executions on which abolitionists based their campaign.

sending wreaths; no interviews with the press. For a self-publicist it is unlikely he would pass up such a splendid opportunity. In its way the two versions run parallel to the Spot and Hill stories of the flushing out of the Whites. The most likely version is an amalgam. The Nashes were then in the ascendancy. Reggie was a friend who may well have helped out, just as Spot helped Hill clean out his rivals in the 1940s.

Whichever is the correct version, it did not take the police long to close down the Double R and Reggie now maintains that every club he and Ronnie owned after that was persecuted – 'And all because we tried to help someone out.'

By the early 1960s, although Reggie claims that he disliked the protection business, feeling it was none too glamorous, he was looking after the remainder of Billy Hill's interests. Any connection with Jack Spot had long since been severed and there is no mention of the Nashes. He was, he says, also looking after Peter Rachman's interests in Notting Hill. Rachman, who provided a new word for the English language with an empire built from prostitution and slum properties, used a collection of wrestlers and strongmen as minders. Reggie says, '[Rachman] was paying us for protection. He had to – it was either that or his rent collectors were set upon. They were big, but our boys were bigger.'

Albert Donaghue, one of the Firm, explains how protection may not really be as bad as it seems to the outsider:

The Krays would know the right guys who would open a club and approach them. Anyone opening a club would go to them. Young guys only respect someone who is a name, otherwise the doorman is a target. It makes sense. I worked the Green Dragon in Aldgate. I got paid and there was £40 to the twins over and above my wages. People who came to the club knew who I was and why I was there.

Then another time I was approached when I was working in an after-hours drinker opposite Stratford Place – the owner of a mini-cab firm down the East End was having scrub calls, you know, you get called out and then there's no one there. Now it can only be people you've interfered with yourself. The fellow asks me to be the manager. Sixty/forty per cent. I'd had a few drinks and I said 'my way' and he said 'yes'. I couldn't believe it. I made a few calls [to locate the people doing it] and said if it didn't stop I'd be round, and it did.

But according to the twins' cousin, Ronnie Hart, another who was to turn against them when the going became rough in 1967, from that percentage Donaghue had to pay a share from his interest in Advance Mini Cabs of £10 per week, rain or shine, to the twins.

The list of clubs in and around North and East London and the West End from which the twins, at one time or another during their reign, were 'on a pension' is staggering. Benny's in Commercial Road, a spieler run by a cab driver, paid £15 a week. The owner of Dodgers in Brick Lane paid £15 and a further £15 for a betting shop. A Club opposite the dog-track in Walthamstow was another. The Krays had invested around £200 to get it started and they took £30 a week plus the wages of the man they had there to mind both the premises and their interests. That £30 went straight to their mother Violet for her housekeeping. The Green Dragon in Whitechapel Road paid £40 protection and when another blackjack table went into the basement a further £10 a week was levied. It was later turned into a betting shop and the payment remained the same. The Little Dragon next door paid £25 a week, and they were not too proud to receive £10 from the Two Aces, a spieler in the Whitechapel Road. Terry O'Brien's club in Cambridge Circus was taken over by them.

In Soho the twins, through their collectors, tapped Bernie Silver for £60 a week from his clubs: the Gigi in Frith Street and the New Life and the New Mill off Shaftesbury Avenue. This pension went three ways, between the twins, Freddie Foreman and the Nashes. In return Johnny Nash gave the twins a share of his pension from the Olympic Club in Camden Town as well as from the celebrated haunts, the Astor and the Bagatelle off Regent Street, an arrangement which left the twins with the lion's share of the take.

In Chelsea there was the La Monde Club in the King's Road and out at Kingston the Cambridge Rooms over the top of the Earl of Cambridge public house on the Kingston bypass. It was here, in one of their well-publicized acts of charity, that a racehorse was auctioned and bought by the actor Ronald Fraser. Then there was a share of the monies Freddie Foreman received from the tables at the Starlight Rooms off Oxford Street. Run by two men named Boot and Barry, the club had been opened after they had quarrelled with the Richardsons. They had gone to the Krays for help and had been installed in the Starlight as managers.

Of the more famous clubs, the Colony in Berkeley Square paid £100 a week and the Casanova, off New Oxford Street, half that sum. But there were occasional reverses. When John Bloom, the Rolls Razor washing-machine king whose empire collapsed in the 1960s, opened the Phone Booth club in Baker Street, a fringe member of the Firm, Eric Mason, an old-time heavy – reputed to be the last man to receive a flogging in prison – was sent round to ask for a 'pension'. He was thrown out and barred from the club. Later Ronnie Hart was dispatched along with Mason to explain the position. Mason could not be barred but the pension would be scrubbed. If Bloom stepped out of line again he 'would go' and his club along with him. The owner of the Monmouth Club in Monmouth Street, Smithfield, was less successful in repelling boarders. He received a beating for his troubles and later paid over a percentage.

The money from all subscribers to the Firm was collected on a Friday by Donaghue, Ronnie Hart, Scotch Jack Dickson and Ian Barrie. It was known as the milk round and the collectors were treated just like the milkman making his weekly call. From time to time the collectors would be given a small gift such as drink or another £10 for themselves. Scotch Jack Dickson and Ian Barrie kept the money from Benny's and the Dodgers as their own wages.

Back in the suburbs there was £10 a week from a scrap metal merchant in Hackney, and the same from another in Poplar. The twins took £15 of the £30 collected by George Dixon from a pub in Leytonstone. A Greek-run casino in Stoke Newington provided a share of its profits and in Leicester, just before the arrest of the twins in May 1967, Rayners Club paid out over a half share of the takings in return for a £500 investment.

In 1960, in accordance with their increasing social status, the twins acquired Esmeralda's Barn in Wilton Place off Knightsbridge. A once smart and fashionable night club, it had declined into producing strip shows and, with gambling legalized by the Gaming Act of 1959, it had applied for and been granted a licence for gambling. The acquisition was brought about by the simple expedient of frightening the controlling shareholder, Stefan De Fay, into signing away his shares to the twins for £1000. They had heard of the vulnerability of De Fay from Peter Rachman and, their implied threats being heeded, the club was theirs within six hours. De Fay stayed on the board of directors for the next two years but drew no salary. In the heyday of the club the twins cleared £40,000 a year, and they had Lord Effingham on the board with the princely retainer of £10 a week or the sum taken from the Two Aces in Whitechapel Road. The day-to-day running of the club and the twins' financial affairs was now firmly in the hands of an adroit long-firm fraudsman, Leslie Payne.

All went well until Reggie was returned to prison, serving his sentence in Wandsworth. Ronnie, not the brighter of the brothers, became lonely and frustrated. As John Pearson says, it was not sufficient for him to sit in a smart dinner-jacket and watch his tables make him money. He started to take an active interest in the club. Indiscriminately he began to grant long lines of credit and, when a punter could not pay, Ronnie took to threatening him. The serious players began to drift away to find other clubs. A lesbian-orientated discotheque was started in the basement. The club continued its decline until 1963, when it collapsed.

De Fay and his co-owners may have been frightened into signing away Esmeralda's Barn but Hew McCowan was made of sterner stuff. His refusal to sell the Hideaway Club coincided with the first of the two major enquiries by the police into the activities of the Krays.

By 1964, as befitted top-class villains, the twins had racked up very little prison record. In the main, witnesses and victims had been straightened. The police, it seems, had been prepared to adopt a policy of live and let live, even to the extent of letting them operate their illegal drinking club next to Bow Road police station. But things could not remain this way. On 12 July the police were galvanized into action by news of a claim that a set of photographs existed of a peer and a gangster. The Commissioner of Police, Sir Joseph Simpson, issued a statement denying a witch-hunt against titled homosexuals. The owner of the photographs obtained an injunction in the High Court to prevent the pictures being printed by the Mirror Group of Newspapers.

On 13 July the *Daily Mirror* ran an editorial: 'This gang is so rich, powerful and ruthless that the police are unable to crack down on it. Victims are too terrified to go to the police. Witnesses are too scared to tell their story in court. The police, who know what is happening but cannot pin any evidence on the villains, are powerless.'

The next day Sir Joseph made a statement that he had asked senior officers for 'some enlightenment' on reports that enquiries were being made into allegations of a relationship between a homosexual peer and East End gangsters.

On 16 July the *Daily Mirror* led with the story 'The picture we dare not print' and described it as one of a 'well known member of the House of Lords seated on a sofa with a gangster who leads the biggest protection racket London has ever known.'

Rumours abounded: the picture showed the peer in a compromising position; there were stories of orgies at Mayfair parties; a coven of homosexual clergy in Brighton; blackmail; surveillance by Scotland Yard.

The picture, which appeared a week later in the German magazine *Stern*, turned out to be totally innocent. The peer was Lord Boothby, one-time darling of the Conservative Party and widely believed to be the true father of one of Prime Minister Harold Macmillan's children. The gangster was Ronnie Kray.

Boothby issued a statement:

I am not a homosexual. I have not been to a Mayfair party of any kind for more than twenty years. I have met the man alleged to be King of the

Underworld only three times, on business matters; and then by appointment in my flat, at his request, and in the company of other people.

He retained Arnold Goodman, of Goodman Derrick & Co, a prominent solicitor and later adviser and confidant to the powerful both in and out of government, to claim damages for libel. The Mirror Group settled for the then very considerable sum of £40,000. Ronnie, for whom Goodman did not act, sold a copy of the picture to the *Daily Express*, and obtained an apology from the *Mirror* but no damages. But, as John Pearson says, the apology kept the *Mirror* away from launching an investigation into him and Reggie.

Nevertheless, prodded by the Labour MP for Brixton, Marcus Lipton, who put down a question in the House of Commons concerning reports he had received about extortion from club owners and what action the Home Secretary was taking, the police began to make active enquiries into the Kray affairs. On 27 July, Area Chief Superintendent Fred Gerrard called on the up and coming young Detective Inspector Leonard 'Nipper' Read at Commercial Street police station and asked him if there was any reason why he should not conduct a detailed investigation into the twins' business and personal interests. Read, rightly taking this as an implication that he might be in their pockets, angrily denied it and a squad was formed.

In his autobiography Read discusses why the police had previously made no serious attempt to break the Krays' hold on the East End:

Over the previous years the Krays had been taken on by the police but not concentrated on. Before Gerrard formed my squad the CID had never taken their actions personally and I think they should have done. If ever there was a shooting and the overwhelming level of opinion amongst detectives was that it was down to the Krays, the attitude had been that you went along to see them first and they said 'No, we got an alibi'. Then you would go and look for the evidence. It should have been the other way round. This is what appalled me even before I started the first enquiry. You'd talk to CID officers and they'd say 'Oh this is down to the Krays', and you'd say 'Well what are you doing about it?' And the answer was they were doing nothing about it. They never sort of took up the cudgels. They never got keen enough or personally involved enough to want to have a go. That was the sort of thing that surprised me.[6]

Read's first move was to go and have a look at the Krays in one of their favourite haunts, the Grave Maurice, where he knew they were to meet a TV interviewer, Michael Barrett. He arrived before six o'clock, the time he had heard was fixed for the meeting, and settled down out of the way.

They came within half an hour, in a large American car. First a man named 'Duke' Osborne got out, his hand in his jacket pocket so it seemed he was carrying a gun. He looked up and down the road, came into the pub and gave the place a swift East to West – I was the only one who was there and he ignored me – checked out the lavatories, went back out on to the pavement, and gave a nod in the direction of the car. Through the open door I watched as Ronnie Kray unfolded himself from the back seat, straightened up, and hurried across the

[6] L. Read and J. Morton, *Nipper*, p. 89.

pavement flanked by minders.

For a moment I could not believe what I saw. His hair was smartly cut and gleaming and his gold-rimmed spectacles firmly in place. He was wearing a light camel coat which almost reached his ankles, the belt tied in a casual knot at the waist. For all the world he looked like something out of the Capone era. Once inside the Maurice the minders selected two booths and Ronnie sat in one whilst the minders collected two gins and a whisky from the bar. Ronnie remained in solitary splendour with his men in the next booth until Barrett arrived. He was wearing a neckbrace at the time and the minders did everything but frisk him. He was escorted by them to Ronnie's table before they went back to collect his drink. At the end of the interview Osborne and the others went out, 'swept' the street, and then Ronnie hurried to the car. I have no reason to think that this was anything other than for show. It was not a period in the life of the twins when they were facing a war with anyone.

In a way it was a joke but, at the same time, it was a bit unnerving. I'd heard all these stories about the Krays and here they were behaving exactly as their reputation suggested they would do. If it had been mocked up for a TV serial you'd have said 'Come on, this is a bit over the top.'

As the months went by little progress was made, although Read's squad contained a talented collection of officers, some of whom were to reach the top echelons of Scotland Yard. Read went to see Jack Spot, but he was now out of the scene; journalists to whom he spoke could add little to the articles they had written; and investigations into the story that an Italian restaurant near the British Museum was paying protection money were abandoned after lengthy observation failed to identify anyone remotely connected with the Firm going within yards of the premises.

Nor did the persistent stories of torture amount to anything. The Krays had been reputed to hold mock trials with the punishment of a razor slashing of the buttocks – known as striping the arsehole and a favourite sport amongst villains of the time – but a combing of the records of every hospital in the Greater London area produced nothing. Read also went to see a gambler whom Ronnie was said to have slashed when he was unable to pay a gaming debt at Esmeralda's Barn, but the man would not make a statement. Read and his men trawled the London night clubs but none of the owners and managers would admit to paying protection money. There was a blank, too, when enquiries were made of local bookmakers who were said to have had to pay into funds of the 'aways', those members of the Firm in prison.

The best that Read could come up with was the information that the main source of the Firm came from long firm frauds. The beauty of a well organized long firm fraud is that goods are bought over a telephone by a 'blower-man', so that identification of the purchaser is improbable, and managers fronting the warehouse or shop are changed weekly or fortnightly, making it difficult if not impossible for the investigations to establish a chain of command leading back to the true operators. Another thing in favour of the LF operator was the laborious way in which an investigation would be conducted. The company had to go bust, then creditors had actually to make a complaint, rather than just lick their wounds and write it off to tax and experience. After that it would go to the Board of Trade for an investigation, which could take a year or more and, if they found grounds for concern, the papers would be sent to the Fraud Squad. By then witnesses would have lost interest and the principals would be long gone.

Read bypassed the Board of Trade and the Fraud Squad, steaming straight into the LFs, which he found fairly easy to identify, and arresting the front operators for conspiracy. By doing this he hoped to find someone who might be persuaded to admit to the involvement of the Krays. But no one would admit anything. Although he mounted six prosecutions for fraud, by January 1965 Read was no nearer to the Krays than when he had started. Gerrard as his superior was under considerable pressure from Commander Ernie Millen to terminate the enquiry. While Gerrard was away on annual leave, Millen called Read to the Yard and asked for a report commenting unfavourably on the progress of the investigation and indicating that it would be shut down. When Gerrard returned Read told him of the conversation and an angry exchange took place with Millen.

Then, seemingly, Read had a piece of luck. He heard through an officer at Paddington that club owner Hew McCowan had been pressured to pay protection money for the Hideaway Club in Gerrard Street, which he had just opened in partnership with Gilbert France, who also owned the restaurant Chez Victor in Wardour Street.

The Hideaway had previously been the Bon Soir, owned by France in partnership with Frankie Fraser and Albert Dimes. There had been a dispute with France over the Bon Soir, which was managed by a young man called Sydney Vaughan, and the club had closed in early autumn 1965. At Vaughan's twenty-first birthday party an agreement had been signed giving Vaughan *carte blanche* to run the premises. For this he had to pay Gerrard Enterprises, France's company, £150 a week. McCowan employed Vaughan as his agent and manager, and spent some £4000 on refurbishing the club, which opened for business on 16 December.

McCowan had already met the twins through both a Johnny Francis and their financial adviser Leslie Payne when they had tried to interest McCowan in an investment in a housing project in Eastern Nigeria. This had been a scam run by the son of Manny Shinwell, the old Labour MP, and was the same project in which they had tried to interest Boothby. In turn this had led to the photographs getting into the hands of the *Mirror*.

McCowan had foolishly mentioned that he was thinking of opening a club and it was arranged he should meet the twins in the Grave Maurice public house. According to McCowan's statement Reggie had maintained it was essential that McCowan have two of his men installed in the club to prevent trouble. Initially a figure of twenty-five per cent was suggested, which was to rise to fifty per cent. A table for ten was reserved for the twins' party on the opening night but no one showed. Three days later a friend of the Krays, a writer called 'Mad' Teddy Smith, appeared, very drunk, caused trouble and did a minor amount of damage in the reception area before being bounced out by the waiters.[7] When McCowan next saw the Krays it was pointed out that this sort of thing would not have happened had their men been there to prevent it. An agreement was reached that now twenty per cent would be payable. McCowan asked for and was told he would receive a written agreement. He telephoned the police.

Once he had taken statements Read liked the way McCowan stuck to his version of events and, even more, he liked the way Vaughan gave his account. He would

[7] Smith, who had written a play for radio and who was a part-time driver for the twins, disappeared in the 1960s and was thought to have been killed in a quarrel over a boy in Steeple Bay, Kent. His body was never found and no charges were brought.

have liked to have had sight of the agreement but what he had was better than nothing. Read thought he had enough for arrests.

They took place at the Glenrae Hotel in Seven Sisters Road in North London, run by Phoebe Woods and her husband. There was a drinking club in the basement originally for commercial travellers but later taken over by the twins as one of their regular drinking haunts. The pattern of events had been remarkably similar to other takeovers. Mrs Woods had run the trouble-free hotel for some five years until in September 1964 her son was attacked by three men. She shut down the drinking club. Three weeks later men came into the hotel threatening that the club must be reopened. She reported the matter to the police. A fortnight later her husband was attacked in the basement kitchen.

Two weeks later matters were under control again with long-time Kray stalwart, the former boxer Billy Exley, in charge of the bar and the doorman none other than Bobby Ramsey. The Krays moved into rooms 1 and 2. It was there that Gerrard and Read arrested them along with Teddy Smith. Of Johnny Francis, who had made the initial introduction, there was no sign. But if Read thought that his troubles were over he was to find they were only just beginning.

The Krays remained in custody until their trial at the Old Bailey the next year, despite a question in the House of Lords from their old friend Lord Boothby, who wanted to know if it was the intention of the government to imprison the Krays without trial indefinitely. Meanwhile Read hoped that with the twins out of harm's way people would come forward. He was wrong but it was a mistake from which he learned two years later. His case now began to fall apart, starting with the defection of Sydney Vaughan, who went to the twins' home at Fort Vallance to retract his statement before a local vicar.

McCowan was offered money not to give evidence but refused.

The first trial came to an abrupt halt on the second day with McCowan still in the witness box. Manny Fryde, the solicitor's clerk who was handling the Krays' cases, said he had a witness who had overheard a juryman discussing the case with a police officer. The witness turned out to be a man who had been questioned about the sale of the shares in Esmeralda's Barn but the juryman was stood down and the case proceeded with eleven jurors. Vaughan maintained that the only reason he had made his original statement was because McCowan had threatened to withdraw his financial support. After three and a half hours the jury announced it was deadlocked. At the retrial things went worse for the Crown. Evidence was produced by the defence that McCowan had spent some time in a psychiatric hospital. Vaughan was called neither by the Crown nor by the defence. The jury took less than ten minutes to acquit.

The same day the Krays purchased the Hideaway Club from McCowan, renaming it the El Morocco. Read and his men went to watch the guests turning up for the celebratory party. Seen by George Devlin, a private detective hired by the Krays, he was invited into the party, an offer he could not refuse. Reggie accepted his presence with something approaching equanimity; Ronnie glowered. Read left after a few minutes. His squad disbanded, it was the last he was to see of the twins for four years. In effect the Krays now had a licence to behave as they wished in both the East and West End.

But possibly the Hideaway trial was the pinnacle of their careers. A month after the case, on 20 April 1965, Reggie married a young girl, Frances Shea; the wedding photographer was the fashionable David Bailey. At the wedding Ronnie believed that not sufficient enthusiasm was being shown by the guests. 'Sing, fuck you, sing,' he ordered them. Frances, increasingly unhappy with her husband, committed suicide just over two years later, on the night of 6 June 1967. At her funeral Albert Donaghue was ordered to make a list for future reference of those who had not sent flowers. Reggie was distraught. Worse, Ronnie was beginning to show increasing signs of mental instability. Another list was compiled, this time of those by whom Ronnie felt threatened. All his energies were being channelled into revenge and retribution.

One of those by whom he felt threatened was George Myers, who changed his name to Cornell. An East London tearaway and one of the old Watney Streeters, Cornell had run a long firm fraud which had been turned over by the twins and he resented it. Now he shifted his allegiance to Frankie Fraser and to the Richardsons. His name too went on the list.[8]

In theory there was no need for the Krays ever to quarrel with the Richardsons. There are stories that years earlier there had been a meeting between the Richardsons, Fraser, the Nashes, the twins and the Foreman family over dividing London between them but it had come to nothing. The failure of the meeting was said to have been caused by the refusal of the Richardsons to co-operate, particularly in relation to the money they were receiving from the National Car Parks fiddle.

Whether such a meeting took place, London should have been quite big enough for both the Krays and the Richardsons. As Nipper Read says, 'There was a natural dividing line – the Thames. Soho had for years been

---

[8] One version of the story has it that Cornell met Fraser in prison and later agreed to join with him in the placing of gaming machines in West End clubs. It is more likely that his allegiance began to change when he married Olive, a girl from Bermondsey across the river.

something of an Open City. There was plenty of pickings for everybody. Each firm had the clubs which they protected. There was no need to muscle in on someone else's club.'

Now with the Cornell–Fraser–Richardson alliance the twins began to feel threatened. Whilst Fraser had been in prison following the Spot affair they had assiduously courted him through his sister Eva Brindle, taking her to see him on visiting days, and when he had been released the twins had thrown a big coming home party for him. But Fraser had not been seduced. Instead Fraser, always interested in gaming machines, had taken over a chain of machines once owned by the twins.

George Cornell they saw as a threat because he took a close interest in the pornography market in both the West End and in Essex. The twins also believed they were on the edge of a big deal with the American Mafia and the Richardsons could interfere with it. At one meeting with a Mafioso chief visiting from New York the Richardsons had been present and had made sarcastic remarks. Ronnie also feared that the uneasy truce between themselves and the Richardsons would end. 'I had a gut feeling that something or someone would force us into a full-scale war.'[9]

Worse, there was personal animosity. A meeting was summoned at that gentlemen's club for villains, the Astor, for a discussion between the twins, Ian Barrie and Ron Hart, Charlie and Eddie Richardson, Frankie Fraser and George Cornell. The meeting became heated, with the Richardsons apparently claiming a substantial interest in the Kray–Mafia business arrangements. It was then that George Cornell, never lacking in courage, called Ronnie a big fat poof and told him to bugger off when he asked to be cut into the blue film

[9] R. and R. Kray, *Our Story*, p. 70.

racket. It was not an insult that could be accepted lightly. Ronnie had already slashed little Johnny Cardew from an Islington family for saying, perfectly pleasantly, that he thought Ronnie seemed to be putting on weight. To be called a poof in front of his friends was far too much. There was a discussion about instant retribution but it was put off and instead Ronnie had Cornell's movements monitored.

Shortly after there was another confrontation. This time it was in Al Burnett's Stork Club in Swallow Street, Piccadilly, and this time it was between Ronnie and Frankie Fraser. As a result the Krays called a meeting with some South-East London rivals of the Richardsons and another smaller North London faction. The old talk of an alliance was revived. It was agreed that a defence union should be formed. The Firm was put on war alert. Donaghue recalls:

> We were each given a name. Ronnie Hart and I had to look after Brian Mottram if it came to it. We were all given the names and addresses of clubs, pubs, girlfriends, where our people could be found. Freddie Foreman had a spy in the Richardson scrapyard. If we went south to see Freddie it was like we were going into Indian country. We would go in a hired car with a gun so if we got a pull it wasn't our car and we could say we knew nothing about it. Going south of the river was like going abroad.

Still the Krays did not believe they were strong enough without help. To counter the ferocity of Frankie Fraser someone just as fearless was needed to be their own private man. The person they chose was Frank Mitchell. There was only one problem – he was serving a sentence in Dartmoor Prison.

In the meantime they began wearing bullet-proof vests and a member of the Firm was deputed to be their personal bodyguard, leaving any public house or club first to survey the street. Although they felt themselves in need of protection they did not carry weapons and were becoming increasingly reluctant to allow members of the Firm to do so either. Wednesday nights were when the Krays went visiting around the various local pubs and before these evening visits, members of the Firm would go to the pub or club and hide weapons in lavatory cisterns. They were right to be careful. Shots were fired at the windows of the Widows, the name for the Lion pub in Tapp Street where the Krays used to drink. A few days later a mini-cab owner who resembled Ronnie was knocked down by a car which mounted the pavement.

There had long been a liaison with gangs in Scotland and a Glasgow hardman was recruited to deal with Cornell. He followed him for some weeks but according to legend succeeded only in stabbing him in the bottom when they met in a basement drinking club. The Glasgow hardman returned to Scotland a couple of months before Cornell's murder.

George Cornell survived the Mr Smith's Club affray which had led to the arrest of the Richardsons, only to die on the next evening, 9 March 1966. Ronnie received word that Cornell was deep in the heart of Kray territory, sitting on a stool at the bar of the Blind Beggar public house near Whitechapel tube station in the Mile End Road. Around 8.30 the door opened and in walked Ronnie Kray and Ian Barrie. Had they been a few minutes earlier they would have met a local Detective Inspector having a drink and sandwich. The story is that Cornell looked up and said 'Look who's here'. If he did say that those were the last words he spoke. Ronnie shot him at point-blank range with a Luger pistol.

He justifies the shooting quite simply:

Richard Hart had to be avenged. No one could kill a member of the Kray gang and expect to get away with it. . . . Typical of the yobbo mentality of the man. Less than twenty-four hours after the Catford killing and here he was, drinking in a pub that was officially on our patch. It was as though he wanted to be shot.[10]

Ronnie went into hiding over a barber's shop in the Lea Bridge Road and the police inquiry got nowhere. Tommy Butler, the senior detective from the Great Train Robbery, now on the Murder Squad, was sent to conduct the investigation. Whilst it was common knowledge that the Krays were behind the killing – 'Everybody knows Ronnie done it,' one East End villain told Nipper Read, 'Christ, they did everything but take the front page of the fucking *Times* to advertise it' – no one was prepared to admit to seeing anything. The barmaid had apparently been in the cellar and everyone else had their heads well down. Butler did, however, organize a dawn swoop on Vallance Road and put Ronnie up on an identification parade. He was not picked out by the barmaid. At that stage she had every reason not to.

Donaghue says he went over to the Three Swedish Coins in Wapping 'to see a man there to arrange a meet to see whether the twins could interview the barmaid at that pub. It never came to anything. I knew that one, she wouldn't show up and two, if they did she would never leave.'

Butler was forced to release the twins to their usual triumphant welcome home. The investigation was put on ice. But though they might be free of immediate police attention they were not free of the Cornell family. George's widow Olive, showing the same courage as her

[10] R. and R. Kray, *Our Story*, p. 72.

husband, mounted a campaign against them, calling at Fort Vallance and smashing the windows. She was brought before the magistrate at Thames Court and fined the derisory sum of £1. At one time the twins seriously considered whether she must join her husband.

Donaghue believes it was then that the twins began to lose touch with reality. Ronnie was on massive doses of tranquillizers and Reggie, besotted with the dead Frances, now believed she had been reborn as a robin he had seen in the cemetery. Ronnie was also putting pressure on his twin to 'do his one'. He would have to wait a year and a half before his brother obliged.

In the meantime, quite apart from managing the day-to-day affairs of the organization, the twins had a long-term and in some ways daring plan. They would arrange the release of the 'Mad Axe-man' Frank Mitchell from Dartmoor where he was serving a substantial sentence of imprisonment. Poor Mitchell, strong as an ox and with the brains of one, had had an amazingly unsuccessful career as a criminal. From the age of eight he had been in special schools, in Borstal at seventeen, and in prison three months later. From then it was downhill all the way, with a flogging for an assault on a prison officer. In 1955 he had been sent to Rampton, certified as a mental defective. In January 1957 he escaped and whilst on the run burgled a house, hitting the occupant over the head with an iron bar. This time he received nine years. Back inside he was sent to Broadmoor, escaped and attacked another householder and his wife. On his arrest he said, 'I want to prove I am sane and know what I am doing.' He received ten years' imprisonment. Involved in the 1962 Hull prison riots he was birched and transferred to Dartmoor.

His behaviour improved and by July 1963 he was removed from the escape list. In May 1964 he was allowed to work outside the prison walls in the quarry party, a small and well-supervised group. In September of that year he was transferred to the honour party, a more loosely supervised group, and now, financed by the Krays, he abused his relative freedom no end. He became a regular in a local pub. Once he took a taxi to Tavistock where he bought a budgerigar. Women were provided by the twins to pass away his afternoons. As one warder said, 'I just could not afford to have Mitchell troublesome.'

For the Krays Mitchell became a special 'away'. Their reputation was on the slide in the East End. Some members of the Firm were now referring to them as Gert and Daisy, after Ethel and Doris Walters, the Cockney music hall act. Others thought they were becoming too dangerous for their own good. Their financial adviser Leslie Payne and his friend Freddie Gore were gone. With the Richardsons in general, and Frankie Fraser in particular, in custody, there was no need for any more strongmen in the Firm. Mitchell was needed more as a rehabilitation or at least damage limitation exercise, showing the East End both how their twins cared for people and, if they put their minds to it, what they could do. On one occasion Mitchell had also protected Reggie Kray against a screw in prison and something of a debt was owed.

Mitchell was becoming querulous about getting a date for his release and the plan was evolved that he would escape from a working party on the Moor and then a campaign would begin to bring pressure for his release. To this end friendly MPs such as the noted homosexual Tom Driberg could be relied on for help. On 12 December 1966 Mitchell went to work at Bagga Tor. The weather that day was too bad for work and the party stayed in a hut playing cards. At 3.30 he asked if he could go and feed some ponies. At 4.20 when the prison officers took the remainder of the party to the bus pick-up point there was no sign of Mitchell. Twenty minutes later the local police were notified. By this time Mitchell was on his way to London. When the hue and cry really went up Mitchell was rather grumpily eating bacon and eggs cooked for him at the Whitechapel flat of a small-time porn merchant and gang hanger-on, Lennie 'Books' Dunn, so named because of the bookstalls he ran in the Whitechapel Road. Mitchell had, it seems, been expecting something more in the way of a red carpet.

When, next morning, his clothing was found in a lay-by some thirty miles from Tavistock it was 'assumed he had made good his escape'. The next and really the last thing the outside world heard of Mitchell was from the newspapers. He wrote to *The Times* and the *Daily Mirror*. Each letter, actually written by Dunn, bore a thumbprint impression to confirm its authenticity and each asked for a release date. At first the Home Secretary agreed to meet with Mitchell but amended this by imposing the precondition of his surrender. The letters dried up. Again it was well known in Barking Road who had helped Mitchell in his escape, but once again, no one was talking to the police.

For a few days Mitchell lived in relative comfort, with the twins trying to keep him happy. A hostess, Lisa, was more or less kidnapped from Winston's night club to provide him with sex and there is little doubt that she became fond of this semi-moron who exercised by holding up members of the Firm two at a time in displays of strength. But Mitchell had in fact exchanged one prison cell for another. Without his surrender he was no nearer obtaining a release date and surrender meant loss of privileges and very probably loss of remission and further time to be served. He began to say he would never be captured alive. And the more he said such things the more of a liability he became to the twins. He wanted to go and see his mother and sister at the family house in Bow and was told a meeting would be arranged, but nothing came of it. He began to rave about going to look for the twins both at Vallance Road and 'all around the clubs'.

On 24 December Mitchell was told by Albert Donaghue that he was being moved to a new address in Kent. He protested at being separated from Lisa but was told she would be following on. He was never seen again, although rather like in the Lord Lucan case, there were reports that he had been sighted in Scotland, Ireland, Germany and, indeed, in most other countries throughout the world. At the trial of the Krays for the murder of Mitchell, Alf Donaghue gave evidence that the axe-man had been shot just as the van left the Barking Road, the gunmen being Freddie Foreman and Alf Gerard, a more or less freelance hitman who died in 1981 in Brighton.

The Firm had a series of codes: 'the dog has won' meant a successful operation had been carried out, 'the dog has lost' meant the reverse. According to the night club hostess Lisa, Donaghue returned to the flat and said, 'The dog is dead.' There was no corroboration of Donaghue's evidence. He himself had been arrested and had turned QE as the trade expression goes. The Krays were acquitted along with Freddie Foreman. Alfie Gerard, who was in Australia at the time of the trial, was never charged.

The third, in chronological order, of the murders for which the Krays eventually stood trial was that of Jack 'the Hat' McVitie, a longtime friend of the family. He disappeared in the autumn of 1967. Apparently he had fallen from favour for a number of reasons.

Tony Lambrianou, one of three brothers and a lesser light of the Kray Firm, who wrote a book on his experiences, described McVitie and his murder:

Reggie didn't do society such a bad turn. Jack the Hat was a known heavy man. He was six feet two and hard as nails. He done a lot of imprisonment in his time. He'd been through the school and he'd hurt a few people along the way.

His stock in trade was crime and he made money out of it. He was an active robber and he cared little for anyone and he was capable of anything. . . . He was on drink and pills and he was unpredictable. . . . Even having a social drink, he could suddenly turn vicious for no reason.

He didn't have a care in the world. He didn't give a monkey for anything, but he should have done. That was his downfall. . . . The twins only tried to help him: they put lots of work his way. But he started making errors, and he brought trouble on himself.[11]

The work from the Krays had included taking over part of a drug-vending operation and spying on the Nash brothers. McVitie was related to Johnny Nash's then right-hand man. After McVitie's death the story was put about that he had died when gelignite in his car had blown up accidentally. It was a story to appease the Nash brothers.

McVitie at one time had a £25 a week pension. He worked as a freelance robber and when asked to donate half the proceeds to the Firm's funds he refused. He was expelled. Later, after a beating, he was reinstated as a fringe member if nothing more. He could not be relied on, however, and he tipped the wink to another independent robber, Bobby Cannon, when Cannon was on the line for, at the very least, a bad beating. McVitie also took to criticizing the twins in public.

[11] T. Lambrianou, *Inside the Firm*, pp. 26–7.

His compounding sin seems to have been his behaviour when given money to kill the Krays' former financial adviser Leslie Payne. He had gone to Payne's house with Billy Exley, an ex-boxer and one-time stalwart friend of the Krays, only to find the potential victim out. McVitie had simply turned away and pocketed the advance fee. Not content with that, he had begun to boast how he had ripped off the twins. It was probably a combination of all these things which led to McVitie's death. They were coupled to one further fact: McVitie was in the wrong place at the wrong time.

He was murdered at a party at Evering Road in the home of 'Blonde' Carol Skinner. She had been sent across the road to a friend of hers for the evening. Tony Barry of the Regency Club had been ordered to tell the Krays when McVitie showed up at the club and to bring to the Evering Road party a gun kept at the Regency. There were advantages in this. The more people who were participants as opposed to mere observers, the more compromised they were and so the less likely to tell the police.

The Lambrianou brothers brought McVitie to the flat and immediately Reggie put the gun to his head. The gun failed to discharge. McVitie began to struggle and to try to escape. Finally Reggie plunged a knife deep into his face and stomach. Reggie commented, 'I did not regret it at the time and I don't regret it now. I have never felt a moment's remorse.'[12]

McVitie's body was wrapped in a candlewick bedspread and taken to South London by Charlie Kray for disposal – something arranged by Freddie Foreman, who, although from South London, was a longtime friend of the twins. Exactly where the body ended is impossible to say. Nipper Read fancied the idea that it

[12] R. and R. Kray, *Our Story*, pp. 85–91.

had returned to East London and had been put in the furnaces of the local swimming baths. Other versions suggest a disposal or burial in farms in Essex or Suffolk. According to Tony Lambrianou, who says the car in which he was taken to South London ended as an Oxo cube in a scrapyard:

> Jack himself is about three miles away from where the car went into scrap, and fifty miles from where we left him. His body will never be found. He and his hat were put in a grave which had been pre-dug, and covered with a layer of soil. A funeral took place the next day, and the grave was filled. So he did get a decent burial.

But by now the gang was splitting. Nipper Read, appointed to the Murder Squad with a special brief to bring down the Krays, had learned from his earlier mistakes. He was not going to move too quickly again. Patiently he began to nip away at the edges of the Firm. Billy Exley, former strong-arm man, was interviewed to no effect. Then Read turned his attention to Leslie Payne, who had after all been the object of the half-hearted attempt on his life made by McVitie and Exley. When would a more adroit one be made? Read obtained an indemnity for Payne against all crimes except those of violence, provided he admitted to them. Over a period of weeks, travelling to town on a daily basis, Payne remained closeted with Read in a police section house away from the eyes of Scotland Yard and other observers as he told the tale of the Firm. Armed with this statement Read was able to obtain evidence from others on the fringes, promising that he would not use the statements unless and until arrests had been made. The inquiries into the murders were shelved as he examined the Krays' involvements with long firm frauds and their dealings in stolen bonds.

Meanwhile at the beginning of 1968 the Krays were moving once more into the international market. They met Angelo Bruno of the Philadelphia family, of whom Albert Dimes was said to be the trusted adviser. Bruno, an associate of American mobsters Raymond Patriaco and Vincent Teresa, and a friend of the financier Judah Binstock, was looking at casino interests in the West End. The Krays promised him a trouble-free life running those interests. They had successfully disposed of a batch of bonds, part of a number stolen in an armed raid on the Royal Bank of Canada in Montreal on 15 April 1965. Now the trade in stolen securities was expanding. They had also met the enterprising American, Alan Bruce Cooper, who effected an entry for them into Europe and the stolen jewellery market in Belgium. It was he who would precipitate the arrest of the Krays.

Read had had Cooper under surveillance for some time when he learned that a man called Paul Elvey was being sent to Glasgow to collect a briefcase. There had long been a two-way trade in villains between Glasgow and London, and there had long been a similar trade of information and assistance between the respective police forces. Elvey was arrested and the briefcase found to contain dynamite, something readily available from the mines around Glasgow. Interviewed by Read, he passed on a story of assassination attempts on Soho strip-club owner George Caruana and others, both in the street and at the Old Bailey. Amazingly, when his premises were searched there was the physical evidence to back it up. Cooper was arrested and to Read's dismay he disclosed that he was being run by John du Rose, a superior officer, as an informer and possibly *agent provocateur*. There was little question of Read being able to charge Cooper; instead he had to use him as a witness.

Read knew that once Cooper disappeared from the streets the Krays would suspect something was up. Luckily the man genuinely suffered from a stomach ulcer and Read placed him in a Harley Street nursing home, from where Cooper telephoned the twins. Read hoped the twins would come and make damaging admissions. Instead they sent one of their henchmen along with Joey Kauffman, a Jewish–Sicilian small-time Mafioso who was dealing in stolen bonds.

In the early hours of the morning of 9 May, after an evening out at the Astor, the Krays went back to their flat and Kauffman to his suite in the Mayfair. At 5 a.m. Read's men swooped, scooping up nearly all the members of the Firm in one hit. Initially they were charged with conspiracy to murder persons unknown. These charges arose from the statements of Elvey and Cooper,[13] and had nothing to do with Mitchell, McVitie and Cornell. It was only after the arrests that Read and his team were able to coax the barmaid to give evidence that she had indeed seen the shooting of Cornell.

The swoop on 9 May had included both the twins' friend Freddie Foreman and their brother Charles. Now, as the police chipped away at the edges of the Firm, several people, including Billy Exley, offered to give evidence. In their book the twins write that they knew their time at liberty was limited; 'the net was closing in. . . . We underestimated the cunning and the cheating of the police.'[14]

With the twins and senior members of the Firm on remand in custody, Read made further progress in obtaining statements from men who might consider turning Queen's Evidence. Although Read thought one of the last who would do so was Albert Donaghue,

[13] Those charges were later dismissed.

[14] R. and R. Kray, *Our Story*, p. 56.

eventually a note was passed to Read at Bow Street asking him to go to see him urgently in prison.

Donaghue, heavily involved in the escape of Mitchell and in the van when he was taken away, had been a well trusted member of the Firm even though he had been shot in the foot by Reggie during an argument in a pub. As far as possible Read had made sure that the members of the Firm were in separate prisons or at least separate wings but, Donaghue says, he went one day for a meeting with Manny Fryde, the Krays' defender:

> We'd been told, don't leave notes about the case in the cell. There were the twins, Charlie and me. I brought out my notes. The girl Lisa had said I had said 'The dog is dead'. I didn't want to dispute it. The dead opposite. We'd had a bull terrier which had to be put down.
>
> Manny Fryde left the room saying he had to go and make a phone call. Reggie just tore my notes up and said 'What we've sorted out is we take all the violence, Scotch Jack takes Cornell, Ronnie Hart takes Jack the Hat and you take Mitchell.' I said 'no'.
>
> Manny Fryde came back and started telling them what he was going to do. 'Just because you're not a Kray don't think I'm not going to look after you,' he said, but I didn't think so. That's when I got my mother to get a note to Nipper. He got me another solicitor, Victor Lissack. I got on all right with him straight away and it went from there.

The trial was split into two sections. The first was that of the Cornell and McVitie murders. The second was for the murder of Frank Mitchell. Trials relating to the charges of fraud and of assault were to be heard at a later date. Before the Cornell and McVitie trial Manny Fryde opened negotiations with the prosecution for deals to be struck over what pleas would be offered by various of the defendants. Nothing came of them.

The Krays received life sentences for the murders of Cornell and McVitie. Charles Kray and Freddie Foreman received ten years each for their part in clearing up after the McVitie killing. Manny Fryde returned to make further offers on pleas before the Mitchell trial. Again they were rejected but this time the twins and Foreman were acquitted of his murder. Donaghue, who pleaded guilty to being an accessory in Mitchell's murder, received two years.

Now that both the Richardsons and the Krays were inside and serving very long sentences, the question was who next fancied themselves as the senior Firm in London.

6

The Dixons
and the Tibbses

Once the Kray trial was over the brass hat brigade at
Scotland Yard had to decide what was to be done with
Nipper Read's squad. In theory, with the Krays and the
Firm put away, there was no need for it to continue, but
once again there were rumours in the press of a takeover
bid for the West End by other interests.

Certainly clubs were paying money to the remnants of
the Nash enterprise but

> it was being done in a very different way from the
> Krays' reign of terror. It was really rather a friendly
> business with this gang – almost a two-way opera-
> tion with benefits to both sides. We thought they
> would jump and occupy the vacuum, but it never
> happened. I think they sensed that if they had done
> that they would have let themselves in for a major
> investigation and consequently all sorts of troubles.
> It was a good example of preventive policing.[1]

Read was sent on the Senior Command Course at
Bramshill, the police training headquarters. He had
been promised the post of Commander when one next

[1] L. Read and J. Morton, *Nipper*, p. 266.

became available. Instead he was bypassed twice and sent into exile as the guv'nor of 'Y' division, North London. Unlike almost every other team that had led a major enquiry and operation, his squad, to his continued disappointment, was not awarded a special tie. The cult of the senior police officer, known on radio, television and in the newspapers, was to come to an end. 'Yard takes Star men out of Limelight' headed a newspaper report, which went on to say that the Commissioner, Sir John Waldron, and Assistant Chief Constable Peter Brodie – no lover of Read – were worried about two recent cases which had resulted in publicity for the officers leading them. The cases were the Great Train Robbery and the Kray case. McArthur had not been a Met officer when he investigated the Richardsons and so, for the purposes, did not count.

It was a curious decision. For years Scotland Yard had traded on its stars, from Chief Inspector Dew who chased across the Atlantic after Crippen, to such great names of the decades as Fred Wensley, who arrested Steinie Morrison in 1911 for the murder of Leon Beron on Clapham Common, and Robert Fabian, whose cases had been made into a series of television films after his retirement. In the 1950s Fabian had a considerable rapport with journalists. He would hold court in the local pub at the time he wanted to release the news, leaving the journalists scrambling to meet the newspaper deadlines, but he always had something for them. Now the Yard was to adopt a more faceless policy, with favoured journalists invited on to the fifth floor on a Friday night for whisky and sandwiches with the top brass.

With the snuffing out of the stars came the disbandment of the Serious Crime Squad. Detective Chief Inspector Harry Mooney, Read's junior officer, had kept a lock on the West End in the immediate aftermath of the Krays. No one had jumped into the vacant seat and so the squad was allowed to run down.

But suddenly the regime changed. Waldron died; Robert Mark took his place. Certain elements in the East End were thought once more to be getting out of hand and there was one Scotland Yard 'star' still left to be pulled out of the locker. His name was Bert Wickstead, variously referred to as the Gangbuster and the Grey Fox. As a young officer he had been involved in the Pen Club killing of Selwyn Cooney in 1960 and had worked his way up with stints in the East End and more lately had been involved in the investigation of the collapse of the Ronan Point building in May 1968.

Just as Read took over the Kray enquiry with a couple of officers and no office space, so Wickstead began with no squad and no telephone. It was then that a decision was made to target the Dixon family. But to the outside world who were they? A friend of the Dixons says:

> George is a reasonably tough man, a family man, not a man I would call a gangster. He's got a couple of medals for bravery. A kid had broken out of the nuthouse and was shooting at everybody. George was driving past and saw what was happening and disarmed him. The second was when a geezer had a gun in the City Arms in Millwall. George knocked it up in the air.

He had also been a friend of the Krays, although that did not stop Ronnie shooting at him one night in a mock trial held at the Green Dragon Club in Aldgate over some alleged misdemeanour. The gun misfired and Kray gave him the cartridge, telling him to wear it as a souvenir on his watch-chain – and he did. 'His brother Alan Dixon is a big clown, always laughing, joking, extrovert, loves a sing and hasn't got an ounce of violence in him,' says the same friend.

171

The so called leader of the Dixons was a publican, the 5 foot 2 inches Phil Jacobs, known locally as Little Caesar, whose pubs were the Bridge House in Canning Town, the Royal Oak in Tooley Street, and the Plough and Harrow in Leytonstone, which George Dixon minded. The Dixons had stood up for him when, shortly before their arrest, the Krays had tried to muscle in on his pubs. Now Wickstead believed the Dixons were expanding their own empire under Jacobs' guidance, specializing in protection and long firm fraud.

Jacobs had left school at the age of fourteen and had worked in various restaurants before he went to do his National Service. Unlike the Krays and the Richardsons he must have rather enjoyed it. He became a Leading Aircraftsman. He married in November 1965 with only ten shillings to his name. His wife's parents bought them the Ship in Aylward Street and from then on, with hard work, he prospered. By the time of his arrest he had a Rolls Royce with a personalized number plate.

George Dixon, with former member of the Kray firm Connie Whitehead, had already been acquitted at the Old Bailey of causing grievous bodily harm to a club owner. The allegation was that injuries had been caused after he had refused the offer to have his club looked after. Wickstead's breakthrough in his enquiries came when a complaint was made to West Ham police station by one of the Dixons' brothers-in-law, Micky Flynn. He was immediately taken round to see Wickstead, who wrote admiringly: 'To say he was big was a little like saying that Rockefeller was rich or that Capone was bad. He was huge, one of the most formidable men I'd ever seen.'

According to Flynn, he was one of the enforcers for the Dixons but now he had left his wife, Lynne, he had consequently fallen out with the brothers. They, he said, had retaliated with a bit of nastiness directed towards his own sisters. One had had her arm broken, another had been threatened.

A friend of the Dixons, and a participant observer in these matters, has it the other way around. 'He'd given his wife a beating and Brian Dixon went round to sort things out.' Translated, this must mean 'sort *him* out'. Despite his size Flynn, the Dixons maintained, ran for cover.

Wickstead sees him in a more heroic light, maintaining that Flynn would have visited each Dixon brother in turn and dealt with him. 'But you see I didn't know how far I'd go,' he told the Commander. 'So I changed my mind. I wasn't going inside for the likes of them.'

It would not have suited Wickstead to have the Dixons as victims: 'If the Dixons had then made a complaint, we would have had to charge him; and with his almost inhuman strength, it might not have stopped at grievous bodily harm. It could so easily have been manslaughter or even murder.' When it came to it no charge was brought over the alleged breaking of Flynn's sister's arm.

It was the familiar pattern of an enquiry. Once one witness came forward it was easier for others. Following a raid on the Greyhound in Bethnal Green, run by a man called Osborne, in March 1971, Wickstead had another witness. Osborne was willing to give evidence about a fight between Michael Young and his cousin Mickey Bailey, which he said had been the usual prelude to a demand for money for protection. The fight was witnessed by two off-duty police officers who were told not to interfere. Instead they withdrew and compiled notes of the incident. Next to come forward was a long-time criminal, Bernard Stringer, who recalled Bailey attacking him in the Court Club in Inverness Terrace.

The arrests came at 5.30 a.m. on 25 August 1971. Wickstead borrowed twenty-nine officers from the Flying Squad and, as a result, nearly came to disaster.

His team was briefed at 4 p.m. and dispersed. Someone leaked the story to the *Evening Standard* which, by the time of the raid, had its early headline prepared: 'Yard swoops on London Gangsters.'

Wickstead learned his lesson. In the future he used only his own squad and the special patrol group. 'We used to get locked in a gymnasium from the time of the briefing until we left for the raid,' one officer recalls.

The Dixon trial began on 12 April 1972 and continued until 4 July. Much of the time was spent challenging the evidence of the police. There had been no written statements of admission and much of the police evidence consisted of verbal admissions. There was also the now fashionable cross-over from the dock to the witness box as some defendants gave evidence against their former friends in return for no evidence being offered against them. Of the defendants who were left, Lambert Jacobs and Brian Dixon were acquitted; Phillip Jacobs, Leon Carelton and George Dixon received twelve years. Alan Dixon went down for nine and Michael Young and Michael Bailey, who had had the fight in the Greyhound, received five each.

Monty Sherbourne defending in the case had called it a 'storm in a teacup' but the judge, Mr Justice O'Connor, had this to say:

> You have mounted a campaign of vilification during the trial against police officers in the hope of saving your skins. Such activity on your part cannot operate on my mind to increase the sentences I have to pass on you. On the other hand, it does show the nature of your guilt. And it removes entirely such compassion as I would have been willing to show.

Moral – plead guilty.

O'Connor called Wickstead forward for a public commendation. 'You and your men deserve the full commendation of the public for bringing this gang to justice. It was a difficult task, thoroughly, honestly, efficiently and fairly discharged.' The encomium did not appeal to the public gallery or the dock, from which someone shouted, 'The end of your reign in the East End is just beginning. We will get you, Wickstead. We will get you.' It was not. They did not. Wickstead and his team were a force to be reckoned with for some years to come.

When George Dixon was released he took a pub in partnership with his father-in-law, then bought a run-down hotel in Hastings, did it up and sold it well. With the proceeds he purchased a caravan park at Frinton and then went into the motor trade. On his release, Alan Dixon first had a wine bar and then expanded into the entertainment business.

The next of the Wickstead successes was the arrest of the Tibbs family. It arose from a longstanding quarrel they had had with a family described derisively amongst some East Enders as 'half gypsies', who were 'not very nice', 'liberty takers' and the ultimate put-down, 'not well liked' – the Nichollses from Stepney.

The feud seems to have begun in 1968 when Georgie 'Bogie' Tibbs, then in his sixties and described by Tibbs' supporters as 'a quiet man', was having a drink in the Steamship public house, managed by a friend of the Nichollses, Frederick Fawcett.[2] He became involved in a row with Albert Nicholls, then in his twenties, who, legend has it, 'smashed into him'. Bogie's eyes were blacked and he lost two teeth. Reprisals were swift and suitable. Albert had a cab office in Poplar near the Blackwall Tunnel where he was visited by Jimmy Tibbs,

[2] B. Wickstead, *Gangbuster*, p. 89.

his brother Johnny and Georgie's son, young George. Nicholls produced a shotgun. It was taken from him, he was knocked down and hit on the head with the stock.

What happened next is variously described. By Wickstead as: 'A shotgun blast inflicted terrible injuries to his legs and to the lower part of his abdomen. There were three large lacerations in the scalp and cuts to the face. The tip of his nose was partially severed and he lost the tip of a finger.' And by an, admittedly partisan, East End historian as: 'Unfortunately the gun went off catching him in the leg.'

That seems to be just how the judge saw it because on his direction at the close of the prosecution case the Tibbs were acquitted of attempted murder and pleaded guilty to minor charges. 'You have been guilty apart from anything else of the most appalling folly. I sympathize with your feelings but at the same time, living in the part of London where you live, there is a great deal too much violence,' said Mr Justice Lyell, handing out suspended sentences of two years' imprisonment coupled with fines of £100 each at the Old Bailey.[3] The Nicholls did not see this as justice being done.

Things simmered for the next two years and then boiled over in November 1970. Robert Tibbs survived having his throat cut outside the Rose of Denmark. Certainly Frederick Fawcett's brother, Micky, was there but just who wielded the knife and who started what, Wickstead was never able to discover.

On Christmas Day one of Fawcett's friends was attacked and severely beaten near his home. Later

---

[3] Albert Nicholls seems to have been out of luck on another occasion. During one of the periods when the Kray twins were seriously feuding with the Richardsons he was knocked down on the pavement outside the Lion public house in Tapp Street. His leg was broken. He had been mistaken for Ronnie Kray.

Michael Machin, brother of Teddy, walked into the Steamship and shot up Freddie's ceiling.

Teddy himself was shot at whilst at home in bed. Two men crept up to his ground floor flat window and blasted him in the backside with a shotgun.[4] Two weeks later Michael Machin was fired on by two men armed with shotguns.

And so it went on. Ronnie Curtis, a friend of the Fawcetts, was badly beaten, as was Lenny Kersey who, it was said, had called the Tibbs pikeys.[5] He was attacked with knives and an axe as he left his flat in Mile End, receiving wounds which required 180 stitches. His wife described the scene: 'I saw the men hacking at somebody on the ground and tried to stop the horrible thing. Then I saw it was my husband. His face was falling apart. I screamed the place down. My friend also screamed and dropped her baby.'

Further attacks took place on the Nichollses and their friends and the Tibbses. Albert and Terence Nicholls were called out of the Rose of Denmark by Stanley Naylor and told to get into their car. As they did so the windscreen was smashed and they were attacked. Albert was stabbed in the leg and a gun was produced. The police arrived and the attackers fled.

---

[4] Teddy Machin, who had been a member of the Upton Park Mob, a friend of Jack Spot and 'a very lucky man', charged in the 1950s London Airport robbery of which he was acquitted, was later shot dead on the doorstep of his home. At the time enquiries were being made into his possible involvement in the death of prostitutes in Soho in the late 1940s. Their deaths were thought to be professional rather than personal. His death was almost certainly a personal matter rather than gang-orientated.

[5] A term of abuse meaning gypsies. The origin is harmless and comes from a user of turnpikes but since the middle of the twentieth century piker has come to mean a thief or cheat.

Terence was taken to hospital but whilst the police were questioning Albert, Jimmy Tibbs returned and drove his car at them. They all jumped for their lives. Albert then drove to the hospital to see his brother. On the way he was hijacked by Jimmy Tibbs and Naylor and hit with a golf club. He managed to push them out of the car as it approached the Blackwall Tunnel. For this attack Jimmy Tibbs was charged with attempted murder.

George Brett, another friend of the Fawcetts and the Nichollses, was shot in the leg.[6] He had tried to separate two men who were fighting in the Huntingdon Arms public house. Eight months later came what he said was the revenge, the incident which determined Wickstead to intervene. Until then, according to his memoirs, he seems to have been observing the situation with something of an Olympian detachment. Quite apart from that, he still had his hands full with the Dixon case.

On 22 April 1971 a bomb was placed under the engine of Jimmy Tibbs' car, near the radiator, and exploded outside a school when his four-year-old son was with him. They would both have been killed had the bomb been positioned properly. The attack came a week after his cafe, the Star in Star Road, had also exploded, although in this case possibly from a gas leak.

'Enough was enough,' wrote Wickstead.[7] Now he augmented his squad and started to liaise with Treasury Counsel Michael Corkery and the late Dai Tudor Price. To the outsider it might have seemed that there was a problem as to which of the rival factions should be prosecuted. Wickstead had no doubts about which faction posed the greatest threat to law and order.

---

[6] For what happened to George Brett, see Chapter 11.

[7] B. Wickstead, *Gangbuster*, p. 91.

The answer to that had to be the Tibbs. They were a highly organized gang. They were becoming steadily more powerful, more ruthless, more ambitious. They were also more wicked and crueller than their opponents. The Nicholls weren't a gang in the accepted sense of the word – more of a loose collection of criminal friends. The same thing could be said about Michael Fawcett and his associates. My decision, incidentally, was agreed and fully endorsed by the DPP.

Nor had he any qualms about taking sides and using one team against another. 'I wouldn't deny it for a moment. In the twilight world of the gangster, archbishops are thin on the ground.'[8] Wickstead settled on Fawcett as the key figure and an arrangement was made with him outside Westminster tube station that he would give evidence.

After the arrests and whilst the Tibbses were in custody awaiting trial, a curious incident took place at Rook's Farm, Stocking Pelham, in Hertfordshire.[9] After the Hosein case the farm had been bought for £17,500 by an East End publican, Tony Wyatt, who also used the name Lewis. On 19 September 1972 a wedding reception for his sister-in-law, Avril Hurst, was held there, at which a number of prosecution witnesses in the Tibbses' case were guests. During the festivities a young man called John Scott was killed with a sickle. The holes in

[8] Ibid, p. 95.

[9] Mrs Muriel McKay, the wife of the chief executive of the *News of the World*, had been kidnapped and held captive there by the Hosein brothers, Arthur and Nizamodeen, in December 1969. They had demanded a ransom of one million pounds. She was almost certainly shot at the farm and her body fed to the pigs. The brothers were sentenced to life imprisonment at the Old Bailey in 1970.

his body were plugged and the corpse was dressed in fresh clothes. It was then placed in Scott's van and driven to the East End, where his body was found the following Monday in Ranelagh Road, Leytonstone, by some schoolboys. A number of people were arrested and taken to Leytonstone police station before being released.

Wyatt was charged with his murder. Scott, he said, had been an uninvited guest who had ridden one of the horses on the farm and had been a general nuisance. He told the police:

> I asked Scott to leave. There was an argument. He pushed me and I fell on the hearth. I got up with something in my hand and I hit him twice with it and he fell down. I realized I had hit him with a sickle. The only reason that this happened was that Scott was making a nuisance of himself to the women of my family and he attacked me when I asked him to leave.

On 9 March 1973 he was convicted of manslaughter and sentenced to three years' imprisonment, most of which was served at Leyhill open prison. He was paroled after twelve months. The farm was sold again, this time for £46,500. Although it is inconceivable that Wyatt managed everything in the way of re-dressing the body and transporting it to Leytonstone by himself, no charges seem to have been brought against any other people.

The month after Scott's death, in October 1972, seven members of the Tibbs family and their friends were gaoled. James Tibbs senior received fifteen years, Stanley Naylor twelve, Michael Machin eleven[10] and Jimmy Tibbs ten. Immediately after the verdict Mrs

---

[10] For footnote, see opposite.

Kate Tibbs, the wife of James Tibbs senior, was taken to hospital suffering from a drug overdose.

This was not generally a popular prosecution amongst the cognoscenti, and the sentences meted out received less than universal approval in the East End. 'They stuck up for themselves, that's all,' was the general reaction Oliver Pritchett of the *Evening Standard* encountered when he canvassed the locals after the case. 'I bet you can go into any pub in Canning Town today and you won't hear a word against them,' said one. 'They've never been liberty takers and that's gospel,' said another.

After the trial a complaint was made that it was Mickey Fawcett who had cut Robert Tibbs. A report was submitted to the Director of Public Prosecutions. Unsurprisingly, he declined to take the matter further.

After his release from prison Jimmy Tibbs worked with the boxing manager Terry Lawless and was eventually given a licence, first as a trainer–second and then as a manager by the British Boxing Board of Control. He is highly respected amongst the boxing fraternity.

Amazingly, the Tibbs' case was the last of the so-called protection racket cases for fifteen years. It was 1990 before Frank Salmon, a market trader from Dagenham,

[10] In October 1973 Machin died in prison after a kidney transplant, donated by his brother Victor, had failed. Robert Tibbs received a short sentence. In June 1991 he received twelve years' imprisonment at Guildford Crown Court. He had left the family's scrap-metal business in 1984 and had run a wine bar. Now he had been convicted following his part in an attempt to smuggle 1.5 tons of cannabis valued at £3.5 million into Britain. Customs officers had foiled the attempt when a yacht, the *Katimavik*, was impounded as she berthed at Oban in Scotland. One-time sculptor and friend of Princess Margaret, Francis Morland, was sentenced to nine years for his part in the importation.

was gaoled at the Old Bailey for seven and a half years. He had been convicted of blackmail, affray and an attack during which ammonia was squirted in a victim's face. Robert Michell, said to be Salmon's right-hand man, was sentenced to three years for blackmail, affray and possession of a firearm, whilst Gary Pollard received four and a half years and Donald Meason twenty-one months.

Salmon had reigned over a part of the East End and Essex for a little over a year, trying to obtain protection money from twenty-three wine bars, clubs and saunas. He had shot up one bar and pressed a gun under the nose of a barman. In 1989 disc jockey Russell Holt, who played the East End pubs, had forty-two stitches in his head and hand following an assault by four masked men. His ankle was broken by a pool cue and he went to the police. He told detectives he had been asked to pay Salmon £1500 as a share in his earnings.

The police used a WPC, Elaine Manson,[11] as the person to trap Salmon. Acting as the friend and business associate of Holt's wife, Denise Seaga, who ran a dress shop, she met Salmon on five occasions, paying out a total of £800. It was thought that Salmon, known as a womanizer, would be less suspicious than if a male officer acted as a decoy. At one meeting she was patted down by him when he came to suspect she was a police officer.

She told the court that one time she was with him he 'shook his arm and a knife slid down inside his left palm'. On another occasion she noticed a bulge in the leg of his trousers and remarked it looked like the outline of a knife. 'Brains of Britain . . .' he replied. 'In this business you get wankers who don't play ball.' On 22 May 1989 she handed over some money and asked Salmon why he

---

[11] A pseudonym.

referred to the cash as a present. 'I am not going to shout out it is protection money, am I?' he replied.

Afterwards a detective commented, 'He tried to model himself on people like the Krays, though he was never going to be as criminally successful as them. He was a plastic gangster, but he was also a dangerous and violent one.'

7

Prostitution and
Pornography

Prostitution, never illegal under British law – the offence is soliciting in a public place for an immoral purpose – has always been a major source of revenue to gangs. It has, however, never really been an 'English crime' and the running of women has been mainly in the hands of Europeans and, in the 1950s and 1960s, particularly the Maltese.

To what extent the operations of the white slave traders have been a fiction of the press is difficult to determine; the pinprick in the cinema, the drugged cigarette undoubtedly made for good copy. There is, however, no doubt that the white slave trade existed in Whitechapel as far back as the turn of the century, when the going price for the vendor of the girl being sent or taken to Argentina was the then very substantial sum of between £200 and £300 per girl.[1]

In June 1912 an effort was made to pass the Criminal Law Amendment (White Slave Traffic) Bill. Supporting it, Ettie Sayer wrote in *The Times*: 'No day passes without several of our girls being duped and trapped and sold into American or continental brothels where life lasts at the most five or seven years, terminating in

[1] B. Leeson, *Lost London*, p. 154.

lingering deaths of the most harrowing nature.'[2] A New York police chief, General Bingham, said in an official government report that at a low estimate 15,000 fresh girls, many from England, were imported in 1909. One syndicate alone was making an annual profit of £40,000.

But whilst prostitution down the East End at the time was certainly rife, it could not necessarily be called a lucrative trade. There were two kinds of girl. Those who went up West and mixed with the toffs would get as much as ten shillings a time or even £1, and they would ride home in hansom cabs. 'The girls who stayed at Spitalfields were very poor. That was what you called a "fourpenny touch" or a "knee trembler" – they wouldn't stay with you all night.'[3]

In the 1920s the white slave trade continued. Advertisements such as: 'Wanted. A few young ladies between the ages of twenty and twenty-five to make up a famous dance act, to travel the Continent and other countries. Apply . . .' The girls who answered were often from the country, with little to recommend them other than a pleasant face. Within a week of their arrival their contract would be torn up by the manager of the club to which they had been sent and, since they had never heard of the British Consul and had no one to whom to turn, they ended up in one of the local brothels.

There has long been a Chinese influence in Soho. Shortly after the First World War a five-foot Chinese, Brilliant Chang, trafficked in women and drugs, and he was almost certainly the supplier of the drugs which led to two well-publicized deaths. After the Victory Ball held at the Albert Hall, Billie Carleton, a pretty young actress, collapsed and died. The inquest showed she had died of cocaine poisoning and was addicted to opium

[2] *The Times*, 11 June 1912.

[3] R. Samuel, *East End Underworld*.

smoking. It was common knowledge Chang had been a close friend but although her companion of the night before, Reggie de Veuille, was charged with manslaughter, nothing was ever proved against Chang.[4] Then in March 1922 Freda Kempton, a dancing instructress, was also found dead from an overdose of cocaine. This time Brilliant Chang did feature. He had been with Freda the night before and faced a hostile series of questions at her inquest. 'She was a friend of mine, but I know nothing about the cocaine,' he told the coroner. 'It is all a mystery to me.'

Chang, gap-toothed with dark hair swept back, was apparently the son of a well-to-do Chinese businessman, and was sent to England to pursue a commercial career. Instead he opened a restaurant in Regent Street and started drug trafficking on the side from his private suite. If he saw a woman he fancied – and he was seemingly irresistible to many – he would send a note with a waiter:

Dear Unknown
Please don't regard this as a liberty that I write to you. I am really unable to resist the temptation after having seen you so many times. I should extremely like to know you better and should be glad if you would do me the honour of meeting me one evening when we could have a little dinner or supper together. I do hope you will consent to this as it will give me great pleasure indeed, and in any case do not be cross with me for having written to you. Yours hopefully, Chang.[5]

---

[4] In one account the death of Billie Carleton is laid at the door of Eddie Manning (see below); V. Davis, *Phenomena of Crime*.

[5] Quoted in A. Tietjen, *Soho*, p. 25.

From there it was, in many cases, a short step to drugs and degradation.

He operated more or less unchallenged until 1924 when two carriers were arrested. Letters in their possession linked them to Chang. Despite police surveillance nothing was established against him, although, in the flurry of unwelcome publicity after Freda Kempton's death, he withdrew his operations to Limehouse. In 1924 the police raided his premises. They found not only a mandarin's palace in the grimy building but, more importantly, they found, in a secret cupboard, a large quantity of cocaine. He was deported after serving a fourteen-month sentence. During his six-year-reign it is estimated he made over a million pounds from drug trafficking.

When he was driven out of Soho his empire there was taken over by another dope pedlar and white slaver, the balding and hollow-eyed Jamaican-born Eddie Manning. Originally a jazz drummer, Manning ran prostitutes and sold drugs from his flat in Lisle Street and the Berwick Street cellar cafe, known as the Black Man's Cafe, which he owned with his Greek woman friend. Cocaine injections were 10 shillings each and he ran illegal and crooked roulette parties. In 1920 he had served a sentence of sixteen months for shooting a man in a fracas at Cambridge Circus. He received three years' penal servitude for possession of opium in 1922 but continued to flourish until he received his final sentence in 1929. By then he too had been chased out of the drug dealing world and was into receiving.

He was also known to be a police informer and, in turn, the underworld tipped off the police. Manning was found with stolen goods worth some £2000 in his flat. He received another three years' penal servitude and died in Parkhurst, apparently from the ravages of syphilis.[6]

[6] For footnote, see opposite.

A third large operator in the drug market was Sess Miyakawa, a Japanese who ran an international ring in 1923–4. He was sentenced to penal servitude of four years after the capture by the Marseilles police of a shipment of drugs worth £250,000.

Apart from Chang, Manning and Miyakawa, who were to a certain extent independent operators, the leader of the Soho prostitution market in the 1920s was Juan Antonio Castanar. Lithe, dark and handsome, he was an accomplished tango dancer who had at one time had a fifty-pound-a-week contract with the great Pavlova. He opened a school for dance in Archer Street, using it as a front for 'white-birding' – selling women to dance troupes abroad at £50 a time. The reverse side of his talent was to arrange marriages of convenience for foreign women wishing to acquire an English passport.

His great rival was Casimir Micheletti, an Algerian, known as the Assassin because of his ability with a stiletto. Micheletti, who gave his occupation as a furrier, is described as an extremely good-looking young man with dark hair, mild of manner and soft-voiced, who could fight with the savagery of a tiger.[7] Both he and Castanar ran strings of prostitutes; each loathed the other and when Castanar was slashed across the face at the 43 Club in Old Compton Street it was common knowledge that Micheletti was the attacker, although no charges were ever brought. He was also strongly suspected of the murder of another French gangster,

---

[6] According to Val Davis, Manning had a terrible superstition about owls. When he was dying in E2 ward in Parkhurst Prison on the Isle of Wight, he heard an owl hooting and his 'body shook and his eyes rolled in abject terror'.

[7] *Detective-Inspector Henry's Famous Cases* (1942), London, Hutchinson, pp. 91–2.

Martial le Chevalier, who was found stabbed in Air Street.

Micheletti was the more or less innocent witness at another murder trial. On 5 April 1926 yet another Frenchman, Emile Berthier, shot and killed an Italian motor car dealer, Charles Ballada, in the Union Club in Frith Street, Soho. The club had a wooden bar along one side, tables and chairs, a couple of fruit machines and some crude murals on the walls. When the police arrived they found Ballada sprawled in the red chimney corner, shot in the stomach.

According to the evidence of a Juan Gabaron, known as L'Espagnol, Berthier believed Ballada owed him money. He went up to him and said: 'My friends, I respect them, but those who owe me money including my partners will have to pay me otherwise I am going to settle with them. I shall do them an injury.'

Ballada replied, 'You must not talk like that. You must do things not talk about them.'

Berthier then shot him dead with an automatic pistol. A member of the club hit Berthier over the head with a billiard cue but Berthier escaped, stopping only to have his wounds cleaned before catching the train to Newhaven, from where the Dieppe packet sailed. It was there he was arrested.

Berthier had earlier written a letter which was produced at the trial:

I know the [sic] Micheletti wants to kill me because I do not give him any more money. You must admit I have given him enough. See, actually that makes £1500 all the money I owe and he is asking for more. Whilst he is away for a month I warn you that if he continues to ask me for money I shall do my best to kill him. He has killed two or three others and this man is an assassin.

That was the story according to the evidence but another version is that Micheletti had swindled Berthier of £2000 and Ballada, who closely resembled the 'assassin', was shot by mistake. On the other hand, Robert Fabian, destined to become the great Fabian of the Yard and who, despite the account in his memoirs,[8] played a junior role in the case, believed a feud between Ballada and Berthier had originated in Paris. At the Old Bailey Micheletti gave evidence to the effect that he was terrified of Berthier. Ballada was, he said, his friend.

The pre-trial medical report on Berthier from a Dr W. R. K. Watson at Brixton Prison included a statement: 'He professes to have no memory of the actual case. This, if true, may be the result of the blows to the head which he is said to have sustained after the event.' Berthier, whose father had committed suicide by throwing himself off a building at the Lyons exhibition in 1904, was found guilty but insane. Later he was repatriated to France.

In April 1929 both Micheletti and Castanar were deported from England but within a few weeks Castanar managed to smuggle himself back for a short period before he was once more thrown out, this time permanently. He made his way to Paris and earned a modest living as a tango dancer and by running a small stable of girls. In February 1930 he and Micheletti met in a cafe in Paris and later that night Castanar shot his rival dead. At his trial he blamed the killing on a mysterious man known to both of them as Le Marseillais. It was he who had shot Micheletti, put the gun in Castanar's hand and run away. Castanar was not believed and was sent to Devil's Island.

Six years later, on 24 January 1936, the bullet-riddled body of Emil Allard, known as Max Kessel or Red Max, was found under a hedge near St Albans in Hertford-

---

[8] R. Fabian, *Fabian of the Yard*.

shire. A friend of Micheletti, this scar-faced – due to a fight in Montparnasse in 1922 – well-built man had been shot five times. All means of identification had been removed.

A Latvian by birth, Allard had lived in James Street off Oxford Street and had the occupation of 'diamond merchant', a cover beloved of the procurer. In and out of London since 1913, he was a prime mover in the pre-First World War white slave traffic, selling girls to Latin American brothels. They may have travelled to Buenos Aires in style but that was the last luxury the girls would have seen in their lives. As the police investigated deeper into Allard's background they traced back his connection to the murders of a number of Soho prostitutes, including Josephine Martin, known as French Fifi, strangled with her own silk stockings in her Archer Street flat. She had been a police informer as well as one of Allard's aides looking after the foreign prostitutes smuggled into this country.

Allard's murder was investigated by Chief Inspector 'Nutty' Sharpe, who found the flat at 36 Little Newport Street where he had been killed. The occupier had been George Edward Lacroix, alias Marcel Vernon. He had lived with Suzanne Bertrand, who had gone through a form of marriage to an Englishman called Naylor. Now she was working the Soho streets. By the time Sharpe caught up with them they had fled to France from where the authorities refused to extradite them, although they agreed to put them on trial there for Allard's murder.

The murder was thought to have been because Suzanne Bertrand was working for both Vernon and Allard, and they had quarrelled over her earnings. Marcelle Aubin, Suzanne's maid, gave evidence at an inquest held in London that Allard had called on her mistress and she had shown him in to Vernon. Later she heard the sound of an argument followed by several shots. Called by Vernon, she and Suzanne rushed in and found Allard shot in the stomach and back. As he was dying he broke two panes of glass in the window with his forearm in an effort to attract attention. It was one of the matching pieces of glass on the pavement that had led Sharpe to No 36. Marcelle Aubin had been told to order a car from a garage in Soho Square owned by another Frenchman, Pierre Alexandre, and the body of Allard had been bundled in the back to be dumped near St Albans.

At the trial at the Seine Assizes in April 1937 the garage proprietor gave evidence against Vernon, who was sentenced to ten years' penal servitude and twenty years' banishment. Suzanne Bertrand was acquitted after she had laid bare the details of Vernon's partnership with Allard as well as Alexandre's agency for marrying off foreign women to threadbare Englishmen. Allard and Vernon, who had first met in Montreal, had worked the white slave trade together for years and the breakdown of their relationship does seem to have been over Suzanne Bertrand, for whom Vernon had left his wife in Paris in 1933.

Bertrand was also able to throw some light on the mysterious Le Marseillais who had featured in Castanar's trial six years earlier. At Vernon's trial, another French gangster, George Hainnaux, known as 'Jo le Terroir', went into the witness box to say that Red Max Allard had confessed to him that he had killed Le Marseillais, really a Belgian called Bouchier, in Canada in 1930, shortly after the Paris cafe shooting. Kessel, Micheletti, Bouchier and Martial le Chevalier, he said, had all been killed in a long-drawn-out battle for control of prostitution and the white slave trade.

This was the end of the French domination of Soho prostitution and there is no evidence that the Sabinis were interested in vice to any great extent. 'I can think of only two girls who went bad in the whole time I lived in Saffron Hill,' says a resident. 'Darby Sabini protected women, he didn't use them.'

However, from the mid-1930s the Sabinis certainly allowed the Messina brothers – Carmelo, Alfredo, Salvatore, Attilio and Eugenio, into the scene. The Messinas' father, Giuseppe, came from Linguaglossa in Sicily and in the late 1890s went to Malta, where he became an assistant in a brothel in Valetta. There he married a Maltese girl, Virginia de Bono. Their first two sons, Salvatore and Alfredo, were born in Valetta. The family then moved in 1905 to Alexandria and Giuseppe built a chain of brothels in Suez, Cairo and Port Said. The remaining sons were all born in Alexandria and their father ensured they were all well educated. In 1932 Giuseppe Messina was expelled from Egypt and two years later Eugenio, the third son, born in 1908, came to England. He was able to claim British nationality because his father had sensibly claimed Maltese citizenship.

With Eugenio was his wife Colette, a French prostitute, and it was on her back that Eugenio founded his London empire. More girls were recruited from the continent and as the empire grew he was joined on the management side by his brothers. Property was bought throughout the West End and the brothers turned their attention to English girls. The technique used was age-old – good looking girls were given a good time; seduction, possibly with the promise of marriage, followed and then it became time to pay. If the good life was to continue the price for it was prostitution. By 1945 the family's business earnings were estimated at £1000 a week.

The girls were under the day-to-day charge of the French-born Marthe Watts, who had conveniently married Arthur Watts, an alcoholic Englishman, to obtain British citizenship. Born in 1913, according to her story she had been placed in a brothel in Le Havre at the age of fifteen after lying about her age.[9] She had been there only a few days before her age was discovered and had been returned to Paris, where she found her mother had remarried. Within hours she had re-met the *placeur*, the tattooed Francois, who had been responsible for sending her to the house in Le Havre, meeting him in a cafe in the Marais, a then louche *quartier* of Paris. Because of her age it was too risky to send her back to Le Havre, he thought. This time she was put on the night train to Barcelona. There followed a career in the brothels of Europe ending with her marriage to Watts.

In April 1941 she met Eugenio Messina in the Palm Beach Club, Wardour Street, and a month later became his mistress. Within weeks she was out working the streets for him. Her loyalty seems to have been remarkable. Despite regular and savage beatings – the favourite method seems to have been with an electric light flex – she stayed with the family, taking charge of the new girls. As a mark of her devotion she had herself tattooed over the left breast: '*L'homme de ma vie. Gino le maltais*'.

Life with Eugenio Messina was no fun for any of his girls. They were not allowed out on their own, they could not accept American servicemen as clients, they were not allowed to smoke, nor, curiously, were they allowed to wear low-cut dresses or even look at film magazines where the male stars were in any sort of undress. They did not take off their clothes with the customers. Worst of all was the ten-minute rule. Clients were only allowed to stay that time before the maid knocked on the door. It seems to have resembled the

[9] M. Watts, *The Men in My Life*.

Paris and Miami slaughterhouses where girls never leave the bed and a bell rings after fifteen minutes. The other Messina brothers seem to have been more relaxed in their attitudes, particularly over the ten-minute rule.

During the war the Messina brothers had evaded military service simply by failing to report. Warrants had been issued but they were never served and the Messinas maintained a low profile as far as the authorities were concerned. Gino Messina, who had worked with his father as a carpenter, built himself a hiding place in the form of a bookcase with a removable bottom shelf in his Lowndes Square flat. Unknown visitors had to be cleared through a series of front men and women before they were allowed in to see him.

By 1946, with the family's weekly earnings at £1000, the girls were earning £100 a night and were being paid £50 a week. Even if takings dropped after the war the business was still a worthwhile target for other ponces. In March 1947 Carmela Vassallo and four other Maltese endeavoured to muscle in on the enterprise, demanding protection money of £1 a girl a day. Retribution in all forms was swift. At a meeting in Winchester Court, South Kensington, Eugenio Messina took off two of Vassallo's fingertips. But it was not sufficient for the girls. Marthe Watts and two others, now thoroughly frightened by the Maltese and what would happen if they gave in to their demands, went to the police.

Carmela Vassallo and the four others stood in the Old Bailey in April 1947 charged with demanding money with menaces. All the witnesses staunchly denied they were 'Messina girls'. For example, Janine Gilson of Cork Street, Mayfair, admitted knowing the Messinas for three years but denied she had ever spoken to them.

'I know them as diamond merchants and I know them as very wealthy people.'

'Do you know the source of their wealth is the money they take from girls on the streets?'

'No.'

'Do any of these Messina men look after you in your profession?'

'No. I don't have anybody to look after me. If I want protection I go to the police.'

This sort of evidence could not possibly be swallowed by any jury. But there was a back-up. The police had been on watch in Burlington Gardens, off Piccadilly, when the five Maltese drew up and one shouted out to the girls, 'It's better for you to give us the money, otherwise I will cut your face!' In the car the police found a hammer wrapped in newspaper, a knife and a life-preserver. At the men's flat there was a knuckleduster and an automatic pistol with six rounds of ammunition.

Convicted of demanding money with menaces, Vassallo and two others received four years' penal servitude.

The thwarted takeover did however spell the very beginning of the end of the Messinas' reign. Eugenio Messina, who had had no takers for his offer of the enormous sum of £25,000 to anyone who could smuggle him out of the country, received three years for wounding Vassallo. The Messina brothers were now known figures and questions were asked in Parliament: in view of what had emerged at the trials where Marthe and the other girls had loyally lied, denying their involvement with the brothers, would the Home Secretary appoint a commission to enquire into organized vice in London? No, replied Mr Chuter Ede:

It is a criminal offence knowingly to live on the earnings of a prostitute and the police exercise all possible vigilance with a view to the suppression of activities of this kind.

Any enquiry would not help the police because their difficulties arise from the fact that, although they may have good reason to suspect such activities, they are sometimes unable to obtain evidence upon which criminal proceedings could be based.

Then as now.

John Foster, MP for Norwich, who was putting the questions, was not satisfied. What about an examination of the Messinas' bank accounts? Was Mr Ede aware they were popularly supposed to be making half a million a year, that they had no fewer than twenty girls working for them and that they owned a West End estate agency? But Mr Ede was having none of it and the remaining brothers continued to flourish.

All, that is, except Carmelo – Marthe's favourite. Conscious of the privations his brother was suffering he tried to bribe a prison officer at Wandsworth Prison, for which he received two months plus a £50 fine and, on his and Eugenio's release, £700 from the takings. The girls had conscientiously been putting their money in the safe for him – watched, it has to be said, by two of the brothers. On Eugenio's release he bought himself a Rolls-Royce. But, for the purposes of the courts, the Messinas went underground. There was no question now of having knife fights with the Maltese opposition. According to Marthe Watts, complainants were simply framed.

I am sure, from some of the remarks passed by some magistrates, that they did not believe there was such a thing as the Messina Gang. They certainly did not when Sally Wright was charged with assaulting Rabina Dickson Torrance with a knife. Sally Wright pleaded that Torrance was a

Messina woman, that the whole charge had been framed by the Messina Gang, and that she was innocent.

She was by no means the first person who had not been believed after pleading that she had been victimized by the Messina Gang. It seems that when anyone upset the Messinas all they had to do was enlist the aid of the Courts, apparently with police assistance, and that someone was conveniently imprisoned, and incidentally discredited for life.[10]

It took three more years before the Messinas were exposed for what they were, and it was the work of Duncan Webb, who had caused so much trouble for Spot.[11] On 3 September 1950 the *People* published the exposure, backing it with photographs of the Messina girls and the flats from where they operated. Eugenio and Carmelo loaded up the yellow Rolls Royce and left for France via Dover. Though they returned using false passports they were never again seen openly in this country.

The next to go was Salvatore. Attilio and Alfredo remained. Attilio lived in Surrey with one of the girls, the same Rabina Torrance who had brought false charges of assault against Sally Wright when the girl had tried to leave the family. His work in clearing things up completed, he too headed for France, leaving behind only Alfredo, living with Hermione Hindin who worked

[10] M. Watts, *The Men in My Life*, p. 207.

[11] Webb was a curious man. A devout Roman Catholic, he believed his mission was to clean the streets of London. After one triumph over the Messinas he put an advertisement in *The Times* offering thanks to St Jude. After the murderer Donald Hume, killer of Stanley Setty, had been convicted Webb married his wife Cynthia.

in Pollen Street, W1, as Barbara.

On 19 March 1951 Alfredo was arrested at his
Wembley home, charged with living on immoral earnings and trying to bribe a police officer. He had offered
Superintendent Mahon, one of the arresting officers,
£200. At his trial at the Old Bailey he naturally gave his
employment as that of diamond merchant. No, he did
not know Hermione was in fact Barbara. No, he did not
know she had over a hundred convictions for soliciting.
When she went out in the evening he thought it was to
see a relative. It was a great shock to him to learn she
was a common prostitute. He had brought his personal
fortune, some £30,000, to Britain at the beginning of the
war and had dealt in diamonds. He had both diabetes
and high blood pressure, which was why he did not really
work. What on earth was this vice ring organized by his
brothers?

Scott Henderson, who appeared for him and who later
conducted the Rillington Place enquiry,[12] did his best for
him but Alfredo received two years' imprisonment concurrent on each of the charges and a £500 fine. In fact
Barbara worked in the next-door flat to Alfredo's real
wife, a Spanish woman, who passed under the name
Marcelle.

For the moment it seemed the hold of the Messina
brothers – one in prison and four abroad – had been
broken. It was not the case. The ever faithful Marthe
Watts took over control of the ever younger girls whom
Eugenio was sending over from the continent, often
after picking them up at tea-dances. Each girl kept her
own accounts and it seems that, such was the mixture of
loyalty and fear, they never tried to skim for themselves.

---

[12] This was the enquiry into whether Reginald Halliday Christie had
in fact killed Beryl Evans, for which her mentally retarded husband
Timothy had been hanged.

Every thousand pounds earned meant a trip to see Eugenio in Paris. The money, however, went over by courier.

But now Attilio was making trips to England. Alfredo's solicitors at his trial had been Webb, Justice & Co, and Superintendent Mahon began to follow the firm's clerk, Watson, as he made trips to Europe. In October 1951 Watson went to his home in Chalfont St Giles for a short time, then left and got into another car which drove off towards Amersham. The car was stopped by Mahon and inside, with Watson, was Attilio. He was charged with living off the immoral earnings of Rabina Torrance. At Bow Street court the next morning he was represented by a young solicitor who would become lengendary in the annals of white-collar crime, a man who spun an evil web throughout commercial London in the 1960s and 1970s. His name was Judah Binstock. Attilio received six months' imprisonment, the maximum sentence.

Certainly this should now have been the end for the brothers but it was not to be so. Eugenio, Carmelo and Alfredo controlled matters from Paris until November 1953, when Eugenio was kidnapped and released only on payment of £2000. In some disarray the brothers moved their headquarters to Lausanne. In the meantime Attilio had completed his short stretch and had set up light housekeeping again with Rabina Torrance under the name Raymond Maynard, in Bourne End. Rabina Torrance leased two flats in London in her own name, with payments for rent and rates being made through the Messinas' agents. Attilio, as Maynard, had another flat in Shepherd's Market and the family had interests in a second flat there. Deportation papers were served on him in 1953 but the Italian authorities declined to have him and, once the *People* had traced him to the Hideaway, his appropriately named cottage in Bourne

End, he moved to South London, reporting daily to the police as an Italian national.

But Eugenio had surfaced again, buying 39 Curzon Street in Mayfair from a Mrs Augustine Johans, who continued to manage it as a brothel. In September she was fined £25 but in the raid the police found £14,000 in a safe there. As a result the premises were taken over by Hermione Hindin and Mrs Johans moved elsewhere. Home, however, is where the heart is and Eugenio yearned for England. He obtained another British passport as Alexander Miller, a merchant, and another as Eugene de Bono. For the purposes of travelling here Carmelo became a Cuban citizen, Carlos Marino.

By now, however, girls from respectable Belgian homes were disappearing to England and the Belgian police were actively pursuing their enquiries. Marthe Watts, who had suffered a collapsed lung, was tiring of seeing an ever increasing harem amassed by Eugenio. She travelled to see him in the Residence Albert in Knokke, where he was staying under an assumed name, and severed her connection as quartermaster sergeant of the operation. She was allowed to work independently from a Messina-owned flat in Chesterfield Street.

On 31 August 1955 Carmelo and Eugenio were arrested in the Horse's Neck at Knokke-le-Zoute and charged with being in possession of firearms, false passports and procuring women for prostitution. It was only then that the extent of their current British empire became apparent. Title deeds to four central London properties were found in a safe-box along with long reports from Marthe Watts and Mrs Johans. One of the reports by Marthe Watts showed that one girl, a former nurse working as Therese, had earned £2400 in six weeks. Eugenio had gone through his prospective fiance routine before marrying her off to a stray Englishman recruited for the purpose. Eugenio received seven years' imprisonment. Carmelo was deemed to have served his sentence; he had been in custody on remand for ten months and was released. He disappeared, but not for long.

At the end of 1956 the appeals were heard in the Belgium case. Carmelo had his sentence doubled *in absentia* whilst Eugenio had seven months knocked off. But where was Carmelo?

In October 1958 he was found sitting in a car in Knightsbridge and was arrested as an illegal immigrant. He received a six month sentence and was deported at the end. He died in the autumn in Sicily. But now where was Attilio?

He was working hard, or rather Edna Kallman, initially seduced by promises of marriage and the good life, was. She had been under his control for ten years, put out to work under the tutelage of Rabina. Attilio knocked her about continually until in sheer terror of a further beating she managed to bring herself to return to her parents' home in Derby. They called the police. He was convicted on 9 April 1959 and sentenced to four years' imprisonment. Edna Kallman had earned between £50 and £150 a week over those ten years and had been allowed to keep £7 a week for herself.

'You made a sumptuous but revolting living from the suffering bodies of the women you trapped, seduced and reduced to a form of slavery,' said the Recorder of London, Sir Gerald Dodson. 'You caused great suffering and it is only right and just that you should also suffer.'

Attilio and Eugenio were eventually accepted by the Italian government. Salvatore lived in Switzerland whilst Alfredo, who could claim British citizenship, died in Brentford in 1963.

The year 1959 should have marked the end of the Messinas as an active force but by the late 1960s Eugenio and Carmelo were still paying the rent and rates of premises in Mayfair.

By the middle of the 1960s Soho had an even uglier face than it has today. Dirty bookshops were everywhere and near-beer joints, clip joints and cinemas showing pornographic films attracted the oddest types, plus tourists wanting to see the naughty bits of London. In turn they became the victims of the unscrupulous operators of these establishments, who picked them clean.

Prostitution, clubs and near-beer joints were controlled by the Maltese, who had taken over the territory after the breaking up of the Messina operation and the retirement of Billy Hill and Jack Spot, and had run it with the initial tolerance of Albert Dimes and Bert Marsh. Over the years there had been a constant struggle to determine power and control, and as a result there were spontaneous bursts of violence as one or other faction tried to establish and redefine territories.

At the time the smoothest operator of them all was not Maltese at all but Jewish. Bernie Silver had seen the disasters which happened when rival operators fell out and had the sense to realize that a rapprochement was necessary between at least some of the operators. He therefore formed a liaison with a Maltese, 'Big Frank' Mifsud, a former traffic policeman and a giant of a man who was considered ruthless by lesser lights. A call to visit 'Big Frank' could strike terror into the heart of the recipient of the invitation, who, like as not, could expect a beating handed out not by the man himself but by an underling.

Together Silver and Mifsud effectively ruled vice in the West End for nearly two decades. Initially they ran prostitutes, brothels and gaming clubs in Brick Lane, in the East End, once the preserve of people such as Tony Smithson and Tony Mella, but Silver and Mifsud had a toe-hold in Soho through a strip club in Brewer Street. From there they began to buy up properties using a string of nominees.

The arrangement had been worked out so there would be no rivalry and inter-club warfare between them. Say A and B owned the Star Club, B and C owned the Spangled Club, C and D the Banner Club and D and A the America Club. If, therefore, premises owned by Silver or Mifsud were attacked the other operators would suffer by it, which removed the incentive for causing trouble in another club. The operation was policed by Silver and Mifsud's henchmen, including Anthony Mangion, Emmanuel Coleiro, Emmanuel Bartolo and Tony and Victor Micallef. They ran what came to be known as the Syndicate, owning nineteen out of the twenty-four Soho strip clubs then operating. It worked after its fashion but there was always an undercurrent of feeling and a belief that violence was never far away.

Near-beer joints, again run by the Maltese under the overall supervision of Mifsud and Silver, and of which there was one or more in every street, yard and alley in Soho, worked very simply. Young, attractive and scantily dressed girls stood outside the premises, which were often on the first floor or in the basement of buildings. Subtly, and sometimes not so subtly, they would lure customers inside with the veiled promise of sexual intercourse. Once inside the men were like moths round a flame, unable to resist the flattery and spiel of these 'come-on' girls. They would pay exorbitant prices for non-alcoholic drinks such as lemonade shandy and blackcurrant juice. Each drink came with a cocktail stick and the girl was paid by the number of these sticks she collected during her stint. Their function was only to rip-off the customer for as much as he would pay without complaining. There was certainly no requirement by the management that the girls had to have sex with the clients, although many did as a side operation. If so, they took the man to a local address or hotel.

Two years earlier the Refreshment Houses Act 1964, which required clubs serving any form of refreshment, including soft drinks and sandwiches, to have a licence, had given the police the right of entry into premises. And enter they did, causing a certain amount of trouble to the 'clubs'. Clubs were closed down on a regular basis by magistrates sitting at Marlborough Street and Bow Street, with the result that many proprietors did not bother to renew their licences. The premises reverted to being clip joints where a version of the 'corner game' was played out.

In this there was no pretence that drinks would be supplied or that the girl was a hostess. Money was obtained on the implicit understanding that sexual intercourse would follow. Most of the girls had no intention of having sex and to avoid the predatory punters a delaying tactic had to be introduced. Mostly the girl would persuade the punter that the address was some form of club and that her employer forbade her to leave before a certain time. She would then ask the man to wait around the corner to meet her as soon as she was free. Often the man would wait two or three hours 'around the corner' before he realized he had been done up like a kipper. Under the clock at Victoria Station was a well-worn favourite; Marble Arch, by Big Ben, Charing Cross, outside the Ritz or the Regent Palace Hotel and Leicester Square were frequently named by the punters who had spent many wasted hours waiting there. The one that Nipper Read, then an Inspector at West End Central, liked best, even though he found it hardest to believe, was Morden, a station at the very end of the Northern Line. He asked the Dutch seaman why he had gone that far to wait for a girl and received the reply, in attractive broken English, that he had paid her £100, adding, 'Well, this is where she tells me she is living.'

These men had of course not been unwilling contributors of their money and even when they reported the matter to the police they were often reluctant to go through with the charges because of fear of exposure to their wives, family, friends or employers. Often they were men from the provinces or sailors who would go home or sail before any proceedings could be processed through the courts. It was better to write off their loss and put it down to experience.

As a result of what they considered amounted to immunity from prosecution the girls became more and more brazen, and so occasionally the clients took reprisals of their own. The most tragic example of this was when, on 25 April 1966, three young men out to celebrate a birthday were tricked at a club in Lisle Street and thrown out by bouncers. They found some rubbish in the street, doused it with petrol and threw it into the passageway of the clip joint at No 23. Far from its being the minor annoyance the boys anticipated, the rubbish set fire to other material and soon the whole premises were ablaze. A perfectly innocent man had decided to try to find a lavatory on the premises and, unable to get out in time, burned to death.

All the police had to go on was the first name of one of the boys who had been celebrating his twenty-first birthday. It was announced that there would be a check on the whereabouts of everyone born that day twenty-one years earlier. It would not have been as impossible as it seemed but it certainly would have been boring police work. But, when it came to it, there was no need. A photograph was published of officers starting to make the list at Somerset House and the boys, thoroughly shocked by what had happened, went into Tottenham police station with a solicitor to confess to what they had done. They were later convicted of manslaughter and received sentences of three and four years' imprisonment.

There were of course many other incidents when punters, frustrated by waiting at one or other of the rendezvous, returned to the club and demanded their money back. The normal course of events was that they would then meet one of the club's bouncers and would sustain a black eye or broken jaw for their pains. Once again the fear of disclosure of the illicit sex behind the assault hampered many a prosecution.

Another common scam at the time was the 'blue film' racket. This was another popular version of the 'corner game'. The scenario was usually that of a smooth-talking spiv standing outside an open doorway and inviting tourists to see a blue film. As a come-on he might have postcards showing explicit sex scenes 'from the film'. After taking the punters' money he would direct them up to the second floor and then simply move on to another suitable doorway. There were variations. Sometimes the spiv would actually go to the second floor with the punters and ask them to wait whilst he went into the projection room to check the film. Off he would go down the back stairs. If their luck was in they saw a film made in Scandinavia showing a woman undressing or nudists playing volleyball in long shot.

With the World Cup coming up in July 1966, Read was afraid that both thefts from visitors and more examples of violence would occur over the summer months. Tens of thousands were coming to London and many who would drift into Soho during the evenings would become the victims of the villains who were waiting to fleece them.

There was not only the problem of the clubs and our own thieves but also the con men who would come from Australia, the fraudsmen and tricksters from Mexico and Venezuela, the pickpockets from Italy, second-storey hotel thieves from the States, drug pushers from Holland

and the heavies, the GBH merchants, from Germany. All these and others travel the world and congregate for any international sporting occasion or world or trade fair of sufficient size which runs for long enough. The World Cup was certainly both of those and the thought of the havoc these kinds of villain could create coupled with Soho's local talent was depressing.

So Read formed a twelve-strong squad of officers from 'C' division (West End Central) with the very positive mission first to harass and shut down the clubs, and then maintain a blanket policing operation on the West End. This, he believed, would keep down the foreign villains to a minimum.

The first job was to visit the clubs and take down the names of the girls present. They were also given the 'warning formula'. In other words, they were told in no uncertain terms that their freedom to fleece the suckers was over. It was also explained to the proprietors, or their front men, that they were committing offences of theft or of obtaining money by false pretences and they had better change their lifestyle. It was all to no avail. The pickings were far too easy and the clubs continued to flourish – for a time.

Soon the girls found that the 'punters' were in fact plain clothes officers. In June seven girls were arrested for obtaining money by false pretences or straightforward theft. In the week leading up to the World Cup a further twenty-one arrests were made by the squad, mainly for theft. From time to time Read would lead part of the squad to raid the premises and all present were logged and cautioned. By the start of the Cup only four of the clip joints remained open.

The West End was now divided into nine crime patrols with three sergeants and two detectives, borrowed from other divisions, posted to each. All had personal radios and Read patrolled the division in a radio-equipped car.

It was later acknowledged to be a good example of how effective saturation policing could be. By the end of the operation on 31 July only one clip joint was still in business and that only on a haphazard basis. During the period reported crimes dropped by nearly a half whilst clip joint complaints had gone down from 205 in the first week to 12 in the last.

The bosses, of the police, if not the clubs, were well pleased. Read's report went to the Home Office and commendations were given. It was announced that the squad should be kept on, although, as with everything, gradually it was allowed to run down because of lack of resources. Even so, the crime rate in the West End was stable for some months to come – until nearly the end of the year.

If Silver and Mifsud thought they had a tight hold on Soho and were immune from outside attack, except by the police, they had a shock when Tony Cauci, a one-time friend of Mifsud, fell out with him over the ownership of the Carnival strip club. At the end of 1966 and in the early part of 1967 there was a series of petrol bomb explosions at the Gigi in Frith Street, the Keyhole Club in Old Compton Street and a gaming club in Greek Street, all of which belonged to the Silver–Mifsud connection in which neither Tony Cauci nor his employee, another Maltese, Derek Galea, had a share.

Cauci and Galea's subsequent trial on a charge of conspiracy to cause explosions took place at a time when links between criminals in Soho and the police in the West End were rife and there was considerable concern amongst some officers that the explosives had been planted. Certainly a witness, Harold Stocker, who said that he had seen Galea running from the gaming club shortly after the fire, had given perjured evidence and, on the advice of Mifsud, Galea had turned against his employer. After a retrial at the Old Bailey and an ugly scene when the police had to be called to deal with two dozen Maltese who had suddenly arrived in the lobby to hear the jury's verdict, they were convicted and sentenced to lengthy terms of imprisonment. Once more a fragile peace was restored.

If living off immoral earnings has never been a wholly British sport there is no doubt that some have joined with enthusiasm into its kin folk, strip-tease and pornography. And none more so than James William Humphreys. Born in Southwark in January 1930, he was one of the porn kings of England throughout the 1960s and early 1970s. He was also a major figure in the downfall of many members of the Vice Squad of the time.

There was nothing particularly remarkable about his early career – a burglary here, an approved school there – until, in March 1958, he received six years' imprisonment at Glamorgan Assizes for stealing £8000-worth of postal orders. Freed in the autumn of 1962 he took the lease of a property in Old Compton Street and started a club, a home from home for the criminal and the quasi-criminal, including one of the boxers from the days of the Pen Club murder. He also met up once more with an old girlfriend, June Gaynor, known as 'Rusty', once a barmaid and now a stripper. In the meantime she had had an affair with a Soho frequenter, Peter 'Pookey' Garfath; now she came to work for Humphreys in Old Compton Street. Six months later they married.

On the advice of Detective Sergeant Harold Challenor, then said to be operating his one-man independent protection racket in Soho, Humphreys moved his club to Macclesfield Street. Humphreys had been paying protection money to Challenor as well as providing him with tidbits of information of Soho life. Once in Macclesfield Street Challenor asked for more money and Humphreys paid over two lots of £25. He also made an official complaint, which came to nothing more than a polite rejection from the Commissioner. Challenor was cleared after a brief investigation. It was, after all, the sort of thing an officer would have to put up with.

In fact Challenor had done him a good turn. The Macclesfield Street club prospered and Rusty Humphreys was a good businesswoman. She heard of premises in Walker Court off Brewer Street and suggested Humphreys open another club. It was an immediate and enormous success. For a start it was in the heart of Soho. Secondly, it had the great advantage of being opposite the biggest and smartest strip club in London, Raymond's Revue Bar. Within a year, with his wife at first performing in the three shows the club ran daily, he had become relatively rich. A neighbour in the same small courtway was Bernie Silver, who, with a front man, Joey Janes, as manager, ran a bookshop.

Silver's operations can be traced back to the early 1950s when he ran clubs and brothels in the Brick Lane area of the East End. In 1956 he was arrested and charged with living off immoral earnings. Along with a man called Cooper and acting as an estate agent, he had been carrying on an extension of the Messina trade by letting out rooms and flats to prostitutes at exorbitant rents. Silver appeared at the Old Bailey in 1956 along with a prostitute called Albertine Falzon[13] and seven others in front of the eccentric Judge Maud, who found there was no case for the defendants to answer.

For three months the police had kept observation, in special vans with peepholes and periscopes, on premises in Romilly Street, watching the girls returning with men to their flats and money changing hands. The rent books provided to the girls showed weekly payments of between £3 and £5 but in fact they were paying £25 or

[13] For footnote, see opposite.

£30 in cash. A surveyor was employed by the police to assess the true rentable value of the flats. Many were what he described as 'orange-box' flats, with no heat, light or water, a truckle bed and two orange boxes for chairs. These, he assessed, were really worth three shillings a week. Much classier were the £2 to £3 flats which were properly furnished with an old-fashioned brass bed, a card table, some linoleum but no chair.

Judge Maud ruled that a landlord or estate agent was in the same position as a shopkeeper, doctor or barrister who received money from a prostitute as a customer or client, and that they were living on these monies as their own earnings, not those of a prostitute. 'It may be that the problem is so grave that Parliament must do something about it – but this is not for me.'

Silver may have had a lucky escape but the lesson was learned both by him and by others. Flat farmers, as they were known, took steps to distance themselves from their prostitute tenants by setting up a network of cut-offs and intermediaries. But rent books still recorded only a fraction of the actual rent and key-money of

[13] Albertine Falzon later married Silver. In the 1970s she committed suicide by leaping out of the flat in Peter Street, Soho, from which she worked. Other similar deaths in Soho included Frank Holpert, who in November 1973 fell to his death from his balcony (he had been a go-between for Silver and Humphreys), and prostitute Odette Weston, who in May 1975 fell to her death when her flat was fire-bombed. Perhaps the most interesting is that of vice queen Irene Micallef, who ran a call girl racket for her estranged husband Victor. She allegedly jumped to her death from a roof on 25 July 1979 when she was about to leave Soho for a new life with a new boyfriend. When her body was flown home to Sweden and taken to a local chapel, the coffin was found to contain the body of a sixty-three-year-old man named Medcalfe. Her boyfriend went into hiding, believing there was a contract out on him.

around £100 changed hands when a girl took over a flat.

In 1969, shortly before Christmas, Humphreys and Rusty were guests with senior CID officers, including Commander Wally Virgo, at the Criterion restaurant in Piccadilly. Humphreys took the opportunity to complain that Detective Chief Superintendent Moody, then in charge of the Obscene Publications Squad, would not give him a 'licence' to use his properties in Soho as dirty book-shops. Silver, also present, arranged a meeting with Moody in a Mayfair restaurant at which negotiations were opened. Could a bookshop be opened in Rupert Street? Nothing was finalized. Silver and Moody would meet the next day when the porn king would make a formal offer.

When terms were agreed they were staggering: £14,000 was to be paid for the licence; Silver would become a partner, so satisfying Moody, who did not want to see outsiders creeping in; and a further £2000 a month would be paid to prevent raids and closure. It was never a particularly happy association, in part because Humphreys took the opportunity of Silver's absence abroad to begin an affair with his mistress, Dominique Ferguson, a move which soon became Soho gossip and went straight back to Silver. Reprisals were threatened, including a suggestion that Humphreys be fitted up for a crime. In turn, he contacted Commander Drury, whom Humphreys had met at a party given to celebrate the promotion of a Flying Squad colleague, and the threats came to nothing. The fee for this service, said Humphreys later, was £1050. From the moment Humphreys met Drury he seems to have had the Commander in his pocket, wining and dining him and taking him to boxing tournaments at the World Sporting Club.

The first cracks in the empire began to appear in 1971 when the *Sunday People* named a variety of operators as the pornographers of Soho, including Silver, Mifsud and Humphreys along with two others, Jeff Mason and John

Mason. The *Sunday People* also made allegations that there were corrupt dealings with detectives. A Detective Chief Superintendent was appointed to investigate the allegations but, with one exception, all the operators denied they had paid over any money to the police. The exception was Humphreys, who refused to be interviewed, ostensibly on the advice of his solicitor but in fact on the advice of a police friend.

The first exposé by the *Sunday People* had come to nothing. Now in 1972 the paper produced a second round. On 27 February it announced that Commander Drury and his wife had recently returned from Cyprus where they had been guests of Humphreys. The gaff was blown in a curious way. When something went wrong in London one person at whom the police looked was one of the boxers charged in the Pen case, the old-time friend of the Nashes and drinking companion of Humphreys. When the police were looking for Freddie Sewell, killer of Blackpool Superintendent Gerald Richardson, they turned over the boxer's home. Nothing was found to link him with Sewell but he was charged with possessing a firearm and ammunition, a charge he strenuously denied and of which he was acquitted at the Old Bailey. He then had the hump with the Met in general and told a reporter of Humphreys' holidays in Cyprus with police officers.[14]

For a time Drury tried to bluff his way out. Yes, he

---

[14] In the summing up of his trial for possessing the gun and ammunition, the judge told the jury that to acquit would mean that the police officers had committed perjury. At Lewes Crown Court on 31 June 1975 one of the officers on the search, Harold Hannigan, who had been on the same regional crime squad as George Fenwick, was found guilty of trying to bribe a Sussex detective. He was given a conditional discharge by Mr Justice Melford Stevenson who called him 'a very, very conceited fool', and advised him to see a psychiatrist. (B. Cox *et al.*, *The Fall of Scotland Yard*, p. 191.)

had been to Cyprus. No, he had not been a guest, he had paid his share. No, it had not been a holiday, in reality he was looking for the escaped train robber Ronnie Biggs. At the time and for what it was worth, Humphreys supported him. It wasn't worth much. On 6 March Drury was suspended from duty and served with disciplinary papers. He resigned on 1 May. Then, foolishly, he turned on his former friend. He sold his story to the *News of the World* for £10,000 and as part of his confessions he named Humphreys as a grass, something guaranteed to destroy his reputation amongst the criminal fraternity, if not to get him a good beating to go with it. It is not surprising Humphreys took umbrage and gave his alternative version, saying that far from being a grass or getting money from Drury it had been all the other way around. The money, the wine, the good life had all flowed from the Humphreys cornucopia.

But now the foundations of the porn empire were cracking and Humphreys was investigated over the slashing of 'Pookey' Garfath in the lavatory of the Dauphine Club in Marylebone as punishment for daring to have an affair with Rusty. Three days before the attack she had been released from Holloway, where she had served a four-month sentence for possessing a firearm. Garfath named Humphreys as one of six assailants and a warrant was issued for his arrest. Humphreys, who was in Holland at the time, launched a counter-attack. He was not involved in the assault on Garfath, rather it was a frame-up organized by a Detective Inspector in concert with some criminals from Streatham as a reprisal over the resignation of Drury. Meanwhile Rusty Humphreys were arrested and charged with conspiracy to pervert the course of justice and conspiracy to cause grievous bodily harm to Garfath.[15]

---

[15] She was later acquitted of both these charges.

Now she went to the Complaints Department of
Scotland Yard to complain about senior detectives,
backing up her claims with details from her diaries which
had been taken from her on her arrest three months
earlier.

Gilbert Kelland, later to become an Assistant Commissioner, was appointed to lead the investigation. At
first he found Rusty Humphreys' statement difficult to
accept. If the diaries were all that revealing why had
nothing been done for the past three months? Why had
they never been sent to the Deputy Commissioner
during that time? 'The explanation I was given for this
oversight was the pressure of work on the senior officers
of the squad dealing with her case, but I have always
found this difficult to accept.'[16]

Kelland and his team began their enquiries in earnest
and in mid-October they visited Humphreys in prison in
Amsterdam where he was awaiting extradition. At first
he was prepared to talk but the next day he refused to
see them and he maintained this stance until after his
conviction on 25 April 1974, when he was sentenced to
eight years for the assault on Garfath. Even when, in
May, he did consent to make statements and later give
evidence, he proved to be a temperamental witness.
Looking for a witness who in police terms would remain
staunch, Kelland turned to John Mason.

On 27 February 1976 Drury, Virgo and Moody were
arrested along with nine other officers. The pool
included two ex-Commanders, an ex-Detective Chief
Superintendent, an ex-Detective Chief Inspector and a
host of smaller fry. It was in any language a major scandal.

In April 1976 at Knightsbridge Crown Court Mason
was fined a total of £25,000 for possessing obscene publications and he now began to make detailed statements

[16] G. Kelland, *Crime in London*, p. 127.

to Kelland. His revelations were remarkable. One ex-Detective Superintendent had attended Mason's offices once a week to advise on articles for the magazine and generally sub-edit the contributions. He had been paid £10 a week until, on his death in 1972, the job had been taken over by DCI George Fenwick. At the other end of the scale Mason recalled how his routine monthly contribution to the Porn Squad, which had been £60 in 1953, had risen to £1000 by 1971. His relationship with the squad had been such that he was lent a squad tie to go to the basement at Holborn police station, from where, at a price of between £500 and £1000, he could buy material confiscated from other shops and dealers.

At the first of the three Porn Squad trials Humphreys, like Achilles, was sulking in his tent and refused to take part. Even so Fenwick received ten years' imprisonment and four other former officers received between four and eight years. In the second trial, which began the next March, Virgo and Moody, together with four junior officers, faced an indictment with twenty-seven counts alleging bribery and corruption totalling £87,485. This time, faced with the story that his 'bottle' had gone and that Mason was by far the more important witness, Humphreys emerged. All six defendants were convicted, receiving between four and twelve years' imprisonment. Later the conviction of ex-Commander Virgo was quashed by the Court of Appeal.

The third trial involved Drury and two others, and again Humphreys had to be coaxed into the witness box. Now he was an essential witness. Arrangements were made for him to see a journalist from the *Sunday People* who had assured him that a full enquiry was taking place into his own conviction for the assault on Garfath.

Humphreys' evidence at the third trial led to the acquittal of one officer, DI Legge, who had admitted he had gone to stay in Humphreys' apartment in Ibiza.

Humphreys gave evidence that he was one of the very few officers he knew who had never wanted or accepted a penny from him. The case was stopped against Legge, who later resigned from the force. On 7 July 1977 Drury received eight years' imprisonment; the other officer half that sentence.

Humphreys was released at the end of August of that year by exercise of the royal prerogative of mercy. In 1982 he was circulated as being wanted over the manufacture of amphetamine drugs in Eire.

Meanwhile Silver had been pursuing something of a parallel, if more violent, course. As far as he and Mifsud were concerned it blew apart in 1973 when Silver was arrested for living off the immoral earnings of prostitutes; Mifsud went on the run. The girls, run by the Syndicate, had been organized on a factory-line basis. One girl would run the flat from 1 until 7 p.m., when the next shift took over until the early hours of the morning. Each girl would contribute £180 a week to the Syndicate. Silver had been responsible for the recruitment and placing of the girls and their clocking on and off their shifts on time. Strip clubs provided up to six shows a day, with the girls travelling from one to the next on a circuit and making six performances a day. The flats above the strip clubs were owned by Silver, Mifsud and their nominees.

Bert Wickstead had now moved his operations from the East End and had been called in to investigate the Soho vice syndicates. His operation ran side by side with one against dirty bookshops and the investigation into the Porn Squad. One of the first men he wished to interview was George Caruana, who over the years had had three separate attempts made on his life, by any standards a risky one. In 1968 he had been the intended target of a Kray-led attack. Although they had interests in Soho this was to be done as a favour to Bernie Silver, with the possible fringe benefit that they would have a substantial hold over him.[17] The plan had been for Caruana's car to be blown up and, perhaps sensibly, he left the country to work a double act with his wife in a strip club in Hamburg. It was in Caruana's house that Smithson had been murdered in 1956. Now in 1973 Caruana was located and made a statement but when it came to it he declined to give evidence. His retraction was to be only one of a series of early disappointments for Wickstead.

In fact Wickstead had considerable misfortune with his witnesses throughout the case. Apart from Caruana's defection, another potential witness, Maltese Frank Dyer, was kidnapped in London and given a beating, with a gun held to his head, to try to make him disclose what he had told the police. In October 1973 the top men of the Syndicate took off on an extended holiday. An offer of £35,000 had been made for the Serious Crime Squad to drop the charge against Silver. It seemed as though Wickstead's work might have been wasted. One of the officers in his squad had given the tip-off that raids were due. Wickstead went through the motions of having warrants he had obtained withdrawn and then leaked a carefully prepared story that his work had been wasted and his investigation abandoned. For the moment he turned his attention to pornographic books.

Three months later the directors of the Syndicate started to filter back and on 30 December Bernie Silver was spotted at the Park Tower Hotel in London. He was arrested, along with his then girlfriend, Dominique

[17] The plan was foiled when as a result of a phone tap the intended assassin, Paul Elvey, was arrested in Scotland with three dozen sticks of dynamite. There had been a considerable trade between the London gangs and Scottish mineworkers, who supplemented their wages by supplying explosives.

Ferguson, as they finished dinner and was taken to Limehouse police station, where Wickstead felt more at home: at West End Central he might run into corrupt officers who could impede his progress.

In the early hours a raid was organized on the Scheherazade Club in Soho. Wickstead had stepped up on stage to announce the wholesale arrest. 'What do you think of the cabaret?' called one reveller. 'Not much,' shouted another. The assembled company, including the band, was arrested and taken down to an East End police station, far from the eyes and ears of the police at West End Central.

But the sweep did not net Frank Mifsud. He had been living in Dublin and was tipped off with a phone call on the night of the Scheherazade raid. By the time the Garda went to arrest him he had gone.

One of the charges against Silver was conspiracy to murder Tommy Smithson. By now Wickstead had most of the story concerning the small-time hoodlum's death. His attempts to blackmail Silver to put up money for Fay Sadler's defence had come at a most unfortunate time. Silver was preparing his moves from Brick Lane into Soho and could not afford any hindrance. Nor could he allow himself to be seen as a weak man. Two contract killers, Philip Ellul and Victor Spampinato, were given the contract and executed their one-time friend Smithson, although they were never paid.

After the murder they had gone into hiding in Manchester, where they received a message from the Syndicate telling them to give themselves up. A deal had been arranged that they would only be charged with manslaughter and once their sentences had been served need never work again. They were betrayed, and both had been put on trial for murder. Spampinato had been acquitted and Ellul sentenced to death before being reprieved on the eve of his execution. He served eleven years and on his release came to London to collect his money. Sixpence was thrown on the floor and he was told to pick it up. Later he was taken to obtain a passport and then to Heathrow.

Spampinato was found by Wickstead's officers working as a wine bar tout in Malta. Ellul was traced by the American police and telephoned Wickstead. Yes, he would come and give evidence. Spampinato gave evidence at the committal proceedings at Old Street Magistrates' Court but did not reappear at the trial. When next traced in Malta he owned a villa on the sea front at Sliema, had a new car and was said to be in possession of £30,000. His contract had been honoured at last.

Ellul was given police protection in a flat in Limehouse. He was kept under close observation but complained, saying that his time in the death cell had left its mark on him and he did not like company. The watch was relaxed and later Ellul said he wanted to return to the States, promising to return for the trial. There is no such thing as protective custody of witnesses in England and so no reason to detain him. He never returned. It is said he was paid £60,000, which would roughly equal the payment made to Spampinato.

Silver was found not guilty on the charge of conspiring to murder Tommy Smithson but guilty to living on immoral earnings. He received six years' imprisonment. Others in the case received up to five years. All that remained was the arrest of 'Big Frank' Mifsud.

He was found in Switzerland, where he had been living in hiding in a small tent on the Austrian border, and was returned to London after fighting a losing extradition battle on the grounds of his ill health. He faced the charge of conspiracy to murder Smithson and also suborning Stocker to give false evidence in the Cauci and Galea case.

Wickstead had already seen both Stocker and Gauci. Stocker admitted he had been promised £100 for his evidence but in the tradition of bilking their employees, Mifsud had paid him only £15. Cauci, a round little man with a cast in one eye, had been set up in a coffee bar in Wardour Mews on his release. He gave his evidence well at Mifsud's trial and a conviction followed. Mifsud was sentenced to five years' imprisonment, only for the Court of Appeal to quash the conviction. He did not remain in England long. He left and returned to Malta to live on the proceeds of his Swiss bank accounts, along with the other members of the Syndicate. Silver returned to the West End but was never again a force with whom to be reckoned.

But, never one door shuts but another opens, and by the 1970s, with the introduction of the escort agency, Soho vice had become an even bigger and more sophisticated business. One of the new kings was not a Maltese but Joseph Wilkins, originally from Stoke Newington but now living the life of a country squire in Surrey. Physically a large man, with thinning and greasy black hair, he had started life as a used car salesman. Following a move to the West End, with interests in fruit machines and night clubs, in 1969 he took over Winston's, then a very fashionable club for tired businessmen and free spending visitors who could be relied on to waste money on indifferent food and expensive drink in return for the opportunity to sit with a hostess, which is what they had come there for in the first place. At one time or another Wilkins had interests in the 800 Club in Leicester Square (formerly the once fashionable 400 Club, home from home for Guards officers out on the town and, in its glory days, frequented by Princess Margaret),[18] the Islet Town Club in Curzon Street and

---

[18] The premises of the 400/800 now houses a large Chinese restaurant.

the Crazy Horse Saloon in Marylebone run by John Bloom, the former Rolls Razor washing-machine tycoon. But Wilkins also had a string of failed clubs to his name, including the Australian Visitors Club and the Minstrel Restaurant, part-owned by one of the Black and White Minstrels.

The circumstances of his inheritance of Winston's were shrouded in mist. At a licensing application before the then Chief Metropolitan magistrate, Sir Robert Blundell, at Bow Street Magistrates' Court, the former owner, Bruce Brace, maintained that Wilkins had terrorized him into handing over the club. Wilkins agreed that he had paid no money for the 27,000-member club but said that instead of payment he had settled debts of £6000. The licence was granted but the club soon closed.

Wilkins' reign in Soho was a relatively short and certainly a troubled one. An aggressive man, on one occasion in Winston's club he is said to have pointed a gun at the former world middleweight champion Terry Downes for making too much noise. Downes simply turned and took it from him. In November 1970 Wilkins was arrested at his farm and charged with conspiracy to pervert the course of justice over obtaining justices' licences. Charged with him was his helpmate Wally Birch.

This was by no means the end of his troubles. With Birch he was then running the Eve International, Playboy Escort, Glamour International and La Femme escort agencies. Eve had a catalogue of 200 girls who were available as escorts at a fee of £14 a night upwards and the business had a turnover of £100,000 a year. For some time there had been rumours that the more drunken punters from the Crazy Horse had found their way to the 800 Club and, following more drink, had been rolled in the alleyways off Leicester Square. Two of the staff of the 800 were arrested and later acquitted. Wilkins was charged with another conspiracy to pervert, this time along with a solicitor and a Detective Sergeant, to give false evidence in the case of one of the club staff. All were acquitted, as were the staff in their separate case.

On 21 March 1972, whilst awaiting trial for the conspiracy, Wilkins and Birch were shot and wounded in the Beak Street offices of Eve International. Later his then wife Pearl was to blame the Krays for encouraging her husband's enemies but, as the twins were in prison at the time, either their influence must have been marginal or they were wielding considerably more power from their cells than the prison authorities would have wished. Certainly in their youth they had quarrelled with Wally Birch and had been charged with grievous bodily harm following a fight with chains outside a dance hall. On that occasion the Krays had been acquitted.

Wilkins was sentenced to two years' imprisonment for his part in the conspiracy over the club licences, whilst Birch received nine months. Released from prison, Wilkins returned to the escort agency business. In November 1975 he was involved in accusations of the theft of a suitcase from currency swindler Ernest Brauch, a friend and acquaintance of the multi-million-pound fraudsman and property tycoon Judah Binstock. There had been a clever plot, said Brauch, involving the switching of a suitcase at Heathrow Airport, so that he was left with an identical but empty case revolving on the baggage carousel. Wilkins and all the other defendants were acquitted. Nevertheless his empire was crumbling and he was said to owe £90,000 in tax. He complained that his former partner John Bloom had put the skids on him over their dealings in clubs.

By now, however, he had been charged with living off immoral earnings, as had his faithful friend Birch, his long-suffering wife Pearl and some of the girls. The evidence showed that the girls were making £400 a week for themselves, let alone for the agency, which had advertised in the *Diplomatic Year Book*; it was what the trial judge called 'a new and sophisticated form of poncing'. A girl charged £40 for 'a quickie' and £100 for 'longer'. In March 1976 Judge Charles Lawton QC sentenced Wilkins to three and a half years. Birch received thirty months whilst Pearl was given a conditional discharge.

Wilkins had his sentence cut to two years by the Court of Appeal. The trial judge had, it said, been prejudiced by information given at the end of the trial which linked Wilkins to both a notorious Soho gangster and 'Mad' Frankie Fraser.

After his imprisonment he turned to a sophisticated long firm fraud and, following his release from a sentence for that misdemeanour, on 17 August 1987 he was caught sunbathing on a boat, *The Danny Boy*, which was carrying £1.5 million in cannabis. The arrest angered Scotland Yard, which had been hoping to follow the consignment to the South London gang who had ordered the drugs. Now Wilkins claimed he was an undercover agent for the Spanish police and in court named Frankie Fraser as one of the bosses behind the Costa del Sol drugs racket. Wilkins, whose only drink was said to be Dom Perignon champagne, had remarried shortly before he received a ten-year sentence. In September 1990 he slipped his guards when on an outside visit to a dentist from Ford Open Prison. It had been said he was worried about a split with his new wife. He was last reported as being back on the Costa del Sol. In March 1991 it was learned that Coral Edgar, Wilkins' sister, had been paid £2000 by Andrew Neil, editor of the *Sunday Times*, for a statement over Wilkins' links with Carmen Proetta, the witness to the shootings of IRA members in Gibraltar.

Nowadays the Soho industry has taken something of a knocking. But whilst the entrance fee to strip clubs advertising double acts and men and women in bed is low, and the lure that of long-legged girls in fishnet tights on the door, the punters get little for their money. 'The price to get in may be only £2,' says Detective Chief Superintendent Roy Ram, 'but at the foot of the stairs another £8 is removed for "membership". No sooner has the punter's bottom touched the seat than he is presented with the menu – £5.50 for a glass of Coke, £8 for an alcohol-free lager.'

In charge of these operations is another Maltese, Jean Agius – 'short and thin with sparse hair, pale and very unhealthy looking. Over a track suit he wore a showy but moth-eaten fur coat. It was all slightly sad.'[19] According to *The Independent* report, however, he is reputed to be wealthy, with a Rolls-Royce Corniche in London and a Bentley in Malta.

[19] 'The Maltese Legacy' by Peter Popham, *The Independent* magazine, 2 February 1991.

8

Robbers and Robberies

There seem to be two ways of setting up a robbery. The detailed perfectionist method of the highly skilled, or the more rough and ready take your, and everybody else's, chance.

Talking of his time, one villain of the 1960s and 1970s says:

> How did we look out the banks? On a Monday Georgie and I would drive round looking for a bank with a side turning. This was in the days before bandit glass – it was us made them put it in. One of us would go and change a note to see what drawers there were and then we'd go in mob-handed with pick-axe handles. One of us would stay by the door. Sometimes Bertie Smalls used to do that because he was fat and unfit and I'd jump on the counter and cause mayhem.
>
> Security vans were often picked by chance. You'd see them collecting and see them again the next week. You'd watch them doing pick-ups and use your judgement about how much each pick-up was worth and just what the van was carrying.

Teams were often picked up on the *ad hoc* basis you

might expect for a Sunday morning kick around in the park.

One of the labour exchanges for robbery work was the Log Cabin Club in Wardour Street, owned at one time by friends of Billy Hill. It was full of robbers, cut-throats and buyers. I was working with a couple then, called Robin and Mickey, and we used to go direct to the club and say to people, 'You fancy going to work tomorrow?' It could have been a porn shop, it could have been a post office.

Sometimes you got set up. One time I was minding the door of a club down the East End getting £100 a night, basically I was keeping the drugs mob out, and the guvnor says, 'Can you get someone for the back door?' I got hold of Tony and after a bit he said he and a mate had a bit of work, a security van. I was to be the driver. What Tony failed to tell me was that the person who stuck the job up to him was someone he'd given a spanking to a few weeks previous and the man had just set him up with the job and gone to the police.

Wasn't that risky?

Not really. In them days the police never had the informants, and they aren't – well they certainly weren't – as clever as they're made out.

Guns we kept in a slaughter – a lock-up garage in Camden Town. Other people had armourers, like the Krays with Colin 'Dukie' Osborne, but we didn't.

We'd never do less than one a week. Sometimes we'd do two in a day. The first robbery I ever did was in about 1961/2 and I was shitting all the night before – literally. I got £500 and to me it was a million. I bought myself a dark blue crombie coat which all the faces wore at the time and a white Fiat 600, and I had money to spare.

In the sixties a small house could be got for £1000 and I could have bought one – week in, week out. But I didn't – it all went on clubs, cars and women.

Robbery is not of course a twentieth-century phenomenon. There have always been robberies. What were those gallant highwaymen but armed robbers? Even then there wasn't much honour amongst them. Dick Turpin, who never actually made the celebrated ride to York, shot his long-time partner Tom King, accidentally perhaps, but he left him to die and escaped just as surely as John Hilton did two hundred years later.[1]

At the turn of the century a favourite form of robbery was with the garrotte. It was not the Spanish form of execution, a mask with a metal pin slowly tightened, but a neck-hold which, properly applied, brought about unconsciousness. Properly applied was the key phrase. Too much force and the victim died. 'You would come up to a man from behind, put your arms around his throat, with your fists on his throttle. If it went on for more than a few seconds he would choke, so you had to be skilled.'[2] A convicted garrotter could expect a heavy sentence: five years and, worse, a 'bashing' or eighteen strokes with the cat o' nine tails.

The Reubens brothers were not sufficiently experienced. On 15 March 1909 two prostitutes under their control took a couple of drunken sailors, McEachern and Sproull, to 3 Rupert Street, off Leman Street, where the brothers, Morris and Marks, attacked them.

---

[1] See Chapter 11.

[2] R. Samuel, quoting Harding, *East End Underworld*, p. 112.

McEachern was found semi-conscious in the street early the next morning. Nearby, Sproull was dead in the gutter. The case was investigated by Frederick Wensley, who later was the senior officer in the Steinie Morrison case. It appeared that after having sex with the girls, McEachern had decided to return to the ship rather than stay the night, taking Sproull with him. The Reubens brothers had been listening outside the room, expecting to roll the sailors while they were asleep, as would have been the normal practice; if they wanted the remainder of the sailors' money – about £5 each – well, they would be forced to attack them as they left. Apart from his other injuries Sproull had been stabbed.

At the trial at the Old Bailey Morris claimed he did not know his brother had a knife. It was not a defence which appealed to the jury, who convicted them both after a retirement of twelve minutes. They were executed on 20 May 1909.

'From that date, robbery with violence grew unfashionable in East London and few unaccountable dead bodies were found in the streets,' wrote Wensley.[3] It may be that a small industry was born with the hanging of the Reubens. A little later Wensley was sent a whisky glass with a hanging man engraved on the base. The inscription was 'The Brothers Reubens – the last drop'.

But the arrival of the motor car revived the flagging armed robbery business. Now thieves could travel at some speed and with comparative anonymity. In his memoirs George Cornish describes the arrest of what he called the first motor bandits in November 1924. He was certainly wrong in describing Reginald Dickenson and his mates as the first because the Recorder of London, sentencing them to terms of up to seven years, commented, 'I had almost decided to have you whipped . . .

[3] F. Wensley, *Detective Days*, p. 92.

I cannot lose sight of the fact that this class of offence is on the increase.'[4]

In fact it had originated in France long before the Second World War. In 1924 the cashier of one of the biggest French banks was shot dead by a gang which robbed him of 300,000 francs before escaping in a waiting motor car. Later the gang was trapped in a Paris suburb and, on conviction, guillotined. One of them, Saudy, said to the executioner as his head was placed on the guillotine, 'It is very cold. Goodbye all.' In French of course.

Indeed in the first year after the Great War there were sufficient smash and grab robberies with teams using motor cars from which a brick or iron bar was hurled through the window of a jewellers to cause Scotland Yard's Flying Squad to get wheels for themselves. Clearly a new version of the sport was here to stay.

The other form of armed robbery was the highly sophisticated, highly organized version executed with military precision – even though often the nearest the executants had been to the army was the glasshouse.

The first major post-war robbery took place at Heathrow Airport – then called Heath Row – on 28 July 1948. The target was the bonded warehouse which contained £388,000-worth of diamonds and was due to receive a further £250,000-worth. The job had been meticulously laid out, with inside help, and the gang maintained a twenty-four-hour watch on Heath Row over a two-month period. Then a warehouseman approached Donald Fish, chief security officer of BOAC, to report he had been offered £500 to dope the coffee of the warehouse staff. The Flying Squad was called in.

Each morning the organizer, who ultimately did not

[4] G. Cornish, *Cornish of the 'Yard'*, p. 143.

take part in the raid, was watched as he left his home in Ealing, with bowler hat, briefcase, umbrella and *The Times* under his arm, to head for a cafe near Waterloo Station. The plan had been to drug the guards at the warehouse and at first the raid seemed to go according to plan. The messenger with the tea was intercepted, and barbitone was dropped in the jug. But at the last minute the guards had been switched and replaced by members of the Flying Squad. The tea was put on one side and the three 'guards' lay on the floor seemingly unconscious. The members of the gang entered, hit one of the detectives with an iron bar to ensure he was unconscious and then took the keys from his pocket. At the same time other members of the squad attacked the robbers. Of the detectives, John MacMillan had his nose broken and a robber broke Detective Inspector Peter Sinclair's arm. Some of the robbers, including Teddy Machin, escaped. One of them hid under a lorry and, scorched by the exhaust, carried the burn on his shoulder for the rest of his life. The remainder were captured and sentenced to a total of seventy-one years' imprisonment at the Old Bailey.

> King Solly came up trumps. He must have caught a fearful cold as the overheads for this job were certainly very heavy. I believe that he had got a large advance payment from the prospective buyer, but even so, he was faced with the prospect of looking after the families of up to nineteen men for several years, if we all went down.[5]

Who was King Solly? The rumour was that it was a Soho gang leader, perhaps on the basis that four of his men were among those on the robbery, but no charges

[5] Shifty Burke, *Peterman*, p. 129.

were ever brought against him.

The first successful major post-war robbery was the Great Mail-bag Robbery of 21 May 1952, when £287,000 in hard cash was stolen from a post office mail-bag van. According to Billy Hill, the night before the robbery nine men, all of whom had been selected and warned of the raid the week before, and who certainly included Slip Sullivan, had been collected and taken to a flat in the West End, where they were locked in before being fully briefed on the operation. Hill had clearly set Wickstead and Read a precedent on the necessity for keeping a tight hold on their men.

The robbery had been carried out with immaculate precision. The mail-van had been followed every night for months as it left on its journey to Oxford Street. Cars had been stolen specifically for the raid. In the early hours of Wednesday morning one of the team had disconnected the alarm system on the van whilst the staff were on their tea-break. The van was kept under observation when it went to Paddington Station and once it left Paddington a call was made to the West End flat. Four men climbed into one of the stolen cars, a green Vanguard, and the other four into the stolen 2½-litre Riley.

As the van turned into Eastcastle Street off Oxford Street the two cars blocked the driver's path. Six men attacked the three post office workers and then drove off in the van, leaving them on the pavement. It was driven to Augustus Street where the cash was transferred into boxes on a fruiterer's lorry parked there earlier. Thirteen out of the thirty-one bags had been taken. 'The thieves were surprised,' claimed the police.

According to Hill the remaining bags were left because there wasn't any more room in the lorry, which was driven to Spitalfields market and parked there under observation for a further twenty-four hours before it was unloaded. The stolen cars were left in Covent Garden.

At the time Hill was seriously suspected of the robbery and it is now generally accepted that he organized it. Rewards totalling £25,000 were put up by the insurance companies but despite intense police activity for over a year, headed by Superintendent Bob Lee, then second in command of the Flying Squad, there were no charges. Hill recalled:

> All my friends were turned over. My spielers were raided and closed down. Friends of mine going abroad on holidays were turned over by the Customs people. One of my lads even had his car taken to pieces, yet he did not have a criminal conviction. All my telephones were tapped for years afterwards. My mail going through the post was steamed open and read.[6]

In the 1940s there had emerged an apparently highly unlikely gang leader but one who, according to journalist Peta Fordham, was to have a seminal influence over the next thirty years. His name was Ernest Watts and he created the South-Western Gang, so called because most of its members came from that area. He served only one short sentence of imprisonment. He must have been a disciple of the American Von Lamm, whose methods he adopted and improved upon.[7] A job would be cased,

---

[6] B. Hill, *Boss of Britain's Underworld*, p. 167.

[7] Lamm (?1890–1930), a German officer cashiered for cheating at cards, has been described as America's most brilliant bank robber, on whose technique Dillinger relied. From the end of World War One until the 1930s Herman K. 'Baron' Lamm's men were the most efficient in the business. Lamm's career came to an end when a tyre blew on the getaway car. They seized another which by mischance had a device fitted by a well-meaning son to prevent his elderly father driving too fast. They were overtaken and Lamm died in the ensuing shoot-out.

procedure worked out, the approach, the commission and the getaway timed to a split second, and the rule kept firmly that nothing was to throw out this schedule. If a safe door stuck or the expected haul was not there the timing was still to be strictly adhered to. Around him young Watts gathered Bruce Reynolds and a small band of trusted criminals who were shortly to lead this south-western part of the underworld.

Apparently Watts was an intellectual *manqué*, the clever boy from a working-class family with a chip on his shoulder. His father was almost literally a quack doctor, selling patent medicines around local markets. Watts, a diabetic, had won a scholarship to Christ's Hospital but his family did not allow him to take it up. He served in the RAF and then, seemingly determined to get his own back on society, he turned to a life of organized crime.

According to Peta Fordham, who made something of a career out of the Great Train Robbery,[8] Watts read everything he could about famous criminals and decided the most paying line was in jewel robberies from private houses and shops. In the main he worked alone and received his only prison sentence, one of two years, early in his career. It was shortly afterwards that he met Bruce Reynolds, one of the masterminds of the Great Train Robbery. Fordham attributes to Watts the use of the 'front man', the one who knew only what he had to do and therefore could not embroil others if he 'squealed'. Watts also introduced into England the system of the buying-in of information as well as the scale of compensation for those sent to prison when caught on a job.

[8] Peta Fordham was the wife of Wilfrid Fordham QC, who defended a number of those accused of involvement in the Great Train Robbery who were subsequently acquitted. A journalist with the *Sunday Times* and author of two books, she had a continuing interest in the fate of those convicted in the Train Robbery.

Watts killed himself, possibly accidentally, at the age of thirty-two. He had made abortive attempts at suicide in previous years; now he gave himself an overdose of insulin after returning from a job in the Home Counties when he had been without his medicine and had been taken ill. He had, however, committed one of gangland's cardinal sins. He had become involved with a close friend's girl whilst the man was in prison. Fordham tells how at the London Hospital where Watts had been taken one man came to see him only to find he had died. 'A good thing,' he said, 'otherwise we might have had to do a mercy killing.'[9]

The name of Watts does not appear in any account of organized crime at the time but he certainly existed, although perhaps not as the great leader painted by Peta Fordham. 'He was a short stocky fellow with short hair, a good dresser, good thief,' remembers one friend. 'But as the organizer – no. Connie Wilkin was the Daddy-O. He was the business.'

But it was Bruce Reynolds, tall, bespectacled, with the intelligent face of a handsome schoolteacher, to whom the leadership of the South-Western Gang devolved. His father was an active Trades Unionist. Reynolds had served his first sentence for robbery at the age of seventeen and another for an attack on a Jewish bookmaker in Park Lane. He drove an Aston Martin and was happy to let it be known that he had been the youngest major in the British Army. It was Reynolds who led the gang's first, and this time partially successful, major operation – the 1952 London Airport bullion robbery. The team consisted of names which float in and out of the London underworld and society for the next twenty-five-plus years. It included his long-time friend Charlie Wilson, described as a humorous, warm-hearted

---

[9] P. Fordham, *Inside the Underworld*, p. 77.

man who lived with his wife and three daughters in Clapham, had originally come from Battersea and had been involved in the West End protection rackets.[10] It was Wilson who was introduced to a man working in Comet House who could tell him of the movement of wages for the staff of BOAC.

Another member was Gordon Goody, later the particular favourite of Peta Fordham amongst the train robbers. An enormous thin-faced man, he had tattooed on one huge bicep the words 'Hello Ireland' and on the other 'Dear Mother'. He had already served a sentence that included twelve strokes of the birch for the rolling of a homosexual, and another for robbing a jeweller in Ireland. He liked West End clubs, women and Jermyn Street shirtmakers. Yet another member was the good-looking Buster Edwards, small-time thief, failed street bookmaker and – the straight job he began and ended with – flower-seller.

The drivers were to be Roy James and Mickey Ball, both small in stature and exceptionally talented. Perhaps, like the drummer in a dance band, being small is a prerequisite for success as a wheelman; Danny Allpress, who drove the getaway cars for the Bertie Smalls Gang at the end of the 1960s, and who was said to be able to make a car do almost anything, was not a big man either. Shortly before the London Airport robbery James and Ball had earned over £90,000 from two burglaries in the south of France. They had also blown £30,000 on the tables there.[11] A reserve driver was John Daly, a member of a powerful South London family, later acquitted of his alleged part in the Great Train Robbery. A safe house was arranged in Norbury. It belonged to Jimmy White, an ex-paratrooper.

[10] Piers Paul Read, *The Train Robbers*, p. 20.

[11] Ibid, p. 22.

Most of the team had already worked together in another highly planned wages snatch which had netted around £26,000. Now the prize was much, much higher; the team estimated they would pick up over £250,000. The plan was that the actual robbers would go to Comet House wearing false moustaches and disguised in bowler hats as businessmen and hide in the lavatories until the wage carriers left the building. Then after the snatch they would escape in the cars in which James and Ball, dressed as chauffeurs, would be waiting.

On 27 November 1962 the raid took place. It had been aborted the previous week when police were seen to be escorting the wage carriers. Now things went almost according to plan. The guards and some clerks with them were duly coshed, the wages snatched and away they went.

When they surfaced they found two things were not in their favour. There was only £62,000 in wages and, worse, the public was appalled by the brutal coshing of the guards. Even worse, it was more or less immediately apparent who had carried out the robbery. For a start Ball and James were the only drivers of sufficient class to have driven the getaway cars. Earlier Gordon Goody's flat had been raided over a receiving matter and theatrical make-up had been noticed. Mickey Ball's Mercedes had been seen with a bowler hat and umbrella on the back seat. It was only a matter of hours before the round-up began. Wilson, Goody, James, Ball and another man were put on identification parades but were not picked out. Reynolds had fled to France. Goody now left for Tangier.

In the middle of November a second identification parade was held, this time with the suspects, including Wilson, James, Ball and the newly returned Goody, dressed up in bowlers and false moustaches. Mickey Ball was identified as one of the coshers and broke down, begging the officers to believe he was only the driver. James was not picked out but Goody and Wilson were charged after further parades. Outside help was clearly needed.

And outside help came in the shape of Brian Field, a managing clerk employed by a confused and disorganized solicitor, John Wheater, who had offices in New Quebec Street near Marble Arch. Field had already helped Edwards out over a small matter of a stolen car. Now he began to work on the concoction of an alibi and the bribing of jurors, one of whom was offered and declined £400. It was helped by the fact that, thanks to a singular lack of proper police objections, Uxbridge magistrates had given bail to all the defendants other than Mickey Ball.

During the trial Wilson was acquitted on the direction of the judge but the case continued against Goody. The jury were unable to agree about his guilt or innocence. Meanwhile Mickey Ball received a five-year sentence.

The only way out for the re-trial was to get hold of a witness and this Goody did, with the help of Buster Edwards. Again it appears the witness declined the £200 on offer. Goody, however, was acquitted.

Within three months the money was spent and Reynolds, Wilson and company were back at work doing, or at least trying to do, what they knew best, robbing trains. Sometimes with some success and on other occasions without. And then for them came the big one.

What view you have of the Great Train Robbery depends on whom you believe for the information supplied. Of one thing there is little doubt – the job had been on offer around the underworld for a number of years. Eight, says Peta Fordham. 'The Great Train Robbery was a job which had been hawked like a film script around the underworld for some time. The blueprint had been carefully worked out and had been offered to a number of suitable clients,' says Nipper Read.[12]

It was the biggest theft the world had then known. At 3 a.m. on 8 August 1963 the night train from Glasgow to London was stopped at the remote Brigedo Bridge, Cheddington, in Buckinghamshire. A gang of armed thieves coshed the driver, Jack Mills, smashed their way into the high-valued package coach and stole 120 mailbags whose contents were estimated to be worth over £2.5 million. Even now the Great Train Robbery has a certain romanticism about it which has not attached to later and bigger raids, such as the Security Express and Brinks Mat robberies. There had been thefts from trains not long before that in 1963, particularly on the London to Brighton line, but these had been relatively small affairs.

The first reports of the Cheddington theft were vague but, as the day wore on, it became clear that this was a major robbery. Buckinghamshire was one of the smallest of the county forces and the Chief Constable, Brigadier Cheney, quickly realized he did not have the manpower at his disposal to deal with such a major incident. He used the facility that was available to all provincial constabularies. He called in Scotland Yard.

Officers from Scotland Yard had been made available from 1907 when the then Home Secretary, Herbert Gladstone, wrote to the Commissioner saying he felt that it was desirable that the services of a small number of detectives should be available for enquiries in difficult and important criminal cases committed outside the Metropolitan Police District.[13] It then fell to the officers of Central Office, New Scotland Yard, to take on this

[12] L. Read and J. Morton, *Nipper*, p. 72.
[13] For footnote, see opposite.

responsibility. As the majority of cases they investigated were murders they soon became known as the Murder Squad but they were not used exclusively in this capacity.

The team consisted of ten Chief Superintendents in charge of squads of men who were committed to investigating a variety of criminal cases. These included extradition and fugitive offender cases, banknote forgery and coinage offences, bribery and corruption, international lotteries and crimes relating to government departments. There was no question that these experienced investigators were simply sitting around waiting for a telephone call from a provincial or overseas force. They were well occupied with their daily responsibilities. But there was a rota system with three men on stand-by awaiting call-out. Being one of the three was known as 'being in the frame' and as a call was taken the next moved up a place. Number one had a suitcase ready packed with a current passport in case of an overseas job and had the famous 'murder box'. It meant that an officer had to be available twenty-four hours a day and ready at very short notice to go anywhere in the world.

The number one in August 1963 was Gerald McArthur, who had only recently been appointed to the squad and who, although he had considerable experience in all manner of investigations, including murder, from serving in various divisions of the Met, had never been appointed to assist a provincial force whilst on the

---

[13] One of the first, if unsuccessful, investigations was undertaken by Inspector Dew who later arrested Crippen. He was sent to Salisbury to find the killer of a crippled boy, Teddy Haskell. Unfortunately by the time he had arrived all the blood had been cleaned away under the supervision of the local police. Flora Haskell, the boy's mother, was arrested and defended by the young Rayner Goddard who later became the Lord Chief Justice. She was acquitted after a re-trial.

Murder Squad. He chose as his assistant Jack Pritchard. Their role was an advisory and directory one, as was that of any member of the Murder Squad when he was called out. Literally he could advise but if that advice was disregarded then too bad. Although this was standard procedure it did not satisfy the press or the public. Why, it was asked, were only two men detached from the Met to solve the world's greatest robbery? It was decided to supplement McArthur and Pritchard with a larger team.

Meanwhile Aylesbury, where the enquiry was based, throbbed with activity, speculation, rumour and excitement. The world's press swarmed everywhere like mayflies on a Hampshire trout river. Nipper Read recounts the political in-fighting which went on amongst senior officers anxious for their five minutes'-worth of glory and exposure to television and the newspapers.

Each officer wanted some of the glory from this, the world's greatest robbery. Each wanted to be seen as the instigator of this or that line of enquiry, preferably when it had turned out to be a successful one. More senior detectives visited Aylesbury than any scene of crime before and probably since. They all gave notice of their arrival to the reporters and made sure their best side was showing when the cameras clicked. Every senior officer was out to make a name with *his* arrests and have *his* photograph in the papers. All gave short crisp quotes suggesting that they were really overlording the operations and then shortly afterwards they were driven back to London.

Through all this Gerald McArthur maintained an air of unruffled equanimity. He knew who was really in charge. Unfortunately the record never gave him any of the credit for the magnificent job he did. Few members of the general public realized that he was the man at the helm.

The robbery job had been on offer so long that when it happened a number of people were not surprised. It was well known at the Yard that an Irishman was responsible for planning robberies and then selling them on to the perpetrators. The first of these was at Ericson's Telephones in Beeston in Nottingham, and was the first big hijack after the war. He went on to plan many others and detectives would say, 'That's got Mickey's stamp on it,' because the planning was meticulous.

Whilst Nipper Read was at Paddington there was one job Mickey told him about. They never met but he either knew or had heard of Read and there was a series of telephone conversations between them.

I was never quite sure why he blew the whistle but I suspect he had not been paid for the plan for this particular job.

It was a nice job really. Each week money was collected from an office block in Eastbourne Terrace by a GPO van. Mickey told me there would be a Ford Zephyr motor car and four people in it and another bloke on the bus stop and so on . . . when the people came out with the loot etc the men in the Zephyr would attack them and the man at the bus stop would be a back-up helper.

It was a perfectly simple operation to mount and when the raid was scheduled to go off there I was standing in my shirt sleeves on the steps of the office block having an argument with my 'girl-friend', a woman detective, Betty Reid. Two of my men were the office workers there to hand the money over to the GPO men.

Sure enough as the exchange was made the Ford

car appeared with four men in it, drove up and then slowed down. After the exchange was made it roared away up the road.

We arrested the only one left, the man at the bus stop, who had a long steel bar up his sleeve and got five years for conspiracy to rob. When I got back to the nick Mickey was on the phone in a rage. 'You've fucked it up completely.' I said, 'What are you talking about? We had everything laid on. They just didn't stop.'

'No,' he said. 'Of course they didn't fucking stop. These two blokes of yours – the ones in the waistcoats who handed over the cash.' 'Yes,' I said, wondering how he knew they were my chaps.

'They came out of the office . . . the real ones never, never do that.' It was an example of how meticulous his planning was. He had obviously detailed in his plan that the office workers handed over the cash and went straight back to their duties. The fact they did not alerted the robbers and the job was off.[14]

Read was sure from all the information he had that it was the same man who drew up the plan for the Great Train Robbery but that it was Bruce Reynolds who honed, polished and fine-tuned it. There is some confirmation of Read's theory. In Piers Paul Read's book, Gordon Goody and Buster Edwards meet a slightly balding, middle-aged man with a Northern Irish accent who tells them of the high-value package coach on the Glasgow to London mail train.

After the robbery Read recalls standing on the embankment at Brigedo Bridge and realizing what a perfect place it was for the unloading operation. Looking

---

[14] L. Read and J. Morton, *Nipper*, p. 72.

around, there was only one building in sight, a farm-house, to which the telephone wires had been cut. A short walk down the track was a white flag resting on an overturned barrow. This was the signal for the driver to stop the train so that the high-value package carriage was precisely above the embankment on the bridge. The carriage had been separated from the rest of the train, leaving the sorters, who may otherwise have been a problem wondering what the delay might be, a mile down the track. The exercise had not only involved the uncoupling of the train but the disconnecting and reconnecting of the vacuum pipe controlling the braking system. Read has always believed it to have been a perfectly planned and well-executed operation. The only flaw was the gratuitous violence meted out to Jack Mills, the train driver.

There have been a number of theories about a sinister and mysterious Mr Big, rather like Steve McQueen in the film *The Thomas Crown Affair*, who masterminded everything but who was never caught. Many police discount this and Read believes that the mastermind as such was Reynolds, with the brilliant Gordon Goody as the quartermaster sergeant, the number two. An operation of this size needed financing and the money for it had been provided by the 'City Gent' job at London Airport. Now the planning for the big one could go ahead.

It was another example of fine planning that Leath-erslade Farm had been selected as a temporary hideaway and that discipline over the job had been very strictly observed. Gordon Goody was thought to be the man who kept the troops under control. Before the job he could do this not only because of his forceful personality but by constantly referring to the rewards on offer when the caper was finally pulled.

Things went wrong, according to one theory, after the

team tore open the mail-bags back at the farm, found they had netted over £2 million and realized they had hit a jackpot beyond their hopes. Discipline then went to the wall and from being a well-drilled and regimented body, the robbers reverted to type and once more became individuals blinded by wealth, each eager to go off and spend it for himself.

They were not helped by McArthur putting out an announcement that he believed the robbers were still within a thirty-mile radius. (Leatherslade Farm was about twenty-seven miles away.) When the friend of a neighbouring farmer circled the area in a plane they really thought the game was up and the exodus from the farm was rapid and frenzied. All this led to a break-up of the tight control which had been exercised by the leaders. Believing that it was only a matter of time before the farm was raided, the team began to split up, taking with them suitcases filled with money.

There has also been a theory that there was a Judas, someone who was meant to go to Leatherslade Farm and set fire to it, destroying all trace of its previous inhabitants, but who failed to carry out his task.[15] One story was that a client of Brian Field, the solicitor's clerk involved, had been paid to burn it. But there were about fifteen men holed up there, eating, sleeping, playing games, going to the lavatory, and yet they left virtually no fingerprints. Had it been their intention to have the place burned down, there would have been no need to worry about prints. One would have expected to find them on door panels, light switches, bathroom fittings, the walls, everywhere. But they were simply not there.

---

[15] The theory was advanced first by Peta Fordham in *The Robbers' Tale*. It was also advanced by Ernie Millen in *Specialist in Crime*. Some underworld sources suggested the Judas was Ginger Marks and that had been the reason for his disappearance (see Chapter 13).

It was only by dusting the most unlikely places that evidence did in fact surface: a sauce bottle, a faint palm print on the tail-board of a lorry, a saucer put out by Reynolds for the cat, and a Monopoly set probably left behind in the mad scramble to get away. In Goody's case there was only the faintest trace of yellow paint on a shoe to connect him to the farmhouse.

Early on at Aylesbury it became quite clear that a London team had executed the job. It had been on offer for some time and informants had done part of their work. Despite the precautions taken by Reynolds and Goody, the Yard knew some major villains were about to pull something big. But it was only after the robbery they knew what.

The police quickly put together a list of those thought to have been involved. After all, there was only a handful of people in the country who were capable of such a job. It was then the real work of finding the evidence began.

Maurice Ray and Ian Holden, the forensic scientists, could provide the foundation on which the detectives could build, but tracing the suspects, their questioning and the breaking of their alibis was left to the Flying Squad under the direction of their newly appointed chief Tommy Butler. It was on this job that he really came into his own. This was what he really loved – chasing top-class villains. It became a personal vendetta. He undertook a totally ruthless and dedicated operation which would finally result in the whole team being netted.

A second base, 'the London End', was established for the enquiry in Old Scotland Yard in the Flying Squad office. Butler, first in in the morning and last out at night, played his cards very close to his chest. His team was given the minimum of information needed for a surveillance operation or to make a quick arrest.

A good example was the way he sent his 'twin', Peter Vibart, the man with whom he was meant to have the greatest rapport, and Read to Leicester after Gordon Goody had been arrested. Goody's had been one of the earliest names suggested as an organizer and prime mover. Police in London had visited his mother's address and some of his known hideouts but with no positive result. On 23 August they had the news that he had been detained in Leicester. Butler sent Vibart and Read to Leicester with no instructions about what they were to do.

> Now usually a superior officer would say either question him in detail there and then, or perhaps ask about an alibi, or just bring the suspect back to the office and talk about nothing but horseracing on the way down. Not so with Tommy. We had no instructions whatsoever. I suppose we were so in awe of him that we didn't ask before we left Aylesbury. Along the M1 Vibart said to me, 'Nipper, stop at the next service station and give him a ring to see what we are to do.'[16]

At first many of the suspects were brought in, questioned and then released. These included Hussey, Wisbey, Goody, Brian Field and Lennie Field. This gave the impression Butler was only on a fishing expedition and that he had no real evidence to back him up; otherwise he would have charged them. This was a most unusual practice for Butler. Normally, and it was well known amongst the villains, once he had his hooks into someone it was seldom they left the police station except to go to court. As a result some of his junior officers

[16] L. Read and J. Morton, *Nipper*, p. 77.

began to be worried that he was going soft. Nothing of the kind; he was merely playing a game of patience. By seeing them and having a quiet, apparently friendly chat he had persuaded them that, so far as they were concerned, it was a routine enquiry. He had opposed the publication of photographs of some of the leading suspects and had been overruled by Ernie Millen. Butler had rightly feared that men of this calibre would simply go underground or flee the country. The others were lulled into a false sense of security.

When it came to some arrests it was only a question of asking them to report to the Yard, which they did quite happily. This time they did not leave. Within a matter of weeks nine of the fifteen finally charged had been arrested and another five had been posted as wanted.

On 11 August Roger Cordery, a man brought in as the electrician to work the signals on the track, and his friend, William Boal, were arrested in Bournemouth where they had had the misfortune to attempt to rent lodgings from the wife of a police officer. They had bought a vehicle and a substantial sum was found in it. The money was lodged in the Chief Constable's safe and the gloom which had descended over the investigating team lifted a bit. Perhaps the use of Boal, who died in prison during his sentence, is an example of the dangers of using unreliable help. No team of robbers in its right mind should have gone anyway near this amiable but unsuitable little man.

There had been a breakthrough the previous day. A Dorking man, John Ahearn, was giving a lift on the pillion of his motorcycle to Mrs Nina Hargreaves when the small-engined machine began to overheat. They pulled off the road into a sheltered area of woodland where only a few yards from the road, sitting on a tree stump rather like an altar, was a beautiful embossed suitcase. They opened the bag and were astonished to find it crammed with used bank notes. Anyone less honest than Mr Ahearn and Mrs Hargreaves might have been tempted to keep the swag but they knew at once they had stumbled on part of the Train Robbery haul and contacted the police. A dog unit arrived with other officers and began to search the ground. A little further into the wood they discovered another bag. The total count was £100,900.

The police were amazed to see how obvious the case must have been. It would have been visible even from the road. It was almost as if it had been put there to be found. Yet right opposite there was a field of fern in which it was almost impossible to see anything. With a bit more planning the case could have remained undetected for years.

At that time anyone seen with a suitcase was fair game for a stop by an officer. Someone stopped with more than an ordinary roll of banknotes would certainly be invited to 'assist the police with their enquiries'. Hundreds of calls were received from up and down the country giving information about this or that person 'acting suspiciously' by spending money freely. The public was in the grip of GTR mania.

At the bottom of the Dorking suitcase a German hotel receipt was found in the name of Herr and Frau Field. This was Brian Field, the solicitor's clerk, and the £100,900 was obviously his share of the proceeds. Field had been fairly easy to link to the job because Wheater's firm had been instructed in the purchase of Leatherslade Farm. For his part in the Train Robbery he was eventually charged with conspiracy to rob and convicted. He was sentenced to twenty-five years' imprisonment but, on appeal, his conviction for conspiracy was quashed and he received five years as a receiver. Later he changed his name and remarried, putting his past behind him. When he was killed in a road accident his new family was shattered to learn his real identity.

It was after the finding of the suitcase that things started to happen. A caravan owned by James White, one of the robbers, was discovered at Box Hill, Surrey, and on 20 August it was found to contain £30,000. From then on arrest followed arrest. Goody, Hussey, Wisbey, one after another Butler had them. He never let up even after the main body of the team had been charged and convicted. His campaign to trace Charlie Wilson after his escape from Winson Green Prison in Birmingham, his persistent dogging of Buster Edwards until the man lost his nerve and surrendered, and his patient tracking of the leader Bruce Reynolds have all been well documented. The accounts bear testimony to Butler's determination. This obsession persisted until the day of his retirement which, at one time, he postponed.

These men were professional criminals of the highest quality who set out on an enterprise they were convinced would be successful. But even had they known before they started out they would be nicked, Read still thinks they would have done it – just to say they pulled the biggest caper of all.

Ronnie Biggs, Charlie Wilson, Tommy Wisbey, Bob Welch, Jim Hussey, Roy James and Gordon Goody each received thirty-year sentences. Lennie and Brian Field received twenty-five years. Cordery received twenty years and Boal, who in reality was probably little more than a receiver, twenty-four years. Wheater, the solicitor who employed Brian Field and who had partly provided an alibi, was given three years. Some sentences were subsequently reduced on appeal. Arrested later, Reynolds received 25 years.

The police investigation of the train robbery was an outstanding success so far as arrests and convictions were concerned. The failure was to recover no more than a fraction of the money stolen. Of the total of around £2.6 million taken from the train only some £400,000 was recovered. There have been a number of suggestions, apart from the mastermind theory, as to where the money went. First there are always other expenses. If someone puts up some money for finance they are in for a share; if someone provides a lorry or a car or welding equipment, then so are they. Escapes from prison are expensive and so is living in the underworld when your face is on a wanted poster. The members of the gang were blackmailed and ripped off for hundreds of thousands of pounds by their friends in the criminal fraternity.[17] Buster Edwards, Roy James, Jim Hussey, Jimmy White, Ronnie Biggs and Gordon Goody all suffered in this way. Piers Paul Read has analysed the lost money. Hussey lost £110,000 in bad investments; Goody – stolen by a minder – £40,000; Welch – appropriated by a minder – £100,000; James – appropriated by minder – £74,500; White – stolen by minder – £10,000; Edwards – expenses in escape, living and lost money – £140,000.

It was another couple of years before the robbery circuit really spread, and when it did it was for two reasons. The first was the growth of the motorway network and the second was the implementation of the Mountbatten report on prison escapes which had recommended that criminals be dispersed around the prisons in the country rather than being kept with their friends in the same prison near their homes. Now villains from, say, Manchester were put in a Liverpool prison and villains from Liverpool moved down south. As a result there was a wide pool of information to be shared and shared it was. Says one criminal:

[17] See Piers Paul Read's *The Train Robbers*, appendix.

We went to Glasgow to do a job. There was a lad
from Wakefield, a guy from Birmingham, me from
London and a lad from Devon. When we arrived
on the plot there was the happy bag. We went to
the scene and fuck all happens. We were all doing
speed. We drop the guns in an artificial lake. If
they ever drain it they'll find enough to start a small
war, and it took us three days to come south. Every
town which had a Marks and Spencers we turned
over.

'Of course it was a London-based job,' says a Stoke-
on-Trent police officer, referring to a major robbery of
the time. 'We went round to see the only man remotely
capable of putting it together almost as a matter of
courtesy and he was flattered we'd been to see him.'

A man eventually put on an identification parade for
that Stoke-on-Trent job and not picked out was Derek
Creighton Smalls, known to both his friends and the
police as Bertie. It was he who led the major London
criminal robbery team of the late sixties; certainly it
became the most celebrated one. He was also the first
person in modern times to become what was to be called
a 'supergrass'.

There were of course many, many other robbery
teams, including that of John McVicar, who in February
1967 received a sentence of fifteen years for a South
London armed robbery which went wrong and in which
shots were fired at the police. Eventually the team was
trapped and one of the members, Billy Gentry, from a
North London family, tried to fire at a police officer at
point-blank range. The gun was empty. Gentry received
a sentence of seventeen years. McVicar later escaped from
Durham Prison and hid out for several years before his recapture. Back in prison, he read for an arts degree and on
his release became a successful writer and broadcaster.

Not everyone was pleased with McVicar's reformation, nor had he been universally popular. Such unpopularity may well be mixed with a tinge of envy. 'He's a preacher now, a reformed character and goes on the telly.'[18]

In May 1967 a robbery went off at Bowling Green Lane, Clerkenwell, when £700,000-worth of gold was stolen. Four months later the famous ex-speedway rider, Francis Squire 'Split' Waterman, England's Test captain and twice runner-up for the world title, and his fiancee, Avril Priston, were arrested and remanded in custody at Lewes on 15 August 1967, accused of gold smuggling. Their arrest began a tale of gold, arms and illegal immigrant smuggling. On 14 August a Triumph Herald car driven by Miss Priston accompanied by Waterman had arrived at Newhaven docks for the 7.30 a.m. ferry to Dieppe. When it was searched, three woollen stockings containing twenty-six gold ingots were found concealed in the chassis. The plate over the entry was cut from a sheet of metal. This had been positioned and covered in such a way that it was very nearly invisible.

Waterman, who had taken up arms dealing in Belgium and Biafra after his retirement from the track, said in a statement he was taking the bars to the George V hotel in Paris where the car would be taken from him. 'I was approached by some men I didn't know at the Mayfair Hotel in London. They offered me £100 to borrow a car before I went abroad and I was to let them have it back again after I got to Paris.'

But it turned out that Waterman was making his fifth trip abroad and Detective Sergeant Algy Hemingway asked: 'Have you been selling arms abroad?'

'No,' was the reply. 'But I know that a lot of money

---

[18] Royston James Smith in G. Tremlett, *Little Legs*, p. 39.

can be made if guns can be smuggled from the Continent to Biafra.' According to Hemingway, Waterman also hinted he had been involved with illegal immigrants.

The same day two men, Michael Kenrick[19] and Ivor Bloom, were stopped at Victoria Station on their way to Dover. Kenrick and Bloom were charged with attempted illegal export of forty-five gold bars worth £10,000 and with receiving the bars knowing they were stolen. Bloom had been found wearing a corset containing the bars and at Waterman's address at 149 Elm Road, New Malden, Surrey, fabric scraps had been found in a sewing machine. One of seven children, the attractive, fair-haired Avril was a dressmaker and had been chosen to make the corsets used to smuggle the gold.

Now attention switched to a 150-acre Bedfordshire farm at Manor House, Bourne End, Cranfield, owned by Avril's father, where the police believed a fortune in gold might be hidden. They were unlucky in that respect but what they did find was a box of arms, four rifles, a sub-machine gun and a gas pistol, as well as a large amount of ammunition. Parked on the estate was a van containing a Gallenkamp electric furnace with traces of gold in it. It had been bought by Waterman fourteen days after the robbery. Waterman's 'non-trade' personal enquiry soon after the robbery to a firm that made high-temperature furnaces had alerted customs officers, who had kept observation on the pair.

Another arsenal including two machine guns, two rifles and pistols had been found under Avril's bed.

[19] Kenrick received a term of imprisonment and whilst serving it was charged with obtaining money by false pretences in the Kray case. He could not face a further term of imprisonment and hanged himself in his cell. Ironically, because of the heavy sentences handed out to the principals in the Kray trials, it was decided not to proceed against the lesser fry.

Waterman admitted receiving the gold but denied it came from the robbery. He had at the time been hard up and, it was accepted, he had been used by the gang rather than being a member of it. It was estimated he had made less than £1000 from his part in the enterprise.

'I cannot express how I feel about this, of what I have done to Miss Priston, to my family and her. I can only plead most earnestly for leniency for Avril and I am sorry for the trouble I have caused,' he told the Court.

'You were a man who was, by character, prepared to face danger and take risks – a gun-runner in Africa and a man with the quick decisive mind of a speedway rider,' said Carl Aarvold, the Recorder of London, sentencing Waterman to four years' imprisonment. Avril Priston received a six-month sentence which meant her almost immediate release.

After his release Waterman married Avril Priston on 15 September 1970. He was later reported to have business interests in tin and copper mines in Guyana. But it was the activities of the 'gang', none of whom was caught, which attracted the attention of the press and public. There were tales of dealing in diamonds, trafficking in arms to rebel organizations in African countries and smuggling immigrants into the country through the Romney marshes.

Scores of Indians and Pakistanis had been picked up at obscure French ports and landed on beaches in Kent and Sussex. Their relatives had paid £100 in gold for the journey. The bullion was then shipped back to France and on to Switzerland. The trade did so well that an approach had been made to a south coast company to rent an additional boat, the *Sea Rod*, for £20 a week on the basis of a sea-bed survey. It was estimated that a successful trip could net the smugglers between £6000 and £10,000 depending on how loaded the boat had been.

The next the owners knew was a letter from the British consulate office in Boulogne saying the *Sea Rod* had sunk in the harbour there after a fishing smack had salvaged it during a storm off the west coast of France. Four Pakistanis had been on board and had been landed in France but it was not known what had happened to them. Doubtless for many of their compatriots it was a miserable journey which may not have ended so fortunately.

These people, mostly illiterate and ignorant of conditions in the West, are often left shivering with cold and terrified of what awaits them. But, almost without exception, their 'fare' for the trip cost them more than a first-class air ticket. In a sense, those who finish up on the deserted beaches are the lucky ones. Many of their fellow countrymen who attempt the cross-Channel journey, police feel, are deliberately drowned by boat owners who 'pull the plug' in panic when they suspect they are being tailed by Customs or immigration men at sea.[20]

The immigrant smuggling racket has continued intermittently into the 1990s. Early in 1992 immigrants were found on the Kent and Sussex beaches apparently having been abandoned by their importers. When on 13 December 1991 Detective Constable Jim Morrison was stabbed to death whilst chasing a thief in Covent Garden, police enquiries included the interviewing of some three hundred suspects, half of whom were illegal immigrants and many of them Algerian. The first stage of their journey is to travel to Barcelona where false identity papers can be obtained for as little as £30. They are then able to fly to Heathrow where document

[20] C. Borrell and B. Cashinella, *Crime in Britain Today*, p. 120.

inspection of their papers may only be cursory.

On 9 February 1970 the biggest daylight raid on a bank took place when a team of eight or nine men attacked a Security Express van while it was making a stop at Barclays Bank, Ilford, Essex. Their gain had been £237,000.[21] A year later in March 1971 the biggest cash haul since the Great Train Robbery had been grabbed when another Security Express vehicle was ambushed and attacked at Purley, South London. The four guards had stopped to relieve themselves in a lay-by. Twenty-eight bags of banknotes with a value of £456,000 were taken in what was known as the Spend a Penny Robbery.

Then on 2 May 1972 a robbery took place which had reverberations throughout the underworld and which harked back to the Krays. A security van containing twenty tons of silver bullion worth £400,000 was hijacked at Mountnessing, Essex. Although it was a high-class attack it was not so much the robbery itself – though that was still a decent amount of loot for a day's work – as

---

[21] One of the men convicted for his part was Arthur John Saunders. The evidence against him consisted wholly of verbal admissions made to Commander Wickstead. Asked if he was on the robbery he had replied, 'There's no point in saying no, is there?' He put up an alibi defence but his witness let him down. His appeal was dismissed in December 1971 but later Bertie Smalls, the supergrass, said in one of his statements that Saunders had not been on the raid. This presented the authorities with a dilemma. How could Smalls be put forward as truthful in one instance and not in another? The Court of Appeal quashed the conviction, pointing out that Saunders had been drinking when he made the admissions. It ordered £1500 taken from him to be refunded. Saunders was later awarded a substantial amount of compensation for his wrongful imprisonment.

In 1985 Saunders was again arrested for armed robbery. He had led a middle-aged team lying in wait for a security van in Baker Street. This time he received fifteen years' imprisonment.

one of the participants that created the interest because, six months later, George Ince was to be charged with the murder of Muriel Patience, the wife of Bob, owner of the Barn restaurant in Braintree, Essex. And as a second prize for criminologists, George Brett, the brother of John, one of the others charged in the robbery case, was to disappear in very worrying circumstances.[22]

The robbery was a straightforward heist of an MAT lorry which always took the same route and was therefore a perfectly good target. The robbers, armed with a gun and iron bars, attacked the van when they blocked it on a roundabout on the A12. Two of the security men were bound, put in a van and taken some two and a half miles to a farm. The police had been targetting one of the men involved and on his arrest he made a statement naming names.

So far as the murder was concerned, both Ince and John Brett were picked out by the Patience family on an identification parade as two gunmen who went to the Barn restaurant in the early hours of 5 November 1972, forced their way in and, when Bob Patience refused to hand over the keys to the safe, shot him, his wife and daughter Beverley in quick succession. Muriel died later in hospital. Brett was never charged. Ince was.

The trial for the murder took place at Chelmsford Crown Court in May 1973. It was presided over by Mr Justice Melford Stevenson, the judge who had tried the Kray twins in their first trial for the murder of Cornell and McVitie, and who was not noted for his sympathy towards defendants.[23] Ince was defended by Victor Durand, who frequently clashed with the judge. Ince continually protested his innocence and was sent down to the cells whilst Beverley Patience gave her evidence that she identified him as one of the attackers. It was

[22] See Chapter 13.
[23] For footnote, see over.

after this that Ince, who had already made an abortive application to change the judge and who, during the trial, had had a telegram sent to the Lord Chancellor asking for Stevenson to be removed, sacked Durand and his junior, Robert Flach. Now he was on his own. Both his barristers remained in court, taking no further part, while Ince stayed in the dock with his back to the court, interrupting the occasional prosecution witness. He offered no defence until he asked whether he could be allowed to take the truth drug. Stevenson said no, but would he like his defence counsel reinstated? Ince replied that he would not and said once more that the judge was both biased and rude. After a retirement of six hours, at 9.30 p.m., before a tense court, the jury returned to say they had failed to agree on a verdict.

Within the week Ince was on trial again. This time before a much more sympathetic judge, Mr Justice Eveleigh. Durand and Flach were reinstated and this time Durand called a crucial witness, a Dolly Gray. Ince had apparently been unwilling for her to appear. He had thought that when her real name was given, it would act against him and also that she would suffer reprisals.

Mrs 'Gray' had bravely gone to see her husband, Charlie Kray, in Maidstone Prison before she testified. It seems that he did not know she had been seeing Ince before she told him and this 'Dear John' was a shattering blow to a man serving a ten-year sentence. To his great credit, however, he did not attempt to prevent her giving evidence to the effect that on the night of the murder she had been in bed with Ince. Reggie Kray, however,

[23] He once sentenced a nineteen-year-old youth to Borstal on his first offence, saying he hoped 'no soft-hearted official will recommend your early release'. He had also earlier appeared for Ruth Ellis when he indicated to the court he could really offer no defence to the charge of murder.

says he had known of the affair for some time. Unsurprisingly he was not supportive of Ince.

> George Ince . . . was always a slag to me, even though he used to frequent our billiard hall in the late fifties. It was I who first tumbled that he was going with Charlie's wife, so I got hold of him outside the Double R Club and butted him in the face. Ron and I then warned him off the manor of the East End and he made sure he stayed away.[24]

On 23 May the jury retired for over three hours before they acquitted Ince, to wild cheers from the public gallery. Three weeks later a northerner, John Brook, was found in possession of the murder weapon and was later convicted of the murder of Muriel Patience.[25]

Ince, together with John Brett, was convicted of the Mountnessing silver bullion robbery and each received fifteen years' imprisonment. Ince had a hard time in prison. He was made a Category A prisoner and while watching a football match at the maximum security gaol, Long Lartin, he was attacked with a knife by another inmate, Harry Johnson, who was serving eighteen years. True to the Samurai code, when Ince appeared as a witness at the Evesham Magistrates' Court and was asked to identify his assailant, he replied, 'I wouldn't like to take a chance on identifying anyone. You know what I think of identification parades.' Nevertheless Johnson received a further three years for the attack.

A year after the George Ince case came the trial of George Davis, the repercussions of which would set the

---

[24] R. Kray, *Born Fighter*, p. 58.

[25] The Barn murder case was one of a number of similar cases of mistaken identity which led the Court of Appeal to formulate guidelines on the dangers of identification evidence.

tone of protests for the next twenty years. A robbery was carried out on the London Electricity Board in Ley Street, Ilford. A PC Groves who was in the vicinity quite by chance ran to tackle the robbers and was shot in the leg for his pains. While he was on the ground another of the team stood over him threatening to shoot him again. Groves' colleague was in the police car alerting patrol vehicles in the area and a series of chases took place. At one time the robbers were cornered by the unarmed police, who were forced to back off as they were threatened with guns. One of the officers involved was Dave Brady, the driver of a Q car from North London who, with his colleagues, had ventured into East London territory to execute a search warrant for some stolen whisky.

As we were coming to a T junction a battered Ford crossed us and I could see there were four men in the car, three of them in crash helmets. This aroused a modicum of suspicion and then a marked police car cut in so we were third in line. Then we heard on the radio that there had been an armed robbery at the Electricity Board.

We all became blocked in traffic and the driver of the Ford swung right across two lanes and then the men bailed out. I ran across towards them and a fellow in a crash helmet poked a revolver up my nostril. Then another came round and they made us kneel down. I had no chance to identify the men in the crash helmets but I looked at the fat fellow who was the fourth man and I said to myself, 'I'll know that sod if I see him again.' I'd done twelve years in the commandos and a few months earlier I'd been shot in the aftermath of a bank raid so though I was frightened I'd had ample experience.

Another car was hijacked and eventually the robbers escaped.

A name in the frame was George Davis, an East End soldier, no great leader but thought of in the hierarchy as reliable. He had recently been acquitted along with Tommy Hole on a charge of robbery of three lorry-loads of whisky. The evidence had been based on that of one of the newest supergrasses, Charlie Lowe, who admitted attacks on the public with hammers, coshes, ammonia sprays, pistols and sawn-off shotguns, and to having made about £100,000 from crime in the previous four years. When questioned in the case about a conspiracy to cash stolen cheques, Lowe piteously replied, 'Coshing people and robbing them is more my game, sir, not cheques.'

Davis was first seen by the police twenty days after the robbery, when he was arrested and gave an alibi that he had been driving a mini-cab. The books of the firm were gone through and one of his passengers was interviewed. Eight days later the same thing happened but this time the log books were taken away by the police.

He was identified by three officers, including Brady, who had seen some of the gang leap out on to the central reservation at Woodford Avenue. Three months after the robbery a second set of identification parades was held at Brixton Prison. Davis was picked out by two police officers, Appleton and Grove, but another thirty-four people failed to pick him out and three made wrong identifications, two after he had changed his purple shirt with another man on the parade.

However, the jury did not accept his alibi and Davis was convicted in March 1975. He was sentenced to a total of twenty years' imprisonment, reduced on appeal to seventeen. Two others, including Tommy Hole, were acquitted and the jury failed to agree in the case of

Michael Ishmael.[26] An enormous campaign began on
Davis' behalf. There were allegations that he had been
fitted up and on his conviction his supporters mounted
protest marches, demonstrations, and the chalking and
papering of most of East London with the slogan
'George Davis is innocent – OK'. In one incident the
cricket pitch at Headingley was dug up during a test
match. Brady says:

> It was funny the DI in the case had been replaced
> with a DS and then one day I got a phone call from
> a copper friend saying, 'I wouldn't fucking go near
> the East End. Your name's absolute shit because
> the hierarchy is convinced you've stitched him up.'
> What hurt me after that was that the coppers came
> up to me and said they believed it as well. No one
> believed me. They all believed I'd fucked him up.
> The next thing I knew I was out on patrol and I
> was told someone was here to see me. It was a DCI
> from Hertfordshire saying he was investigating an
> allegation of perjury and stitch-up. Now this was

[26] Ishmael was not having a great deal of luck at the time. Shortly before
the Bank of Cyprus raid his former lover had run him down in Commercial
Road, Stepney, following a row. Unfortunately she also hit a bystander.
As Judge Edward Sutcliffe QC pointed out when sentencing Brenda Orsler
to two years' imprisonment, 'This was a really dreadful case of using a car
as a weapon and injuring not only your man friend but also a nun.' Sister
Joan West of the Convent of Mercy, Stepney, had a fractured leg and a
cut on her head which required twenty stitches. Ishmael, who sustained
injuries to his left knee and arm, but who recovered sufficiently to take his
part in the Bank of Cyprus raid, was another to observe the Samurai code.
He had been about to leave the pregnant Mrs Orsler at the time and wrote
to the judge trying to exculpate his former girlfriend. He had, he said,
taken terrible liberties with her and for that reason she would have been
so upset she would not have known what she was doing.

the first time I'd been involved in an allegation like this and what surprised me was there was no old boy network. I was with them for three hours and I was giving a right tousing. I was accused of being as bent as arseholes and this made me even more angry than when it started.

Then after a bit I started getting iffy calls at home. 'You stitching bastard, watch your back,' and things like that.

Then I thought I was being followed but I didn't know if it was by villains or by the investigation branch so I got in touch with the DCI in Hertfordshire and told him I was getting iffy calls. Two days later he came back to me and said, 'It's nothing to do with them but it won't happen anymore.' I still don't know who the calls had come from.

Just as Rosie Davis was fantastically loyal to George so my missus stuck by me, but most people were sure he'd been stitched up. All I'd done is made what I thought was a correct ID. After all I was just a uniform copper from another division. I'd got nothing to do with it really.

The 'George Davis is Innocent – OK' campaign was successful. On Tuesday, 11 May 1976, he was released by the Home Secretary in a blaze of publicity after the publication of the Devlin report on the dangers of convicting on identification evidence alone. It appears an additional alibi witness had also come forward. Davis travelled back from the Isle of Wight with Charlie Kray, whom he had met on the ferry; Charlie had been visiting one of the twins. 'That is my last brush with the law, never again – never,' Davis told the *Daily Mirror*.

Unfortunately the rejoicing was short-lived. He seriously blotted his copybook as folk hero when, on 23 September 1977 along with Micky Ishmael, he was captured *in flagrante* during a raid on the Bank of Cyprus in the Seven Sisters Road, Holloway. This time the police were armed. One of the robbers grabbed an eighty-two-year-old man as a shield as the officers approached. Another passer-by, Mr Albert Carney, grabbed the robber from behind, forcing him to release his hostage.[27] The gang received sentences of up to sixteen years and a number of policemen wrote in their memoirs of the naivety of Davis' former supporters.[28]

Dave Brady's colleagues made sure he wasn't involved this time:

> I got a phone call from a bloke at Holloway saying it was a good idea if I didn't go out on the Q car that day. He said he couldn't tell me why but not to go out. A bit later he rang back and said 'cancel that' and that he would let me know what it was all about. Then I got another call and so I stayed in the nick. Sure enough I got a call to say there'd been a blagging [armed robbery] and Davis had been nicked. They just didn't want there to be any chance I was in the vicinity when it went off.
>
> I don't know if it's true but the story goes that he got away and into a van and a copper poked a pistol through the window. 'I'm only doing a bit of shopping,' George said. 'Well take your balaclava off then,' said the copper.

From the police point of view this was a major success, but the cream turned slightly sour. The next day when the *Daily Express* published a picture of a robber standing outside the bank with a shotgun, it was apparent from the angle that it had been taken from the police control room

---

[27] He later received the Queen's Commendation for gallantry.

[28] Including G. Kelland, *Crime in London*, p. 205.

from which the bank was being staked out. A Detective Sergeant was suspended. He said he had taken the photograph and passed it to the *Express* because he thought it would be good for the image of the force. He resigned before disciplinary proceedings could be brought.

Davis' sentence in the Bank of Cyprus case was reduced to one of eleven years on appeal. But that was not his last brush with the law. On 21 January 1987 he received another sentence, this time of eighteen months with nine of them suspended, following a raid on the London to Brighton mail train in March 1986. Police guarding postbags on the train tried to enter the mail-van and found Davis blocking the door. He pleaded guilty to attempted theft, while his partner, John Gravell, was sentenced to ten years on his conviction on five charges of theft, attempted wounding and assault.

So far as Brady was concerned the Electricity Board robbery never went away. Years later he was seconded to a police driving school in Norfolk when he heard a young CID officer recounting his time on a course in London and reminiscing about Davis. 'He was bang to rights on the Bank of Cyprus but he was stitched up on the first fucker,' he said. 'I think I became a better officer because of the case,' says Brady.

The decade ended well for the police with the capture and conviction of one of the most successful robbers, Billy Tobin. He was taken in November 1980 when about to rob a security van carrying £1 million in Alleyn Park, Dulwich. The van was to be rammed with the jib of a mobile crane, the driver of which had been kidnapped and tied up in a van. Tobin, on bail at the time for two other armed robberies, was watched by the police following a tip-off. He and another man were shot at by a Detective Sergeant as they approached him moving their hands towards their pockets.

After a re-trial Tobin received a total of sixteen years'

imprisonment. Convicted with him was a member of the team who would himself be executed a decade later, Ronnie Cook. But the police cannot have been wholly satisfied with the outcome of the Tobin case. They had known in advance that he would be on the raid but they had not known the identities of the others. They were not pleased to find that two of the gang came from East London. Now, instead of the polarization which had existed over the years between North and South London firms, it appeared the Thames was being forded.

9

Supergrasses

The early 1970s introduced a new word – supergrass – into the English language.[1] It also gave a new phrase to criminal slang – to do a Bertie, or inform to the police.

Grassing is perhaps the principal method by which the police obtain information which will lead either to the prevention of a crime, or to the arrest of the villains and recovery of stolen property. Any good detective keeps a small, or sometimes large, string of informers who may be active thieves themselves or who may simply hang about on the fringes of the underworld. In the past they were paid out of a police information fund or sometimes out of the pocket of the officer who ran them. It was regarded as a good investment towards promotion. Sometimes in the case of a drug bust the informer was given a part of the bust itself as his reward. Sometimes an informer had a licence to commit crimes, short of violence, in a particular area. Sometimes all three.

One singularly corrupt Flying Squad officer of the 1960s, Alec Eist, is described in admiring terms by a former colleague: 'He was the best informed police officer in London. What he took off one criminal he gave

---

[1] The origin of the term is in doubt. It might come from rhyming slang, grasshopper–copper.

back to another. If he got £200 from a villain for giving him bail, Eist would give £195 to cultivate an informant.'[2]

And another says of the practice: 'You find three pounds of heroin and put only one on the charge sheet. The villains are pleased; less they're found with means less bird, and you give the other two to the informant. The job won't pay the informant so the only way is you give it back.'

The grass could also expect help from his runner if he was arrested. This might well take the form of an intercession to prevent a charge being preferred.

But grassing changed gear on to a wholly different level with the arrest in 1970 of Derek Creighton Smalls. It became the era of the supergrass, the criminal who, to dig himself out of trouble, would inform not just on his colleagues on a particular job but on his associates and their efforts going back years and years. In turn he could expect to receive a minimal sentence compared with that handed out to his former friends. He could also expect, through a nominee, a share of the insurance rewards.[3]

In the late 1960s and early 1970s Bertie Smalls led a highly successful team of armed robbers in a series of attacks on banks, mainly in North and North-West London but on occasions as far afield as Lloyds Bank in

[2] Eist, a florid, handsome, black-haired man, was acquitted in one of the trials of police officers and solicitors in the 1970s. Later he had a dress shop. 'It did no good. He was always having fires and burglaries – it was an embarrassment.' Later he owned a public house near Newmarket. He died of a heart attack.

[3] Although Bertie Smalls was undoubtedly the first of the modern supergrasses, in 1706 John Smith, a convicted housebreaker known as Half Hanged Smith because he had survived an attempt to hang him, was pardoned after he had accused about 350 pickpockets and housebreakers. He may well have been the original supergrass.

Bournemouth. Each time the operational method was almost identical. The robbers wore balaclavas, possibly with a nylon stocking underneath, and masks. The raids were in banking hours. A ladder was used to get over the security grilles put up in the 1960s but not yet made ceiling to counter, and a sledge-hammer was used to smash them. A shotgun would be fired into the ceiling to concentrate the minds of staff and any customers there might be in the bank. There would be one or two getaway cars waiting. The haul was usually substantial.

Smalls' name was in the frame. He had been wanted for the Bournemouth Lloyds Bank job in September 1970 and his wife, Diane, had been arrested along with others, including a Donald Barrett who had made a confession naming names. At the trial at Winchester Crown Court, Barrett pleaded guilty. His reward was a sentence of twelve years and a card posted from Spain from the others, who had all been acquitted, reading 'Wish you were here'.

Smalls had also been identified from a photograph in the Rogues Gallery at Scotland Yard as being involved in the National Westminster raid at Palmers Green in May 1972. The number plate of a Jaguar car which had been used in a trial run had been noted by an off-duty police officer. It was traced back to a garage at Tower Bridge in which Smalls was known to have an interest. That was certainly not sufficient to bring a charge. After a robbery at Barclays Bank on Wembley High Road in August 1972, which had netted over £138,000 in old notes, a special unit was formed by the police under the direction of Jim Marshall. It would eventually become the nucleus of the Robbery Squad.

The team began to accumulate snippets of evidence against Smalls. A woman clerk picked out his photograph as being involved at a robbery amassing £296,000 at Ralli Brothers in Hatton Garden in March 1969. Now the Bournemouth robbery was cross-checked even though he had never been arrested for it. Indeed at one time the Hampshire police had thought he had done away with the principal witness, Stella Robinson, the Smalls' au pair. Only the production of her to the police in London after the acquittal of Diane Smalls and the others had prevented a murder enquiry.

Three days before Christmas 1972 Inspector Victor Wilding went to see Smalls at his home in Selsdon. They now had sufficient evidence to justify an arrest. The only person there was Stella Robinson, who allowed them to look around and who, when pressed, told them Smalls was spending Christmas near Northampton. She did not know the address but she could show them. At 5.30 a.m. the police grouped outside the house and DCI Brewster of the Regional Crime Squad knocked on the door. Smalls in his underpants opened it and the police rushed forward, knocking Brewster over in the rush. Smalls said he had opened the door to let the cat in. It had a trick of scratching to gain admission. Diane Smalls commented, 'You let the rats in, not the cat.'

The arrest was totally unexpected. Members of the gang had paid £5000 each to a 'bent copper' to get an early warning of any arrest. Bertie had not paid his whack. Whether there was such a police officer able to obtain information is doubtful. It may have been a double scam to lure the robbers into a false sense of security.

Smalls was arrested for the Wembley bank robbery and was taken from Northampton to Wembley where he was questioned. On the journey he had made a tentative suggestion about doing a deal but when formally questioned he had said nothing. He was remanded in custody by Harrow Magistrates' Court for committal papers to be prepared. It was when the papers were served on the defence that Peter Donnelly, the solicitor's managing clerk who had acted for Smalls over the years, noticed a reference in them to 'outers'. Smalls would, so the statement of a police officer read, give names if he had 'outers'.

I went to see him in Brixton and asked, 'Did you say it?' He's hedgy. 'I've got to have guarantees,' he said. I went to see either Marshall or Wilding and asked if it was a serious proposition. 'Yes,' was the reply, 'but we don't believe he'll do it.' 'If he does what will you give us?' I asked, and it's then they start thinking it's possible. I went back to Smalls and said, 'Go and sit tight, keep your trap shut.' Then I got word they were interested.

I went and saw him again and told him he's got to put his cards on the table. They wanted robberies, names and so on, but not unnaturally he was reluctant to go into details at this stage. Finally we got a skeleton of the jobs from him in areas.

Then I arranged a meeting with Marshall and Wilding at Wembley. I went up there with Peter Steggles, the senior partner. They've got a clipboard with a list of names and robberies I could see upside down.

I said that everything on the board they could have plus XYZ additional robberies. That seemed to take them off guard. From then we had the advantage. They were reluctant and thought it would be difficult to have anything in writing. Nothing in writing – no deal. They said they'd take instructions. It was then going to have to go to Deputy Commissioner or Commissioner level.

We then tell them that we will draft heads of agreement as to our conditions and the main concerns were, one, the immunity from prosecution and, two, the security. There was no question of a reduced sentence. Another term was that it had to be agreed on by the DPP. We had two more meetings before they agreed to write a letter which was the final document and was basically word for word our heads of agreement.

It was then lined up that on receipt of that letter Smalls was to be produced at Harrow Court. The Bench had been squared to grant him bail – that had been dealt with before we arrived – and he was bailed into police custody and we're taken down to Wembley. We sat down twelve to fourteen hours a day while he reminisced.

By this time I had spread the word I was going on holiday, but the day he appeared people were asking what was happening. Where was he? Where was I? The word was out. That's why I think the rest of the team had paid their money.

Diane Smalls was never happy with the whole business. Donnelly met her on Brixton Hill one afternoon when he had been to see Bertie in prison and explained things. She stood by Smalls but their relationship was effectively over at this time anyway.

By now Smalls had given so much detail – the statement ran to sixty-five pages and covered eleven other suspects and twenty crimes – the police were starting to look for corroboration.

They heaved in Stella Robinson, got a statement from her as to how various robbers, including Bertie, had descended on a flop and when they were playing around with one of the sawn-offs had mistakenly fired it into the floorboards. They managed to identify the address, took the carpet up and the damage was still there with the pellets. But they still needed Diane and I went to her and said, if you don't do it the deal won't be accepted, because we didn't know whether they'd say the evidence was sufficient. Very reluctantly she made the statement, but she then refused to take the oath at court.

One of the final conditions was that if Smalls' statement wasn't used and he was not to be a witness and immunity given, then what amounted to a total confession would remain on police files and not be used against him at a trial.

But there was such a level of corruption at that time that sooner or later it would have got out and he'd have been dead.

During those three days Smalls stayed at Wembley with an armed guard. On the third day the police had to say yes or no. They said yes and Smalls was then produced at Harrow, granted formal bail and taken to a hotel by Wembley Stadium where he and his family were put in the suite in which David Cassidy had stayed the week before. It seemed to please him. Later he was moved out to a couple of addresses, being guarded by shifts of police officers. The only time Donnelly could see him was at an arranged point which he would be given half an hour beforehand. 'I'm sure there was a contract out. Publicity had it that it was £100,000 but I heard from Smalls' friend Jacky O'Connell that it was only £50,000.'

The sweep took place in the early hours of 6 April 1973 when over a hundred police officers rounded up twenty-seven of Smalls' former colleagues. Then the problem was whether Smalls, who was drinking heavily, would actually go through with things when it came to it.

The committal proceedings took place in a heavily guarded gymnasium in Wembley and Smalls appeared to give evidence minutes after his formal acquittal at the

Old Bailey. Jack Slipper, who had chased Train Robber Ronnie Biggs to Brazil and was now one of the senior officers in the case, recounts:

> He stood in the witness box, looking towards the magistrate, resting on his elbow. His eyes seemed dead and he almost mumbled his answers, so that a couple of times the magistrate had to ask him to speak up. I was really worried at that point that Bertie might be about to crack but, just in time, there was an incident which completely changed the picture.
>
> One of the prisoners was a Danny Allpress, a real comedian and a live wire, who had always run around with Smalls and had virtually been his assistant. Danny kept quiet at first then suddenly he leaned across the dock and said in a loud whisper, 'Well, Bertie, who's been having Slack Alice while you're away?' The remark got a lot of laughs from the prisoners, but Danny couldn't have made a more serious mistake. The remark brought Bertie to life. You could see the determination come into his eyes.[4]

Diane Smalls was not popular with the rest of the wives. Once because of friction she had left a holiday in Torremolinos early and had later chosen to spend her time in Tangier. But was the Slack Alice joke as crucial as Slipper believes? Says Donnelly:

> I don't think the Slack Alice joke enamoured them to him, but I don't think it was the end of the world. His attitude was that most of them when pulled in had tried to do exactly the same but he

[4] J. Slipper, *Slipper of the Yard*.

got in first. From that point of view he felt justified. There had also been some trouble earlier when he was on remand for possession of a firearm. He got out but he was skint and one of them was meant to have given Diane money to look after her. He hadn't and I think that annoyed him as well.

In July 1974 at the Central Criminal Court, Danny Allpress received a sentence of twenty-one years' imprisonment, reduced on appeal to eighteen years. Donald Barrett, who had already received twelve years for the Bournemouth job, received another seventeen years, reduced to twelve on appeal. Others had sentences of up to twenty-one years, reduced by the odd couple of years on their appeals.

One of them, Philip Morris, had been involved in a raid in February 1973 on the Unigate Dairies Depot in Ewell, Surrey. Morris had the job of standing guard over a young man, Frank Kidwell, who had just been named Milkman of the Year. The shotgun went off and Kidwell died. The raid netted £148,000. Morris pleaded guilty to Kidwell's manslaughter and received a seventeen-year sentence. For his part in the Wembley raid he received a concurrent sentence of twenty years, reduced by the Court of Appeal to twelve. His appeal against the seventeen-year sentence for manslaughter was dismissed.

The Court of Appeal was none too pleased with the Director of Public Prosecutions, Sir Norman Skelhorne, and his deal with Smalls. 'Above all else the spectacle of the Director recording in writing at the behest of a criminal like Smalls his undertaking to give immunity from further prosecution is one which we find distasteful. Nothing of a similar kind must happen again,' said Lord Justice Lawton.

After the trial Smalls had an armed guard for some

months, but eventually this was phased out and from then on the family lived more or less normally under another name. 'No one ever made threats to me,' says Smalls. 'Of course I didn't put myself about and if I went into a pub and saw someone who was a friend of the others I just left, but no, overall I had no trouble.'

Trouble or not he had set the tone for the 1970s. The opprobrium attached to most supergrasses never seems to have stuck to him. In a curious way he seems to have been regarded as an innovator.

John McVicar, talking about supergrasses in general and Smalls in particular, comments: 'Some of them are very strong people. Look at Bert. He was a good worker, although there was always something odd about him.'

What he did have was a sense of humour. After one bank raid in the Wood Green area a woman witness who was shopping in the High Road ran more or less slap-bang into the men escaping after the robbery. She had heard what she thought was a car backfiring but when three men wearing stocking masks rushed past her she knew exactly what had happened. She backed up against a wall and then started to walk to the end of the alleyway when a fourth man also wearing a mask loped towards her. Again she backed up but as he went past he stopped. 'What a way to earn a fucking living, eh girl?' said a sweating Smalls as he disappeared down the alleyway.

Smalls never did as well as he could have from his story. There was a short serialization in the newspapers, but a book he was planning never came to fruition due in part, perhaps, to both his and his ghost writer's current predilection for vodka.

The next in line to repeat, recant and recount all was a man who did publish his memoirs, designating himself King Squealer. Maurice O'Mahoney had been suspected for the attack on a Securicor van at Heston in West London. The van had been rammed with a tipper truck but the take had been a disappointing £20,000. He had been the victim of a tip-off that the raid would take place. After his arrest and that of other members of the gang the whisper went around that O'Mahoney was going to squeal. Two members of the team threatened to gouge out his eyes if he talked. O'Mahoney says that this is in part true but he was also worried by the contract of £2000 put out on his girlfriend Sue and his children. He also says he discovered a cyanide capsule had been smuggled into Brixton and the plan was to put it in his tea.[5] According to Jack Slipper, in whose charge O'Mahoney was, this was the turning point. He asked to see a senior officer. In his turn O'Mahoney's evidence led to some two hundred convictions and from then on the floodgates were opened.

After the Court of Appeal's comments on the Smalls deal, supergrasses could not expect to walk free. What they could expect was a sentence of around five years – the supergrass tariff – instead of one of twenty, during which time they would be kept in police custody while they gave their evidence and, allowing for remission and parole, released immediately or very soon after they had completed it. They could expect reasonable accommodation visits from their wives and sometimes the opportunity to go out to the local pubs with the detectives guarding them. There would be reward money and a new identity at the end of their sentence. It is hardly surprising that there has been a steady queue of men – Charlie Lowe, Leroy Williams, Donald Barrett (twice), John McCabe (who claimed to have made £8 million in four years) and many, many more – willing to testify against their former colleagues.

---

[5] M. O'Mahoney, *King Squealer*, pp. 129–30.

But whatever successes Marshall and Slipper had had with Smalls and O'Mahoney it was nothing to the success which would come to a rising star in the Met, Tony Lundy. In May 1977 Detective Chief Inspector Tony Lundy rejoined the Flying Squad, soon to be reorganized in part as the Robbery Squad with its headquarters at Finchley. It was Lundy who developed the supergrass into a whole business of its own.

Within six months he had his first major success with David Smith, arrested for an attack in September 1977 on two elderly men who collected their company's wages near the Thatched Barn, a restaurant at Borehamwood in Hertfordshire. The money was snatched but then one of the team, Alf Berkley, tore off the glasses of one of the men and squirted ammonia in his eyes. The man was almost completely blinded.

Smith turned supergrass, confessing to over sixty armed robberies. He was kept at Finchley police station for over fifteen months, at the end of which, as a result of his efforts, sixty-nine people were charged, of whom ninety per cent pleaded guilty. Two of the other robbers in the Thatched Barn team were also allowed to become supergrasses. One of them, George Williams, who had been offered the supergrass deal before Smith had rolled over but had initially held out, also received five years for a total of eighty robberies.

His evidence was necessary because there was a small problem with Smith. He had actually killed a man and the DPP's policy was to require a plea of guilty to a murder – which carried a mandatory life sentence – and so he could not be considered a credible witness. Smith had coshed Kurt Hess, an elderly factory owner, during a robbery in Shoreditch. Hess had died three weeks later. However, Smith's luck was in. A statement was obtained from a pathologist which showed that Hess' poor health had contributed to his death. A charge of manslaughter was sufficient and so Smith could be reinstated as a prosecution witness.[6] Later the rules were relaxed and supergrasses who had pleaded guilty to murder were allowed to give evidence for the Crown, in one case with fairly disastrous results.

In fact George Williams' hands were none too clean either. In 1967 he and Smith had kidnapped the manager of a North London supermarket, Walter Price, to get the keys from his safe. The 16-stone Williams, known as 'Fat George', coshed Price, who died eight weeks later from heart failure. Price had staggered home with a lump on his head described by his widow as 'as big as an egg'. When she heard Williams had received the tariff five years she commented, 'That seems a very light sentence for murder.'[7] Judge Michael Argyle, his hands tied by public policy, commented that he considered Smith and Williams as 'two of the most dangerous criminals in British history', adding that whilst he accepted they were telling the truth 'it was nauseating to hear these hypocrites and that as a matter of policy they have only been sentenced to five years each'.

But Smith did not last long on the outside. Throughout his adult life he had been an unsuccessful career criminal and he only spent short periods out of prison. On 29 September 1986 he was caught in a raid on a Securicor vehicle in Golders Green along with another

---

[6] Smith was also reputed to have killed a bookmaker, Harry Barham, found shot in the back of the head in his car in Hackney; £40,000 had been stolen from him. There was no hard evidence against Smith and he was never charged. In fairness many a name was put up for the Barham killing including that of the ubiquitous Teddy Machin.

[7] For a detailed account of the successes and more importantly the failures of the supergrass system, see Andrew Jennings, Paul Lashmar and Vyv Simson, *Scotland Yard's Cocaine Connection*.

former supergrass, Ron Simpson. Smith again turned supergrass but this time he did not live long enough to testify. In a cell which had been hung with balloons for his birthday five days earlier, Smith cut his throat with a razor blade on Monday, 13 October. Simpson was gaoled for twenty-one years. Perhaps, when it came to it, Smith was the better off.

Recruit followed recruit through the Lundy supergrass factory, some thirty of them defended by Roland Pelly, a Bishop's Stortford solicitor who had been outside the mainstream of criminal defence practice. In fact he had been the DPP's agent in Hertfordshire in the early 1970s when the DPP used to send cases to local firms of solicitors.

One of Lundy's less successful supergrasses was Billy Amies who, dressed as a policeman, had threatened his victim in a robbery with castration and had the man's daughter stripped to her underwear, asking, 'How would you like to see your daughter raped?' Amies served only twenty-four months in prison, but although he had named fifty-eight criminals it seems he was responsible for the conviction of only five.

But in many ways, the seemingly prize catch was nothing to do with Lundy. This was Maxwell Thomas Piggott, who was to turn what the police thought would be the major supergrass and would give evidence against Ronnie Knight, considered by the police to be one of the top figures in London's underworld. Bradshaw, as Piggott became known, had a long and interesting criminal career. In September 1965 he was charged with housebreaking and in November of the same year with throwing acid at the police, for which he was sentenced to seven years' imprisonment. He escaped from Wormwood Scrubs in 1968. In 1969 he popped up in Brighton running a long firm fraud for which he received six years at Lewes Assizes. When on 17 January 1980 he pleaded guilty before Mr Justice Comyn to his part in the Zomparelli murder and numerous armed robberies, he was praised for his courage in naming 105 criminals in a long confession. He was gaoled for life. This was to be the start of a major breakthrough in the war against professional crime. However, when Knight and his co-defendant Nicky Gerard were acquitted of the Zomparelli murder, plans to use Bradshaw in other trials were quickly shelved and he was returned to prison. He served ten years for the murder before his release.[8]

On 24 March 1980 a robbery went off which surpassed the Great Train Robbers' caper. It was also one which would have the greatest repercussions on the credibility of Scotland Yard and, in particular, Tony Lundy. Three hundred and twenty-one silver ingots of bullion, worth £3.4 million, were stolen from a lorry on its way from London to Tilbury Docks, when a gang of bogus traffic officials together with a man wearing a police uniform flagged down the lorry and held up the crew at gunpoint.

The instigator of the enterprise was Michael Gervaise, six foot, a fluent linguist and a skilled burglar alarm engineer, described as a 'balding figure with the mild air of a retail tobacconist'; he was another who would become a supergrass. He had received eighteen months for his part in the 1975 Bank of America robbery but otherwise had no record worth speaking of. Together with an old friend, Micky Sewell, who had been given bail on a charge of armed robbery so that he too could act as an informant, Gervaise put together a team which included Lennie Gibson, Rudolpho Aguda and Aguda's nephew, Renalto 'Ron' Aguda. Ron's specialities included the ability to uncouple trailers from their tractor units at speed.

Gervaise had on his team a number of bent police

[8] See Chapter 12.

officers who were paid to overlook his activities. One, Terence Donovan, who later served a prison sentence, was employed as a 'security adviser' after his retirement from the force. His job was to advise Gervaise of suitable places to burgle. Another bribed by Gervaise was the notorious Alec Eist.

The lorry was stopped by Gervaise, flagging it down wearing his policeman's uniform – supplied by a sergeant in the Met to Billy Young, who had passed it and some other uniforms to Lennie Gibson – and directing it into a lay-by for a bogus traffic census. The guards were threatened that their kneecaps would be blown off if they did not co-operate and away went Gervaise and co with the silver to store it in a slaughter, a rented lock-up garage, near Oakwood tube station at the northern end of the Piccadilly line. Gibson and Aguda senior were the only ones to hold keys to it and they had them on them when arrested.

Sewell was on bail at the time for a £200,000 wages snatch and was being used as a snout by the then DCI Bill Peters, a large and flamboyant officer on the Flying Squad. His mission for Peters was to infiltrate another robbery team headed by Ronnie Johnson and his information led to the arrest of that team hours after they had shot a guard in a robbery at a bank in East Finchley.[9] One of the men soon accepted Lundy's offer to turn supergrass and he named Tony Fiori, an Islington thief, who graduated from grass to supergrass with some facility. In turn he named Gervaise.

It was only a matter of time before Gervaise joined the supergrass circuit. And it was only a matter of time before someone claimed the £300,000 reward being put

[9] Peters was one of the few police officers to sue for libel. On 24 July 1985 he was awarded £10,000 for false allegations of corruption by the *Observer* over the silver bullion robbery.

up by the insurers. The claimant would be Roy Garner, part-owner of a thoroughly disreputable night club, Eltons, which more or less backed on to Tottenham police station, and a man closely associated with Lundy as well as Gibson. He had turned down an approach to do the silver bullion job.

The important thing was the recovery of the silver. Gibson when arrested held out for some time as to its whereabouts until he had spoken with Aguda senior. Quite clearly there was much to be discussed because Gibson then had a two-hour private meeting with Lundy.

On the night of 4 June 1980 the police went to the lock-up at Oakwood, kicked in the door and recovered the silver – all but twelve bars worth £120,000. No one has ever been able to establish where they went to, but there again no one has ever seemed to worry too much about it. Nor has anyone ever satisfactorily explained why it was necessary to kick the door down. After all Aguda and Gibson had been arrested with their keys to the slaughter on them. Gibson and the Agudas received ten years each on pleas of guilty, rather more than the seven they had been half-promised. Micky Sewell had long disappeared – tipped off by a police officer – and Gervaise had his five years. 'Dave Granger', a pseudonym for Roy Garner, the close drinking companion of Lundy, received the £300,000 reward. Garner also submitted claims through Lundy for payment for information relating to a Brinks-Mat security van hold-up in Hampstead in December 1979 and a fraudulent insurance claim based on a faked armed robbery, the reward for which was £75,000. After much haggling Garner received £178,000. Over the years he is believed to have accumulated over £500,000 through rewards recommended by Lundy.

By then the supergrass system was becoming more and

more complicated. There seemed to be competing teams of supergrasses: those who gave evidence under Lundy's aegis and those, such as John Moriarty, who gave evidence against Lundy's friend Garner. Moriarty had twice been shot by rivals and had served periods of imprisonment. Now he decided to give evidence and to implicate Roy Garner.

'I never knew why he did it,' says Dave Brady. 'I was the officer called to the Favourite, the pub in Hornsey Rise where he'd been kneecapped. I asked what had happened and all he said was, "I fell down the fucking stairs, didn't I?"'

In the early 1970s Garner, together with a friend, Kenny Ross, had purchased premises in Upper Street, Islington, and then tried to evict the tenants. When this failed the premises were fired. Now Moriarty was prepared to name them in his statement as the organizers of the arson attacks.

Yet another series of supergrasses was being run from Reading by Number 5 Regional Crime Squad, under the name Operation Carter. In 1977 a security van at Hemel Hempstead in Hertfordshire had been taken for £34,000 and three years later a North London robber, Freddie Sinfield, was arrested. The name he put in the frame was Billy Young, Gervaise's police uniform supplier. And this time a supergrass was prepared to talk about corrupt police officers.[10]

Perhaps 1979 was the Year of the Supergrass. At least twenty leading villains had queued up to give evidence for the prosecution. According to Scotland Yard, serious crime had tumbled from an all-time high in 1977, when it had netted £166 million. James George Gallant had joined the list of supergrasses following the discovery of £1900, his share of a £4600 robbery, in a cornflakes

---

[10] See Chapter 10 for the continuation of this enthralling saga.

packet. He informed on twenty-one major criminals. Assistant Commissioner David 'Crazy Horse' Powis observed, 'London's criminal fraternity is experiencing its lowest ebb ever.'[11]

Another attraction for the supergrass was the attitude of the Home Secretary. In that year, using his 'prerogative of mercy', he cut the prison sentences of seventy-two informers for their 'assistance to the authorities'. Leroy Davies was a particular beneficiary. For his role as informant the Court of Appeal had cut his ten-year sentence to one of seven. The Home Secretary cut it further to four years, seven months and seven days, and released him on parole, after which he gave his life story to the *Daily Express* describing how he had 'repaid his debt to society'.

He disappeared in the 1980s after he had been acquitted of a robbery at the French Revolution public house in Putney. His brother Glanford, who pleaded guilty and implicated Leroy, received five years' imprisonment. It was alleged that Davies had escaped after firing one barrel of a sawn-off shotgun at the police. He had told the jury, which took only ninety minutes to acquit him, that he would never have participated in such an inefficient robbery. Judge Lawson was not so impressed. 'I have no doubt as to the true identity of that gunman,' he told the jury as he invited them to stay behind and listen to the confession of Glanford which had not been in evidence at the trial.

But were the supergrasses all that major? One criminal lawyer commented, perhaps a trifle sourly, 'We seem to be catching the big fish as informers but they in turn are only netting the minnows.'

In recent times supergrasses have not had it all their own way.

---

[11] *Daily Telegraph*, 29 November 1979.

Supergrass trials have fallen into disrepute and supergrasses aren't used quite as much. But what they did was present to your stock gangland criminal a real threat. Gangs haven't stayed together because of that risk. The risk of being supergrassed got very high about seven or eight years ago. Then jurors started to acquit because supergrasses were being offered immunity or extremely low sentences, money was being offered or facilities in custody, so they died off.[12]

More recently life has become more dangerous for supergrasses than in the days of Bertie Smalls. In April 1991 Dave Norris was shot dead in the driveway of his home at Belvedere, Kent. He was reputed to be a grass and, worse than that:

> He used to set people up on jobs that he had done himself. He would carry out a warehouse job, tell somebody there was still stuff to be taken and then tip the police off.
> The police won't say he's a grass because being bumped off is not a terrific advert for a career in grassing. He was on Rule 43 inside which tells its own story.[13]

---

[12] Michael Mansfield QC in D. Campbell, *That was Business, This is Personal*.

[13] Duncan Campbell, 'Gangland Britain', *Weekend Guardian*, 14–15 December 1991. Rule 43 is protected accommodation away from the mainstream of the prison and is used to house sex offenders and informers along with convicted police officers.

10

Helpers and Hinderers

The underworld cannot flourish without the active co-operation of those in the half-world which straddles crime and respectability. They are the people who, whilst they might not dream of committing a robbery themselves, will assist in covering up, helping obtain bail, standing surety, providing an alibi, giving succour to the relatives of the 'aways'. They are publicans, garage proprietors, scrap-metal dealers, owners of small businesses, betting shop owners, barristers, solicitors and their clerks and, above all, policemen. Sometimes the help is provided for friendship, sometimes for fear, sometimes for money, sometimes innocently, and often for a combination of reasons. Sometimes the helper is a criminal groupie who just does it for kicks.

Jimmy was a bloke who had shops all over London and one of them was a really good one. He used to drink with me and Lennie and then one day just says, 'Can I come with you on a job?' just like that. He was in his early thirties at the time, never done anything wrong at all. He got hooked. From that day he never went back to the shops. Now he's in his fifties doing fifteen years.

Bail has always been an essential requirement of the arrested person. Just as the prudent traveller will settle domestic affairs before going away on a holiday, so will the professional criminal. In essence there is no difference between a trip to the Isle of Wight by a holidaymaker or business person and one by the professional criminal, except that the latter's visit is likely to be of longer duration. It is only sensible that he should provide for his wife and children by doing another couple of jobs while on bail, arranging for their comfort and, if necessary, providing a beard[1] so that the wife will not be tempted to take up with another man during his absence.

On a Friday night we used to collect for the 'aways' in five or six pubs. We each had a book coded to show what people gave and when it was nice and busy we'd start collecting. People would put their hands in their pockets and give what they had. It might be a quid or two or, if they'd done well, a fiver or even a tenner. If they didn't they'd get a hard look and if that didn't do any good then, when they went to the toilet, we'd follow and give them a spanking. Then we'd go with a girl to see the wives and give them the wages. You never visit a woman on her own whilst the old man's away. It looks bad for her and a neighbour might get the wrong impression and say something out of turn.

Sureties would be publicans, garage owners, wives and mothers, anyone without recent convictions to whom the police could not reasonably object.

Sometimes the easy part was getting bail for the client. The most difficult part was to find a surety

---

[1] A paid escort, usually homosexual.

who was acceptable to the police. In the days before the advent of the Crown Prosecution Service in 1985, when the officer opposed bail himself, if bail was granted he would regard the provision of a surety as a sort of re-match and oppose those proffered on the slightest grounds. The only way round this was to put the surety before the magistrates and see if they were brave enough to overrule the officer's objections.

Although illegal, a sensible surety would require indemnification.

I stood for Harry in £10,000 and the day of the trial he goes back to Ireland. I'm there at the Bailey telling the judge that I'm now out of work and I'd seen him up to the night before so the judge only takes £3000 which I have to pay in a year. Harry's given me the £10,000 and has told me to keep what I'm not fined. He was a real gentleman.

Of course, outsiders as opposed to 'family' would not stand bail without a fee, particularly if they had been required to negotiate with the police in the first place. They were also required to try to eliminate or have watered down certain damaging pieces of evidence.

The first time I ever knew about the police being bent was in 1963 in Borehamwood. A mate and I were nicked in a stolen car with pickaxe handles. The copper comes into the cell and asks if I'm from Kentish Town and I say yes. Then he asks me if I know GB. I think he's on the pump [seeking information] but I still say yeah. That evening I get a visit from a friend who says, 'I've done the business'. And he had. It cost £300 to get six

months and it was good value. We pleaded to the
car and offensive weapons. It could have been a
conspiracy. In them days the police stood by their
word. They dropped evidence or you wound up
with a very small sentence.

Sometimes half the money would be paid in advance
but often it was unnecessary. 'If a publican or bookmaker could get the business done for £500 then I would
expect to pay £1000. In those days the police were
honest. If they agreed something they honoured it.'

There were professional straighteners including one
who owned greetings card shops and was said to have a
lock on a Commander at the Yard. But some could do
better than others.

Old Bill knows you've got a few quid and it's not
your time to go – they can save you for a better
day. They've got two or three of you so they can
afford to leave you out. A friend'll go to a known
man and he'll straighten it up. You get bail to show
good faith. How much? Depending on what you're
on and how much they know you've got in your
pocket. Can be anything. Likely you never see
them. They've got the SP[2] and they won't take
money unless they know you're not iffy.

Sometimes it went wrong. 'I only recall one case when
the cozzer went bent and that was when a West End
copper agreed to get my mate out of a drink driving for
£1000. It all went wrong but I think that was because my
friend was a spade and the copper didn't like spades.'

Sometimes it appeared to have gone all wrong but
hadn't. A solicitor relates:

[2] Literally starting price, but in this context knowledge.

I attended an identification parade at Brixton Prison in the late 1960s for two of my clients charged with bank robberies. The parade took hours with probably about twenty witnesses. Just at the end they were picked out by one person. I telephoned one of the wives to tell them what had happened and she just wailed down the telephone. 'They can't have been; we paid £6000 for that parade'.

Of course, for a variety of reasons criminals like to pretend they have the police in their pockets but I think she was telling the truth for two reasons. The first is that the person turned out to be a police constable who later made a statement saying that whilst he believed the two he had identified were the people he had seen, he could not be sure. The second was that I met one of the wives twenty years later and the first thing she said was, 'I haven't seen you since we paid all that money for the ID.'

On other occasions it was never quite clear whether the money had been well spent.

Just before a bail application in a very substantial jewellery robbery the defendant's wife came up to me and said, 'He's sweet as a nut. You can ask him anything you want.' But any question I asked got a wrong answer. Like: 'He's married with two children? and the reply came: 'I don't think he's married to the woman he's living with. I know the children are by a different father.' It took me half an hour to convince the bench to give the man bail. The client's wife ran up to the police officer afterwards and said, 'Thank you, you were wonderful.' Personally I thought I was the wonderful one. I thought she'd have been better giving her money to me. But then at the trial the officer got up and said the principal witness had gone to Switzerland. There was no point in having an adjournment because he had told him he wouldn't come back.

Negotiations took place in clubs like the Premier off Wardour Street where detectives, barristers, solicitors' clerks and the underworld mixed, or in public houses such as the Prince of Wales in Lant Street in the Borough once run by a member of the Foreman family. Peta Fordham wrote:

> At one end sit the bloods – a lot of failed boxers etc. who are gang strong-arm men. At the other sit the wives, chastely excluded from the conversation of their lords, and drinking port and lemon. This is where the dishonest police get their wages.
>
> The Prince of Wales is a well-known place to fix surrender bargains, as well as to pay over, so that the Flies[3] have legitimate grounds in being there. X and Y [senior police officers] are said to get their wages there through an informer called Z.

But the underworld accepts that in a relationship with the police they are the underdogs. They must expect a certain amount of harassment as part of the toleration of their activities. As one officer says:

> Now this family is a great example. The old man was a great rogue, in fact some of the most spectacular robberies in Kent were his doing, but he lived in abject squalor. There was a huge family.

[3] Police officers. Fly was a Victorian term for a police officer and also for a cadger or beggar. Peta Fordham had something of a sense of humour.

The wife was a prolific breeder and it seemed like there were kids from two to forty. Anyway one of the youngsters gets nicked for some shoplifting and we want to give him a caution. You've got to have a parent there and so I was sent to get the old man.

I go round in the car and at his gate is a fucking mongrel Alsatian standing like the Hound of the Baskervilles. I thought 'Fuck, he's going to bite me,' but I got to go in so I ease past him and he follows me up the path.

I go in, dog behind me, and the place stinks. My feet stick to the carpet, and they're burning bits of furniture in the grate and drinking tea out of jamjars.

So I say to Freddy, 'Look we've got the kid, come down the nick and get him.' And he's humming and hawing because he doesn't like nicks and he's pissed off the kid's got caught, when the Alsatian wanders over to the grate and drops three great turds on the fire. Freddy doesn't say a word. Doesn't give the dog a kick or nothing. Doesn't bat an eyelid.

Now, I'm choking and gagging with this dog shit cooking in the fire and eventually I get Freddy to agree that I go on back and he'll follow down in the van in five minutes.

So off I go, get in the motor and there's a rapping at the window and it's Freddy. I wind it down and say, 'What's up now?' and he says, 'Mr Smith, Mr Smith, you've forgotten your dog.'

And if the police could not or would not help, then there was always the possibility of a spot of jury-nobbling to ease passages; and the longer the trial went on the easier it was. Charlie Richardson describes his reaction to the jury in the Mr Smith's Club case:

We was in court and we heard all the names read out and we looked as they come in and you look at the people as the kind of people you can get into. If a man comes in from the East End you find a man who lives in the next road and you ask him what he is like. If they are nice people they go round and fucking see them for you, you understand what I mean. It's all right that way . . . [4]

The jury had been got at in many major trials, including the Heath Row robbery, before the police discovered that, despite the apparent cost in manpower, it was sensible to protect jurors. The jury was protected in the Kray case and has been in most of the major cases thereafter. Nevertheless it was left unprotected in the Dulwich robbery case of 1981, which went to a re-trial. In the first round it was discovered that no less than ten of the jurors lived on Tobin territory in the Greenwich–Bermondsey area and on the third day a juror told the judge her son knew one of the defendants. In the re-trial two members of the jury complained they had received threatening telephone calls but Tobin was still convicted. Now in major trials jurors are kept out of sight of the public gallery.

Even so, with a little ingenuity juries can be got at. For example, a solicitor can obtain names and addresses of jurors quite legitimately. After a re-trial John Reed and Peter Mitchell were jailed for twenty-two years each for a raid on a Brinks-Mat van near Brentwood in Essex – they had sealed off the road, smashed the van open with a hijacked crane and fired at the guards inside, escaping with £500,000.

At the first hearing, after a list of the jurors had quite properly been obtained, a second list came into the

[4] R. Parker, *Rough Justice*, p. 310.

hands of nobblers and they assigned a team to each member of the jury. The trial was halted when four jurors were seen in the same pub as relatives of the two defendants. The solicitor refuted suggestions made by the officer in the case that he had handed over the list for nobbling purposes. 'There had been widespread publicity about the robbery in Essex and we wanted to make sure that no one on the jury came from that area,' he said. He invited the officer to repeat the allegations made in court outside, where legal privilege against defamation does not run.[5] There appears to be no record he did so.

In the pre-PACE days, when access to legal representation was denied to suspects until the questioning had finished, solicitors instructed by major families were expected to have sufficient rapport with a senior officer to be able to get into a police station to provide succour and encouragement. A senior managing clerk says:

This was a murder and a very bad one – a security guard – and my junior clerk is sent down. He rings me at 4 p.m. and says, 'I'm at Leman Street; it's hot in the kitchen and they won't let me near the front door. Can you pop over and see what you can do?'

As I went in, there was a most disagreeable atmosphere and then the DCI walks in with his hat on the side of his head.

'Hello, Sam boy,' he says, 'what you doing here?' And when I explained he told the officers in the case to let my boy in. So then the DCI takes me up to his office and asks for two brandies. When an aide brings them he tells him to take them away and get a proper bottle. 'That's for visitors – bring my stuff,' he says and he pours and pours

[5] *Today*, 11 April 1987.

them out. I was emptying half mine into the rubber plant; it was shameful really. He was legless by the time we finished chatting.

But whilst the underworld is convinced that if things seem to be going badly in a trial the police are not above alleging jury interference even if none has occurred, then help can sometimes come from unexpected sources. According to the *News of the World*, an Acton Crown Court usher boasted he could help if a defendant needed to 'sort out a trial' and would provide jurors' names and addresses.[6] He certainly had the right connections. A relation was the man paid by Jack Spot to mind him when he fell out with Hill and who was out with his girlfriend the fateful night his employer was slashed.

Apart from the police, the occasional too-close involvement of solicitors or barristers in the crime has always been a source of concern. It is still used by some judges as an argument against allowing solicitors rights of audience in the Crown Court.

The first and certainly the most infamous case in modern, or at least Victorian times was that of a fashionable barrister, James Townsend Saward, known in the underworld as Jem the Penman, who employed a gang of safebreakers and con artists to obtain blank cheques. He would then obtain the genuine signature of his proposed victim. He worked on a world-wide basis and on one occasion was able to cash forged cheques in London drawn on a Hobart bank in Tasmania before they had even been missed. Saward was deeply involved in the first Great Train Robbery and when the thieves on that operation fell out he went down with them. He was sentenced to transportation for life.[7]

[6] 25 March 1990.

[7] For footnote, see opposite.

In the early 1900s one of the most adroit and dishonest lawyers was the ex-public school, handsome, charming Arthur Newton, a man with great gifts of advocacy, who duped Crippen into retaining him and who sold both a forged 'confession' to the *Evening Times* and a forged letter said to be by Crippen to the Horatio Bottomley-owned *John Bull*. Newton was suspended by the Law Society and in 1913 was sent to prison for three years over a forged stock deal involving the title deeds to timberland in Canada, a case he defended himself. On his release he became a marriage broker, matching the impoverished holders of titles to those without the titles but with the cash to buy them.

But Newton was eclipsed in the 1920s by the activities of a Charles Sharman, a well-known police court advocate working in the East End. The judge, Sir Travers Humphreys, father of Christmas, recalled that Sharman earned his sincerest respect. 'He struck me as one of the few natural lawyers whom I had come across. He never talked nonsense and seldom repeated himself, with the result that the magistrates, whether lawyers or laymen, always listened with respect to his arguments.'[8]

It came therefore as something of a shock to Sir Travers to find that Sharman, in the best tradition of Saward, had been the head of a gang of international thieves which specialized in stealing mail-bags. In 1922 there had been an incident when a mail-bag containing a consignment of £50 bonds had been stolen from a train somewhere between London and Liverpool. These had been cashed in Belgium by an old gentleman giving the

---

[7] There is a full and most entertaining account of Saward and his associate Edward Agar, who actually carried out the robbery on the London–Folkestone train, relieving it of gold being sent to France, in Donald Thomas' *Honour amongst Thieves* (London, Weidenfeld and Nicolson, 1991).

[8] Sir T. Humphreys, *A Book of Trials*, p. 134.

name of Johnson. Sharman, who was then in his early seventies, was identified by a bank clerk but nothing came of it. Nor did a second incident come to trial. Within a month another mail-bag went missing, this time between Birmingham and London. Sharman was again implicated but said a poor man had picked up the bond certificate and brought it into his office. Next year he was identified as cashing a stolen Mexican bond in Manchester but he provided an alibi. Finally his luck ran out when he was identified by nine people who placed him in Canada selling a stolen war bond from the same bag which had contained the Mexican bond. Because of his age – he was then seventy-five – he received a sentence of three years' penal servitude and was ordered to pay the costs of the prosecution.

Lord Goddard believed there were eleven dishonest solicitors in London and five barristers, and he knew the names of them all. For years Scotland Yard kept a black list of solicitors believed to be too actively involved in helping their clients. Says a solicitor:

> The old question asked at parties, 'How do you defend people you believe are guilty?' is easy to answer. Whatever you may think of a client or his case, if he says he didn't do it then you defend him. If you start trying to be judge and jury and only defending the ones you believe to be innocent then you shouldn't be in the game anyway.
>
> I think over all the years I've only defended about a couple of dozen whom I've really thought were innocent and they're the really worrying ones to defend. I remember one who was said to be on a bank robbery begging and praying us to believe he was innocent, and I did. After he was acquitted he was unsporting enough to tell me he was the driver. He was killed in a car accident about three

months later. Sometimes I do wonder if there is such a thing as divine retribution.

It's very difficult to walk a line. You are meant to advise the client that he has no defence, so you point out that this and that are fatal flaws in his case so why doesn't he plead guilty? The next thing you know is he comes back and says now this version is the truth, or even worse goes off to a solicitor down the road and says his brief doesn't believe him and you're sacked. Frankly if I couldn't invent better defences than they come up with I'd be ashamed.

Solicitors are at risk from their clients. In 1955 one of the first post-war solicitors found to have been 'middled' was Ben Cantor. He had been one of the solicitors who acted for the Messina brothers and was then acting for Joseph Grech, another Maltese who was sent to prison for three years for a housebreaking offence. Grech had seemingly had an unshakeable defence. Part of the evidence against him had been that the key to the burgled premises had been found on him. Grech maintained that it fitted his own front door and therefore was of no significance. The jury found it was and, from his cell, Grech unloaded a series of legal bombs.

He had, he said, given a Morris Page around £150 to hand to Detective Sergeant Robertson, who had been in charge of the initial case and who made the key to the burgled premises available so that a locksmith could make a lock to be fitted to Grech's front door. There was to have been a further £150 given to Robertson on an acquittal. He also alleged that Robertson had coached Ben Cantor about the questions to be put at the trial.

When Robertson, Page and Cantor appeared at the Old Bailey charged with conspiracy to pervert the course of justice, Grech unloaded some more bombs. His conviction, he said, had been brought about by perjured evidence of other officers acting on the instructions of an Inspector Charles Jacobs, attached to West End Central.[9] Jacobs, he said, had asked him for £2000 so that none of his flats or brothels would be raided. After negotiations the terms were set at £500 down and £30 a week. Cantor, said Grech, had been the bagman taking the £100 to give to Jacobs. According to Grech, Cantor came back saying, 'He wants £500.'

When he came to give evidence Cantor was in difficulties over his relationship with Tony Micallef, a brother-in-law of the Messinas, who had been accepted as a surety by Robertson.

'Can you imagine any honest policeman agreeing to take Micallef as a surety for this man Grech?'
'That is a difficult question to answer.'
'I think it is a simple question. Try to answer it . . .'
'It depends on the circumstances.'

Cantor received two years' imprisonment, as did Robertson; the intermediary, Morris Page, fifteen months.

In November 1955 the *Daily Mail* revealed that Detective Superintendent Bert Hannam had lodged a report with the Commissioner, Sir John Nott-Bower, revealing 'a vast amount of bribery and corruption

---

[9] In February 1956 Jacobs was dismissed from the force, having been found guilty by a disciplinary board of assisting a prostitute to obtain premises, of failing to disclose in court a man's previous convictions, and of failing to account for property taken from an arrested man. His application to the High Court for an order quashing the verdict, on the grounds that by reason of his mental health at the time he was unfit to prepare his defence, was rejected.

among certain uniformed officers attached to West End Station'. According to Hannam's report the corruption involved 'club proprietors, prostitutes, gaming-house owners, brothel-keepers and men living on immoral earnings'. It appeared that Hannam had interviewed no fewer than forty men serving prison sentences arising out of West End vice.

The extent of corruption can be gauged by the fact that it was found that some uniformed patrolmen in the vice-ridden streets of Soho were receiving up to £60 a week in bribes. Hannam found, so the article said, that 'evidence was "cooked" by police officers to benefit accused people. Details of previous convictions were suppressed in many cases so that men standing on charges were fined nominal sums instead of going to prison.'

Under a heading 'Tipped Off?' readers were treated to the following:

Gaming houses, where faro and chemin de fer were being played quite openly, were tipped off at a fee when a raid was to take place. Proprietors were warned to get 'mugs' in on a certain day, so that the regular customers could escape arrest. Brothel-keepers were told that certain evidence could be adjusted for a price. Huge sums of money changed hands. The 'adjustment' was for an officer to say in evidence that upon the raid taking place he found a number of fully clothed women on the premises, whereas, in fact, they were nude. That gave the premises an air of respectability – and halved the fine.

The hundreds of prostitutes who infest the West End streets are included in the bribery racket. One officer is pointed out by them to be the richest policeman in the Force. Most of these unfortunate girls appear on a special 'roster' due for appearance at a magistrates' court on a certain day for the usual £2 fine for soliciting. If the day does not happen to suit the woman, a 'fee' is paid for postponement.

Nott-Bower acted swiftly. Summoning effectively the whole of 'C' Division, he climbed on to two tables and gave his men a pep-talk.

I wish to tell you how much I deplore the imputations which have recently been made in the press which reflect on the reputation of the whole force and, in particular, all of 'C' Division.

In one of today's papers reference has been made to certain statements regarding the officers of 'C' Division in a report submitted to me by Detective Superintendent Herbert Hannam.

I want it to be known that there is no truth whatever in this, and that none of the subjects referred to in that report have been so much as mentioned in any report submitted to me by the Superintendent.

There was something of what would now be called a damage limitation exercise approach from the authorities. In a statement to the press, Nott-Bower went on to deny that 450 men might be transferred from Central London. 'Nor is there any truth in suggestions that "many officers" have come under suspicion.' Certain confidential papers had gone missing but 'neither is there truth in reports that "top secret" or even "secret" papers have been missed from Scotland Yard. Those that were found in a house have no security importance whatever.' The next day the then Chief Magistrate appeared at Bow Street to scotch the rumours. The aim could not, he said, 'be other than to sap the confidence of the public in law enforcement, both outside and, perhaps of even greater significance, inside this court.' He went on to exculpate 'C' Division, adding that the article so far as it purported to reproduce the report was 'utterly misleading and most mischievous'. He had not, he said, read the report.

And in the House of Commons Sir Hugh Lucas-Tooth commented that the 'general accusations made in certain quarters against the police are unwarranted and unsubstantiated'.

The newspapers were not satisfied. Cassandra in the *Daily Mirror* and the then *Manchester Guardian* both rose in defence of the *Mail*. Cassandra wrote: 'The Police Commissioner, the magistrates and the Home Office should reserve some of their congratulations for the day when Central London is cleansed of blackguards, thieves, and pimps who publicly flaunt their power and their riches.'

In December 1955 it was revealed that the wardrobe locker of a Detective Sergeant who had been assisting Detective Superintendent Stephen Glander, who was either helping Hannam or working independently on an enquiry investigating 'allegations of professional misconduct among policemen', had been forced. Papers had been disturbed but nothing had been taken. An enquiry which involved a number of officers submitting their fingerprints for comparison seems to have come to nothing.

Sometimes, of course, the information came out unwittingly. 'We had our own inside tap,' says a surviving member of the Billy Hill organization. 'One of the Assistant Commissioners was having it off with a bird on the strength and she used to tell us everything he told her in bed.'

The next famous name to go was the barrister Patrick Marrinan who had defended so ably in the series of Spot trials. He was disbarred on 28 June 1957 for his association with Billy Hill. His telephone had been tapped and conversations between him and Hill had been recorded. This was in clear breach of the code of conduct of members of the Bar that they should not have direct contact with the client. It is also fair to say that he did not enjoy the respect of the Establishment, with whom he regularly quarrelled. It cannot have helped him that on one occasion he fought Edward Clarke, later an Old Bailey judge and scion of the great legal family, in the robing room at Chelmsford Assizes. He returned to his native Ireland where, with his brother, he enjoyed great success in a criminal practice there.

Throughout the sixties and seventies efforts were made to prosecute dishonest solicitors but, as with police officers similarly accused, juries were unwilling to convict. Solicitors can also, of course, be used innocently.

In the 1960s, the heyday of the Friday bank robbery, you would find your waiting room full of clients who'd brought their friends in to see you. 'Mind if Tommy comes in with me?' they'd ask. Then one of them would ask the time and say 'I didn't think it was so late.' When you went out at lunchtime you'd read a bank had been robbed. There you were providing an alibi if needed. The reason was that all the known faces would be pulled in rather like the round-up of suspects after the German officer has been shot in *Casablanca*. At least the alibi was a genuine one and you did get to take some instructions from the real client.

But it didn't make for a good reputation.
Some solicitors would actively assist:

I had a client accused of an LF in the early 1970s and the principal Crown witness was his former girlfriend. Her statement was to the effect that she had gone with her boyfriend (my client) to see a solicitor in Wembley and the conversation had gone sómething like this.

'The gentleman asked my boyfriend his name and he said, "John Smith". "Like that is it?" asked the solicitor. "What is it – an LF?" My boyfriend nodded. "Is it too late for a fire then?" asked the solicitor.

Over the years, Norman Beach of the firm Beach and Beach fell foul both of the coùrts and the Law Society. Unimpressed with the identification evidence against his client, he sought to test the ability of the principal witness to recognize the defendant when he was wearing a ginger wig in the dock. The client was acquitted but Beach was convicted of conspiracy to pervert the course of justice. The jury's finding was overturned in the Court of Appeal in September 1957.

His solicitor son Martin Beach believes his father's action, in the days when identification of a defendant in the dock at court was common, was important in proving that in many cases it was the simple fact of being in the dock which caused the identification. 'The wig case was to prove that by changing the person's appearance the witness may have been briefed that this was the guilty person,' he says. Rules regarding the identification of defendants have been toughened over the years and a dock identification is now almost worthless.

Norman Beach acted in any number of the big criminal trials of the time. Unfortunately for him in 1977 the Disciplinary Tribunal of the Law Society struck him off the Rolls of Solicitors. This time it was alleged that, in a major trial, he had brought a defendant's Uncle Bertie out of the public gallery to sit in the well of the court with solicitors the better to intimidate witnesses. In January 1959 the Divisional Court upheld the decision. Martin

Beach again believes his father was the victim rather than the transgressor.

Perhaps the only real success the police had during this period in prosecuting a solicitor for conspiracy to pervert or related offences – as opposed to those who disappeared with the client account – was with De Mesa, who was involved in the case of Soraya Khashoggi, former wife of Adnan, arms dealer and friend to the mighty. De Mesa received a four-year sentence.

But the most spectacular of convictions of a solicitor has been that of Michael Relton, educated at Westminster, and principal of a very successful practice in Horseferry Road near the magistrates' court. He had made something of a speciality of defending police officers accused of corruption. It is said that of the twenty-eight he defended only one was convicted.[10]

In 1984 Relton was approached to launder the Brinks-Mat money and effectively retired from his practice – leaving it in the hands of a clerk who had served four years for fraud – to run a property company, Selective Estates. In two years using the Brinks-Mat money, say the police, Relton turned £7.5 million into a property portfolio worth £18 million, admittedly with the help of the property boom.

When the balloon went up Relton was interviewed and decided to co-operate with the police to become the first solicitor supergrass. In October 1986 he was charged and remanded on bail with the usual condition he reside at a police station in a suite, where he was visited by his second wife, a barrister's clerk. But, unfortunately for the police, he had a touch of seconds. He declined to assist further and when he appeared at the Old Bailey in July 1988 he pleaded not guilty.

His problems were that he had become too close to

[10] M. Short, *Lundy*, p. 231.

his clients. He had defended a man in 1973 on a drugs trial at Middlesex Crown Court. When the client received three years, Relton had continued to act for him whilst he was in Ford Open Prison, including the purchase of a recording studio in New Cross and a hotel on the Isle of Wight. Relton became his partner.

During the trial Relton said he thought the money had come from the man's father who owned twenty-six betting shops. But even so he should have been alarmed when his client was questioned about the robbery in June 1985, when his clerk, Emmanuel Wein, had acted for him. Instead of demanding a full explanation from his client and declining to act further, Relton had disposed of the money by an even more circuitous route, bringing the money back from abroad to purchase even more property. On his conviction in July 1988 Relton received twelve years' imprisonment. He was released shortly before Christmas 1991.

However astute Relton may have been when dealing in the Brinks-Mat investments, he pales into insignificance beside a man now reportedly living in Switzerland and the subject of a variety of warrants should he care to return to the United Kingdom. 'Judah Binstock is probably the most bent person the world has ever known,' says one City solicitor, not wholly unadmiringly, of the former Messina defender.

Prior to the Gaming Act he sold his businesses for £19 million. He is one of the few people I know who boosted his company by putting his own money into the company and paying tax on it. He owned the Victoria Sporting and the New Brighton Towers in Blackpool.

I went to see him once with a client in Paris. He spoke execrable French – and he gave a small party for about twelve of us. Towards the end he said,

'You're in luck. Madame – I can't remember her name – has got these three girls including this fantastic Eurasian. She's been with Kennedy. We'll have them £150 each the night' – this was late 1969–1970. My client and I looked at each other and Binstock said, 'No, my treat.' And then the client said, 'No, my brief has to go back to London this afternoon for a very important meeting.'

The criminal link was Judah Binstock – George Dawson – Albert Dimes – others. Binstock was not close to clubs; he was a brilliant man with a brilliant mind. He could use criminals in the same way as he used straight people.

Dawson would know all the heavy mob; if something happened Binstock could always talk to him.

Binstock invested a lot of money with Dawson. The deal was they would buy a company which on paper was full of assets, mainly machinery, and when you bought it it was worthless.

At that time I had a substantial indebtedness to a fashionable London solicitor – a dated IOU over a property deal. I had to find the money or extend the note, which would cost more. This got to the ears of Binstock and he approached me to say he would pay off the loan. In return would I guarantee a company in which he had invested to manufacture orange juice for a similar sum. I had already learned the machinery there was worthless and the company was going into liquidation – I didn't take him up. With friends like that you really don't need enemies.

I've never been approached by someone with such a blatant fraud. I knew him – what a rotten thing to do, but that was Judah. Yet a lot of people made money standing alongside him.

But when it comes to it the best helpmate is the police officer, and historically it has always been so. The Met, founded in 1829, was staffed by recruits from the working classes, and they were literally butchers, bakers, plumbers and sailors as well as old soldiers. The aim was to provide a body of honest, sober and unobjectionable men, wearing an innocuous non-military uniform. The pay had been fixed at a deliberately low level to deter the officer class. Immediately, however, there was a high turnover amongst these recruits. In eighteen months, out of a total strength of 4000, some 1250 had resigned and a further 1986 had been dismissed, mainly for drunkenness.

Then in 1877, at what became known as the Trial of the Detectives, one third of Scotland Yard's detective force (admittedly totalling only fifteen) were arrested and stood trial. The reasons for the downfall of Inspector Meiklejohn and his colleagues – associating with criminals, taking bribes, suppressing evidence and giving advance information of impending raids – were no different from the hundreds of their colleagues who followed them down the following decades.[11] As a result the Criminal Investigation Department of Scotland Yard was formed. Fifty years later it was described as a thoroughly venal army.

The Met survived a Royal Commission set up in 1908 to investigate corruption in street crime, and the next major public scandal came in 1928, when a uniform sergeant, George Goddard, stationed at Vine Street and detailed to clean up vice in the West End, did so with such success that when he was investigated he was found, on pay of £6 15s a week, to have a £2000 house. He also had £500 in a Selfridges deposit box and £12,000 in an account in Pall Mall. He had been a police officer for

---

[11] Each detective received two years' hard labour.

exactly twenty-eight years.

From where had the money come? Sir Percival Clarke, for the Crown, said it had come from the person in the dock with him, Kate Meyrick, the undoubted Queen of the Night Clubs. Known throughout the upper echelons of English society as 'Ma', she ruled principally at the Forty-Three Club in Gerrard Street,[12] although in her time she opened dozens of clubs, including Dalton's (in Leicester Square), Brett's, the Silver Slipper and, after her release from Holloway, the Bunch of Keys.

She was by no means a conventional Irish beauty; sad-eyed, drab and dowdy she would sit behind her desk in the narrow entrance hall collecting the £1 entrance fee. But she was an astute businesswoman even if she had not taken up her career until her forties. From the profits she educated her eight children well; one son went to Harrow, the daughters to Roedean. Time and again her clubs were raided, mainly for selling drinks after hours and running unlicensed premises. Kate Meyrick first went to prison in 1924 and continued to do so sporadically throughout much of the next decade, but her most celebrated appearance in court was in 1929 with Goddard.

Goddard certainly could not have come by his money honestly and it was said he had acquired his considerable fortune by gifts from Mrs Meyrick in return for tip-offs over raids. It was something he denied throughout the trial, maintaining he was no more than a successful gambler – £7000 had come from winnings on the turf – and an investor in a music publishing business, which had netted him another £5000. Ever the astute business-man he had invested money in a scheme to sell rock – edible rather than audible – at the Wembley Exhibition

---

[12] She was immortalized as Ma Maybrick in the novel *Brideshead Revisited* by Evelyn Waugh.

of 1924 and then he had dabbled on the foreign exchange market. These ventures had produced £4000 and £2000 each. He had, he said, reported irregularities in the running of the Meyrick clubs.

He was done for by the evidence that a secret observation had been kept by senior officers without letting him know so that in turn he could not tip off the night club queen. Goddard was sentenced to eighteen months' hard labour and ordered to pay £2000.

On his release he was back in court, this time as plaintiff. After his conviction the Commissioner of Police had, somewhat prematurely, confiscated all his money, claiming it to be the property of the Crown. In fact he had been convicted of taking only some £900 in bribes and an order was made that a substantial part of the money be returned to him. Goddard retired to the country and lived off his investments.

After her sentence Kate Meyrick returned to the West End, opening fresh clubs until in 1932, following yet another spell in Holloway, she promised to stop. She died the next year at the age of fifty-six. Dance bands throughout the West End observed two minutes' silence in her memory.

That may be the attractive part of the story. What was unattractive was the fact that as early as 1922 a young officer, Josling, who had arrested a bookmaker, had been warned by Goddard to 'leave the betting boys alone'. In return Goddard would 'see him all right'. The young officer reported the matter to his seniors who charged him with making false statements about Goddard and dismissed him from the force.

Throughout the pre-war period when Sir Hugh Trenchard was Commissioner corruption flourished undercover.

Trenchard, for example, while deluding himself

that he had stopped the rot, had constantly shirked the issue. Detectives played the game according to their own rules, confident that neither their superiors nor the courts would accept the word of known or convicted criminals.

He was constantly alive to the extent of CID corruption and his correspondence with Gilmour during 1934 is a curious commentary on his intellectual cowardice. The man who could talk to kings seemed frightened of corrupt constables.[13]

In 1933 Leopold Harris, a notorious fire-raiser, was sentenced to fourteen years' imprisonment after pleading guilty to eighteen counts of arson, conspiracy to commit arson, conspiracy to defraud, and obtaining money by false pretences. His brother David had received a term of five years following his conviction on two counts of arson. After his conviction Leopold Harris was interviewed at length in Maidstone Prison over allegations that senior police officers, mainly from the East End, had suppressed evidence in return for bribes, participated in mock burglaries for insurance purposes and dropped charges in exchange for cash. Harris told the investigating officer how money had been handed over at a billiard hall in the East End and at a police sports ground. He named two Chief Constables, six Superintendents and three Chief Inspectors. No prosecutions were ever brought.

During and after the war so far as the public was concerned the police were epitomized by George Dixon, the officer who in the guise of Jack Warner was gunned down by the young tearaway Dirk Bogarde near the Metropolitan Music Hall in the film *The Blue Lamp*. There was no point in criminals suggesting that the

---

[13] D. Ascoli, *The Queen's Peace*, pp. 306 and 240.

police had fabricated evidence, that their confessions were not what they had seemed; the magistrates or the jury, guided by the trial judge, would not believe them. The police were 'our police' and whatever they said and did was beyond both reproach and question.

It was not until the great *Times* exposure in 1969 that the public raised a serious question mark over the behaviour of the police. On Saturday, 29 November, an article was published which led to the convictions of Detective Sergeant John Symonds and Detective Inspector Bernard Robson. It also gave rise to the phrase 'a firm within a firm'. Symonds, Robson and a third officer had been systematically blackmailing a small-time Peckham thief, whilst offering him help if he should find himself in difficulties.

> Don't forget always to let me know straight away because I know people everywhere.
> If you are nicked anywhere in London . . . I can get someone on the blower to someone in my firm who will know someone somewhere who can get something done.[14]

Robson received seven years, Harris six. Symonds fled the country before his trial but was sent to prison when he surrendered seven years later.

The Times' enquiry led, inexorably, to a full-scale investigation into the Met. In a blaze of publicity Frank Williamson, then Her Majesty's Inspector of Constabulary for Crime, was appointed as adviser to oversee the enquiry. However, Williamson, who had a reputation as an honest and painstaking detective, was seen by the Met as an intruder who, it was feared, would ensure that a positive rather than an inconsequential report was

[14] Garry Lloyd and Julian Mounter, *The Times*, 29 November 1969.

produced. His views on police corruption were well known and he had stated at many detective training schools that until the words 'except police officers' were written into certain statutes, they must be dealt with in just the same way as any other offender. Nipper Read recounted:

> At the time of the enquiry I was a Chief Superintendent at Scotland Yard and Frank, a good friend of mine, would confide in me both the difficulties he was experiencing and the attitude of some of the top brass of the CID. It can be summed up quite neatly. One day he asked to see me and I said, 'I'll meet you at the Yard.' 'Good God,' he said, 'we can't do that, Nipper.' And when asked why ever not, he said, 'I'm *persona non grata* at the Yard.' I was dumbfounded. Here was a man who had been a provincial Chief Constable and who was now an Inspector of Constabulary whose presence in the Yard was being questioned.
>
> We had to meet in a pub and there he expressed his concern at the quality and ability of officers seconded to his inquiry from the Yard, giving as an example Detective Chief Superintendent Bill Moody.[15]

The Drugs Squad was the next to cop it, so to speak. In November 1972 Victor Kelaher and four other members of the squad were charged with conspiracy to pervert the course of justice and, with the exception of

---

[15] Williamson's fears were fully justified. Even whilst engaged on *The Times* enquiry, Moody was taking vast sums of money from pornographers in the West End. He later received a sentence of twelve years' imprisonment for his part in an extensive corruption racket. (See Chapter 7 and also L. Read and J. Morton, *Nipper*, pp. 44–5.)

A family snap of Jack 'The Hat' McVitie.

below: Eugenio Messina arriving handcuffed for the trial, accused of illegal possession of firearms and attempted procuring.

1970: 'To a fine gentleman': the wreath sent by the Twins to Albert Dimes's funeral.

Soho Rangers F.C. Left to right includes: Stanley Baker, George Wisbey, William Stayton, Tommy McCarthy (Bert's brother), Albert Dimes, Frankie Fraser. Front row includes: Bert McCarthy (boxing promoter) Eddie Richardson and others.

'The Sinister Scrapyard' said the newspapers. The Richardsons' yard
at New Church Road, Camberwell.

Charles and Eddie Richardson.

left: Frank Fraser, friend to the mighty, doyen of both Soho clubs and the British prison system.

November 1980: a delighted Ronnie Knight leaves court after his acquittal on a charge of killing 'Italian' Tony Zomparelli.

right: George Brett, victim of Henry 'Big H' Mackenny

below: Terence Eve: victim of Big H flexes his muscles.

Friend of the famous, Ronnie Knight (left) with his wife Barbara Windsor and Frank Norman, author of 'Fings Ain't What They Used to Be'.

The Great Train Robbery case remembered: Gordon Goody (in dark glasses back right) Bruce and Frances Reynolds, Micky Ball and, far left, Roy James.

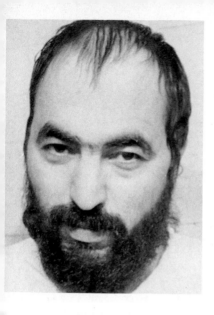

left: 1991: Dennis Arif, acting head of the Arif family jailed for 22 years after the shoot-out with the police in Surrey.

below: The scene of the Arif-police shoot-out.

Off to prison goes the Black Widow Linda Calvey after her conviction at the Central Criminal Court.

Mrs Meyrick's coming out party from Holloway Prison.

Kelaher, with perjury. The prosecution was not helped in its case by the evidence of Wally Virgo, whose testimony favoured the defence, but in the end three of the junior officers were convicted of perjury. One received four years, the others eighteen months each. Kelahar, in one of the smart cover-ups favoured by the Yard, was allowed to resign and given a medical discharge. In the shades of Challenor he had spent a year attending St Thomas' Hospital for treatment for a nervous complaint. It did not work as well as it might have. 'I am allowed by the Commissioner to say that, had he not done so, serious allegations would have been made against him in disciplinary proceedings,' said Alex Lyon, Minister of State for the Home Office.[16]

Meanwhile, things were not going well in the City of London police. Following allegations by a supergrass in August 1978, Operation Countryman was set up originally to look into the City of London police but later extended to cover the Met as well. The officers conducting it were derisively referred to by the Met as the Sweeney. In the end eight Met officers were all acquitted of charges brought against them. Three of them were dismissed following disciplinary proceedings, one resigned and four resumed duty.

Nor was there much success for the three-year-long enquiry under the control of Detective Chief Superintendent Stagg. Although the Director of Public Prosecutions was quite content to allow common criminals to be convicted on the evidence of supergrass Billy Young, he was not happy with the prospect of putting serving police officers at such risk. One officer was suspended and, in May 1983, served with internal discipline charges. Would he possibly become the first police supergrass? No, was the emphatic answer. Only traffic policemen

---

[16] *Hansard*, 14 May 1974, p. 1262.

bite their colleagues. He knew nothing. He was allowed to resign and a reference was given to him by the Yard, enabling him to become a member of the Institute of Professional Investigators.[17]

The rise and fall of Roy Garner, together with the eclipse of Superintendent Tony Lundy, came with Garner's increasing involvement in the cocaine trade. Before that, in 1982, he had been involved in a VAT fraud which worked by importing exempt coins, such as Krugerrands under £50,000, and then selling them on with the VAT added. This in itself was perfectly legal. The only problem was the VAT had to be repaid within three months. It was not. Given that flights were being made on an almost daily basis the profits were enormous.

In November 1984 Garner went to prison for the maximum term of two years consecutive on two counts and was fined, as well as being made the subject of a criminal bankruptcy order. The Court of Appeal later reduced the sentence by a year and quashed the fine. The Court expressed the hope that the criminal bankruptcy would be pursued by the authorities. It was something of a vain hope. Garner's stud farm belonged to his father, the family home was mortgaged to the hilt, his share of Elton's, the night club behind Tottenham police station, went to repay a loan on the club, and as for the reward money – well that had gone too, probably on his string of racehorses.[18]

By now Garner was well into the cocaine trade – of that there is little doubt – and it is here that the pro- and anti-Lundy camps become polarized. Just what did Lundy know about Garner's dealings? A very great deal, say Jennings, Lashmar and Simson. Nothing at all that

[17] A. Jennings et al., *Scotland Yard's Cocaine Connection*, p. 104.
[18] A. Jennings et al., *Scotland Yard's Cocaine Connection*, p. 112.

was improper, says Martin Short.[19] In any event Garner, put forward as the grass over the Brinks-Mat laundering, was arrested along with a Nikolaus Chrastny and Mickey Hennessey (one of the South London family), over the importation of 57 kilos of cocaine found in suitcases in Chrastny's flat in Harley Street. After sixteen days in custody Garner, through his wife June, got a message to Lundy asking for help. Matters moved quickly. One version is that Lundy was suspended for telling June that 'certain information had been passed at a very senior level from Scotland Yard to senior personnel of the agency dealing with his case'. Lundy says it was for making a complaint about the Chief Constable of South Yorkshire.

Chrastny was given conditional bail. He was to become a supergrass on the usual terms of residence in a police station. Off he went to the wilds of Yorkshire where his wife was allowed to give him £500 in cash for his daily needs, and to while away the time he was given modelling plasticine, paint and glue. By the morning of 5 October he had finished sawing through the bars of his cell, making his escape through the doctor's room and out of the window into a waiting car.[20]

Lundy appeared at Garner's trial, giving evidence *in*

---

[19] *Ibid and M. Short, Lundy.*

[20] Mrs Chrastny was given a seven-year sentence for conspiracy to import and distribute cocaine. She was also charged with helping her husband to escape and was acquitted. It was put on her behalf that of all the people who had an interest in the escape of her husband, Scotland Yard came top of the list. Perhaps one should not think too hard of the officers at Dewsbury police station from which Chrastny disappeared. After all, when O'Mahoney had been in the custody of Jack Slipper he had accumulated a pile of empty cans and bottles which he had hidden in his cell. He only told the police after his release. Chrastny was probably much smarter than O'Mahoney.

camera along with another officer, Detective Chief Superintendent Roy Ramm. The trial judge, Keith Machin, had allowed an application by Michael Corkery QC, former Treasury Counsel who had turned his hand to defence work, to hear this part of the case without the scrutiny of either public or press. Later the *Observer* published an account of the *in camera* part of the trial:

> Lawyers representing HM Customs accused a senior Scotland Yard detective of corruption in a secret session during an Old Bailey drugs trial. . . . Lundy was cross-examined *in camera* about two leaks to the cocaine smugglers which occurred after he allegedly gained knowledge of the case. His answers were inconsistent with subsequent statements by Florida police.
>
> Mr Derek Spencer, cross-examining him for Customs, said the nature of the corrupt relationship was that Garner gave Lundy information to further his career and Lundy gave Garner police information. He told Lundy: 'You found out Garner was being inquired into and you told him.' Lundy denied the allegations.[21]

On his conviction Garner received a twenty-two-year sentence. Lundy was investigated up hill and down dale and in the end a disciplinary matter over the receipt of some fencing for his home was brought against him. He decided not to contest the allegation, maintaining it would cost him over £20,000 to do so. He was allowed to retire on the grounds of ill health and sold his two part story, 'Bent or Brilliant?', to the *News of the World*. There are no prizes on offer for correctly guessing his answer. He is now living in Spain.

[21] 23 April 1989.

Was he bent? Along with journalists, serving police officers are divided on this point.

'He couldn't have done what he did if he was,' says one fervently.

'He had very bad breath,' says another enigmatically.

11

The Killers and
the Killed

'We were none of us nice, but you wouldn't turn your back on him,' said Albert Donaghue mildly.

'I thought of him as an original member of Murder Incorporated,' said an acquaintance.

Peter Kelly, a face of the eighties, was more forthright. 'He was a very hard man. Most hateful, frightening man because he was so fucking ugly. He had a horrible disposition. In fact he was the most hateful man God ever put breath into.'

They were all talking about Alfie Gerard, murderer, armed robber, one-time owner of a jewellery business and, amongst the fraternity, a noted cook who at one time ran a restaurant in Bermondsey, the Blue Plaice, in partnership with Mickey Hennessey. He was also noted as probably the nearest London had known to a hired killer who operated for any length of time. Rather like the boots in the film *All Quiet on the Western Front*, the restaurant was passed down the criminal hierarchy as first one and then the next proprietor fell foul of the law.

Since Gerard was acquitted on a number of occasions and not tried on several others, it is not possible accurately to pin the number of murders on him, but the likelihood is at least half a dozen. He also claimed to have disposed of the body of Jack 'the Hat' McVitie.

The killing of Ginger Marks on 2 January 1965 was not one of his better moves since it was clearly a mistake. Marks just happened to be in the wrong place at the wrong time and when the name Jimmy was called it sounded like Ginger, so he answered. Marks, a small-time thief, disappeared and immediately there sprang up a whole series of rumours about him and his whereabouts. First there was a story he had been involved in the 'Jack the Stripper' nude murders.[1] Almost immediately petrol bombs were thrown into the office of a suburban newspaper after it had run a story linking those murders to Marks.

From a chip found in the wall in Cheshire Street in the East End, the police believed Marks had been shot in the stomach. A dig took place on a local bomb site but there was no trace of the body. Three weeks later no one was any nearer a solution. Now came a suggestion in the *Sketch* that his body had been thrown in the Thames in concrete. Next the police thought the killing had a link with the Great Train Robbery.[2] The *News of the World* offered a reward of £5000 for information leading to the

[1] The Jack the Stripper murders occurred in the Shepherd's Bush and Hammersmith areas over a period of a year in 1964. A series of prostitutes were found naked and strangled. Almost all had had oral sex. No arrests were made but a man whom the police linked to the murders committed suicide and the case was closed. A rumour was put about that the man was the former world light-heavyweight champion Freddie Mills but neither John du Rose, who investigated the murders, nor Nipper Read, who investigated the death of Mills on another occasion, could find any grounds to support this rumour (see J. du Rose, *Murder was my Business* and L. Read and J. Morton, *Nipper*).

[2] In one version of the Great Train Robbery story Marks was the man engaged to burn down Leatherslade farm and who failed to do so. His is one of several bodies said to have disappeared into the parlour of a South London undertaker.

recovery of Marks or his body. A couple of days later the paper was on the right track. 'It is accepted that he was the unintended victim of a "crime of passion" feud between two South London gangs,' wrote their major crime reporter Peter Earle.

It was ten years before George Evans, known as Jimmy, a hard and quick-tempered Welshman, was arrested for the attempted murder of George Foreman, who at one time ran a club with Buster Edwards and whose brother Freddie was a close friend of the twins. The prosecution's case was that on 17 December 1964 George Foreman was allegedly shot by Evans because he had suspected his wife was carrying on with another man. The prosecution's case was that by hiding out in the boot of her car he had discovered George Foreman. He borrowed a single-barrelled 12-bore shotgun but returned it because it was not powerful enough. He then borrowed a double-barrelled shotgun from a man named Sands and shortened it.

On 11 April, Evans was acquitted both of shooting Foreman and having a shotgun and triumphantly gave an interview to the *News of the World*. He claimed he was continually being framed by police because he would not talk about the disappearance of Marks. 'Think what happens when a car breaker compresses a car into a cube box of metal no bigger than a cornflake box,' said Evans in the witness box, going on to deny that he and Ginger had been up to no good that night.

On 10 January 1975 the police arrested Jeremiah Callaghan, Alf Gerard and Ronald James Everett. By now Evans, serving a seven-year sentence for man-slaughter, was prepared to give evidence. He said that he, Marks and three others had been involved in a night raid on a jewellers. When they failed to get in they noticed a red car of the 1100 type following them near the Carpenters Arms in Cheshire Street, Bethnal Green.

The car drew up beside them and a voice called out, 'Jimmy, come here.' Three shots rang out and Ginger fell. Marks thought the call was 'Ginge' and was shot as he stepped forward. Evans ran round the corner and climbed under a lorry, clinging to the transmission link. Marks' body was bundled into a car and driven away. The other two had gone. He named the attackers as Alf Gerard, Ronald James Everett, Jeremiah Callaghan and Frederick Foreman.

On 30 October 1975 Gerard, Callaghan and Frederick Foreman were acquitted by Mr Justice Donaldson. Ronald Everett had been acquitted earlier in the trial. Donaldson said, 'The problems with identification are very real. This crime is ten years old. The first time Mr Evans condescended to say it was these three men who were in the car was last year.' Outside the Old Bailey Alfred Gerard commented, 'This is the end of a nightmare for us. Justice has been done at last.'[3]

In December of the same year as the killing of Marks came the disappearance of Frank Mitchell, the man whom the Krays had at first anticipated would help them if the Richardsons and their allies became too troublesome. Mitchell was killed, so Albert Donaghue said at the trial, after he left the house in the East End where he had been sheltered after his escape from Dartmoor. Reluctantly he had got in the back of a van waiting for him. Alf Gerard was in the van and almost immediately shots were heard.

---

[3] Marks' wife Anne remarried and never told her son Philip of his father's career. He obtained seven 'O' levels and won a medal for encouraging children to help the police. On 10 February 1987 Philip, then aged twenty, was sentenced to twelve years' imprisonment for masterminding a security van ambush in Limehouse, East London. His stepbrother Robert Judd (twenty-two) received ten years for the same offence. John Samson of Plaistow received eight years.

At the subsequent trial Ronnie and Reggie Kray, Freddie Foreman and others were acquitted of Mitchell's murder, but at the time of the arrest of the Krays and their associates in May 1968 Gerard had fled the country. He only returned after they were acquitted. As a result he was never charged with the murder.

In some camps Gerard is credited with the killing of bookmaker Harry Barham, shot and relieved of over £30,000 in Hackney one evening. But without doubt the most complicated if not the most famous incident in which he was involved, if only parentally, was that of Tony Zomparelli.

In August 1981 Alf Gerard was found dead in a flat belonging to the Callaghans in Brighton, that town of Max Miller and the fading gangster; it was the year his son was put on trial for the killing of Zomparelli. An inquest showed he had died of cirrhosis of the liver. The preferred version, more in keeping with his lifestyle and culinary artistry, is that he choked over a lobster.

The Zomparelli killing came after the death of David Knight, whose brother Ronnie, at one time married to Barbara Windsor, owned the Artists and Recreation Club off the Charing Cross Road. David Knight was badly beaten in a fight with a Johnny Isaacs in a pub at the Angel, Islington. On 7 May 1970 when he was out of hospital, Ronnie took him round to the Latin Quarter night club off Leicester Square to see Isaacs to whom he, Ronnie, had already given a retaliatory beating. He also took with him his brother Johnny and David's friend Billy Hickson, who had, it seems, been the cause of the original fight. As Ronnie Knight put it, 'I wanted they should say sorry to my David, promise him that it was all a big mistake. Then everything would be squared. Then I could forget it. It would be forgotten.'[4]

[4] R. Knight, *Black Knight*, p. 100.

According to Knight, Isaacs was not there and whilst he was making his peace with Billy Stayton, Hickson attacked Stayton. In the ensuing fight Alfredo Zomparelli, run-around man for Albert Dimes and bouncer for the Latin Quarter, stabbed David Knight twice in the chest.

Three weeks later Zomparelli, who had fled to Italy, returned and gave himself up. He claimed that the Knight contingent had walked into the club and violence had erupted. He had grabbed a knife to defend himself when two men attacked him. Looking back to the case of Tony 'Baby Face' Mancini, he seems fortunate that he was only convicted of manslaughter, for which he received a sentence of four years. To rub salt into Ronnie Knight's emotional wounds he, his brother Johnny and Hickson were charged with making an affray. Hickson was given a suspended sentence. The jury disagreed in the case of the brothers and the next day the prosecution offered no evidence. The witnesses had either gone abroad or declined to give evidence a second time.

The police version of why the fight took place does not quite match that of Ronnie Knight. According to them the Latin Quarter had been paying protection to David Knight.

After serving his sentence Zomparelli ran a bucket shop travel agency in Frith Street. Much of his leisure time was spent playing the pinball machines in the Golden Goose around the corner in Old Compton Street (and not far from the A & R Club). It was in the pinball arcade he was shot in the head and back by two men wearing dark glasses and moustaches on 4 September, a few months after his release. Appropriately he was playing a game called 'Wild Life'.

'He was a most likeable man,' said Augustus Tedeschi who had known him for fourteen years. 'I cannot understand why anybody should want to do this.'

It is not surprising that the police fancied Ronnie Knight for the killing. He does not seem to have hidden either his loathing of Zomparelli or his intention of seeking revenge. His alibi was that he was in the A & R Club and he named a substantial number of witnesses.

As in all these cases there were a number of theories offered for what was clearly a professional hit. One was that Zomparelli was trying to muscle in to the highly profitable amusement arcade business; another that he was involved in a stolen car racket involving the theft of Lancias and Ferraris in Italy and their resale in London, with claims on Italian insurance companies completing the scam; and a third that he was a drug courier. A Mafia expert, Captain Francisco Rosato of the Rome police, was sent to London to collaborate on the investigation. The police interviewed over a thousand people including Knight but the enquiry came to nothing.

There the file remained shut, if not fully closed, until in 1980 Maxie Piggot *aka* George Bradshaw became the supergrass with most to confess in his generation. On 17 January 1980 he received a life sentence for the murder of Zomparelli with a ten-year concurrent sentence for all the rest. Then he became one of the last of the all-star supergrasses. In his long confession, in which he admitted to over a hundred armed robberies, he named Nicky Gerard, son of Alfie, as his co-hitman, the one who pulled the trigger of a .38 revolver. The shock of hearing gunfire made him involuntarily pull the trigger of his own .22.

He and Gerard had left a flat in Clerkenwell and bought their disguises at a theatrical costumiers on the way to Soho. He also named Ronnie Knight as the financier of the reasonably priced £1000 contract and the supplier of the .38. He said that night he and Gerard received £250 of the promised £1000. He went to his parents' home near Winchester and buried the guns.

Later he would claim that it was not the money which had tempted him but the added prestige in the underworld which such an execution would bring him.

Of course the police were bound to check the story and at least they found the guns buried, as Bradshaw had said, in Hampshire. Forensic examination would match the guns with the spent cartridges found at the Golden Goose.

There is no doubt that Knight had met Bradshaw at the A & R Club. He had been there as a friend of Knight's 'old mate' Alfie Gerard.

'He was a right weirdo, this Maxie character. He had dark, long curly hair, a funny little drooping moustache and a beard.' He reminded Knight of the 'Cisco Kid. 'He must have been blind as a bat because he wore those thick, jam-jar glasses . . . and contact lenses on underneath. Mad as a March hare on the funny powder.'[5]

But by 1980 supergrasses did not always have the ear of the jury. Ten years of practice had taught defence barristers how to overcome the witnesses' all-consuming repentance and a desire to bare their souls so that justice could at last be done. The public was also becoming a little tired of hearing the evidence of men who had committed the most outrageous crimes, and who were serving relatively nominal sentences, which would put away others involved in a single offence and who would then get double or even treble that of the supergrass. They did not like hearing how brave these men had been by telling all, and when they sat on a jury they were rightly sceptical. Knight also had the bonus of his wife Barbara Windsor on his side. The jury acquitted both him and Nicky Gerard.

The Director of Public Prosecutions declined to continue with any further proceedings against the dozens

[5] R. Knight, *Black Knight*, p. 108.

of others Bradshaw had named. Once the police had seen him as a major supergrass he had been placed in police custody at Twickenham outside the prison system under the name of John February. Now he was returned to prison to serve the rest of his sentence.

Gilbert Kelland, the head of the CID at the time, commented:

> Whilst he had been held by us he had been well behaved and co-operative, although he seemed completely cynical about his involvement in murder and other violent crimes. In my view it should be many years – if ever – before such a ruthless criminal is considered suitable for parole.[6]

With hindsight it does seem odd that Knight would have chosen Bradshaw to execute Zomparelli, particularly when his old friend Alfie Gerard was alive and shooting well. For his part Bradshaw complains that the judge was senile and should have listened more closely to his evidence.

The newspapers reported Tony Zomparelli junior, middle name Alberto as a mark of respect to Albert Dimes, as saying, 'The day Ronnie Knight dies, I'll throw the biggest party East London has ever seen.'

Tony Zomparelli believes they exaggerated.

> What I did say was I'll open a bottle of champagne. It wasn't right what was reported. My dad was there [at the Latin Quarter] as a peacemaker. He was hit on the head with a hammer himself. They went round tooled up. I was only eleven when my father died. He was a bit div. There's a story he glassed his best friend but I don't know if it's true.

[6] G. Kelland, *Crime in London*, p. 228.

He was a bad gambler. He and my mother were separated and one day he would have a car full of toys for us and then we'd never see him for three months. When he went to Italy after the killing in the Latin Quarter it was Albert Dimes who told him to come back. He told him he'd only get four years.

Zomparelli went on to say that Knight had loathed his father because Barbara Windsor was always flirting with him.

Bradshaw was released from prison in 1990.

Nicky Gerard did not last that long after his acquittal. In June 1982 he was shot dead in South London. Peter Kelly says that 'Nicky Gerard was a very good friend of Billy Dixon. He was the dead spit of his father but he had a much nicer nature. Personally I liked Nicky. Alfie, when he died in Brighton, was not missed by many. He was a hateful bastard.'

'He [Nicky] would lean on anybody who took liberties,' said another acquaintance. 'But he wasn't only a muscle for hire man. He was known and feared throughout the East End.'

Prior to the Zomparelli trial, in May 1978, Nicky Gerard had been gaoled for seven years for an attack on boxer Michael Gluckstead at the Norseman Club in Canning Town. He had been found not guilty of the attempted murder of Gluckstead, who, widely regarded as a local bully, had his cheek slit from ear to nose and had been shot twice, as well as being hit about the head and being stomped. Gerard would say nothing of his instructions or reasons for the Gluckstead beating. John Knight, brother of Ronnie, was acquitted of all charges relating to the attack.

While he had been in prison Gerard had been sentenced, *in absentia*, by a kangaroo court. Certainly his wife Linda had received threats and a wreath with the message 'Nicky Gerard, Rest in Peace'. Now, on 27 June 1982, when leaving his daughter's eleventh birthday party, he was ambushed by gunmen wearing boiler suits and balaclava helmets at the lock-up garage to which he had driven his Oldsmobile. Shots were fired through the windscreen and Gerard was hit in the stomach. He managed to get out of the car and to stagger a hundred yards but his attackers followed him, smashing him so hard on the head with a gun that the stock shattered. He was beaten unconscious before the gunmen reloaded and shot him.

Gerard had not been sufficiently careful. Over the previous few days he had known he was being followed but he had thought they were undercover police.

'Gerard was one of the most feared men in the London underworld. Although he was acquitted of being a hit man in the Knight case, he was the man who did the heavy business,' said former Commander Bert Wickstead. '. . . His death could easily spark off a gangland war.'[7]

On 22 November his cousin and 'best friend' Thomas Hole was arrested and charged with his murder. Hole's criminal career traced back to his friendship with George Davis and ended on 12 July 1989 at Snaresbrook Crown Court when he acquired a thirteen-year sentence for conspiracy to manufacture drugs, to run concurrently with an eighteen-year sentence for armed robbery.[8] On the way he had acquired a sentence of seven years for the attempted murder of a James Venton. Together with

---

[7] *News of the World*, 27 June 1982.

[8] The prosecution alleged that sufficient chemicals to make 40 kg of amphetamine sulphate had been found at Colney Hall, an isolated mansion near Norwich. The drugs were said to have a street value of millions.

Billy Williams he had been instrumental in holding Venton down whilst a car was driven over him in Daveney Street.

Hole was tried at the Old Bailey in April 1983. He had been picked out on an identification parade by a 'Mr Fisher', the pseudonym given to a protected witness, who said he had seen a man with one rubber washing-up glove acting suspiciously. 'But,' he added, 'I am not sure it was the man I had seen that day in June in the car park.' Despite protests that the Crown had more evidence it had not been allowed to produce, on 27 April 1983 the judge stopped the case at the end of the prosecution evidence.

Thomas Hole was acquitted by the direction of the trial judge, Mr Justice French, who said, 'This, of course, was an appalling gangland murder, and any right-thinking citizen must be dismayed at the thought that no one has been brought to justice for that murder.' Hole, who left court with his friends, said, 'My head is reeling.'

The 'war' had not been long in coming. Within six months of Nicky Gerard's death, Patrick 'Paddy Onions' O'Nione was also executed. On 30 November 1982 he was shot near his son's wine bar, Caley's, in Tower Bridge Road. He had been hit in the back of the head, the right shoulder, the chest and the abdomen. A Detective Sergeant who was passing gave chase to the killer but the man escaped. Paddy Onions had been a major, if shadowy, figure in the South London underworld for some years. As long ago as March 1951 he had been acquitted of being the decoy in a brutal attack in which the Gregory brothers, Ernest and Andrew, received twelve and seven years. In March 1963 he had not been so fortunate. At Lewes Crown Court he received five years in a conspiracy to smuggle watches. The jury failed to agreed in the case of Alfie Gerard, one of three others charged with him.

As always a number of explanations were offered for the execution. O'Nione was thought to be a grass; he was thought to be deeply involved in a drug racket embracing both Europe and the Middle East; perhaps it was a revenge killing for that of Peter Hennessey, one of the South London brothers, who had been stabbed at a Boxing Gala dinner at the Royal Garden Hotel, Kensington.

Two of the Hennessey brothers, Peter and Bernard, after a series of convictions for robbery, had bought a public house, the Dog and Bell, in Deptford. Of course they had a manager in whose name the licence appeared but the pub was theirs. Peter would sit on a stool in the corner of the pub and watch the proceedings. An officer who worked the area says:

> He had a frightening temper. I was scared of him and I was Old Bill. But he did have a better side. At Christmas he and his brother would get a coach and round up all the old-aged pensioners of the area whether they drank in the Dog or not and take them to C & A's in Lewisham and buy them a new hat and coat. It cost them thousands. I think it all went back to Peter being fond of his mother.

Hennessey died at the Royal Garden Hotel at the end of a charity evening designed to raise money for a well-known South London amateur boxing club. 'Every villain in South-East London was there,' says an officer who was involved in the enquiry. 'If the roof had fallen in, South London crime would have been cleared in a moment.'

Towards the end of the boxing, Peter Hennessey, described as 'well drunk', decided to have an informal extra collection in aid of a friend's wife who had multiple sclerosis. He went round the tables and an argument broke out between him and O'Nione. They fell to the floor and during the fight, in which others were involved, Hennessey was stabbed sixty times. James Coleman, a brother-in-law of the Arifs, and O'Nione were charged with his murder. Both were acquitted.

So far as O'Nione's death was concerned, despite the tales of protection of wine bars and pubs in South London and the story that he had been instrumental in financing a web of violence and intrigue spreading as far as Miami and Milan, the likelihood is that he was executed on the instructions of friends of Peter Hennessey.

On 11 March 1983 Jimmy Davey was arrested in Coventry and held in custody to await the arrival of the London police for questioning over O'Nione's death. On their arrival Davey, who had already served a six-year sentence for a brutal attack on a Coventry-based policeman, is said to have lunged at one of the officers, who put him in a choke-hold. Eleven days later, with Davey still in a coma, the life support machine was switched off. The police gave out that they were convinced that Davey had undertaken the hit for £5000.[9]

Seemingly independently of the troubles of O'Nione and Hennessey, John Darke, then aged thirty-two, had fatal difficulties on 21 November 1978. A medium-quality gangster, he had been charged back in 1969 with the BOAC wages snatch and had been acquitted at the Old Bailey in the October. Reputed to be the leader of a South London team known as the Wild Bunch, as well as being a police informer for the last three years, Darke, hacked to death with a machete, had died in a

---

[9] The going rate for a hit in the 1960s had been £1000, with half that for a shattered arm or leg, but inflation had crept in and in the early 1980s the basic contract was £5000 with a price of up to £50,000 for the death of one of the supergrasses who were proliferating.

pool of blood at the Ranelagh Yacht Club, Fulham – it was also known as Bobby's Club. Tough guy TV actor John Bindon, friend of the model Vicki Hodge, from West London, was arrested and charged with what the prosecution alleged was a contract murder. He was said to have undertaken the contract for a fee of £10,000.

Bindon disappeared immediately after Darke's death and was found a fortnight later in a Dublin hospital. He was said to have staged an amazing escape to foil a gangland execution squad. The *News of the World* thought the amazing escape had been with the full co-operation of the police, who had let him leave hospital after giving vital information about the feud. Bindon, one of whose television programmes had to be post-poned whilst he was in custody, walked free from the Old Bailey in November 1979. 'There is a hell of a lot behind this – villains who I'd made enemies with in the past,' he told the *Sun*.

He appeared in various courts throughout the 1980s, mainly on petty matters, and in November 1982 he appeared before the West London magistrate, Eric Crowther, who fined him £100 for possessing an offensive weapon. 'I regret I have not had the pleasure of seeing you act to my knowledge, except here,' said Crowther, with one eye on the evening papers.

Bindon's name came up again in 1984 when the ex-boxer charged in connection with the Pen Club murder of Selwyn Cooney back in 1961, was alleged to have been building an empire of pubs and clubs in South London – and running them through fear. The claim was made by the police at a hearing of an application for a licence in the name of former Bolton Wanderers star, Alvan Williams. The police alleged that the boxer was mixed up with major criminals at home and abroad in organizing serious crime. 'I'm no gangster,' said the boxer angrily, adding that he was taking legal advice. 'Of course I know villains but I also know very respectable people.'

In the late 1980s, the boxer, who always maintained an interest in the sport, was involved in the contract of a promising South London light-heavyweight boxer. In 1991 he was arrested and charged in connection with a major drug smuggling operation.

In 1991 both Alfie Hinds and Stephen Jewell died peacefully. Their lives had been rather less so. Hinds' criminal career had led to a change in the law, while his great friend and business partner, Tony 'The Magpie' Maffia, was killed by Stephen Jewell, who served a life sentence on his conviction. Throughout his trial Jewell constantly implicated Hinds in the killing.

Alfie Hinds, who died in January, had a number of claims to fame. With an IQ of 150 he certainly had the intelligence to qualify for the dubious epithet Master Criminal – his old adversary Chief Superintendent Herbert Sparks thought he was 'the most cunning and dangerous criminal' he had met. In those pre-Ronnie Biggs days of the early 1960s he was certainly the best known prison escaper and he was generally regarded as the best non-lawyer advocate of his time who appeared on his own behalf in the criminal courts.

Hinds was born in 1928, the son of parents who had both seen the inside of prison. Indeed his father had been sentenced to ten strokes of the cat on being convicted for a bank robbery in Portsmouth. He had died soon after and Hinds believed that the flogging had contributed to his death. As a young man and a skilled safebreaker, he was in and out of Borstal and army detention centres but after the war, apart from what he described as 'a foolish incident in 1946', he had seemingly settled down and worked in the demolition business for his brother. He had a small bungalow (or the largest on the island depending upon whether the commentator is pro-Hinds or not) at Wraysbury on the Thames. On Thursday, 24 September 1953, the furniture and department store, Maples in Tottenham Court Road, London, was burgled. The thieves struck lucky. When the safe was blown there was a considerable amount of jewellery discovered. Four days later Hinds was arrested at his bungalow along with two others. For his part in the burglary he received a sentence of twelve years' preventive detention from Lord Goddard.

Hinds bitterly and continually protested his innocence. The theft had been an inside job and the evidence against him consisted of that of accomplices, some scientific evidence (particularly dust in the trouser turnups of a suit Hinds said he had not worn since it had been cleaned) and some verbal admissions. He maintained that he had had poor representation – a last-minute change of counsel with the substitute refusing to call his alibi witnesses – as well as suffering at the voice of an interrupting Lord Chief Justice whose interjections and questions ran into the hundreds in a two-day trial. And, he maintained, perjured police evidence.

There is no doubt, however, that, at best, Hinds had been in the wrong place at the wrong time. On the Monday prior to the theft he had gone to Tottenham Court Road to buy a carpet from one of the co-accused in a pub. He had lent the man his Land Rover and when it had not been returned had telephoned the police and reported it stolen. He maintained that had he been involved he would never have put himself on offer. The counter-argument was that this was a diabolically cunning move to divert suspicion if his vehicle had been seen on a reconnoitre – just the sort of thing a Master Criminal, class of '53, would have thought of doing.

Hinds was nothing if not resourceful. While in prison he wrote a leaflet detailing his innocence, and had it printed and circulated. His first escape came two years later when he left Nottingham Prison in November 1955 using a hacksaw blade and a prison workshop key he copied from memory. He stayed on the run for 245 days, circulating his pamphlet and recording interviews for later use on the television and radio.

The newspapers and the public loved him. Almost all the popular papers recruited 'experts' to comment on his escape. Major Pat Reid from Colditz wrote for the *Sunday Dispatch*, Geoffrey Household, author of *Rogue Male* – the story of a man on the run from the Nazis – had his say in the *Daily Mail* and even the now released 'Mad Parson' John Allen, who had himself escaped from Broadmoor and had stayed out for two years before recapture, gave his comments. Hinds, caught in Dublin on 31 July 1956, successfully defended himself on a charge of prison breaking and continued to use the legal process to try to have his case reopened and provide the opportunity for another escape. In the meantime the *Star* published his version of events, 'This is My Case', in July 1957.

His next escape chance came when he went to the Law Courts in the Strand to argue a case against the Prison Commissioners. With the help of a friend, Tony 'The Fox' or 'The Magpie' Maffia, he locked his escorts in a lavatory and was gone. This time he did not last long on the outside. He was caught in Bristol, recognized by an alert stewardess who later said she felt mean for giving him away, about to board a plane to Ireland. For his part in the affair, Maffia was later sentenced to twelve months' imprisonment. It was back to prison for Hinds and this time he stayed until in 1958 he escaped from Chelmsford with another copied key. His old safebreaking experience was standing him well. Two years later, as William Herbert Bishop, he was arrested, again in Ireland. Back in prison he continued to seek the reopening of his case, at one time arguing in person before the House of Lords.

In June 1961 one of his co-accused gave his story to the *News of the World* saying 'Alfie Hinds wasn't in on the deal but he had been promised a cheap carpet.' Hinds was still trying unsuccessfully to have his case reopened when a short time later Herbert Sparks, on his retirement from the police, published his memoirs in the *People*. In them he said Hinds 'couldn't admit that he had been out-thought by the police', adding, 'I think it is a pity that Alfie did not take his medicine manfully.'

Now on the hostel scheme under which prisoners go to a halfway house before their release, Hinds sued for libel, offering to withdraw the case if his appeal against conviction could be reopened. This time his case was far better prepared and he was represented by James Comyn, later to become a High Court judge, who called experts to throw cold water over the scientific evidence. His alibi witnesses stood up and, in a test of will, Hinds came over much better to the jury than an emotional Sparks. Hinds was also fortunate in that the police were going through one of their bad patches. The Challenor case had not been forgotten and when at one point during cross-examination Sparks buried his face in his hands, a wag in the gallery called 'Watch out! He's doing a Challenor.'

Despite an unfavourable summing-up the jury awarded Hinds the then huge amount of £1300. Disregarding James Comyn's advice not to put his head in the lion's mouth again, the award emboldened him to go one more time to the Court of Appeal. But that court was not as easily persuaded as a jury. For the last time his appeal was rejected. By now, however, he had been released and for some time he lectured on the criminal justice system at polytechnics. The law was later changed so that a criminal conviction was effectively a bar to subsequent civil proceedings to claim it was wrong.

In the Channel Islands Hinds became not only the Secretary of Mensa for the islands but a successful property developer. 'Plumbers are like lawyers,' he said. 'I found I couldn't rely on them so I learnt to do it all myself.'[10]

Throughout the rest of his life he kept in touch with his friend and helpmate, the small but flamboyant Tony Maffia. They acquired a coppermine in Portugal together and worked in various enterprises. They also both knew Stephen Jewell.

For outside purposes Maffia was a car trader with a small firm, Justice Motors. His card carried a drawing of the Old Bailey figure but with the scales of justice weighed down rather than evenly balanced. Described as having bundles of personality and a man who couldn't keep his hands off a quick deal, he was one of the largest receivers of stolen goods to be found.

He disappeared in 1968 soon after he returned from Belgium, where he had shown an interest in forged notes over which he might have been deceived. On 27 May he met a recent acquaintance, Stephen Jewell, a Manchester coal merchant, who hoped to sell him forged £10 notes and to whom Maffia hoped to sell his cruiser, the *Calamara*, then in a marina at Wallasey Island. The price for the notes was £8000 in real money against £32,000 paper value.

According to Jewell, when he saw Maffia's house in Buckhurst Hill he liked it so much he suggested buying it. The price, which now seems nominal – £12,000 – was even then a bargain. Maffia was separated from his wife

---

[10] Sparks outlived Hinds and at the end of 1991 was in retirement in Sussex. On Hinds' death he wrote a rueful letter to the *Police Pensioners* magazine warning ex-officers against publishing their memoirs.

and a sale was needed. They then drove in Maffia's green Jaguar MCC 932 to the marina to see the boat. Jewell carried a gun which, he said, Maffia had instructed him to bring. The gun, with its magazine housing bullets with a hole in every nose, was put on the front seat covered with a cloth. Jewell's car was then left in a pub car-park. They certainly went to the marina, where Maffia reversed a call to London to say he would be back in about an hour. After they left the marina he was never seen alive again. Maffia had been planning to fly to Jersey later that day. Apparently he had important papers to sign.

'Everybody's wondering what happened to Tony,' says a friend. Well, the Krays were no friends of his. When Charlie Kray was in a spot of trouble in Africa and needed money to repatriate him, a whip had been organized. Maffia had told them to bugger off and get the money the hard way as he had done, by grafting.[11] However, the twins were in custody and, for once, blame could not be laid at their door. Tony's older brother, the much shyer Arthur, was missing as well. He was wanted for questioning over a spot of LF.

Negotiations were opened with the police by a retired wrestler, 'Man Mountain' Dean, who arranged the surrender of Arthur Maffia. The long firm enquiries came to nothing but Arthur could not explain where his brother might be.

Four days later on 1 June it became quite apparent where he was. On the Whit Saturday one of the staff at the Midway Restaurant, so called because it was between Southend and London, saw a dog sniffing at a

[11] It was over this that Buller Ward was striped. He warned Maffia in the Regency Club that the Krays were about to do him over. Maffia escaped through a back door, but for his treachery Ward received 110 stitches in his face.

green Jaguar which had been in the car-park for the last few days. In the front passenger seat covered by a tarpaulin was Maffia. It had been a hot few days and his body was so bloated it was recognizable only by fingerprints and a gold ring he wore. He had been shot twice, by the right eye and behind the right ear.

Two days later Jewell, of his own volition, arranged to see Detective Chief Inspector Kenneth Drury.[12] His story was that shortly after he and Maffia had left the marina, they were stopped by three men in a Ford Zodiac who told Jewell to go away while they talked to Maffia about a deal. When he returned both Maffia and the Zodiac were gone, as was the pistol and ammunition from the Jaguar. The car itself was still there. Jewell's overcoat which he had left in the car was blood-stained. He described the men, saying that one had a scar on his cheek.

He said he drove off in the Jaguar for London and after a time stopped to throw the overcoat into a field. It was just as well he admitted that, for the coat was found containing a live bullet and sale particulars of Maffia's house. A witness would later say he saw Jewell wipe the passenger door with the coat before it was thrown away. He agreed he left the Jaguar in the car-park of the Midway Restaurant.

It was not a good story. Quite apart from the forensic evidence against him, how did Maffia's body get into the Jaguar if it was not in it when Jewell drove to the Midway? It is impossible to believe that when Jewell dumped the Jaguar at the restaurant, the killers then happened upon it quite by chance and in full view put Maffia's body in the passenger seat. Or had they

---

[12] Drury was later implicated in the great Porn Squad enquiry, convicted and sentenced to eight years' imprisonment, reduced to five on appeal.

followed him all the time, watching what he was going to do? Jewell was convicted by a ten to two majority. Throughout the trial he had repeatedly sought to implicate Hinds, answering questions by saying that Hinds should be asked about the subject. After the trial Hinds was allowed to have counsel, Mr Roger Frisby, make a statement in court denying any knowledge of the murder.

Why did Jewell go to the police in the first place? There were probably enough local candidates to keep the police happy in their enquiries for months. Presumably he wanted to get his story in first in the hope it would be believed. Unfortunately he changed the details on a number of occasions, although he stuck to the basic details throughout his trial and sentence. Whilst he was in Wandsworth he wrote to Arthur Maffia denying, yet again, that he had been his brother's killer and giving descriptions of the men whom he said had stopped the car. Arthur Maffia and other friends made what are quaintly described as 'their own investigations' and were satisfied the killer was Jewell. But Jewell could still find supporters for his story and in 1991 a television programme was made advancing his version of events.

Once the police began their investigations into Maffia's background they unearthed a series of safe-boxes containing the proceeds from a string of robberies in the Home Counties, including a gold bar from the £750,000 gold bullion robbery in Bowling Green Lane, East London, a year earlier. There were coins, diamonds, Dresden porcelain and jewellery. His name 'The Magpie' was completely justified.

There seems no really good reason why Jewell should have killed Maffia. It certainly wasn't a robbery. When the body was stripped, cash and cheques totalling over £700 were found, together with some rare gold coins. As always a number of theories were advanced. It was a contract hit – in which case it was extremely clumsily executed; Maffia was shot because he would not join in a forgery racket, which seems unlikely as offers such as this are made and declined on a daily basis without such major reprisals; Jewell had swindled Maffia and Hinds, which doesn't account for why he then shot Maffia; that he was swindled by Maffia and Hinds, which would. There is no suggestion that Maffia was a grass. Another theory advanced by friends is that Jewell showed Maffia three £10 notes and said pick the right ones for £4 each. They were all genuine and Maffia put £12 on the table saying he was not being taken for a mug and that was all he was going to buy. The theory is that on the way back to London Maffia ('he had a spiteful tongue') taunted Jewell, who shot him in temper.

Maffia was thirty-eight at the time of his death and, assuming you count other people's property as his, was worth well over £500,000.

Another killing which brought back the past was that of fashion expert Beatrice Gold, who on 8 September 1975 was shot through the head at point-blank range at the dress factory she owned in Islington. The killing was certainly a contract one and thirty-one-year-old Errol Heibner, a self-confessed jewellery store robber, was gaoled for life with a recommendation that he serve a minimum of twenty-five years for the killing. But why was she killed?

The link with the past was the second defendant at Heibner's trial, Robert 'Battles' Rossi, who had previously been sentenced to seven years for the slashing of Jack Spot. Now it was alleged that he was the contact man who had set up the murder, for which Heibner had been paid £8000, and had provided the pistol with which Mrs Gold was shot.

But there were many things to muddy the waters. Her lifestyle had been bizarre. She was the author of two unpublished novels on sex and was what was impolitely known as a fag hag, a woman who favoured the company of homosexuals, whose parties she and her husband regularly attended. She was also said to be involved with the Soho porn market and was thought by Bernie Silver to have documents which could be used for blackmailing purposes. Indeed, according to the evidence at the trial, there had been a meeting between Silver, Zomparelli and a Frankie Albert (who later fell to his death from a roof during a police raid) to discuss her position. There had been nearly fifty keys to her factory floating around to make it easy for the killer to gain entry, but who but an intimate would know she would be alone and in position at exactly the right moment?

Rossi was an old friend of a Hatton Garden villain, George Miesel, himself a friend of Albert Dimes and one-time bookmaker on the point-to-point courses. Rossi lived over Miesel's spieler at one time. The case was that Rossi had handed a package containing the gun to Heibner in the Strand only a few hours before the killing. In evidence Rossi told the court he thought the package had contained jewellery. He was found not guilty.

For some years after the murder a television producer worked on the theory that a prominent London solicitor had been involved in the killing. The proposed documentary programme was never shown.

Other killings were definitely linked to past crimes. Sid Kiki, the betting shop proprietor, was a regular police informant, providing them with good information. One evening in May 1967 he telephoned Nipper Read. 'Listen,' he said, 'you've got another Ginger Marks on the manor.' Did Read know of a man, Jack Buggy? When Read said he had never heard of him Kiki asked if he knew of the Mount Street Bridge Club. At one time it had been quite a fashionable card club but as the years had passed it had become little more than an illegal gaming club run by Franny Daniels and his nephew Charles 'Waggy' Whitnall.

'Well,' said Kiki, 'this fella Buggy was knocked off in there a few nights ago and his body has been done away with. Apparently he was making a right nuisance of himself. Albert Dimes was called in at the end.'

American-born John 'Scotch Jack' Buggy had come to England with the American forces and had become a Glasgow hard-man. In 1961 he had been sentenced to nine years' imprisonment following the shooting of Robert Reeder outside the Pigalle night club in Swallow Street. Buggy had endeavoured to go backstage to invite singer Shirley Bassey, who was the cabaret act that night, to attend a private party. He was turned away shouting loudly. Reeder, who was dining in the club, complained and Buggy smashed a plate over his head. Both men were ejected and Buggy shot Reeder at point-blank range. He was acquitted of shooting with intent to kill but convicted of shooting with intent to cause grievous bodily harm. During the time he had been in prison Buggy had served part of his sentence, and become friendly, with one of the Great Train Robbers, Roy James.

Read and his Superintendent, Arthur Butler, walked round to the bridge club from West End Central to see what was going on. Both noted that there was a new carpet on the club's floor. But there were no signs of nerves from either the punters or the staff. The club was hardly a hive of activity. Butler sent Read to make some enquiries and he went to Buggy's address in Kilburn. He discovered that his girlfriend, Ann Phillips, had received a telephone call from him on 12 May telling her to meet him at her mother's stall in Kingston Market. Buggy had not shown up and two days later she had told the police in Sutton he had gone missing.

Now all sorts of rumours started to fly around the West End. The night before Buggy disappeared a gelignite bomb had gone off in the hallway of the club in Mount Street. He was known to have been involved in protection rackets in the past. Could the bomb and his disappearance have been connected to them? Ann Phillips told the *Evening Standard* that he had given up that part of his life, but could she really know that? Then there was a suggestion that he owed £20,000 to a big-time syndicate. Another version was that it was a Mafia-backed killing and yet another that Buggy had been protecting a man who had turned against him.

There was also the story, and it was the one which lasted the longest, that he had gone in search of money belonging to Roy James and said to be held, but unaccounted for, by a man who frequented the club. It was also said that the man had been given the money to mind but when the Train Robbers' appeals were dismissed he had gone on a spending spree and blown it all.[13] Buggy's mission was to try to recover at least part of it. As to Buggy's death, the firm rumour was that he had been shot in the club at around 3 p.m., his body wrapped in a carpet and taken away. There was yet another story that he had eventually been killed in a garage in Kingston upon Thames.

Buggy's red MGB sports car turned up in Maida Avenue by the Grand Union Canal. In it was a key to a safe deposit box which he always carried. It was now clear that he was dead and a murder investigation was started. Police frogmen dived into the muddy waters of the canal while other police, along with forensic

---

[13] In his book, *The Great Train Robbery*, Piers Paul Read endeavours to account for the total monies stolen in the raid, apportioning shares to each man. He lists £76,000 as having been stolen by the man deputed to guard Roy James' share.

scientists, began the search of the club's Regency-striped walls and its spanking new carpet.

There was no help at all from the members who had been in the club. They knew nothing or, if they did, they certainly would say nothing. It had all the hallmarks of a gangland execution. Two men whom the police thought could assist and so wished to interview were out of the country.

The body surfaced, so to speak, in a slightly unusual fashion. Two off-duty police officers out fishing off Seaford in Sussex had seen something floating. They had cast for it, hooked it and reeled in Buggy's body. It was wearing his black polo-neck sweater and the arms had been bound with baling wire. He had also been gagged. In his back pocket was his driving licence and some correspondence. An examination by the pathologist Francis Camps showed he had been shot twice.

The police made little more progress the second time around. One of the men whom they wished to interview, Waggy Whitnall, was in Vienna, where after negotiations he agreed to be interviewed in the presence of a London solicitor, Andrew Keenan. Nothing came of that interview and he remained in Austria. When it came to it no one was arrested and charged that year, nor for the next six.

There was, however, an interesting sequel to the story. On his deathbed in 1973 Albert Dimes is said to have ordered that the police be told the truth about Buggy's death. In any event enquiries were renewed and then Donald Wardle, a member of a team of Australian shoplifters who was serving nine years for blackmail, made a statement. As a result Whitnall's uncle, Francis Daniels, then aged sixty-three, and Abraham Lewis, who was two years older and had been working at the club at the time of Buggy's death, were charged with his murder. Wardle maintained that he had been in the gaming room of the club on the afternoon of Buggy's death when he had heard three shots. Daniels, he said, had come out and told him and other players to go home.

In November 1974 both men were acquitted and so the death of 'Scotch Jack' Buggy still remains a mystery. Like all unsolved crimes it has been taken out and dusted down over the years and even more reasons have been put forward for the slaying.

Read still believes it was something to do with the Train Robbery money. Shortly before he left 'C' division a Mr Field had called at Savile Row asking to see him. Read was surprised to discover it was the former solicitor's managing clerk, Brian Field. He told Read he knew Buggy because he had served part of his sentence in the same prison and that there was no doubt in his mind that Buggy had heard the story of the handing over of the money from the robbery for safekeeping. According to Field it was common gossip in the prison.[14]

A final footnote is provided by Tony Lambrianou, one of the Krays' runners. He had been turned over and questioned in the investigations into Buggy's death. Years later he met Roy James in Gartree.

> And the Weasel was asking me why Buggy had to go.
> He said, 'The money doesn't matter to me. I just wouldn't like to think Buggy died for it.'
> I was happy to tell Roy that we genuinely hadn't had anything to do with the murder.[15]

One murderer managed to evade justice for so long that the warrant against him was eventually withdrawn.

[14] L. Read and J. Morton, *Nipper*, p. 124 et seq.
[15] T. Lambrianou, *Inside the Firm*, pp. 118–19.

John Gaul, procurer to the rich and with a conviction for living off immoral earnings, set up the contract killing of his estranged wife Barbara, a former children's nanny, who was shot outside the Black Lion Hotel, Patcham, near Brighton, where she had been visiting her daughter Samantha on Monday, 12 January 1977. She died eleven weeks later.

On the basis that when a wife is killed the first person to be questioned is the husband, John Gaul was taken in to Cannon Row police station but was later released. Almost immediately he fled to Rio de Janeiro. Later that year he was found with a new nanny, Angela Pilch, in Switzerland before moving on to Malta.

Originally Gaul had been a property dealer, who diversified into motor trading and then returned to his first love when in 1952 he took over Sun Real Estates, a publicly quoted company which had not paid any dividends for some time. In 1958 it had paid an 8.5 per cent dividend and had a trading profit of £37,000. In 1962 the profit was £122,000 with premises worth £3 million.

On 11 October 1962 Gaul had been fined £25,000 for living off prostitution. Through a firm called Rent and Management he had leased out flats in Soho to prostitutes, charging £20 a week for old squalid properties with poor furniture. Of the £20 only £8 8s was entered in the rent book. It was collected by a pair of old Soho characters, Thomas Jenkins and Anthony Deguilio.

Now, in theory, all that was behind him. In practice it was not. His name came up in both the Profumo and Lambton vice scandals.

It was not difficult for the police to trace the actual killers of his wife. On the way from the killing the shotgun used was dropped from a car window and later the car was traced to a breakers yard in East London. The contract had been arranged in Norfolk with two

East End brothers, Roy and Keith Edgeler.

The brothers were gaoled on 24 June 1976. In the witness box Roy said that from his limited knowledge he did not believe it was John Gaul who had arranged the contract for which he was to have been paid £10,000. Roy Edgeler was given a recommendation of a minimum of twenty years to serve.

On 3 April 1978 Gaul was arrested in Malta, where he was living on a boat in the harbour, having defied efforts to have him returned to the United Kingdom. There had been troubles with the United Kingdom's extradition treaty with Malta because the Home Secretary had refused to extradite a Maltese woman on a forgery charge. Gaul had high political connections in Malta.

Why should he be involved in the killing? he asked. Barbara had agreed to an undefended divorce, claiming neither alimony nor costs, and had already relinquished claims to the child, Samantha. There was no reason why he should have had her killed, he argued plausibly.

On 24 April 1978 a blast destroyed a mini-cab office and flats in Hackney Road, owned by Printing House Properties Ltd, a £100 company owned by Gaul. It was thought that a Maltese, John Borg, who had been involved in West End properties over the years and who had been gaoled for ten years for gunning down another Maltese outside a Stepney cafe in 1953, had died in the blaze. This turned out to be correct. Borg's body was found in the wreckage on 3 May. Curiously, no smoke was found to have been in his lungs, a clear indication he had died before the fire. Things were made more complicated when it became known that a Portuguese, Carlos Amazonas, had made a statement to the police that Borg had been approached to kill Mrs Barbara Gaul. This statement had somehow found its way into the Soho underworld.

By 1981 Gaul was assumed to be safe in Malta because

of his political connections. Officially the explanation was that insufficient evidence had been supplied by the British police, but Gaul was now well established – he had built and leased out a 240-room hotel. In March that year he was reported to have had a serious heart attack. On 17 July 1981 a magistrate in Malta said the prosecution case was weak and refused to order extradition.

By April 1984 it was reported the English police had given up. Even if he came back, the passage of time had made witnesses' memories unreliable. Gaul was said to be ill and medical certificates were sent to the Director of Public Prosecutions and the warrant was dropped on his orders. Gaul at once flew to Switzerland and then came back for his son Simon's wedding in September 1984. He died in September 1989 in Italy. He had been reported missing but it was three days before it was realized he had died in a Milan hospital.

According to the *Sun*[16] Keith Edgeler, then in Ford Open Prison, named Gaul as the man who had ordered the contract. It was, he said, because Gaul feared Barbara was about to expose shady deals. He said he never received the payment for the murder. Despite offers by the police for a deal he had refused to talk on the basis that if a man could have his wife murdered, his own family was in danger.

In two connected gangland killings there still seems to be no general consensus of opinion as to why the victims were executed, nor for that matter is there complete certainty amongst the cognoscenti that the right men were put away. The Legal and General Murders was the last major case investigated by Bert Wickstead and it concerned the deaths of two second division robbers –

---

[16] 31 October 1989.

the gaunt, gangling Billy Moseley and his close friend, Micky Cornwall, the first of whom disappeared in the autumn of 1974 and the second in the spring of the following year.

The Legal and General Gang[17] was headed by Reginald Dudley, a hard-man with convictions for violence, and a most unlikely villain, Bobby 'Fat Bob' Maynard, a roly-poly amiable man who had a terrible speech impediment caused, it was said, by being severely beaten in a fight in a club in Tottenham Court Road. He spoke extremely slowly with long gaps between words and was seemingly unaware of this problem because if interrupted by the recipient of his telephone call with a 'Hello Bobby', he would reply 'How-do-you-know-it's-me?'

By the mid-1970s Dudley had become a professional receiver. 'He didn't mess about with anything except high-quality stuff', dealing alike with the underworld and the police, for whom he was also said to be an informer.

'He was well respected in the fraternity. I always thought he could go as far as the Krays and the Richardsons. He had a team and he had the ability and the sense of purpose to do to North London what the Krays did to East London,' says one police officer who knew him.

On his release from prison in September 1974 Moseley was horrified to find his old schoolfriend Maynard had teamed up with Dudley. On 26 September Moseley set off for a meeting at 6.30 p.m. with Ronnie Fright at the Victoria Sporting Club in Stoke Newington. He had been having an affair with Frankie, Ronnie's wife, whilst

[17] The soubriquet Legal and General Gang came about when Dudley and Maynard appeared in a Kentish Town public house wearing identical overcoats which resembled a popular television commercial for the Legal and General insurance group.

Fright was serving a seven-year sentence for armed robbery and the meeting was to clear the air between them. Moseley was never again seen alive. Parts of his body started to surface a week later in the Thames near Rainham. Although the head and hands were missing it was possible to make a positive identification of the body since Moseley had suffered from a rare skin disease. The autopsy also showed he had been tortured. His toe-nails had been pulled out and he had been burned.

Moseley's other great friend, Micky Cornwall, was released from prison a fortnight after the bits started floating along the river. He was tied in to Dudley through a short liaison he had been having with Dudley's daughter Kathy. Kathy had once been married to a John Dann, known as Donuts possibly because he had worked in a bakery but also because it was said he cut holes in people who offended him. That marriage had broken down and she had taken up with a Ray Baron. When, in turn, he went to prison, she took up with Cornwall. In theory this was just as heinous a crime as Moseley's affair with Frankie Fright but neither Baron nor the paterfamilias, Dudley, seems to have objected.

Cornwall, along with any number of criminals before and after him, was looking for a 'big one'. He now had a new girlfriend, Gloria Hogg, and was looking for sufficient money to buy a place in the country. Cornwall, again like many other criminals, lacked discretion. He confided his plans to John Moriarty, hardly the best person because Moriarty later turned supergrass after being shot in the leg for the second time. Cornwall left Gloria for the 'big one' on Sunday, 3 August 1975. He had been renting a room from another police informer, Colin Saggs, and left shortly before two men came looking for him. Sharon Saggs, his daughter, would identify them as Dudley and Maynard at the trial. Moriarty saw him at a bus stop in Highgate on 23 August and that seems to have been the last sighting of him before his body was found in a newly dug grave at Hatfield, Hertfordshire. He had been shot in the head.

The old 'gangbuster' Wickstead's last swoop was on 22 January 1976. Seven people out of eighteen taken were charged. They had been interviewed over a period of four days[18] and included Dudley and his daughter Kathy, Maynard and Ronnie Fright. During the period in custody they were said to have made admissions which amounted to evidence against them. Dudley was alleged to have said of Cornwall, 'I told him if he had sex with her, I would kill him.' Maynard allegedly admitted going to the Saggs' house looking for Cornwall. 'It was business,' he said. As for the question put to him that he had told Fright to be late for the rendezvous at the Victoria Sporting Club, he is said to have replied, 'I'm not answering that, otherwise I'm finished.' Apparently, Wickstead had had a tape-recorder fitted into his desk at the police station but had never switched it on. Why not? asked the defence.

'I am a police officer who believes in police methods and tape-recorders are not used in police interviews,' replied the Commander.

The prosecution's case was that the killings had occurred because (1) Moseley had had an affair with Frankie Fright, (2) he had fallen out with Dudley ten years earlier, (3) Moseley had been suggesting Dudley was a grass, (4) he, Moseley, was sitting on the proceeds of a large jewellery robbery, (5) out of sheer sadism, (6) Cornwall had set out to avenge Moseley's death, (7) he

---

[18] The effective implementation of the Police and Criminal Evidence Act of 1984 was nearly ten years away. At the time suspects in serious cases could be interviewed almost endlessly. Then such protection as was available to suspects was the informal Judges' Rules. These did not include the right to the presence of a solicitor during interview.

had discovered Dudley and Maynard were the killers and so (8) had had more than a brief liaison with Kathy in order to find out the truth. It was said Moseley had been shot with a single bullet. The case against Ronnie Fright was that he was deliberately late for his meet with Moseley outside the Victoria Sporting Club and so had lured him to his death.

Apart from the confessions and the liaisons between the various dead and accused there was not, as the judge, Mr Justice Swanwick, told the jury, 'evidence on which the Crown could ask you to convict'. The police had stated on oath the confessions were accurate and the defence had said they were fabricated. Whom were the jury to believe?

Much of the rest of the evidence was the rag-bag of serving prisoners who, having seen the light, were able to give evidence against their former cell-mates.

In the end Ronnie Fright was acquitted, as was another defendant, while a third had been acquitted at the direction of the judge. Bobby Maynard was found guilty on a majority decision on the third day of the jury's retirement. He and Dudley were sentenced to life imprisonment; Kathy received a suspended sentence along with an old-time villain, Charlie Clarke. Six weeks later Moseley's head, wrapped in a plastic bag, was found in a public lavatory in Barnsbury, North London. Perhaps significantly the copy of the *Evening News* wrapped around it was dated 16 June 1977, when the jury had been in retirement.

Some facts emerged from the inquest. The head was in 'extremely' good condition, Professor James Cameron, who had undertaken the initial autopsy, told the coroner. Traces of car paint indicated it had been in a garage for some of the three years since Moseley had choked on his own blood. That removed one of the pillars on which the Crown had based its case. It had also been in a deep freeze, for it was on the thaw when it was discovered.

After the appeals were rejected the families of both Dudley and Maynard launched a campaign to prove their innocence. It did not take the extreme course adopted by the friends of George Davis. T-shirts were sold and there was a march through Camden Town to Hyde Park Corner. Bobby Maynard junior stood as a candidate in the European Parliament elections in June 1984. Inevitably, however, the campaign suffered with Davis' conviction for the Bank of Cyprus raid. Dudley appeared on television in the 1984 BBC programme *Lifers*. Nor was the North London underworld convinced of their guilt. Whilst it was accepted that Dudley was capable of great violence, few could believe that Maynard had the same capacity. Over the years various names have been put up as the potential killers but no real enquiry has been undertaken by the authorities.

In 1991 'Liberty' adopted the Maynard–Dudley case as one for special consideration in a campaign against wrongful convictions. With the passing of the Police and Criminal Evidence Act of 1984 it is doubtful if there would have been convictions in the Legal and General case.[19]

Several years later, in November 1985, two more heads turned up. They seem to have been thrown one night at the door of Harold Hill police station, Essex. They belonged to hard-man David Elmore and James 'Jimmy the Wad' Waddington (so named because he always carried a wad of money) who had vanished on St Valentine's Day 1984, thereby giving the press a good deal of licence to use the word 'massacre'. Elmore, a night club bouncer, and Waddington, who happened to

---

[19] For a more detailed account of the case, see B. Woffinden, *Miscarriages of Justice*.

be in the wrong place at the wrong time, were bound
hand and foot, then attacked with a ceremonial sword
stolen from a sports club and throttled with a tablecloth
in the Kaleli restaurant in Station Road, Barking.
According to a witness, Brian Wilson, Elmore began
reciting the Lord's Prayer and when he reached 'Thy will
be done', he was interrupted by one of his attackers who
said, 'You're dead right, son'. The killing was said by the
prosecutor, William Denny QC, to be the culmination
of a longstanding feud between the Elmores and another
East End family, the Maxwells, which had included an
axe attack on a relative, Mickey Maxwell, ten years
earlier. An alternative theory was that Elmore had been
running a protection racket and that he and Waddington
had been attacked as they had finished their meal at the
Turkish restaurant.

Bar steward David Maxwell was acquitted of the
murder in January 1985 after just an hour's retirement
by the jury. 'I am off to celebrate with my family,' he
told reporters.

I have been held in prison since March for crimes
I had nothing to do with. The jury accepted what
I told them about prosecution witnesses lying
through their teeth. We had only got the word of
the police that these two men were murdered in the
first place.

The only reason that I can put forward as to why
the staff at the restaurant implicated us is that they
have something to hide and they wanted a fall guy.

David Reader, who was acquitted of assisting in the
disposal of the bodies, added, 'It's all been an ordeal.
The allegations against us and my brother are totally
without foundation.'

His brother Ronnie Reader was in Spain at the time

of David's and Maxwell's arrest, and in November 1984 announced that he would be returning to England. 'I'm giving myself up,' he told the *Sun* in an exclusive article, in which he said he would return home after Maxwell and his brother had faced their trial. 'I'm taking a terrible chance,' said Ronnie, who at the time lived in a small flat in 'picturesque Nerja' on the Costa del Sol. 'If I am found guilty, it means life imprisonment.'[20] He wasn't.

After his acquittal the senior detective in the case said the police 'are not looking for anyone else'.[21]

After the heads were found, Jimmy Waddington's mother Winifred told the *Daily Express*, 'I felt desolation not knowing where his last resting place might be or what exactly happened to him. I wanted to have him found in one piece but it looks like it could be him.'[22]

Others victims, such as Tony Mella, seem to have been killed almost pointlessly. Mella, a small-time thief and one-time proprietor of a spinner,[23] had been a boxer. In his early days he thought he had promise as a heavyweight. He fought at the Mile End Arena where his friends had arranged that his opponent should throw the contest. In the next match he came up against Dennis Powell, a southern area champion, who would not agree to the fix. Powell gave him a bad beating before knocking him out.

Later he became semi-respectable and took to running

[20] *Sun*, 7 November 1984.

[21] *Today*, 21 March 1986.

[22] *Daily Express*, 6 November 1985.

[23] A spinner, now rarely seen, was a cross between the three-card trick and a roulette wheel. Played outside racecourses and dog-tracks, it consisted of the punter betting on which suit of cards came up. It was, of course, fixed by using a stick, known in the trade as a Haley, to stop the wheel.

clubs such as the El Ababi in Soho. He was heavily involved with gambling machines with interests throughout England. There are a number of colourful stories about him. One is that a bayonet was rammed into his backside and left there for several hours. The metal cauterized the wound and it healed. He also fell foul of the dwarf Roy Smith, who wrestled as Fuzzy Kaye:

> . . . I opened this club for dwarves in Gerrard Street. Tony Mulla [sic], who was a big villain in those days, had two clip joints down the street. He thought I was taking away his business. He was angry and was wailing up and down the street, just across from my club, shouting at me: 'You think you're Jack the Lad', 'Midget mafia', and so on, trying to tell me that I was being cheeky and was out of order opening a club on his patch. . . . Anyway I wasn't having that and took him up the stairs above his clip joint, took his trousers down and slashed him across the arse with a razor; gave him noughts and crosses.[24]

Another story is of his death. He had, the story goes, offended a rival organization and a button man had been sent from America to carry out the hit. He went to Mella's office, asked if he was Mella and shot him. The gunman turned and walked calmly down the stairs. Mella, badly injured, managed to take his own gun from his safe, followed the American on to the street, shot him and then died himself.

The truth is more prosaic. One of Mella's minders was Big Alf Melvin, another man with a long criminal history. Over a period of time Melvin was treated appallingly by Mella both in front of the hostesses and

[24] G. Tremlett, *Little Legs*, p. 100.

friends and the punters. 'Like he was a serf,' said Buller Ward. There was also the possibility that Mella had pulled a fast one and deprived Melvin of his interest in one of the clubs.

One afternoon in the Bus Stop Club in Soho, Melvin said to Tony Mella, 'You've took a right fucking liberty there. We been pals all these years. I been more like a brother to you and now you've gone and took a liberty like that.'

He fired at Mella, who ran out of the club shouting, 'The silly bastard's shot me.' Mella died on the pavement with his head being held by one of the hostesses who had followed him outside. Melvin sat in the club for some time and then put the gunbarrel in his mouth and pulled the trigger.[25]

English criminal law has always been a bit squeamish about convicting defendants of murder if no body has been found. It dates back to the seventeenth century when a man was executed for murder, only for his supposed victim to appear some years later. For a long time it was the case that there could be no conviction for murder without a body. Then in the 1880s came the case of Dudley and Stephens where the cabin boy was eaten at sea. In the case of James Camb, he was convicted although the body of Gay Gibson had been pushed through a porthole.

Then after the war came the case of Onufrejczyk, who was convicted of the murder of his partner in a farm even though the body was not found. From then on there was a series of cases where death was presumed beyond a reasonable doubt from the surrounding circumstances. Mrs McKay (killed by the Hossein brothers), Frank Mitchell, Jack 'the Hat' McVitie and Ginger Marks were

[25] H. Ward, *Buller*, p. 130.

all cases where there was no body. However, perhaps the most amazing series of cases where no bodies were found resulted from the killings by John Child, Henry MacKenny and Terence Pinfold.

Unlike Gerard who seems to have been a one-man hit squad, the three set themselves up as a team of contract killers and, for a time at least, they appear to have been very successful. In 1972 John Childs, more usually the getaway driver on armed robberies, discussed the prospect of providing contract killing with Henry MacKenny, a huge man who had his fingers tattooed with LTFC on his right hand and ESUK on his left, and Terence Pinfold. These two were partners in a firm which made both life-jackets and cuddly toys, working out of a small hall belonging to St Thomas' church in Haydon Road, Dagenham, Essex.

The idea met with mutual approbation but it was not until two years later that it was put into execution, partly because Childs was given a prison sentence for burglary in October 1974. The third partner in the cuddly toy firm, Terence Eve, was thought not to be pulling his weight. According to Childs, who became the chief prosecution witness, he and MacKenny were waiting when Eve returned to the church hall in Dagenham one October evening after making some deliveries of toys, coincidentally to Bob Patience at the Barn Restaurant in Braintree. Eve was beaten senseless with a metal pipe and then strangled with a rope. There were two witnesses, Pinfold and Robert Winston Brown, an odd job man in the workshop but a one-time none too successful professional wrestler who had worked small halls as one of the many masked White Angels about at the time. The police made enquiries but they came to nothing.

The first actual contract, according to Childs, was George Brett, a haulage contractor and receiver. He disappeared along with his ten-year-old son Terence on the first Saturday of 1975. The fee was said to be £2000 and was paid by Leonard Thompson, who had been beaten up by Brett. It was a fee reduced by ten per cent because, so Childs told the court, Thompson supplied a sten-gun and two hundred rounds of ammunition. Brett's wife had been approached earlier in the week by a man who gave his name as Jennings. He had asked her to make sure Brett was about on the Saturday. He turned up again, this time as a 'city gent' wearing a Homburg hat and carrying an umbrella. Brett said he would follow him in his own car to look at a load the man had for disposal. As he was leaving, Brett's son Terence ran out and climbed into his father's Mercedes. Neither were seen again but the car was found near King's Cross station.

There were considerable rumours about his disappearance. Brett was believed to have been a police informer and it was said he had informed once too often. Another version was that he had stumbled on a crime syndicate ready to take over the remainder of the Krays' operations. Or he was the victim of a 'group who organize revenge beatings and shootings from prison' – a clear and erroneous reference to the Tibbs family, who were named in the newspaper article. Nevertheless it was announced that Bert Wickstead had been called in to the investigation. Finally it was suggested that he was enquiring too deeply into a bullion robbery which had netted £400,000 and for which George Brett's brother John was serving a fifteen-year sentence.[26] Yet again the police enquiries came to nothing. It was even thought possible that Brett would return one day.

Childs' version of events was that he had been the city gent. He had taken Brett and his son to the workshop,

[26] For footnote, see over.

where only three rounds had been required out of the
two hundred. MacKenny had fired the shots at George
Brett whilst Childs gave the child a worn teddy bear to
hold as he was killed.

In November 1975 the White Angel was the next to
go. Brown had earlier escaped from prison, where he
was serving a short sentence, and it was feared that when
recaptured he might trade off information about the Eve
killing. He was lured to Childs' council flat in Poplar,
where he was shot and then stabbed and struck with an
axe. As befitted a man able to take punishment in the
ring he survived these injuries and only died when run
through with a sword by Childs.

Nearly three years later the team pulled off another
contract. This time it was conducted, so Childs said, on
behalf of Paul Morton-Thurtle who had had sour
business dealings with a Frederick Sherwood, a constant
companion of criminals, who ran a nursing home in
Herne Bay. On 31 July 1978 Sherwood took his Rover
car to a potential purchaser and was never seen again.
The car was found in Earls Court. Childs' story on this
occasion was that the price of the contract was £4000,
payable by instalments of £1500 down and £500 a
fortnight. Sherwood was taken to MacKenny's bungalow, near the workshop, given the £480 he had asked for
the motor and shot while he checked the money.

The team's last success was on 12 October 1978 when
a roof-repairer, Ronnie Andrews, disappeared. He had
been having marital troubles with his wife Gwen. The

---

[26] On 29 November 1973 John Brett, together with three others
including George Ince, was convicted of the hijacking of a £400,000
consignment of silver bullion at Mountnessing, Essex. 'You played for
very high stakes – something over a third of a million pounds – and
the penalty must be severe,' said Mr Justice Milmo sentencing them.
(See Chapter 8.)

police made enquiries and also spoke to his best friend, Henry MacKenny, who was able to confirm that Andrews had both personal and business problems and might have moved on. What he did not say was that he was himself infatuated with Gwen. Andrews' Lincoln Continental was found the next day in the River Nene in Lincolnshire. A postcard signed Ann and postmarked nearby Wisbech was produced by Mrs Andrews, who said her husband had received it. The implication was that he had left home to set up a new life. A more convincing theory advanced by the police was that he had accidentally driven into the river while drunk and the body had been swept out to sea. The deep tidal currents were extremely strong and a half-empty bottle of vodka lay on the back seat of the car. Despite the connection of MacKenny with two of the victims, again the enquiry lapsed. Childs' version was that he had been given £500 to lure Andrews to his own flat, where MacKenny shot him whilst Tina, Childs' wife, made a pot of tea.

It was only when Childs was arrested following the hijacking of a Security Express armoured van in Hertford in June 1979 that he began to talk. He was arrested through his own carelessness in what had otherwise been a well-planned and executed robbery. The robbers had cleared £500,000 by impersonating Security Express employees. After the robbery they changed out of their uniforms in a public lavatory, leaving the clothing behind. In the pocket of one of the overalls were the keys to a BMW. It was not difficult for the police to trace the vehicle to its owner, an East End greengrocer. In a deal for a light sentence he returned the money which had been left in his care and then implicated both John Childs and MacKenny as part of the robbery team.

The case was initially investigated by Tony Lundy, then a Detective Inspector. He rightly supposed that this was not the first raid the team had carried out and interviewed each member with a view to getting confessions of other jobs. One of the team was even more forthcoming and named Childs and MacKenny as being involved in the killings of Andrews, Eve and the Bretts.

Lundy's initial inclination was to laugh at him but the man went on:

'There's going to be another murder shortly – and you know the victim.'

'What are you talking about?'

'Do you know a police officer called Treen?'

I said 'yeh' because John Treen had been one of my inspectors on the Flying Squad in 1977, so I knew him well. Treen had arrested MacKenny and Terry Pinfold in December 1976 but then the Director of Public Prosecutions dropped the case against MacKenny.

He said, 'MacKenny is going to murder Treen and Butcher,' who was the sergeant on the same case.[27]

Lundy recalled that MacKenny had been arrested in December 1976 over two bank robberies at Romford and Woodford. He was then placed on a total of eight identification parades but was not picked out. Nevertheless he was detained on the basis of witnesses' remarks of a big man – he stood 6 feet 6 inches. He was an associate of Terence Pinfold and, so the detectives investigating the case said, he had made verbal admissions. MacKenny denied these verbals and wrote out a statement giving a detailed notice of alibi.

The case against him had been dropped in July of the next year, whilst Pinfold was gaoled for ten years. When

[27] M. Short, *Lundy*, p. 74.

the allegations were dismissed he shouted threats at Treen, the officer in charge of the case. Later MacKenny had endeavoured to interest the media in a number of cases in which he said miscarriages of justice had occurred.

In turn Lundy had difficulties in getting senior officers to accept that the stories told by his informant were credible and it took him some time to persuade Commander Arthur Howard that the matter should be investigated further.

In December 1979 Childs became the first serial murderer in modern times to confess and give evidence against his accomplices. He had a hard time in the witness box, saying that he was drinking a bottle of whisky a day to try to obliterate the memory of killing Terence Brett. He did admit he had thought about writing a book on the killing but denied the potential title 'East End butcher'.

The juries' verdicts were curious. As to the murder of their partner Eve, Pinfold was convicted and MacKenny acquitted. Both were acquitted of the murder of the White Angel, Brown. MacKenny was convicted of the murder of Brett and his son, while Leonard Thompson, charged along with him, was acquitted and left court without a stain on his character, as did Paul Morton-Thurtle, acquitted in the case of Sherwood, the nursing home owner. MacKenny was convicted in that case as he was over the killing of Ronnie Andrews. He and Pinfold received life sentences, with, in MacKenny's case, a recommendation that he serve not less than twenty-five years.

He was not happy, shouting that he had never killed anybody but that through his life-saving jacket he had saved plenty. 'Straight people need protection from you,' he told Mr Justice May, 'and from mongols and mugs like you,' he added to the jury before the court was cleared.

But where did all the bodies go? Although there had been considerable forensic evidence of bloodstains and traces of hair which went to corroborate Childs' story, there was no trace of any of the six bodies. According to Childs, initially the idea had been to cut up the bodies using a butcher's mincing machine. This had proved too blunt to deal with Eve and the idea was abandoned.

The next suggested method was simplicity itself and extremely efficient. The bodies were cut up and then burned in a standard-size fireplace with an anthracite fire augmented by a gas burner. Bones which did not dissolve could be pounded on the hearth. The ashes were then emptied on waste ground. The disposal of a complete body took about twenty-four hours.

Professor James Cameron, the pathologist, was asked whether it would be possible to cremate a body in this way and tests were carried out. An 11-stone male pig, calculated as being the equivalent of a fully developed average-sized man, was taken to Childs' home. Cameron, using brute force, sawed up the carcass, taking just over five minutes. He described it as 'perfectly simple, requiring no anatomical knowledge'. The police and the pathologist then sat down to burn the body. Later Cameron told Philip Paul:

The temperature in the fire reached over 1000 degrees but the room never went above 75. It was all properly measured, logged and photographed. But when we put the intestines on the fire it almost went out. Because, as soon as it burnt through, the fluid ran. Later on we were told that MacKenny had washed out and dried the intestines before they were burnt.

The total burning of the pig took thirteen hours. We ended up with remains of ash, bone and whatnot which filled two large plastic bags. We then went over it twice with a hammer, as we were told MacKenny had done, and eventually finished up with a small plastic bag of ash with not a remnant of teeth or bone visible to the naked eye.

Repeated checks had been made outside the building during the burning, but no smell of roasting pork or other odour had been detected.[28]

Death from a striping, traditionally a slashing of the buttocks and anus rather than the face, was uncommon but on 24 August 1986 Michael Collins of Canning Town, said to have been trying to install a protection racket in the area, bled to death on his way to hospital. He and a friend, Mark Natrass, had been over powered in the Moonlight public house in Stratford Broadway, once owned by former England and West Ham football star Bobby Moore, when they were first sprayed with ammonia and then slashed by four men. One of the cuts to Collins severed an artery in his left leg.

A week later wealthy night club owner Peter Morris died after being stabbed with a flick knife, hit with an axe and finally shot three times as gangs battled outside the Telegraph pub, also in Stratford Broadway. The incident was said to be a revenge attack following the death of Collins.

[28] P. Paul, *Murder Under the Microscope*, p. 156.

12

The Last
Decade

Over Easter bank holiday 1983 a particularly unpleasant
robbery took place. A gang led by a 'toff' with a 'posh'
accent carried out what came to be called the Great
Banknote Raid in Curtain Road, Shoreditch, East
London. Seven million pounds was removed from the
Security Express headquarters when six masked bandits
burst in at about 10.30 a.m. One guard had petrol
poured over him and was threatened that if he did not
hand over the combination for the safe, he would
become a human torch. The guards were then tied and
blindfolded for the duration of the raid, which would last
a further five hours.

As with the Great Train Robbery it was a job which
had been on offer for some years and one which had
taken a considerable time in the planning. The Security
Express building had been known as Fort Knox and had
been thought to be a virtually impregnable fortress. The
underwriters put up the then staggering sum of £500,000
as a reward. But it was police work which paid off. One
of the men involved had been under observation for
some time and when he was being questioned about
another major robbery he told the police he had stored
Security Express money at his home. This led to the
arrest of an Allen Opiola, who was later given three

years and three months with a recommendation he serve this in police custody. Opiola was to turn Queen's Evidence against the rest of the gang.

He had allowed his home – the money would fit into most people's living rooms – to be used for counting and laundering the money. For this service, and for providing suitcases, making coffee, fetching a Chinese take-away whilst the money was being counted and later doing a certain amount of laundering, he received £30,000.

On 10 June 1985 John and James Knight – brothers of Ronnie who was aquitted of the murder of Tony Zomparelli and was once married to actress Barbara Windsor, herself a former girlfriend of Charles Kray – were arrested along with Billy Hickson.[1] Hickson, who had been shot accidentally by 'Colonel' George Copley, and the brothers were three of five men convicted. John Knight received twenty-two years, James eight for handling stolen monies and Hickson six. With his new wife, Ronnie Knight now lives in Spain, one of the so-called Famous Five from the Kray days, unwilling to return to England. The Five were reduced to four with the conviction of Frederick Foreman, who in 1990 received a nine-year sentence for his part in the handling of the Security Express monies. The remaining three are Ronald Everett, once a close friend of the twins, John James Mason, who was acquitted of conspiracy in the £8 million robbery of the Bank of America in 1976, and Clifford Saxe, one-time landlord of the Fox in Kingsland Road, Hackney, where the robbery is said to have been planned. Saxe is reputed to have bought two villas for just under £170,000 with part of his share.

Within six months the Security Express robbery had

---

[1] For further details of some members of the Knight family and friends' alleged involvement in organized crime, see Chapter 11.

paled into insignificance. On 26 November 1983 at 6.40 a.m. the biggest of the biggest of robberies took place when £26 million in gold was lifted from the Brinks-Mat warehouse on the Heathrow trading estate. Its ramifications would run for nearly a decade. Again the guards were threatened: one with castration; others had petrol poured over them; another was coshed for not producing keys sufficiently speedily and was then punched in the stomach as he lay on the ground. The gang drove off with 6400 bars of gold. It was clearly a job executed with help from the inside. The premises had been opened with a key and the gang knew the guards' names as well as the workings of the vaults and locks.

It was only a matter of days before the police latched on to the last guard to arrive that morning – Tony Black – who had missed the robbery because he was ten minutes late for work. Black confessed. His sister was living with Brian Robinson, who had been on the Williams & Glyn's robbery in 1978 and in 1981 had benefited through the mistakes of the No 5 Regional Crime Squad.[2] Black identified two more of the team, Tony White and Michael McAvoy.

---

[2] Robinson was one of a number of criminals who were known as 'The Colonel'. The most famous example is Ronnie Kray and another is George Copley. It was Copley who was instrumental in sabotaging the efforts of the No 5 Regional Crime Squad when in June 1981 he and Frankie Fraser junior were on trial at Oxford on charges of robbery. Three months previously a Sergeant Pook visited him in Reading gaol and was secretly taped by Copley in a conversation in which Pook confirmed an offer that if Copley was to admit his part in the Williams & Glyn's robbery and also give evidence of corruption against certain London detectives, he would receive only a five-year sentence. The tape was produced at the trial and the case was stopped. It was 'hopelessly compromised' said Stephen Wooler for the Director of Public Prosecutions.

In December 1984 Robinson and McAvoy received twenty-five years each; White was acquitted. Later there was said to be £50,000 on offer to free McAvoy and Robinson. Black, who had given evidence for the Crown, was handed a six-year sentence. That still left a number of villains at large and a very large amount of property missing. The gold, in the form of marked ingots of extremely high quality, could not be offered to legitimate dealers; instead it was being smelted by a small bullion firm, Scadlynn, on the outskirts of Bristol.

A surveillance operation on a Kenneth Noye ended in disaster. An undercover police officer, John Fordham, clad in a balaclava helmet, was stabbed to death in the grounds of Noye's home at West Kingsdowne in Kent. Noye, charged with the murder of Fordham, gave evidence that 'I just froze with horror. All I saw when I flashed my torch on this masked man was the two eyeholes and the mask. I thought that was my lot. I thought I was going to be a dead man.' He stabbed Fordham eleven times.

In November 1985 he and Brian Reader, who was with Noye at the time, were acquitted of murder. In July 1986 both were convicted of handling the Brinks-Mat gold, along with Garth Chappell, a Scadlynn director. Reader received nine years and Noye, whose defence was that he was a gold smuggler and VAT fraudster as opposed to a thief and receiver, ended up with fourteen years. However, there are still plenty of figures in the underworld who believe that his defence was correct. No Brinks Mat gold was ever found on his premises and, although £100,000 of gold was discovered, tests showed this could not have been from the Brinks-Mat robbery.

Garth Chappell received ten years, whilst Matteo Constantino, sixty-eight, a longstanding Hatton Garden villain who had allowed his company to be used in a false VAT claim, received a suspended sentence of twelve months for conspiracy to evade VAT on the gold. After being melted down it had then been delivered in small parcels to London. The gold was sold on the legitimate market to dealers who were charged VAT at fifteen per cent. Constantino had been acquitted of dishonest handling and was suffering from cancer at the time.

The convictions of Noye and Reader were the greatest successes the police had on the Scadlynn side of things. The next year John Palmer, a former director of Scadlynn who had been invited to leave Spain by the authorities and who chose to be deported to Britain from Rio de Janeiro, was put on trial at the Old Bailey. He was charged with conspiring with Noye and Reader dishonestly to handle the gold. He was acquitted and went to live off the proceeds of his time share business in Tenerife.

Nor was there any greater success in the case of John Fleming, who was deported from Florida in 1986. In March of the next year, with evidence given against him by a new supergrass, Patrick Diamond, Fleming was charged with dishonestly handling nearly £500,000 of the Brinks-Mat proceeds. At the committal proceedings at Horseferry Road Magistrates' Court he was found to have no case to answer. Fleming told reporters, 'I feel a great relief. It has been a bad year,' before he returned to Spain where he was involved in a car accident and again deported.

The year 1991 proved fatal for Noye's former friend, forty-three-year-old Nick Whiting, who ran a garage at Wrotham in Kent. Whiting had been questioned back in 1983 over a Range Rover sold to Noye and bought back. Now on 6 June Whiting vanished from the garage along with five cars. At first it seemed to be a straightforward kidnapping but when all the cars stolen in the raid on his garage were recovered within a few days, unkind suggestions came on offer, including one that Whiting had staged his own disappearance over the Brinks-Mat spoils and that he had gone on the run with a friend of his, Lennie 'Little Lew', who was also wanted in connection with Brinks-Mat.

Ex-racing driver Whiting had secured a plot of land during the period of falling property prices and had borrowed bent money to finance a building deal. One suggestion was that the mortgagor wanted his money back. A variation on the theme is that Whiting owed money on the cars. At the beginning of June his body was found in marshland in Essex, nearly a month after his abduction. It appeared he had been beaten up, bound hand and foot, and stuffed in a car boot. He had then been shot in the back of the head, seemingly after being frog-marched across at least three miles of boggy ground.

Throughout the late 1970s and 1980s the police had adopted a more aggressive policy towards armed robbers. Stake-outs were followed by shoot-outs. One of the first to go was Micky Calvey, shot in a robbery in 1978. The old-timers didn't have it so good any more. On 9 July 1987 Nicholas Payne and Michael Flynn were shot dead in Plumstead as they tried to attack a Securicor van. Four months later, in November, Derek Whitlock died in a hail of bullets in Woolwich as he mounted a similar operation.

On 13 April 1989 Terry Dewsnap and James Farrell failed to batter their way into the post office strongroom at North Harrow and died. They had been staked out by the police for over a month. Dewsnap, once related by marriage to night club owner Joe Wilkins, had served six years for receiving monies stolen from the Dunstable branch of Barclays Bank following the kidnapping of the manager in 1976. Farrell had served twelve years for holding up the National Westminster Bank at Isleworth after his conviction in June 1977. 'They needn't have shot him quite so many times,' said one of the relatives.

One of the oldest surviving armed robbers of recent times has been John Hilton who, in September 1991, was jailed for life. He was then sixty-two, frail and grey-haired, but he had killed three people during his thirty-year career which had ended in Burlington Gardens, Piccadilly. In 1963 he had been given a life sentence for the murder of a man in the celebrated raid on the Co-op dairy in Mitcham, South London. He was freed on licence in February 1978 and a month later he and Alan Roberts robbed a Hatton Garden jeweller, Leo Grunhut, outside his home in Golders Green. He accidentally shot his partner in the thigh and as the jeweller tried to escape shot him in the back. The proceeds of the raid were £3000 in cash and £277,000 in diamonds. Hilton managed to get his partner into their getaway car and drove him to a garage in South London where he bled to death. Roberts was buried on a railway embankment at Dartford, Kent. Grunhut died a month later.

Hilton told the police, 'The course of history of armed robbers is littered with bodies. If it had been me then Roberts would have done exactly the same thing. Roberts got in the way and I shot him in the thigh. The jeweller was running to his front door so I shot him in the back from three feet.'

In June 1981 Hilton had received fourteen years for seven robberies, an attempted robbery and two charges of conspiracy. On 6 October 1990 he escaped from Kingston Prison in Portsmouth and raided a jewellers shop in Brighton. The haul this time was jewellery worth £90,000. His career has seemingly closed with a raid by him and his partner on a jewellers in Burlington Gardens when, on 4 December 1990, they terrorized two brothers into handing over £420,000 in jewellery. The brothers gave chase and Hilton fired three shots before he was tackled and overpowered by police, the brothers and other jewellers. At his trial he refused to allow his counsel to put forward any mitigation.

With the police on the alert for armed robbers, the pattern changed. The year 1987 was that of the international inside job, which surpassed, on paper at least, even the Brinks-Mat robbery. In July of that year the Knightsbridge Safe Deposit Box Centre, opposite Harrods, was robbed of £40 million by American antiques dealer Eric Rubin working with Italian Valerio Viccei and the manager of the deposit company, Parvez Latif, the black sheep of a wealthy Pakistani family who had been promised a third share of the proceeds and had taken out £1 million insurance on the company.

Latif, then in serious financial difficulties, agreed to let Rubin and Viccei into the building. The guards were tied up and threatened and the 120 safety deposit boxes were stripped. Once again it was a grass who brought about the team's downfall. Rubin, a shadowy man who held neither bank account nor credit cards, had commuted from New York for the robbery. Valerio Viccei, who had links with neo-Fascist terror groups in Italy going back to his teens, had lived the life of a playboy with tastes in women, Gucci shoes, fast cars and cocaine, not necessarily in that order. He was wanted in Italy for a series of bank robberies. In January 1987 Rubin had teamed up with Viccei to rob Coutts Bank in Cavendish Square, the first time in its three-hundred-year history that Coutts had been robbed. To make things even cosier amongst the conspirators Viccei was also sleeping with Latif's girlfriend, Pamela Seamarks. Viccei, whose fingerprint was left at the scene when he cut himself – some police think deliberately – had intended to return to Colombia, taking with him his black Ferrari Testarossa. He had difficulties in obtaining an export licence, delayed his departure and was arrested. He received twenty-two years while Latif received sixteen. The member of the gang who turned Queen's Evidence to put them all away had the now almost statutory five. Later Rubin, said to be a dying man, was extradited back to Britain and received a twelve-year sentence.[3]

On 24 April 1990 the Great Train Robber Charlie Wilson was shot dead beside his swimming pool at his home in Marbella. He had been hosing down the pool area when his wife, Patricia, answered a knock on the door. There was a man with a South London accent asking for her husband. She fetched Charlie and he and the young man went off together.

At the inquest held in London in November 1991 Patricia Wilson said:

> I heard the man say 'I am a friend of Eamonn.' I had a feeling there were two people there, although I couldn't say why.
>
> I heard two very loud bangs and at first I thought it was from the building site next door, but then I heard the dog screaming.
>
> Charlie was lying at the side of the pool face down. The man had gone and the gate was open.
>
> I saw blood coming from his mouth and Charlie did a sort of a press-up and gestured in the direction the man had gone.

Initially it was reported he had been killed with a single karate blow but the autopsy showed he had been shot in the side of the neck and the bullet had lodged there. As the shot passed through the larynx it would have caused heavy bleeding and as he inhaled blood he would have been unable to cry out. The dog had a

---

[3] Viccei wrote his own account of the affair whilst in Parkhurst in *Knightsbridge* (pub. Blake hardbacks).

broken leg and had to be destroyed.

The inquest was told by Detective Superintendent Alec Edwards that although there was no direct evidence to link Wilson with drug dealing, there was much circumstantial evidence, such as his lifestyle and his visits to Morocco.

> As far as the Spanish police and the British police are concerned, there is circumstantial evidence that this is a drug-related incident.
>
> We know of his meeting British criminals who are known drug dealers and who have since been convicted of drug dealing and with one who has also been executed in a gangland killing.

A verdict that he had been shot by persons unknown was recorded. Paul Spencer, a solicitor for the Wilson family, said after the inquest that the drug allegations were strongly denied.

After his release from prison in 1978 – he was the last of the Great Train Robbers to be freed – Wilson had led something of a charmed life so far as the courts were concerned. In 1982 he had been one of seven men charged in a £2 million VAT fraud involving the melting down of £16 million-worth of gold Krugerrands. Charges against him were dropped when the jury had disagreed twice and he paid £400,000 to Customs and Excise. In 1984 he spent four months in custody awaiting trial for the alleged armed robbery of a security van. He was freed amid allegations of police corruption.

The executed man referred to by Edwards was Roy Francis Adkins, whose inquest was heard the next day. In the convoluted way of life in the underbelly of society, James Rose had pleaded guilty to drug offences at Chelmsford Crown Court in January 1990, naming Adkins as the leader of the gang. Apparently Rose had been authorized to say this by Wilson and it was something which, not surprisingly, upset Adkins, who then had ordered the execution of Wilson. There was, however, no suggestion that any of Wilson's friends had killed Adkins by way of reprisal. It was an entirely separate matter.

On 28 September 1990, the night of his death, Adkins had met two Colombians in the Nightwatch bar of the American Hotel in Amsterdam. He had been the middleman in selling parcels of stolen emeralds in Amsterdam; he had been approached by a Sean O'Neil and several successful runs had been carried out. Then one of the parcels had been stolen from O'Neil and the Colombians wanted their money as a matter of urgency. Adkins persuaded O'Neil to attend a meeting to explain in person what had happened.

According to O'Neil he had gone to the Nightwatch bar and had seen Adkins with the Colombians. Adkins gestured to O'Neil to continue walking. O'Neil had then heard eight gunshots and had run out of the hotel. He had not known Adkins was dead until he read the papers the next day.[4]

In the 1970s some members of various families had great influence in South London: the Tobins, the Hennesseys, the Smiths in Deptford, the Frenches in Lewisham and the Porritts and their quasi-cousins, the Reddens. 'Flash' Harry Hayward had the Harp of Erin, the Frenches had the Deptford Arms, and Peter and Bernie Hennessey, with a manager firmly in place to

---

[4] This evidence was given by a Customs and Excise officer. Earlier in 1991 O'Neil had been acquitted at Isleworth Crown Court of charges relating to £10 million-worth of cocaine. Three Colombians co-accused were sentenced to terms of up to eighteen years' imprisonment. Now, although he had previously made a statement, O'Neil could not be found to give evidence in person at Adkins' inquest.

hold the licence, ran the Dog and Bell. In 1966 Peter Hennessey had served a sentence of ten years for warehouse breaking and his brother Bernard had a conviction for conspiracy to rob. The third brother, Micky, friend of Alfie Gerard, would later be a party in the big drug-smuggling case involving Nikolaus Chrastny.

During the decade a new name appeared on the South London scene, that of the Arif family from Stockwell, originally from Turkish Cyprus and now the kings of the Old Kent Road. 'It doesn't matter whose name it is over the door of the pub in some areas,' says one police officer, 'it's the Arifs who own it.' Pubs, restaurants and clubs, including the Connoisseur in the Old Kent Road, are said to have been bought with the proceeds of a series of major armed robberies.

The head of the family is forty-two-year-old Dogan Arif, currently serving fourteen years' imprisonment for his part in an £8.5 million drug-smuggling plot. At the time of his sentence he had followed the tradition of porn king James Humphreys (Hastings United) and master fraudsman Robert Maxwell (Oxford United) in owning a football club, non-league Fisher Athletic, in South-East London. During his time as chairman, the club, which at one time rose to the so called Fifth Division, the Gola League, was involved in paying substantial transfer fees for well-known players and had as its manager Malcolm Allison. In 1983 Dogan was acquitted of taking part in a bogus arms deal plot to swindle the Ayatollah Khomeini out of £34 million.

The family first came to some sort of national prominence when in May 1977 Osar Arif was acquitted of the murder of security guard David Cross in a robbery when £103,000 was stolen from a security van on the A2. The windscreen was smashed with a sledgehammer and the crew blasted with a shotgun. Photographs of the fleeing robbers were taken by a passer-by while other onlookers chased them up a bank at the side of the road before they too were fired upon. Bekir Arif was convicted of disposing of guns which had been found in the Surrey Docks; he received five years.

In 1981 Dennis and Bekir Arif were seen in the market square in Bromley near a Securicor van by an off-duty police officer. He was suspicious of their behaviour and went to intercept them in his car. A chase ensued, with the raiders throwing away crash helmets as they drove. They were convicted of conspiracy to rob.

On 27 November 1990 the police shot dead Kenny Baker, one of a four-man gang armed with enough weapons for a small war, including a Brazilian-made revolver, a 12-bore Browning self-loading shotgun, a US Army self-loading Colt, an Enfield Mark II revolver and a Browning 1922 pistol. He and three of the Arif family had ambushed a Securicor van parked on a garage forecourt in Reigate whilst the woman guard and a colleague went to buy drinks from a cafe. It was due to deliver some £750,000 to various branches of Barclays Bank. They were forced back into the van at gunpoint by Dennis Arif wearing a 'grandfather' mask. The plan was for the van to be driven away followed by a pick-up truck driven by Mehmet Arif, Dennis' brother, with Kenny Baker in the passenger seat.

The police, however, working in Operation Yamato – named after the Japanese sneak attack on Pearl Harbor – had been targeting the Arifs. Squad members rammed the van and Dennis Arif and his brother-in-law, Anthony Downer, threw down their weapons. Mehmet Arif and Kenny Baker did not do so.

'I felt a muzzle blast across the left side of my face and realized he [Baker] was shooting at me and I could tell my life was in danger,' PC William Hughes said in a statement at Dennis Arif's trial. 'I fired two shots at

Baker and then I heard two shots on my left and saw the passenger window disintegrate.'

Mehmet, who was wounded, and Downer both pleaded guilty to conspiracy to rob and possession of a firearm with intent. Dennis Arif ran the defence of duress, saying that he owed Baker £60,000 because of gambling debts – he had lost over £100,000 gambling in the previous twenty years – and that Baker had threatened to shoot him if he did not pay it back.[5] He had taken it seriously when he heard that Baker had previously shot a man. He was not believed. Earlier in the year both men had attended an Arif family wedding at the Savoy along with the other powerful South London families, the Colemans, Frasers, Whites, Adams and Hiscocks.

The jury took only an hour to convict him and afterwards friends of Baker pooh-poohed the idea that he would force anyone into committing a robbery. 'But Kenny wouldn't have minded being an excuse,' one of them told reporter Duncan Campbell. 'It is accepted that if someone is on their toes or dead you can drop them in it.' Perfectly sporting behaviour. Dennis Arif received a sentence of twenty-two years; Mehmet and Anthony Downer eighteen years each.

At the trial Dennis had asked to be tried under another name because of the prejudice the name Arif might have on a jury. After all, in the 1981 case involving Dennis Arif for conspiracy to rob and firearms offences, the police were convinced that there would be an attempt to nobble the jury. The first sign seems to have been as early as the first week of that trial when Michael

---

[5] In English law the defence of duress is extremely difficult to establish. In essence the accused must show that he, or his family, was in a life-threatening situation and had no opportunity to report the matter to the police. It was a defence run with success by Tony Barry in the Kray trial.

Arif, another brother, was seen with a man who could be described as a minder outside the court waiting for the jury to come in. On the road outside, a BMW was seen moving slowly. Michael Arif may have seen the police observation and he jumped into the car, later traced to the ownership of a defence witness. The next day a woman approached a woman juror on the underground offering money for a favourable verdict. The juror had the courage to report the incident.

In hindsight it seems incredible that the trial judge did not order blanket protection of the jury, or that the prosecution did not think to ask for it, but when the judge asked who wanted protection only five said they did. They included the woman who had been approached. In the end the jury failed to agree and when the police took the woman home she broke down, saying she had done a terrible thing in pressing for an acquittal because she was in fear of her safety. She claimed she had been terrified by a large man sitting in the public gallery. At the re-trial the following year Dennis was convicted.

Despite his sentence for drug-smuggling it was believed that Dogan Arif had masterminded his empire from prison and according to some sources the aim of the 1990 robbery had been to accumulate sufficient funds to organize an escape attempt.

'The Arifs are undoubtedly feared,' a detective told the *Independent*. 'People are not daft enough to cross them. There will be a void in the Old Kent Road area now which will be filled. It will be the survival of the fittest.'[6]

'We reckoned they made millions,' said another detective. 'We believe they have been active armed robbers for about twenty years. Every job was always

[6] *Independent*, 10 December 1991.

meticulously planned and ruthlessly executed.'[7]

But by now the sensible families had moved into drugs. So even if the aim was to put together enough money to free Dogan, what were the Arifs doing with an attack on a security van?

The explanation of one police officer is, 'They're dinosaurs, that's why. Look how old that Kenny Baker was.' He was fifty-three.

Others do not agree. 'For every drug man who succeeds he has to have the stake money from somewhere and drug deals are financed by money from armed robberies. Robbing security vans is the best way. You can pick up £1,000,000 without too many problems,' says a senior South London officer.

The theory is that the exodus from armed robberies by the sensible gangster came about with the rise of the supergrass, the lengthy sentences which were being imposed by the courts and the fact that the police were now very often armed and were adopting a tougher line with gangsters they encountered.

These days are very different from those of the early 1970s. Between 1971 and 1973 shots had been fired on only three occasions by the police. On the other hand the number of occasions when firearms were issued in connection with a particular incident had more than doubled, from 1072 to 2237 in 1973.

In that year PC Peter Simon, armed with a Webley revolver and on his way to guard the Israeli Embassy, was told that the National Westminster Bank in Kensington High Street was being robbed by three armed men. He walked into the bank to be confronted by a robber with a sawn-off shotgun. Simon stood in the middle of the bank and shouted, 'I am a police officer. I am armed.' He was shot in the arms and chest before he shot

[7] *Sun*, 10 December 1991.

and killed one of the raiders and injured another. Public reaction was all praise for this young officer.

It was not the same for two other members of the Special Patrol Group three months later when they encountered three young Pakistani men holding hostage the staff of the Indian High Commission in the Aldwych. They shot and killed two of the men. The third gave himself up unharmed. It was then discovered the weapons had only been imitations. Now the public was less pleased and there were suggestions that the police should have used tear gas or rubber bullets.

Public support had been fickle, but in 1966 Harry Roberts had shot dead three policemen in Braybrooks Street, Shepherd's Bush. He, together with his two friends, John Duddy and John Witney, had been on their way to rob a rent collector when the police approached Witney about the out-of-date tax disc on his car. Roberts shot DC David Wombwell through the head and DS Christopher Head through the back before going over to the police car where he shot PC Geoffrey Fox. Roberts and the others were sentenced to life imprisonment with a recommendation they serve at least thirty years. Previously Roberts had been fortunate. In November 1958 he had attacked and robbed a seventy-nine- year-old man, who died a year and three days after the attack. Had he died two days earlier a murder charge could have been preferred. Roberts was saved by the time limit. He received a seven-year sentence. It was after his release from that sentence that he teamed up with Witney and Duddy, ensuring they were always armed for their work. It was this predilection for guns that caused the death of three police officers during a routine stop and questioning.

On 23 August 1971 Frederick Sewell shot and killed Superintendent Gerald Richardson, head of the Black-pool Borough Police, in an armed robbery in The Strand in Blackpool. Sewell and four other South London gangsters undertook what they considered to be a simple job which would net them £100,000 of jewellery. Things did not go simply. One of the staff managed to set off the alarm, the first police officer on the scene saw the men escaping and followed them, and others joined the chase. Finally Richardson caught up with Sewell, who shot him twice at point-blank range as the officer wrestled him to the ground.

Sewell escaped and hid out in London for the next six weeks until a succession of offers of reward, including £10,000 from the *Daily Mirror*, brought about his betrayal. He was sentenced to life imprisonment, again with a recommendation that he serve a minimum of thirty years. Sewell's comment on the man he killed – 'He was too brave.'[8]

On 20 October 1979 Peter Bennett became the first customs officer to be killed on duty for nearly two hundred years when he was shot by Lennie 'Teddy Bear' Watkins, proprietor of Edward Bear Motors, Fareham. Bennett, married with a one-year-old son, had been part of a stake-out team on a surveillance known as Operation Wrecker.[9] Some well-known faces were fringe members of the enterprise. In 1976 Watkins was serving a sentence in Maidstone Prison for a supermarket snatch when, together with his minder Graeme Green, he planned to switch from armed robbery to drug smuggling. Deals were set up in Pakistan and secret compartments fitted to the containers shipped abroad. With high-quality cannabis being imported – blocks were embossed with the Rolls-Royce symbol – the trade was

[8] There are few accounts of these cases but one does appear in C. Borrell and B. Cashinella, *Crime in Britain Today*.

[9] There is a memorial to him in the form of a pair of doors at All Hallowes Church in Mark Lane, London EC3.

highly lucrative. Four runs brought in £10 million-worth at street prices. Watkins bought his garage. High living was his downfall. Reports began to filter through to the police that £20 notes were being used to light cigars. A joint police and customs observation was mounted.

The customs officers watched as a container was fitted with a false bottom and despatched by lorry with sanitary ware to Karachi. They waited until its return when, driven by Watkins, it was filled with shoes and with £2.5 million-worth of cannabis in the false floor. It meandered for a period of days around the Suffolk countryside after unloading at Harwich. The shoes had been dropped off in Saffron Walden and one morning a bag containing guns was seen to be handed to Watkins as the lorry was parked.

The surveillance ended in the Commercial Road when it became apparent to the officers that there had been a 'show-out' and their cover was blown. Watkins, who knew he was being watched, had doubled back and forth in an effort to shake the observers. Now he parked the lorry, leaving two sawn-off shotguns inside, and called his team for further instructions. He was told to stay near the telephone box and wait for an orange van which would guide him to a slaughter in Limehouse. Watkins was by a bus stop when he was approached by Bennett and Detective Sergeant John Harvey. Watkins had a Lady Beretta inside his parka and he fired at both officers, hitting Bennett in the stomach. A seventy-six-year-old pedestrian came to the men's aid and began beating Watkins with his stick as other officers surrounded him.

At his trial for murder at Winchester Crown Court in October 1980 Watkins endeavoured to leave the witness box. 'I am not going to answer any more questions from made-up note books and rubbish from your firm, from the trickery department who pull more strokes than an

Oxford blue,' he told prosecuting counsel. His defence
was that he thought a rival gang was about to hijack the
lorry and he had shot in self-defence. It was not a story
the jury accepted and Watkins left the dock hoping the
judge would die of cancer, after he had been given a life
sentence with a recommendation that he serve a minimum of twenty-five years.

If there was not too much in the newspapers about the
case it is not surprising. It was a vintage month for trials.
On the day Watkins was convicted, Ronnie Knight was
acquitted of the murder of Zomparelli whilst the jury in
the MacKenny case was hearing about the time it took
to reduce the carcass of a pig to ashes.

But there were a number of differing verdicts at the
trial of the others said to have been involved in the
conspiracy to import the drugs in the container. Brian
Bird and James Johnson, who both pleaded guilty, were
sentenced to six and five years' imprisonment respectively. Green received six years. Frederick Foreman,
recently released from his sentence in the Kray trial,
received two years on a plea of guilty at a later trial,
whilst George Francis was acquitted after a re-trial.

Within a month an effort to free Watkins had failed.
A ladder had been left propped against the wall of
Winchester Prison and a yellow lorry had been parked
nearby.

One man who did not stand trial was Colin 'Duke'
Osbourne, one-time armourer and gofer of the Krays.
Immediately after the arrest of Watkins it was made
known that the Duke was wanted for questioning as a
potential organizer of the enterprise. He was sought by
both the police and other firms who believed he held a
list of pushers. Osbourne was never arrested. On 3
December 1980 he was found dead on a playing field at
Hackney Marshes. He was aged fifty. It was said in some
quarters he died from natural causes, that he had had a

heart attack. A less charitable view is that he died of a drugs overdose. An open verdict was returned at the inquest.

In February 1987 Dennis Bergin had died in a raid on the Sir John Soane's Museum in Lincoln's Inn Fields. In July of that year Nicholas Payne and Michael Flynn were killed by police officers as they threatened the crew of a Securicor van in Plumstead, and four months later Anthony Ashe was shot dead and Ronald Easterbrook was wounded after a robbery of a Bejam store in Woolwich, South London.

If this was not sufficient to spread alarm through the underworld, the generation who had executed the great armed robberies of the 1970s and early 1980s, even if they weren't in prison, were getting a bit arthritic for this kind of pavement work.

If you're organizing an armed robbery too many people know about it – there's often the man inside, then there's the people you approach who may decline because they're on holiday or have another bit of business, but now they know what you're doing on a particular day and there's always the chance they'll grass you up for the reward money. Then there's the fact the police would fucking shoot you if you were caught in a stake-out. And even if they don't end up dead, you end up with a twenty.

So what did these old South London villains do?

First there was the refinement of the bank robbery by kidnapping the bank manager and his family, holding them hostage overnight and then taking the manager down to open the safe in the morning. The team could be a relatively small one. Three to guard the hostages and two to go to the bank. In a kidnapping for ransom the team would be of the same number, again with three members guarding the victims, the fourth negotiating with the police and the fifth administering the technical details such as supplying cars etc.

Until the mid-1970s kidnapping had never been a part of British crime. As Mark Bles and Robert Low point out, 'Almost all the major kidnaps for ransom in Britain since the first in 1969 were carried out either by foreigners or by loners who were outside the criminal mainstream.'[10] However, in 1985 the British underworld kidnapped Shirley Goodwin who was taken from her home in Hackney. At the time her husband, John, was in prison.

In the early 1980s John Goodwin had been a regular visitor to the Old Bailey, first as defendant and then as prosecution witness. He was charged with the burglary of a bank in Whitechapel in 1982 and on his first trial the jury could not agree. The second was abandoned when he feigned a heart attack and on the third, when he produced a tape-recording of a detective taking money from him, the case was stopped. But in April 1982 he was back again in the dock along with Brian Reader, later convicted of handling some of the Brinks-Mat gold and acquitted of the murder of John Fordham. This time Goodwin's accuser was the redoubtable Micky Gervaise and the charges related to burglaries totalling over £1.25 million. Gervaise by now had become a double agent supergrass and was saying that not only did he not wish to give evidence but also that Robbery Squad officers had told him to implicate Reader and Goodwin and give false evidence against them.

---

[10] M. Bles and R. Low, *The Kidnap Business*. They cite the cases of the Hossein Brothers from Trinidad, Greek Cypriots in abductions in 1975 and 1983, and Donald Nielson as the loner in the kidnapping of Lesley Whittle in 1975.

Despite Gervaise's turnaround the trial judge abandoned the trial amidst claims of jury nobbling and on a retrial in October 1982 both Reader and Goodwin were acquitted. In March 1983 Goodwin was convicted of nobbling and received a seven-year sentence. This was quashed by the Court of Appeal on 25 May 1984. 'However suspicious we are, we have to look at the quality of the evidence and the quality was lacking,' said Judge Lawton. As for the detectives Goodwin had taped, two were acquitted, one after putting up the ingenious defence that he had taken the money but had told the truth so he could not have committed perjury. The third had his conviction quashed by the Court of Appeal.

In the meantime, however, Goodwin had fallen out with yet another old-established South London family, the Pitts, and Shirley was kidnapped. At 11.30 one evening four men with sawn-off shotguns burst in, grabbed Mrs Goodwin, took £1500 from the wall-safe and handed over a ransom note reading, 'If you call the law then I will teach you mob a lesson you will never forget.'

Mrs Goodwin was kept chained up in a deserted holiday camp from which messages were sent by the gang demanding £50,000, a sum it appears the team thought Goodwin owed them and which, it was believed, he had in an account in a Jersey bank. Goodwin was provided with a telephone in his cell and he, together with the family solicitor, Jeffrey Gordon, co-operated fully with the police. Negotiations continued and the gang was lured into collecting a letter from Goodwin's sister which, it was said, was of vital importance. The mini-cab in which the letter was collected was followed to an address in Rennethorne Gardens. From then on it was relatively easy to trace the gang to the Isle of Sheppey in Kent where Mrs Goodwin had been held.

She had been released in Mitcham, South London, in the meantime.

Charles Pitts and his son-in-law, Sean McDonald, were charged and appeared in May 1984. On 22 June 1984 Pitts was gaoled for eighteen years and McDonald for eight.

Whilst hostage-taking of bank employees had become relatively common during the 1970s, it was not until the £1 million Millwall Security Express robbery in 1983 that a security guard and his family had been taken hostage. But there are real problems with this line of work. A Robbery Squad officer says:

> You need at least six people for a successful hostage situation and you have the logistical problem of keeping them overnight. Straight attacks on security vans are so much easier. If cash is being transferred there is little the carrier can do to protect himself. He has to rely on the honesty of the people who work for him and who are often paid peanuts. He has also to rely on their self-discipline. And even then, no matter how impregnable you think you make the van the people have to get out of it some time. Hostage taking will only take off in a big way if other robberies become too difficult to do.

Where one door opens another shuts. The great days of the commercial burglary are probably gone for ever. A former participating expert says:

> All the major commercial burglaries throughout the country in the sixties and seventies were carried out by a loosely associated team of eight. If you look back you'll find they end in 1982. I'm not talking about the Knightsbridge job because that

had shooters and was an inside job anyway. I'm talking about the proper burglaries. The last one was Lloyds Bank at Holborn. There hasn't been one since. They're things of the past. Security is tightened and to be frank the professional expertise isn't there. Nor is the money.

But what of those off the field of play down there in Spain? A Drugs Squad officer says:

They were sitting down in Marbella, which anyway was the cannabis route, and they've got to do something with their money. In the old days no self-respecting villain would have had anything to do with drugs but now it's different. We've had flower power and we've had the permissive sixties and so cannabis is not that bad. And even if it is, they're not actually doing the villainy, all they're doing is putting up a bit of scratch to finance it. It's not hands on so to speak.

But, of course, once the apple had been bitten it was realized the money behind the taste of cocaine was considerably greater than that of cannabis. The old-timers were sitting on top of an even more lucrative trade. Moreover, possession of cocaine for one's personal use was not an offence in Spain, which provided the bridgehead for the Colombians into Europe. A kilo of cocaine may have weighed the same as a kilo of heroin but the profit was many times greater, and so shipping in bulk was not the problem it was with the Class B drug.

One drugs deal is worth £3 to £4 million. Drugs is a victimless crime; there's no one embellishing the figures. With drugs there's no one screaming.
It's greed, pure greed, why people go on in

drugs. You'd think after one go they'd have enough. Put it in the bank at ten per cent and it's £100,000 a year – but no. A pal of mine and me received information that our car number had been taken. Now it was a straight car and so we put ourselves about and found it was tracked when we went to see a man we knew. They'd been on him for three months for drugs. So we say to him, 'Look, why don't you give the game up?' And what does he say? 'How do you turn up winning the pools every week?' He got caught on his sixth 10-ton run. His whack must have been £5 to £6 million. He got a ten and he's been done again since. They think it's for ever.

There wasn't even all that much risk.

You had a man pick it up in Spain, drive through Customs into France, which are a joke anyway, with the van or truckload. Sometimes it's concealed in the skin walls of the caravan and sometimes in the roof of a Range Rover. It's a three-day job and £5000 top whack for the driver for a big load.

Anyone except a totally amateur drug smuggler will employ a cut-out system so that the courier knows only his or her superior, and perhaps not even them. Nor will they know what is in the package. The drugs can be compartmentalized. Once the main cargo has been imported then the drugs can be left to sleep until the time personally chosen for the pick-up. With a robbery there is no knowing just how secure the operation is.

And the police see the sentencing in drug cases as rather a joke. 'It's all cock-eyed. You give a bimbo courier twelve years and in reality the same for the organizer. It may look great on paper but with parole and remission it's about one and the same.'

They are also unhappy about the press handouts which magnify out of all proportion the value of the quantity of drugs seized.

You buy a kilo of cocaine in Colombia for $2500. Now to buy that in the UK will cost £28–30,000 from the importer. That will have cost him £5–10,000 in Spain. Once it's on the streets in the East End then it can realize between £80,000 and £100,000 in gram deals, but it's still really only $2500 of drugs.

And what happens to the money from a successful drugs run? It is laundered back to Spain where a bigger villa, a better bar may be purchased or, more likely, it is changed into dollars or Swiss francs. And what is the discount – bearing in mind the Train Robbery money was laundered at ten shillings in the pound? Probably a fee of between ten and twenty per cent depending on the amount, together with an up-front fee of between £20,000 and £30,000 for a one-million-pound launder.

But as the traditional English gangs shifted their position from robbery to drugs there grew up two other major operations: the Triads and the Yardies. The first would work independently and the second, sometimes at least, in a reluctant partnership with their traditional counterparts. Although some police officers decline to accept the existence of the Triad operation in London and the United Kingdom, the late 1970s and the 1980s have produced a rise in this and other ethnic minority gangs.

I was reluctant at first to accept that any Triad groups existed in London. I was anxious that any

criminal elements that existed did not have their
street credibility, and in consequence their ability
to intimidate, enhanced by being labelled Triads,
with all the fear that such a term generates.[11]

But Detective Superintendent James Boocock soon
changed his mind.

Quite distinct from these street gangs, however,
there exists a number of very close-knit groups
whose criminal empires are networked throughout
the United Kingdom and beyond. They are
shrewd, ruthless individuals who have no compunc-
tion in resorting to extreme violence in order to
punish, intimidate or impose their will on vulner-
able Chinese businessmen.

In February 1976 Mr Kay Wong, a restaurant owner
from Basildon, was kicked to death in an illegal
gambling club in a basement in Gerrard Street as he sat
playing Mah Jong. He suffered fourteen broken ribs as
well as a ruptured spleen. The kicks were so savage that
the toe of one of the attackers' shoes had split, and later
the police were able to trace a shop in Leeds where a
new pair of shoes had been bought and to retrieve the
old ones.

Just what was it all about? The attackers had wanted
to know the address of Wong's son, Wong Pun Hai,
whom they believed to be a member of the 14K (a Triad
gang formed in the 1950s, named after 14 Poh Wah
Road, Kowloon) and partly responsible for the murder
in December 1975 of one of their relations, drug dealer
Li Kwok Bun (sometimes Pun), in Holland. Li Kwok

[11] Detective Superintendent James Boocock, *Police Review*, 21 June
1991.

402

Bun had failed to make a heroin delivery and the 14K had displayed its displeasure by putting eight bullets into the man's chest.

There had been no problems with the Amsterdam police. The body, decomposing quietly in the dunes at Schevingen, was not found until a fortnight after Kay Wong's killing. In Bun's pocket 1500 guilders (then £300) had been left, indicating to all who could read the message that it was not a robbery gone wrong. Bun may also have died because of his involvement in the murder of the so called Godfather of Amsterdam, Fookie Lang, who was believed to be an informer who had co-operated with the Royal Hong Kong Police in one of their periodic and often unsuccessful blitzes on Triad crime. Lang had been shot dead outside his own restaurant on 3 March 1975. After exacting their revenge on him, 14K had fled to London where in turn they became the hunted.

Kay Wong was unfortunately in the wrong place at the wrong time. His attackers headed north to Leeds where they split up. Two returned to Amsterdam whilst one went to Wales. They were charged with murder and appeared at the Old Bailey in November 1976. Convicted of manslaughter they received terms ranging from five to fourteen years.

Some days after his father's death Wong Pun Hai went to Vine Street police station with the dual purpose of claiming his father's body and clearing his own name of the death of Li Kwok Bun. In turn he was arrested and put on trial for murder in Amsterdam with two others. All were acquitted.[12]

The following year, on 11 January 1977, Shing May Wong, educated at Roedean, was sentenced at the Old Bailey for conspiracy to deal in drugs. With one of those

[12] For footnote, see over.

splendid passages of hyperbole which judges love to use when they can see the morning papers in their crystal balls, Judge Michael Argyle had this to say:

> When your tiny shadow fell on Gerrard Street, metaphorically the whole street was darkened and you and your confederate walked through the valley of the shadow of death. When you drove to the West End of London it was to become spreaders of crime, disease, corruption and even death.

He was rewarded. The *Daily Mail* faithfully recounted, 'At that her serenity was gone, she sobbed.'

Hers was a curious story. The reason she gave for becoming involved in the drug world was to avenge her father. He was a bullion dealer who had been kicked to death in Singapore by a gang of nine youths who lured him to a deserted spot when he was carrying a hundred gold bars. Six of the youths were hanged but for May Wong that was not sufficient. She told the court she believed he had been murdered on Triad orders, so she decided to infiltrate the group.

She abandoned her business, a beauty salon and boutique, and became a hostess in Singapore. Here she met Li Mah, the man who was to become her lover and who also received fourteen years' imprisonment. He, it was said, had fallen foul of the Triads when he owed them money and had agreed to work for them when his family was threatened. He was sent to Britain to peddle

[12] According to Fenton Bresler in *The Trail of the Triads*, Wong Pun Hai returned to England where in the late 1970s he was running a fish and chip shop in the Midlands. In September 1984 he was later alleged to have been involved in an attempt to extort £2000 from a Soho waiter but was acquitted.

drugs coming in from the Golden Triangle of Laos, Cambodia and Thailand. May Wong left her husband and came with him.

Their first consignment was to sell low-grade heroin and when they proved themselves they were issued with two pounds weight of good-quality 'smack', then worth £92,000 on the London streets at £15 a fix. Over the next six months she and Li Mah brought in £500,000. In two years her gang brought in £20 million. They were promoted, replacing a restaurateur, Chin Keong Yong, known as Mervyn, who had become an addict himself and had started stealing from the Triads.

May Wong's third partner was Molly Yeow, a beauty consultant whom Judge Argyle described as 'chief of staff'. She received ten years. It was during a search of Molly's home in Montpelier Grove, Kentish Town, that the police discovered May's address to be in St Mary's Avenue, Finchley. May was away in Singapore but she had left behind two little red books setting out in neat columns the names of retailers, stocks of heroin and the price paid for supplies. To lure her back the police gave out that Li Mah and Molly Yeow had been seriously injured in a car crash. She returned and was promptly arrested.

Argyle was not convinced by her tale. 'I cannot judge the truth of this,' he said.

By June 1990 four Triad gangs, Wo Sing Wo, Wo On Lok, 14K and San Yee On, each said to have a hard core of ten members, were systematically working the six streets of Chinatown – Wardour, Gerrard, Macclesfield, Lisle, Newport and the southern side of Shaftesbury Avenue – demanding protection money from restaurant owners and the gambling interests. As an indication of the amount of money involved, 14K are said to control a multi-million-pound racket of gaming and protection. A swoop was made in Glasgow in July 1990 and a number of restaurateurs there were charged in a multi-million-pound credit fraud said to be masterminded by 14K. However, they may be under siege. A Singapore-based group is said to be taking over from them.

Wo Sing Wo are undoubtedly seen as the most powerful of the London Triad operations, a position they established in August 1977 with a ruthless attack on their then principal opponents, Sui Fong. It came in the Kam Tong restaurant in Queensway, the second most important London base of the Triads after Chinatown. Three customers were slashed with traditional swords and another who ran into the street was chased by a man carrying a meat cleaver. In those few seconds Wo Sing Wo established a control they have not relinquished. Sui Fong have been effectively banished to operations in West London.

By June 1991 the situation in London had deteriorated substantially, with the intimidation of Chinese restaurant owners rising to such an extent that the chairman of London's Chinatown Association called for the government to proscribe the different Triad gangs.

Triad organizations require the euphemistically named 'tea-money' as a tribute, and the traditional chopping using a 14-inch beef knife is regarded as the ultimate sanction. If, for example, the restaurant owner does not pay on the first approach a negotiator is sent in. This meeting will be formal with tea and perhaps a meal in the private room of a hotel. Before a chopping takes place a knife wrapped in a Chinese newspaper may be presented as a final warning. If the man remains intractable then he will be killed.

Apart from protection and straightforward blackmail the Triads offer such services as loan-sharking. In certain areas of Glasgow, permission from a high-ranking Triad member is required before a Chinese businessman may approach a bank for a commercial loan – and such permission is only granted in return for tea-money. Also on offer are credit-card fraud, gambling, video-pirating and prostitution. The Chinese-operated brothels throughout the country are staffed by Malay or Thai girls usually brought into the country as secretaries or tourists who work a three-month stint before returning home.

As with most communities the problem the police have is in persuading victims to come to court. After a number of arrests in a very serious case in 1990 the victim left Britain and simply disappeared. No evidence was offered.

It is feared that the Triad problem will get worse as 1997 approaches and Hong Kong reverts to China. The Chinese Intelligence Unit based in the West End has no doubt that Triads resident in Great Britain are arranging for other gang members to join them here.

The second major operation, the Yardies, basically Jamaican-run gangs, merged at some point with their more powerful American equivalents, Posses, a name taken from the Western film, with their leaders known as Top Guns. The influence of the Yardies in Britain can be traced back to around 1980. They were blamed for up to 500 murders during that year's Jamaican election campaign in which they supported Michael Manley's People's National Party. When that regime was toppled by the more moderate Labour Party they fled first to New York and Miami and then further afield, including England.

Suggestions of the meaning of their name are diffuse. The Yard can mean home in general, a patch of territory or manor, Jamaica more specifically and a dock area in Kingston quite specifically.[13] Membership of the senior ranks is restricted to between thirty and forty men from Jamaica who are said to rule their members with iron

---

[13] In American prison slang it is also the exercise area.

discipline. 'Quite a few gained admission [to England] saying they were reggae musicians but their main aim was to take over drug supply lines,' said an observer.[14]

They were reported as having established a base within the year in Railton Road, the scene of the Brixton riots in 1981, running protection in the drinking she-beens and prostitution as well as illegal gambling and drugs. Two years later they were reported as having moved the scene of their operations to the All Saints Road area of Notting Hill Gate.

Three years on there were reports that they were back in South London attempting to hijack the booming cocaine market. In May, June and July there were six shootings which included two murders, the second of which, on 23 May, bore the hallmarks of a cold-blooded drugs execution. The victim, a thirty-one-year-old man, was standing in the doorway of the Old Queen's Head public house in Stockwell Road, London, when a blue Mercedes pulled up. A man got out, walked up to the victim and shot him at point-blank range with a sawn-off shotgun. The other victim was a doorman at Cynthia's night club in Acre Lane. He was shot through the head when trying to stop a gang entering the club and shooting their real target. At that time street robberies were running at around twenty-five a day in the Brixton area alone.

The same West Indian observer commented: 'Even among the violent elements, the Yardies are known as the worst. They first moved in on All Saints Road in Notting Hill, then into Hackney and now they are trying to take over Brixton. They are well armed and highly dangerous.' A detective said, 'They won by being totally ruthless and the situation in Brixton is looking like a carbon copy.'

[14] *Evening Standard*, 8 July, 1991.

On 25 May 1987 what the press described as the first Yardie killing took place. The deaths in Brixton three years earlier seem to have conveniently been forgotten, but perhaps they were just killings by the prior incumbents. Michael St George Williams, thirty-one, from Stoke Newington, was found slumped over the steering wheel of his car in Stamford Hill with gunshot wounds in his back after leaving a night club. Williams, who had left Jamaica at the age of three, had convictions for minor drug dealing but there was no hard evidence to link him with any criminal group. Described perhaps accurately as a street trader – in fact he ran a small baby-clothes stall – he was known for his lavish spending. He drove a Porsche.

The Yardies were closely watched by the police throughout the late 1980s but to no great effect. One problem was the adoption by members of street names such as 'The Scorcher', or 'The Executioner', which would be changed at will. A second problem was, and still is, that many of their assaults would go unreported both from a fear of further reprisals and a general mistrust by the black community of the police. In the summer of 1991 two events came to light. In one an armed gang had raided and robbed three hundred people at a disco. In the other an armed gang had fired shots at a fund-raising event attended by over four hundred people in a South London community centre. Neither had been reported to the police at the time.

At present the home of the Yardies is in South London, where a gang can consist of as little as four and as many as forty loosely associated people. Each will have one or two leaders, known as the Big Man, who will return to Jamaica for a month or two to buy and supervise the despatch of drugs. Then he will exchange positions with his opposite number.

Back in London, where police believe up to a hundred

people a day are dealing crack on the streets, there are
the generals, who supervise the gangs' particular activities such as the dealing and prostitution, and the
enforcers, lower in the hierarchy, who will collect money
owed by drug dealers.

'In gang fights over territory, they don't take out the
top man. They'll hit the second in charge to show how
close they are. Otherwise they would lose all power and
information.'[15] Kidnappings are relatively common. The
Yardies 'are always ripping each other off. Someone
might owe money for some drugs, but won't pay. So he's
kidnapped until relatives, or other gang members, pay
the ransom.'[16]

In October 1987 a swoop was made in Dallas, Texas,
and thirteen other American states, rounding up the
major Shower Posse, based in New York, and other
Posses throughout the country. From documents seized
it was apparent that the Posse operations stretched into
Great Britain. The documents showed clear links with
Yardies, not only in London but also in Birmingham and
Bristol as well as in Sheffield. It appeared they had
moved on from cannabis and cocaine to heroin dealing.

Three months later Scotland Yard began its first
organized major offensive against the Yardies when a
lengthy surveillance was undertaken on the New Four
Aces, a club in Dalston. On 25 February 1988 it was
announced that Commander Roy Penrose, formerly of
the Drug Squad, was to head the new team. Two weeks
later it was learned that one of America's top Yardies,
Lester Coke, aged forty, known as 'The Executioner'
and leader of the Shower Posse, had flown into Heath-

---

[15] Detective Superintendent Bob Chapman, quoted in 'Living on the
Front Line' by Ken Hyder, *Police Review*, 22 November 1991.

[16] Detective Superintendent John Jones in 'Living on the Front Line',
op. cit.

row on false papers. Happily throughout his visit he was tailed by the Jamaican Defence Force.

Six months after Penrose took over, the strength of his squad was doubled and a week later the so-called Godfather of British Yardies, Errol 'Rankin Dread' Codling, was deported to Jamaica where he was taken into custody. But the killings continued. On 1 September 1988 Rohan 'Yardie Ron' Barrington Barnet of Vaughan Road, Harrow, died from two shots in his chest after an exchange of gunfire in Harley Road, Harlesden. On Christmas Day Steven Mendez, twenty-two, was shot dead as he sat in the rear of his car during a street battle between rival gangs in Camden.

Penrose and his men had rather more success throughout 1989. On 21 July Philip Baker, described as a 'top Yardie drug trafficker', was sentenced to fifteen years' imprisonment for conspiracy to import cocaine and possession with intent to supply. On 4 August 'The Scorcher', Neville Edmond August Grant, also known as Graham Johnson and Noel Folkes, was arrested. A week later four men, Hubbert Millwood, Courtney Murray, Paul Lemmie and Stephen Fray, were convicted and sentenced for running Britain's first 'crack' factory. On 13 August 'The Scorcher' was deported. Altogether he would be deported four times in four different names.

In 1992 it has become clear that the problem of the Yardies–Posses is no longer an isolated one but is at the very least on the fringes of big-time crime. In November 1991 Leroy, from Rankers, the New York Posse, and Victor Francis were arrested while selling crack on the third floor of a council block in White City, London. Leroy, who claimed to be Norman Smith, and Victor, who gave his name as Ivan Thomas, were both wanted for questioning involving a murder in the United States.

Romeo Hugh Dennis used his real passport to come to England in late 1987 and when here acquired the

passport and identity of Andrew Clarke, a serving
soldier. Dennis set up home with his girlfriend and
claimed social security. It was only when he was arrested
for a failed bank raid that his identity became known.
He had served two sentences totalling thirty years in
Jamaica before being released on parole in 1981.

Genuine passports are now being obtained for the
price of a single £30 hit of cocaine, Detective Superintendent John Jones announced. Drug pushers are offering
addicts a deal they can't refuse – free drugs or a
substantial discount in exchange for their birth certificates, which contain the necessary details to obtain a
passport. One Yardie is known to have entered Britain
eight times in a year, on each occasion using a different
passport.[17]

At the same time, with shootings in South London
averaging two a week, there has been a substantial
increase in the use of firearms. Prices are incredibly low.
An average semi-automatic pistol with ammunition costs
about £250, with a sawn-off shotgun a bargain at
between £50 and £100. On the other hand a sophisticated
handgun such as a 9mm automatic costs £600.[18] For

[17] *Daily Mail*, 3 December 1991.

[18] The price of an automatic in 1954, according to Robert Fabian in
London After Dark, was £10, with a big revolver costing £5. Most were
war souvenirs or were smuggled in from France, Belgium and Eire. In
the *Sunday Times*, 8 March 1992, Simon Bell wrote that he obtained
a Smith and Wesson handgun for £300 on three days' notice. Ten years
ago, he wrote, the price of a Browning was £60, reflecting its age and
its probable involvement in several crimes. The following week it was
said in an East End spieler, 'Shotguns are easy to buy and if you want
a handgun then you can get one for £150, but you can guarantee it's
been used. If you want to do a bit of work then you've got to buy it
off someone sensible. There's a drought at the moment and you might
have to go as high as £800.'

those who cannot afford the purchase price, guns can be rented from armourers for the night or week. Certain named guns, as opposed merely to makes, are highly favoured. 'I want Brown Annie tonight.'

In the three months to November 1991 the specialist squad aimed at tackling the problems of the Yardies made fifty-eight arrests. There were six charges of armed robbery, a kidnapping, two threats to kill, five of attempted murder and twenty-six drugs offences. Ten firearms were recovered along with ammunition and £40,000-worth each of heroin and cocaine.

The killings have continued throughout 1992. It is believed there have been some forty to fifty shooting incidents in Brixton alone, most of them unreported. Seizures of crack have risen from around two hundred rocks in 1990 to two thousand in 1991.[19]

But not everything has been centred on London. In 1991 in Manchester the Yardies, with the Gooch Close Gang and the Pepperhill Mob, were fighting for control of the lucrative Moss Side estate, dubbed Britain's Bronx by some newspapers. On 29 October, in the fourth gang-related murder there that year, Darren Samuel tried to escape the Mountain Bike gang, who chased him into a baker's shop and fired six shots at him as he tried to leap over the counter.

Yet just as there has been no general acceptance amongst police officers of the Triads as a force in the underworld, nor is there of the Yardies. A senior officer told journalist Duncan Campbell:

It is the Jamaicans who come over here and are not worried about using guns to sort things out who are the most dangerous. They use their baby-mothers to bring drugs over. But what happened was that

---

[19] *The Times*, Saturday review, 14 March 1992.

every time a West Indian guy was done for drugs or firearms, it was described as a Yardie thing, so their reputation grew. Some of the blokes themselves took advantage of it because their name had a certain menace to it which worked for them.[20]

'In a way the Yardies are the only real gang operating,' says Bill Waddell, curator of Scotland Yard's notorious Black Museum, perhaps a trifle optimistically.

Certainly Asian gangs have never been a threat to London's established hierarchy although they have been around nearby Southall for the last 20 years. There two classic styled gangs, the Tooti Nung and the Holy Smokes, operated more or less unchallenged except by each other from the early 1970s until the beginning of the 1980s. The Tooti Nung, possibly a rough translation of the Punjabi words for worthless or no good, were regarded by the community as downmarket Sikhs. Primarily groups of youths with membership handed down from brother to brother they and their arch rivals the Holy Smokes lived in comparative anonymity, with their sport consisting mainly of gang fights, stealing cars, 'and the rather less palatable abduction and rape of unaccompanied women, usually Sikh girls, whose families never reported the attacks to the police', according to one local solicitor.

Another area of activity was the financing of trips to India.

The way to do this was to report a lost Cortina (there wasn't a youth in Southall who didn't have a complete set of Ford keys), take it to a garage where it would be stripped, the parts stored and the shell dumped in a side street. The police would

[20] 'Gangland Britain' in *Weekend Guardian*, 14–15 December 1991.

then find it and the insurance money would be paid
out. The car would be reassembled by the garage
and returned to the owner less a fee. The de luxe
version of this is for the garage to dump the car
with one sports wheel so the loser could claim for
the other four.

The gangs, whose origins dated back to 17th century
Indian groups, surfaced so far as the police and public
were concerned in 1982 when outsiders became involved
in the fights and were injured. In 1989 there was
something of a police crackdown on Tooti Nung–Holy
Smoke crime which had expanded to stolen credit cards
and traveller's cheques as well as drug dealing and
immigrant smuggling. Shopkeepers in the district,
mainly Indian or Pakistani, were also the victim of minor
protection rackets run by the gangs. In the view of the
solicitor:

> They dominate communities like Southall . . . it's
> a place where as soon as you have some money you
> go and live in Hounslow or Wembley. What there
> is is drug dealing. It's a way of escape. A high
> percentage of businesses in Southall have been
> financed by drugs. Restaurants are a particularly
> easy way of distributing drugs. There is a high
> turnover of staff, storage space and no one needs
> an excuse to go into a restaurant.

In August 1989 the police announced that more than
165 suspects had been held in the crackdown which had
begun in January.

> This is organised crime on a grand scale with many
> of the participants having amassed large sums of
> money. Several are now multi-millionaires leading

apparently respectable lives,

said Detective Superintendent Roy Herridge.

Until recently the London gangs seemed to honour the supposed Mafia tradition that women were left unharmed. Well, maybe they were threatened and worked over but at least they were left alive. This now appears to have gone by the board and the so-called Colombian mob method of wiping out everyone in sight is beginning to prevail.

In October 1991 Mick Smithyman was gaoled for life for the killing of his former girlfriend, April Sheridan. On 6 January 1990 he had shot April, mother of three young children, in a Kentish wood, because she knew too much about his underworld activities. Following a conviction he had burgled a neighbour's house and provided the shotgun used in the contract killing of another woman, Kate Williamson. Smithyman was afraid April would inform on him. Two others, Paul Smith and Ygar Salih, were in the car which took her to the fields where Smithyman marched her into nearby woods and shot her.

She pleaded with Smithyman, telling him she was pregnant. 'Just shut up. You know you are going to get it anyway. You know where grasses go and you don't deserve to live,' was Smithyman's reply according to Michelle Miles, Salih's girlfriend, who gave evidence at the trial. In turn she was told she'd get what April had got. 'Say goodbye to my kids and give them a kiss and tell them their Mummy loves them,' were April's last words to Miles.

Women gangsters are rare. At best, or worst, they are normally minders of property, cheque fraudsters, alibi givers and general supporters, trailing to prison taking food, changes of clothes and until a couple of years ago a half bottle of wine or a pint of beer a day to the men on remand. Now they pass drugs as they kiss their husbands and lovers goodbye. Fay Smithson, the Black Widow of the 1950s and 1960s, seems to have been in that mould. Much tougher was Linda Calvey, another 'Black Widow', who boasted she was the original of one of the characters in the popular ITV series, *Widows*.

In 1978 her husband Micky was shot dead during an armed raid and she earned her nickname by shouting 'murderer' at the police officer who stood trial for the shooting. He was acquitted and given a bravery award. Shortly after that she became involved with robber Ronnie Cook, going with him on trips abroad, including one to Las Vegas in which it was said they spent £30,000 in just over a week. He lavished gifts on her – clothes from Harrods, jewellery, money, a car, even £4000 for cosmetic surgery. There was, however, a down side. Cook's wife Rene was almost in penury and he was obsessively jealous, forbidding Calvey to speak to other men, beating her savagely and, according to reports, subjecting her to sadistic sexual practices.

Three years later he was jailed for sixteen years for his part in what was described as one of the 'most spectacular and well-planned robberies in the history of crime'. Whilst this is quite often a phrase used by prosecuting counsel opening the case to a jury, this robbery did have the hallmarks of brilliance. It was in fact Billy Tobin's Dulwich raid, when a hijacked mobile crane was rammed into the back of a security vehicle containing almost £1 million near a school in Dulwich.

Calvey promised to wait for him and as a mark of her fidelity had 'True Love Ron Cook' tattooed on her leg. But, it seems, she could not give up the lifestyle to which she had grown accustomed. Almost certainly Cook had had money salted away and she began to spend it, taking up with one of his friends, Brian Thorogood, whom

Cook had arranged to act as a 'minder' for him whilst he was inside. Thorogood left his wife, bought a house in Harold Wood, Essex, and moved in with her. Later he too was sentenced and served three years of a five-year term for conspiracy to rob. Linda also seems to have supplemented her income by being the armourer for various robbery teams.

Fearful that on his release Cook would find out about both her infidelity and her dissipation of his money, she planned to kill him, offering a £10,000 contract. Finding no takers, she turned to Daniel Reece, a convicted rapist whose evidence had assisted the police in convicting David Lashley, the killer of Australian heiress Janie Shepherd. Quite apart from the money Reece too was enamoured with Calvey and agreed to do the job.

In theory Ron Cook had a cleaning job outside the prison but, as with so many before him, he took to more palatable days out. Linda Calvey collected him on 19 January 1990 from Maidstone Prison and drove him to London, whilst Reece, whom she had already collected from another prison, waited outside her flat. Cook brought in the milk and as he stood holding it Reece followed him in and shot him in the elbow. He could not, he later told police, bring himself to kill the man. 'I shot to his side and he fell backwards into the kitchen. I moved forward and stood over him. I could not kill him. I have never killed anyone.' Linda Calvey had no such qualms. She grabbed the gun from him, ordered Cook to kneel and then shot him in the head.

Reece took a train back to the West Country to continue his thirteen-year sentence for rape, buggery and false imprisonment.

At first it seemed as though Calvey had been successful. The police appeared to accept her story that an unknown gunman had burst in and shot Cook whilst she cowered in a corner. Then it was discovered Reece had been with her over the weekend and had been her lover. It was curious he had not been mentioned in the statement. Under questioning Reece cracked first, telling all.

Reece, who was not notedly popular in prison following the evidence he gave against Lashley, thought twice about squealing again and withdrew his confession in court. Linda Calvey told the jury his confession was a fabrication. 'Ron meant everything to me,' she said. This gesture of solidarity did Reece no good. They both received life sentences for murder. Just as the men in Fay Sadler's life had ended up dead or in prison so did those in the life of Linda Calvey, a classic gangster's moll turned gangster.

1991 might be described as a vintage year for violence in what *Today* called the Bermondsey Triangle,[21] and much of it related to the Arif family and their rivals. Possibly some of the violence dated back to the shooting of Stephen Dalligan, a nephew of Tony White, at the Connoisseur Club. He had gone there by invitation to try to calm things down between his brother Mark and Ahmet Abdullah, known as Turkish Abbi, a suspected drug dealer and adopted son of the Arifs, who had quarrelled earlier. Stephen was shot in the mouth and back. He was unable to give a full description of his attacker and no charges were ever brought. Although there had been a number of witnesses none of them was able to make any identification. Dalligan would not even authorize the release of the bullets which had lodged in him.

On 11 March Ahmet Abdullah himself was killed in the William Hill betting shop in Bagshot Street, Walworth. Hit in the back after pleading with his attackers not to kill him, he had tried to use another customer as

[21] 4 December 1991.

a shield and had managed to escape from the shop before he was shot. He reached a nearby flat and then died within a few minutes. Tony and Patrick Brindle were acquitted of Abdullah's murder at the Old Bailey on 16 May 1992. Witnesses had given evidence from behind screens and were themselves only identified by number. Tony Brindle gave evidence that he had been playing cards and drinking in The Bell. Patrick did not give evidence. After the hearing Grace Brindle, their mother, told how the boys helped old ladies across the road and cried when their pet budgie died. In turn, the police said the enquiry was closed.

The next month, on 28 April, David Norris, a South Londoner suspected of grassing on gangsters, was shot at his home in Belvedere, Kent. Two men wearing crash helmets approached him and one opened fire with a handgun. Things cooled down for much of the summer until, on 3 August, David Brindle, another of Tony's brothers, was shot dead in the Bell public house in East Street, Walworth. Two masked gunmen burst into the crowded pub shortly before closing time and screamed 'This is for Abbi' before they fired on Brindle as he tried to scramble over the counter. No one is quite sure if the cry was something of a blind.

It was a shooting to be followed a few days later by that of the now legendary Frankie Fraser, apparently well out of his ground outside Turnmills night club in Farringdon. When questioned by the police about the shooting, which had removed part of his mouth, the sixty-seven-year-old fiance of Train Robber Tommy Wisbey's daughter gave his name as Tutankhamen and said 'What incident?'

Over the years his relations had shaped up nicely. In July 1984 David, then thirty-seven, received a sentence of fourteen years' imprisonment for his part in the hold-up of a director of an airline and his family in Hyde Park

Gardens. In November 1986 James, who had an interest in the Tin Pan Alley club, a wine bar off Charing Cross Road, was sentenced to a term of imprisonment in Bruges, Belgium, for his part in a drugs conspiracy.

Ten days after the shooting of Fraser, William Walker was shot in the leg and arm as he was out walking with his wife in Rotherhithe. It was reputedly another gangland incident.

A man who typified the term footsoldier, John Masterson, one-time Scots hard-man and a friend of the Krays – he has a watch inscribed 'To John from the Kray brothers' – was more fortunate. On 17 October 1991 Masterson, a miner from Hamilton near Glasgow, smartly turned out in suit, shirt and tie and thick spectacles, had been drinking in the Heaton Arms and other pubs in South London with his and the Krays' friend Bernard O'Mahoney. On the way home they were attacked with ammonia sprays and there was a report a shot had been fired. Masterson was bundled into a car and disappeared. He reappeared at the Royal Infirmary, Edinburgh, three days later, doused in petrol. 'He was a walking petrol bomb,' said a member of the staff. It was a case of mistaken identity, said Masterson.[22]

In November Perry Donegan, a friend of David Brindle, was shot in the leg in the Green Man in the Old Kent Road. On 3 December Kenneth Neal was shot dead with a bullet in his chest and two in his head by a man described as young and blond who jogged away laughing. At first it was thought Mr Neal had been killed by mistake. Later it transpired that he had been involved with a married woman and had recently resumed the relationship.

[22] For an account of his career, remarkable for his prison experiences rather than work on the ground, see 'The Footsoldier' in D. Campbell, *That was Business, This is Personal*.

By the end of 1991 there had been forty murders in the South London area, a hundred per cent rise on the figure for 1990. But not all the violence has been confined to South London. There has been just as much violence across the river and in Essex, but with no press magnet such as Frankie Fraser, the North London gangs have been able to go about their business almost unreported, as two longstanding families, one with substantial South London connections, have waged war for control of a drug and protection market.

If I knew they knew the Xs I wouldn't deal with them. They are today's equivalent of the Krays and the Richardsons. Say a man owes you £15,000 for a legit piece of business, then he goes to the Xs and says he doesn't want to pay. They say they'll get you off his back for £5000 and they do. I'm not frightened but I'm not going up against them. Why don't the police do something about them? I don't know. There's three of them on bail at the moment. One for a big drugs thing and the others for possessing shooters. Maybe the police have a grander plan. I don't know.

Mad 'Scouse' Alan Smith, a moneylender and enforcer, was shot in a pub in Islington, as was former armed robber Brendan Carey in September 1990. He went down in the bar of the Prince of Wales in the Caledonian Road, shot at point-blank range. At first the police had difficulty in making an identification and a neighbour said of him, 'I believe the victim was Irish and named Jimmy. I think maybe the shooting was a punishment or something to do with drug dealing.'[23]

---

[23] *Evening Standard*, 28 September 1990.

On 2 January 1990 a shooting took place in Huntingdon Street, N1, which led to the arrest of a former footballer, now a garage owner in the area. He was later released and brought a number of libel actions against the newspapers which alleged he had been part of this gangland shoot-out.

Later that month, William Fisher was shot dead on the doorstep of his home in Islington when a man in a motorcycle outfit opened fire. Fisher had long been a name in the frame and the police had interviewed him over a bogus Hatton Garden robbery, although drugs and not the spurious insurance claim were thought to be the reason for his death.

Masseuse Debbie Lee Parsons (forty-three) disappeared on 23 June 1990 and was found shot with a cross-bow in Epping Forest. She had been due at her boyfriend's restaurant to help out at a special party that evening. She never arrived. Despite wide-ranging police enquiries and the attention of the *Crimewatch* programme, no one was arrested and charged. The officer in charge of the case, Detective Superintendent Harvey, said it was an execution by any other name.

That month the former supergrass John Moriarty was dragged out of a bar in Benalmadina on the Costa del Crime and thrown under the wheels of a 32-ton lorry. Moriarty, who had survived two shooting attempts, did not on this occasion.

In December 1990 at Southwark Crown Court, high-living Peruvian Rene Black – he had wanted to be both a top-class racing driver and show jumper – who had planned to flood the market with cocaine, earned a fifteen-year sentence and the stripping of his £1.5 million fortune. His slightly reduced sentence was an acknowledgement that he had turned Queen's Evidence. His distribution partner, James Laming, was gaoled for eleven years and stripped of £23,950 of his profits. The defence of former car dealer Laming had been an ingenious one. He had not been dealing with Black at all over cocaine, about which he knew nothing, but rather over an attempt to organize horse-racing coups. He had, he said, invented an ultrasonic stun gun which could bring down a horse at three furlongs distance. All you had to do was point and shoot. Laming tested this at Royal Ascot in 1988 when jockey Greville Starkey was brought down on Ile de Chypre when leading the field in the Kings Stand Stakes. Very sportingly Starkey allowed the defence to test out the machine again, this time in the peace of his paddock. But the jury would have none of it. Laming was found guilty on two charges to supply cocaine and one of conspiracy to supply.

In December 1990 Laming's partner, John Lane, alias John Gobba, was found shot in the back. Lane had been arrested along with Laming at his Holborn flat but had been released when no drugs were found on him. He had been a close associate of Lionel Webb. In January 1991 Webb, supposedly an estate agent, was shot at his premises in North London, which he used as a front. His safe was found to be stuffed with narcotics.

On Sunday, 24 March 1991, antiques dealer and cocaine user Peter Rasini was shot dead at his home in River Avenue, Palmers Green, a North London suburb. A sole gunman came up behind Rasini as he walked down the path and shot him four times in the back. Loyally, his family said they knew he had no enemies in the world. A re-run of the events on *Crimewatch* has failed to produce a charge and Detective Chief Superintendent Bill Peters told *Time Out* that 'the cold-blooded way the murder was executed, the lack of clues, the absence of any motive at all, point towards a hired killer'.[24] One theory is that Rasini may have stumbled

---

[24] *Time Out*, 22 January 1992.

across a major criminal activity, whilst another is that he angered a member of the criminal fraternity and had to be killed.

On 17 July 1991 publican Alan Brooks was dragged from his bar at the Clydesdale pub in Loughton and hacked to death by a six-man gang with machetes. He had only taken over the pub two weeks earlier.

Whether innocent by-standers who have suffered include Maxine Arnold and her boyfriend Terry Gooderham, found shot dead in their black Mercedes in Epping Forest on 22 December 1989, is open to speculation. Certainly she was a bystander; he may have been more of a player, which resulted in what was certainly a gangland execution. As always a variety of suggestions were offered. Terry had an active life, for he shared it with Maxine part of the week and another blonde, Carol Wheatley, for the remainder. One suggestion was that there was a third Ms Gooderham in the background and she had organized the hit, but enquiries came to nothing. Nor did they in relation to the theory that he was involved with Brinks-Mat monies.

Gooderham had been a stocktaker for a number of clubs and pubs in London and Hertfordshire, and one anonymous friend put it: 'It is nothing to do with his love life or his own business but a lot of money is involved.' There were claims that he had been the victim of part of a drugs war and indeed a small amount of drugs were found in the car, but the police became convinced these had been planted and were a red herring. Then there was a claim in the *Daily Mirror* on 4 January 1990 that he had tried to muscle in on the lucrative Spanish ice-cream market and had so upset suppliers that a £50,000 contract was put out on him. Finally there was yet another solution offered. This time it was that the killing was over £150,000 which was euphemistically described as having been redirected.

Possibly the killing related to the North London gang war which had been simmering throughout the 1980s. 'Sometimes we take out one of them, and then they take out one of ours. Or the other way around,' said a fringe participant.

Commentators have seen the gaoling of Freddie Foreman, Eddie Richardson and Dogan Arif, along with the death of Charlie Wilson, as the basic causes of the present instability in the underworld. 'Two or three new gangs started to take over, with drugs as the base of their power. One of them has been ruthless in its bid to get to top dog position,' reported Jeff Edwards in the *People*.[25]

Life is cheap in North London at present. According to the *Sunday Mirror*,[26] contract killers will carry out the murder of a top criminal for £25,000, down to as little as £1500 for a surplus wife or boyfriend. According to the article the gang, so far unpenetrated by the police because of a wall of fear, operates on a kill now pay later basis. If this is correct they are the legitimate descendants of Henry MacKenny.

With spoils on offer of which Darby Sabini, the Cortesis, even Billy Hill, the Krays and all the other long dead or imprisoned heroes can never have dreamed there are likely to be more killings and near-misses. It promises to be a long struggle for power.

[25] 7 October 1990.
[26] 5 January 1992.

And then...?

It would not be right to finish this saga without at least a comment on the relationship the gangs have had with their national and international counterparts, in particular the so-called Mafia. There must also be some effort to lift the curtain of the future and to see if, and how, things will change over the next decade. Although there has been organized crime on a large scale in some provincial cities, the police usually seem to have stepped on the participants sufficiently hard and sufficiently quickly to stamp out gangs similar to the Krays and the Richardsons. One case in point was Sheffield, where gang wars raged in the 1920s and where Sir Percy Sillitoe, later head of MI5, suppressed them in a way that is quite alien to today's liberal attitudes.

The gangs there, led by George Mooney and Sam Garvin, controlled organized betting in the area. The game was called tossing and odds were laid against which of five half-crowns landed heads or tails. According to Sillitoe, each gang had hundreds of members who, quite apart from running the pitching rings, controlled the poor quarters such as the Crofts, Norfolk Bridge and the Park, collecting protection from the publicans.

I called my senior officers together and asked them

to select very carefully for me some of the strongest, hardest-hitting men under their commands. . . . It was not difficult to pick a dozen of the best of these to form a 'flying squad' specially to deal with the gangster problem. These men were taught ju-jitsu and various other methods of attack and defence, and it was surprising how little teaching they needed. They had just been waiting for the chance to learn![1]

Motorways and airports have certainly contributed to the improved mobility of the London-based criminal. France, Spain and in particular the Mediterranean have long been happy haunts of teams, initially of burglars and shoplifters, now of drug smugglers. On the other side of the coin there have always been visiting teams. Describing the build-up to the World Cup in 1966 Nipper Read wrote:

There was not only the problem of the clubs and our own thieves but also the con men who would come from Australia, the fraudsmen and tricksters from Mexico and Venezuela, the dipsters from Italy, drug-pushers from Holland and the heavies, GBH merchants from Germany.[2]

If there is any doubt that travel broadens both the mind and the opportunity, the case of Jamaican gunman Leon Virgo should assuage it. Virgo lived more or less quietly in a council flat on the North Peckham estate in South London whilst commuting to New York on false passports using the names of Kenneth Smith and Kenneth Barnard to carry out contracts for the Jamaican

---

[1] P. Sillitoe, *Cloak without Dagger*.

[2] L. Read and J. Morton, *Nipper*, p. 122 and see Supra p. 161.

Spangler Posse. In July 1987 in Manhattan he killed James Fernandez, shooting him nine times, and a week later he shot drug courier Tanya Lang, who was believed to be an informer. A further fifteen cases were left on the file at his trial at the Manhattan Supreme Court.[3]

And on the subject of travel there has been a resurgence of immigrant smuggling. Throughout the winter of 1991–2 there were reports of immigrants being found on the beaches of the Kent and Sussex coasts and in March 1991 fifteen Indians were found in a lorry at the Heston service station on the M4 west of London, the latest in the lucrative immigrant racket. In 1991 over four hundred people were found to have been smuggled into England – well over twice the number for 1990.

According to a report in *The Times* most of those smuggled are from Bangladesh, India, Turkey and Pakistan, with suggestions that between £1000 and £3000 is paid per person for the trip made by air to Germany or Denmark before being loaded into lorries for the crossing of the Channel.[4]

How far does basic street-level crime reach up into the world of the City and finance? One London solicitor traces the hierarchical structure of the 1960s from solicitor Judah Binstock, one-time owner of the Victoria Sporting Club, then protected by Corsican connections, to George Dawson, the orange juice king who later went to prison for fraud, through to Albert Dimes. John Bloom, the washing-machine tycoon, was deeply involved with Joe Wilkins, relative of Bert Wilkins who stood trial with Bert Marsh for the Wandsworth dog-track killing of 1934, who in turn was the man behind Dimes, and so on. Even the seemingly small-time Tony Mella of the one-armed bandits mixed socially with his

---

[3] *Daily Mail*, 5 March 1992.
[4] *The Times*, 24 March 1992.

solicitors and the directors of publicly quoted companies. The links are both endless and indissoluble.

And as for the Mafia? There can be little doubt that from the days of the Sabinis there have been close links with Italy and later with American-organized crime both at blue- and white-collar level. Dimes was closely linked with Angelo Bruno, whilst Bert Marsh assisted the Giotti family from New York when they were trying to establish a foothold in English gaming. Although Bruno seems to have declined close involvement, saying the English ways were 'quaint', his friend Meyer Lansky, the Mafia financier, was a friend of the malevolent Binstock and together they went to Brazil with Sir Eric Miller, chairman of the Peachy Corporation, not long before Miller shot himself on the Jewish Day of Atonement. The Krays had close links with New York crime. When they were endeavouring to shut down Nipper Read's enquiry, a hitman was brought over from New York. He was arrested at Shannon and put on the next plane home. The Richardsons had interesting deals in South Africa. The Soho connections have always been with France, Malta and Cyprus. When Gaul, the property magnate, wanted a hitman to remove his wife, Barbara, he knew where to find one – in the East End underworld.

It was only the vigilance of the immigration authorities which kept the Mafia out of London when the Gaming Act of 1960 was passed. The big junkets of American gamblers which followed provided an opportunity to launder money through the casinos. According to Peter Gladstone Smith it was then that Angelo Bruno endeavoured to forge links through Albert Dimes – and Judah Binstock. Apparently he wished to establish the American numbers racket in the United Kingdom. Basically the numbers game is a variation of the Italian National Lottery or the Pools. For a very small stake the

punter has the opportunity to bet on a single three-digit
number with the winner determined by the results at a
major race meeting that day. The odds against winning
are 1000 to 1 whilst the pay-out is a maximum of 599 to
1 less ten per cent commission on winning bets. Punters
will choose their lucky numbers, birthdays, houses in
which they live, etc, and it is possible to buy part of a
ticket, when the odds paid out are considerably reduced.
Bruno, along with film actor George Raft and other
prominent American-organized crime figures, was subsequently refused entry to the United Kingdom.[5]

More and more the really intelligent criminals are
turning to computer fraud. It is less dangerous to subvert
a bank employee into passing over the numbers of an
account than it is to attack a security van and risk being
shot at by the police. Moreover conviction, which may
be rare, carries less in the way of a sentence.

Of course such computer crime is not new, and one of
the first exponents was Roderic Knowles, who in 1968
came within an ace of removing $600,000 from the Bank
of America. Knowles, an Old Etonian, led a team – of
all people, public schoolboys could never be called a
gang – of gold smugglers. To finance the enterprise, one
Sunday he obtained entrance to the Bank of America in
Seoul and photographed the documents needed for the
fraud. He and his colleagues obtained the Bank's secret
code which authorized the branch's immediate payment
from an account to a person named in the message.
Knowles decided to try the scam on two branches, one
in Zurich, the other in Amsterdam. The money was
obtained from the Zurich branch but the innate cautious-
ness of the Dutch in paying out a large sum of cash close
to a weekend led to Knowles' arrest.[6]

[5] P. Gladstone Smith, *The Crime Explosion*.
[6] P. Deeley, *The Manhunters*, p. 119

Perhaps even easier is the money to be made out of cloned credit cards. *The Times* reported a worldwide card fraud involving the embossing of personal account details on to a 'cloned' card and using a non-existent bank. The profits are said to be channelled into drugs and pornography.[7]

On a smaller scale it is possible to rent a stolen credit card at certain London clubs and public houses for an hour or for a day. The days when forgery, for this is what the scam amounts to, brought about a three-year sentence are long gone. The girls who are involved at the mule end of the trade can, at the worst, expect a fine or probation for a first, second or third offence unless they are extremely unlucky with their choice of magistrate. It is rare that they know the person from whom they obtained the card in the pub or wine bar for £25.

Now, with the booming cocaine and heroin trade, international co-operation between criminals is essential. Already there are tenuous links between Yardie gangs and the traditional London underworld. The immigrant smuggling racket requires cross- border co-operation. There is evidence that the Peruvians and Colombians have moved into the London drugs market. Once these presently tenuous links are properly forged we could see a whole new game. The only major criminal organization which does not seem to have established any real hold in London – possibly because of the relatively small community here – is the Japanese Yakuza, but no doubt, despite the country's new laws to kill off organized crime, it is only a matter of time before that happens.

[7] *The Times*, 23 March 1992.

Bibliography

Ascoli, D., *The Queen's Peace* (1979), London, Hamish Hamilton

Ball, J., Chester, L. and Perrott, R., *Cops and Robbers* (1979), London, Penguin Books

Beveridge, P., *Inside the CID* (1957), London, Evans Brothers

Biron, Sir Charles, *Without Prejudice* (1936), London, Faber and Faber

Black, D., *Triad Takeover* (1991), London, Sidgwick & Jackson

Bles, M. and Low, R., *The Kidnap Business* (1977), London, Pelham Books

Borrell, C. and Cashinella, B., *Crime in Britain Today* (1975), London, Routledge & Kegan Paul

Bresler, F., *The Trail of the Triads* (1980), London, Weidenfeld & Nicolson

Burke, S., *Peterman* (1966), London, Arthur Barker

Campbell, D., *That was Business, This is Personal* (1990), London, Secker & Warburg

Cannon, J., *Tough Guys Don't Cry* (1983), London, Magnus Books

Cater, F. and Tullett, T., *The Sharp End* (1988), London, Bodley Head

Challenor, H. with Draper, A., *Tanky Challenor* (1990),

London, Leo Cooper

Cherrill, F., *Cherrill of the Yard* (1953), London, Harrap

Cheyney, P., *Making Crime Pay* (1944), London, Faber & Faber

Chinn, C., *Better betting with a decent feller* (1991), Hemel Hempstead, Harvester Wheatsheaf

Cole P. and Pringle, P., *Can you positively identify this man?* (1974), London, Andre Deutsch

Cornish, G., *Cornish of the 'Yard'* (1935), London, Bodley Head

Cox, B., Shirley, J. and Short, M., *The Fall of Scotland Yard* (1977), Harmondsworth, Penguin

Davis, V., *Phenomena of Crime*, London, John Long

Deeley, P., *The Manhunters* (1970), London, Hodder and Stoughton

Dew, W., *I caught Crippen* (1938), London, Blackie

Dickson, J., *Murder without Conviction* (1986), London, Sphere

Divall, T., *Scallywags & Scoundrels* (1929), London, Ernest Benn

Du Rose, J., *Murder was my Business* (1971), London, W. H. Allen

Fabian, R., *London After Dark* (1954), London, Naldrett Press

— *Fabian of the Yard* (1955), London, Heirloom Modern World Library

— *The Anatomy of Crime* (1970), London, Pelham Books

Felstead, S., *The Underworld of London* (1923), New York, E. P. Dutton

— *Shades of Scotland Yard* (1950), London, John Long

Finmore, R., *Immoral Earnings* (1951), London, M. H. Publications

Fordham, P., *The Robbers' Tale* (1965), London, Hodder & Stoughton

— *Inside the Underworld* (1972), London, George Allen

& Unwin

— Gladstone Smith, P., *The Crime Explosion* (1970), London, Macdonald

Goodman, J. and Will, I., *Underworld* (1985), London, Harrap

Greeno, E., *War on the Underworld* (1960), London, John Long

Grigg, M., *The Challenor Case* (1965), London, Penguin

Henry, J., *Detective-Inspector Henry's Famous Cases* (1942), London, Hutchinson

Higgins, R., *In the Name of the Law* (1958), London, John Long

Hill, B., *Boss of Britain's Underworld* (1955), London, Naldrett Press

Hinds, A., *Contempt of Court* (1966), London, Bodley Head

Hoskins, P., *No Hiding Place*, Daily Express Publications

Humphreys, Sir Travers, *A Book of Trials* (1953), London, Pan Books

Janson, H., *Jack Spot, Man of a Thousand Cuts* (1959), Alexander Moring

Jennings, A., Lashmar, P. and Simson, V., *Scotland Yard's Cocaine Connection* (1990), London, Jonathan Cape

Kelland, G., *Crime in London* (1986), London, Bodley Head

Knight, R., *Black Knight* (1990), London, Century

Kray, C., *Me and my brothers* (1988), London, Grafton

Kray, R., *Born Fighter* (1991), London, Arrow

Kray, R. and Kray, R., *Our Story* (1988), London, Pan

Lambrianou, T., *Inside the Firm* (1991), London, Smith Gryphon

Laurie, P., *Scotland Yard* (1970), London, Bodley Head

Leeson, B., *Lost London* (1934), London, Stanley Paul & Co

Lewis, D. and Hughman, P., *Most Unnatural* (1971), London, Penguin Books

Lucas, N., *Britain's Gangland* (1969), London, Pan Books

McConnell, B., *The Evil Firm* (1969), London, Mayflower

Millen, E., *Specialist in Crime* (1972), London, George G. Harrap

Narborough, F., *Murder on My Mind* (1959), London, Allan Wingate

O'Mahoney, M., *King Squealer* (1978), London

Parker, R., *Rough Justice* (1981), London, Sphere

Paul, P., *Murder under the Microscope* (1990), London, Macdonald

Payne, L., *The Brotherhood* (1973), London, Michael Joseph

Pearson, J., *The Profession of Violence* (1977), London Granada, (1985), London, Grafton

Read, L. and Morton, J., *Nipper* (1991), London, Macdonald

Read, P., *The Train Robbers* (1978), London, W. H. Allen

Richardson, C., *My Manor* (1991), London, Sidgwick & Jackson

Samuel, R., *East End Underworld* (1981), London, Routledge & Kegan Paul

Short, M., *Lundy* (1991), London, Grafton

Sillitoe, P., *Cloak without Dagger* (1956), London, Pan

Slipper, J., *Slipper of the Yard* (1981), London, Sidgwick & Jackson

Taylor, L., *In the Underworld* (1985), London, Unwin Paperbacks

Thurlow, D., *The Essex Triangle* (1990), London, Robert Hale

Tremlett, G., *Little Legs, Muscleman of Soho* (1989), London, Unwin Hyman

Tietjen, A., *Soho* (1956), London, Allan Wingate

Tullett, T., *Murder Squad* (1981), London, Triad Grafton

Viccei, V., *Knightsbridge* (1992), London, Blake Hardbacks

Ward, H., *Buller* (1974), London, Hodder & Stoughton

Watts, M., *The Men in My Life* (1960), London, Christopher Johnson

Webb, D., *Deadline for Crime* (1955), London, Muller
— *Line up for Crime* (1956), London, Muller

Wensley, F., *Detective Days* (1931), London, Cassell & Co

Wickstead, B., *Gangbuster* (1985), London, Futura

Wilkinson, L., *Behind the Face of Crime* (1967), London, Muller

Woffinden, B., *Miscarriages of Justice* (1987), London, Hodder & Stoughton

Index

Aarvold, Carl 258
Abdullah, Ahmet (Turkish Abbi) 419–20
Adams family 388
Adkins, Roy Francis 384–5
Agar, Edward 301n
Agius, Jean 227
Aguda, Renalto 'Ron' 285, 287
Aguda, Rudolpho 285–7
Ahearn, John 251–2
Albert, Frankie 349
Allard, Emil (Max Kessell, Red Max) 191–3
Allen, John ('Mad Parson') 342
Allpress, Danny 239, 278, 279
Amazonas, Carlos 355
Ambrose, Billy 79–80
Amies, Billy 284
Anderson, Det. Chief Insp. Michael 127n
Andrews, Gwen 368–9
Andrews, Jimmy 99, 123

Andrews, Rev. Basil Claude 59–61
Andrews, Ronnie 368–9, 371
Antiquis, Alec de 97
Apostolou, John 89
Argyle, Judge Michael 283, 404, 405
Arif family 338, 386–90, 419
Arif, Bekir 387
Arif, Dennis 387–8, 389
Arif, Dogan 386, 389–90, 426
Arif, Mehmet 387–8
Arif, Michael 388–9
Arif, Osar 386
Arnold, Maxine 425
Ashe, Anthony 395
Avory, Mr Justice 12

Bailey, Mickey 173–4
Baker, Philip 411
Baker, Kenny 387–8, 390
Ball, Mickey 239–41

Ball, Patrick (The
    Professor) 93–4
Ballada, Charles 190–91
Barham, Harry 283n, 329
Barnet, Rohan Barrington
    ('Yardie Ron') 411
Baron, Ray 358
Barrett, Donald 273, 279,
    281
Barrett, Michael 144
Barrie, Ian 141, 153, 155
Barry brothers 135
Barry, Tony 135, 388n
Bartolo, Emmanuel 205
Beach, George 309
Beach, Norman 309–10
Bell, Simon 412
Bending, Joan 80, 82–3
Bennett, Peter 392–3
Benneyworth, 'Monkey' 18
Beresford, Walter 21, 22
Bergin, Dennis 395
Berkley, Alf 282
Berman, Alfie 114, 125
Berthier, Emile xvi, 190–91
Bertie Smalls Gang 239
Bertrand, Suzanne 192–3
Bessarabians 2–5
Beveridge, Chief Supt.
    Peter 45, 62
Biggs, Ronnie 216, 253–4,
    278, 340
Bigland, Reuben 20
Bindon, John 339–40
Binstock, Judah 164, 201,
    225, 311–12, 429–30
Birch, Wally 224–6

Bird, Brian 394
Birkett, Norman, K.C., 26
Biron, Sir Charles 10
Black, Rene 423–4
Black, Tony 377–8
Blind Beggar gang 5
Bloom, Ivor 257
Bloom, John 140–41, 224,
    225, 429
Bloor (Blore), Jimmy
    112–13, 114
Blue Lamp, The 316
Blythe, Billy 54–5, 65–6,
    131
Boal, William 251, 253
Bogard, Isaac (Darky the
    Coon) 8–9, 12
Boocock, Det. Supt.
    James 402
Boothby, Sir Robert 143–4,
    149, 150
Borg, John 355
Bottomley, Horatio 20, 301
Botton, Henry 122, 125
Bouchier (Le
    Marseillais) 191, 193
Bradbury, John 105, 106,
    110, 112, 113, 117–18, 119,
    125
Bradshaw, George *see*
    Piggott, Maxwell Thomas
Brady, Dave 264–7, 268–9,
    288
Brauch, Earnest 225
Brett, George 178, 261,
    366–8, 370, 371
Brett, John 261, 263, 367

Brett, Terence 367–8, 370, 371

Brewster, Det. Chief Insp. 274

Bridges, Bunny 110, 115, 126

Brindle family 97–8

Brindle, David 420, 421

Brindle, Eva (née Fraser) 98, 99, 126, 153, 309

Brindle, Grace 420

Brindle, Jimmy 98, 103

Brindle, Patrick 420

Brindle, Tommy 'Tom Thumb' 97–8

Brindle, Tony 420

Brinks-Mat hold-up 287, 298, 310–11, 321, 377–80, 382

Brodie, Asst. Chief Constable, Peter 170

Brook, John 263

Brooks, Alan 425

Brown, Robert Winston 366, 368, 371

Brummagen Boys 15–16, 19–21, 95

Bruno, Angelo 72–3, 164, 430–31

Buggy, John ('Scotch Jack') 73, 166, 349–53

Burge, James 93

Butcher, Sgt. 370

Butler family 135

Butler, Supt. Arthur 350

Butler, Tommy 156, 249–51, 253

Callaghan family 82, 97, 329

Callaghan, Jeremiah 79, 80, 327

Calvey, Linda (Black Widow) 417–19

Calvey, Micky 380, 417

Camb, James 365

Cameron, Prof. James 360, 372

Campbell, Duncan 388, 413

Camps, Francis 352

Cannon, Bobby 123, 161

Cannon, Joe 62–4, 68

Cantor, Ben 303–4

Capoccii, Harry 36

Carelton, Leon 174

Carey, Brendan 422

Carleton, Billie 186–7

Carney, Albert 268

Carter family 65, 69

Carter, Johnny 65

Caruana, George 47, 49–50, 164, 219–20

Casey, James ix–x

Castanar, Juan Antonio 189, 191, 193

Cauci, Tony 210, 222–3

Challenor, Det. Sgt. H.G. 76, 85–8, 89–92, 211–12, 319, 343

Chang, Brilliant 186–8, 189

Chapman, Det. Supt. Bob 410n

Chapman, Eddie 56

Chappell, Garth 378

Cheeseman, Alan 86, 91
Cheney, Brigadier 242
Chevalier, Martial le 189–90, 193
Cheyney, Peter 28–9
Childs, John 366–72
Childs, Tina 369
Chin Keong Yong (Mervyn) 405
Chrastny, Mrs 321n
Chrastny, Nikolaus 321, 386
Christie, Reginald Halliday 200n
Clarke, Charlie 118, 360
Clark, Tommy 125, 127
Clarke, Judge Edward 308
Clarke, Sir Percival 314
Codling, Errol 'Rankin Dread' 411
Coke, Lester ('The Executioner') 410–11
Coleiro, Emmanuel 205
Coleman family 388
Coleman, James 338
Collette, Joseph 36
Collins, Michael 373
Comer, Jack *see* Spot, Jack
Comer, Rita 51–2, 61, 62–3, 64, 67, 68
Comyn, James 343
Comyn, Mr Justice 285
Constantino, Matteo 378–9
Cook, Rene 417
Cook, Ronnie 270, 417–19
Cooney, Selwyn Keith (Jimmy Neill, Little Jimmy) 78–80, 81, 83–4,

171, 339
Coons 8–9
Cooper, Alan Bruce 164–5
Copeland, Florence 'Fluffy' 95–6
Copley family 96, 97
Copley, Edwin (Cadillac Johnny) 95–6
Copley, George ('Colonel') 376, 377n
Cordery, Roger 251, 253
Corkery, Michael, Q.C. 178, 322
Cornell, George (George Myers) 5, 99, 112, 113, 115, 123, 152–4, 155, 156–7, 166–7, 261
Cornell, Olive 152n, 156–7
Cornish, George 232
Cornwall, Micky 357, 358–9
Cortesi brothers (Frenchies) 23–5, 31, 426
Cortesi, Augustus 23–4
Cortesi, Enrico (Harry) 23–4, 31
Cortesi, George 23–4
Cortesi, Paul 23
Costello, Tommy 106, 107, 108, 111–12
Coulson, Benny 126
Crippen, Dr 170, 243n, 301
Cross, David 386
Crowther, Eric 339
Cummins, Chief Supt. John 123
Curtis, Ronnie 177

Dalligan, Mark 419
Dalligan, Stephen 419
Daly, John 239
Daniels, Francis
(Franny) 66, 350, 352–3
Dann, John ('Donuts') 358
Darke, John 338–9
Darling, Mr Justice 16, 24–5
Davey, Jimmy 338
Davis, George 264–9, 335,
361
Davis, Rosie 267
Davis, Glanford 289
Davis, Leroy 289
Davis, Stanley Clinton 88–9
Dawson, George 27, 109,
312, 429
Dean, 'Man Mountain' 345
Deguilio, Anthony 354
De Mesa 310
Dennis, Romeo Hugh
(Andrew Clarke) 411–12
Denny, William, Q.C. 362
Devlin, George 151
Devlin report 267
Dew, Chief Insp. 170, 243n
Dewsnap. Terry 380
Diamond, Bill 56
Diamond, Patrick 379
Dickenson, Reginald 232
Dickson, Scotch Jack 141
Dimes, 'Italian' Albert ('Big
Albert') 27, 36–7, 56–66,
68, 65–73, 98, 115, 119,
132, 148, 164, 204, 312,
330, 333–4, 349–50, 352,
429–30

Diplock, Mr Justice 83
Distleman, 'Big Hubby'
35–6
Distelman, Harry ('Little
Hubby', 'Scarface') 35
Divall, Chief Insp. Tom
21–3
Dixon family 171–2, 173,
178
Dixon, Alan 171, 174, 175
Dixon, Brian 173, 174
Dixon, George 141, 171–2,
174–5
Dodson, Sir Gerald 36–7,
203
Donaldson, Mr Justice 328
Donegan, Perry 421
Donnelly, Peter 274, 276–7,
278
Donoghue, Albert 70,
138–9, 152, 154, 156–7,
160, 165–7, 325, 328
Donoghue, Steve 20
Donovan, Mr Justice 65
Donovan, Terence 286
Dover Road Fighting
Gang x
Dower, Dai xv
Downer, Anthony 387–8
Downes, Terry 224
Driberg, Tom 158
Drury, Commander 214–16,
217, 218–19, 346
Dryden, Sir Noel 115, 117
Du Cann, Richard 126
Duddy, John 391
Dudley and Stephens

case 365
Dudley, Kathy 358–60
Dudley, Reginald 357–61
Dunlop, James 66
Dunn, Lennie 'Books' 159
Durand, Victor, Q.C. 262
Duval, Jack 108–15, 127, 220
Dyer, Frank 220

Earle, Peter 327
Easterbrook, Ronald 395
Ede, Chuter 197–8
Edgar, Coral (née Wilkins) 226
Edgeler, Keith 355, 356
Edgeler, Roy 355
Edwards, Det. Supt. Alec 384
Edwards, Buster 239, 246, 253–4, 327
Eist, Alec 271–2, 286
Elephant and Castle Boys (Gang) 18, 28, 31, 51, 65, 97
Ellis, Ruth 262n
Ellul, Philip 49–50, 221–2
Elmore, David 361–2
Elvey, Paul 164–5, 220n
Emmanuel, Edward 7, 19
Emmanuel, Philip 19
Evans, Beryl 200n
Evans, George (Jimmy) 327–8
Evans, Timothy 200n
Eve, Terence 366–7, 370, 371–2

Eveleigh, Mr Justice 262
Everett, Ronald James 327–8, 376
Exley, Billy 150, 162, 163, 165

Fabian, Robert xvi–xvii, 170, 191, 412n
Falco, Thomas ('Big Tommy') 66–7, 100, 132
Falzon, Albertine 212
Farrell, James 380
Fawcett family 177, 178
Fawcett, Frederick 175, 176–7
Fawcett, Micky 176, 179, 181
Fay, Stefan De 141–2
Fenwick, Det. Chief Insp. George 215n, 218
Ferguson, Dominique 220–21
Fernandez, James 429
Field, Brian 241, 248, 250, 252, 253, 353
Field, Lennie 250, 253
Fiori, Tony 286
Fish, Donald 233
Fisher, William 423
Flach, Robert 262
Fleming, John 379
Fletcher, Eddie (Eddie Fleicher, Joseph Franks) 34–6
Fletcher, Ronald Gordon 85
Flynn, Micky 172–3, 380,

395

Ford, John 86
Fordham, John 378, 396
Fordham, Peta 236–9, 241, 248n, 296
Fordham, Wilfrid, QC 237n
Foreman family 152, 296
Foreman, Freddie 140, 154, 160, 162, 165, 327–9, 376, 394, 426
Foreman, George 327
Fox, PC Geoffrey 391
France, Gilbert 148
Francis, George 394
Francis, Victor (Ivan Thomas) 411
Fraser family 97, 388
Fraser, David 420–21
Fraser, Eva *see* Brindle, Eva
Fraser, Francis 51, 55, 61–5, 67, 69, 76, 93, 98–100, 103, 112, 115–16, 118, 119–23, 124, 126–8, 131, 148, 152–4, 158, 226, 420–21, 422
Fraser, Francis Jnr 377n
Fraser, James 421
Frater, Mark 29
Fray, Stephen 411
Fredwin, Donald 129
French, Mr Justice 336
French family 97, 385
Frett, Richard ('Dicky Dido') 65
Fright, Frankie 357–8, 359
Fright, Ronnie 357–60
Frisby, Roger 347
Fryde, Manny 81, 89, 151,

166–7

Fuller, Jimmy 135
Fulton, Eustace 12

Gabaron, Juan (L'Espagnol) 190
Galea, Derek 210–11, 222
Gallant, James George 288–9
Galliers, Thomas ix–x
Gaming Act 1959 141, 311
Gaming Act 1960 430
Gardiner, Wilfred 86–7
Gardner, John xv
Garfath, Peter 'Pookey' 211, 216–17, 218
Garner, June 321
Garner, Roy (Dave Granger) 287–8, 320–22
Garvin, Sam 427
Gaul, Barbara 354–6, 430
Gaul, John 354–6, 430
Gaul, Samantha 354–5
Gaul, Simon 356
Gaynor, June *see* Humphreys, June
Gentry, Billy 255
Gerard, Alfie 160, 325–6, 327–9, 331–4, 336, 366, 386
Gerard, Linda 335
Gerard, Nicky 285, 329, 332, 334–5, 366
Gerrard, Det. Insp. Leonard 144, 148, 150
Gervaise, Michael 285–8, 396–7
Gibson, Gay 365

Gibson, Lennie 285–7
Giotti family 430
Gladstone Smith, Peter 430
Glander, Det. Supt.
  Stephen 307
Glinski, Christopher 59, 61,
  119
Gluckstead, Michael 335
Glyn-Jones, Mr Justice 58
Goddard, Lord Chief
  Justice 243n, 302, 341
Goddard, Sgt. George
  313–15
Gold, Beatrice 348–9
Goldstein, Morris ('Moisha
  Blue Boy') 61
Gooch Close Gang 413
Gooderham, Terry 425
Goodman, Arnold 144
Goodman, Jean 106, 109,
  125
Goodwin, John 396–7
Goodwin, Shirley 396,
  397–8
Goody, Gordon 239,
  240–41, 253–4
Gordon, Jeffrey 397
Gorman, Mr Justice 82–3
Grant, Neville Edmond
  August ('The
  Scorcher') 411
Gravell, John 269
Gray, Dolly 262–3
Great Bank Note Raid
  375–6
Great Mailbag
  Robbery 235–6

Great Train Robbery xvii,
  73, 90, 117, 118n, 156, 170,
  237–54, 260, 285, 326, 350–
  53, 375, 383, 384, 401, 420
Grech, Joseph 303–4
Green Gate Gang x
Green, Graeme 392
Greeno, Det. Chief Supt.
  Edward 15
Greenwood, Anthony 71
Gregory, Andrew 336
Gregory, Ernest 336
Groves, PC 264
Grunhut, Leo 381

Hackney Gang 28, 31
Hainnaux, George ('Jo le
  Terroir') 193
Hall, Roy 102, 103, 110,
  111, 114, 125, 127–8
Hannam, Det. Supt.
  Herbert 304–5, 306, 307
Hannigan, Harold 215n
Hanratty, James 89
Harding, Arthur xi, 6–10,
  12–13
Hargreaves, Mrs Nina
  251–2
Harris, David 316
Harris, Leopold 316, 317
Harris, Lucien 109–10,
  114–15, 118
Hart, Richard 120–23, 124,
  156
Hart, Ronnie 139, 140–41,
  153–4, 166
Harvey, Det. Sgt. John 393

Harvey, Det. Supt. 423
Haskell, Flora 243n
Haskell, Teddy 243n
Haward family xi, xiii, 97, 120–22
Haward, Billy 120, 121–2, 125
Haward, Flash Harry 120, 385
Hawkins, Mr Justice ix
Head, Det. Sgt. Christopher 391
Heibner, Errol 348, 349
Heilbron, Rose 58
Hemingway, Det. Sgt. Algy 256–7
Hemming, William 49, 90–91
Henderson, Scott 200
Hennessey family xiii, 97, 321, 385
Hennessey, Bernard 337, 385–6
Hennessey, Mickey 321, 325, 386
Hennessey, Peter 121–2, 337–8, 385–6
Herridge, Det. Supt. Roy 416
Hess, Kurt 282
Hickson, Billy 329–30, 376
Hilbery, Mr Justice 29
Hill, Maggie ('Baby Face, the Queen of Forty Elephants') 53
Hill, William xvi, 1, 22, 27, 28, 33, 44–7, 51–6, 61–4,

66–8, 69–70, 71, 72, 78, 82, 83, 93, 100, 103, 131, 138, 204, 230, 235–6, 300, 307–8, 426
Hilton, John 231, 381–2
Hindin, Hermione (Barbara) 199–200, 202
Hinds, Alfie 340–44, 347–8
Hiscock family 388
Hodge, Vicki 339
Hogg, Gloria 358
Holden, Ian 249
Hole, Tommy 265–6, 335–6
Holford, Christine 72
Holford, Harvey 72
Holt, Russell 182
Holy Smokes gang 414–15
Hosein brothers (Arthur, Nizamodeen) 179, 365, 396n
Household, Geoffrey 342
Howard, Commander Arthur 371
Hoxton Mob 8, 18, 28, 29, 31
Hubbard, Peter (King of the Dog Dopers) xv
Hughes, PC William 387–8
Humphreys, Christmas 301
Humphreys, James William 211–12, 213n, 214–19
Humphreys, June 'Rusty' 211–12, 214–17
Humphreys, Sir Travers 250, 253–4
Hussey, Jim 250, 253–4

Ibbotson, Barbara 81–2
Ince, George 261–4, 368n
Isaacs, Johnny 329–30
Ishmael, Michael 266, 268
Italian Gang (Mob) 34–6,
 57, 131

'Jack the Stripper'
 murders 326
Jacobs, Insp. Charles 304
Jacobs, Lambert 174
Jacobs, Phillip (Little
 Caesar) 172, 174
James, Arthur, QC 90
James, Roy 239–41, 253–4,
 350, 351, 353
James, Vicky (Blonde
 Vickey) 78
Jeffrey, Ronnie 122, 125
Jenkins, Thomas 354
Jewell, Stephen 340, 344–8
Joannides, Peter 116
Jockey Club 21, 23, 42
Johans, Mrs Augustine 202
Johnson, Harry 263
Johnson, James 394
Johnson, Ronnie 286
Jones, Billy 132, 136
Jones, Det. Supt.
 John 410n, 412
Jones, Judge Mervyn
 Griffiths 124
Jones, Reggie 103
Judd, Robert 328n

Kallman, Edna 203
Kauffman, Joey 165

Kay Wong 402–3
Keenan, Andrew 352
Kelaher, Victor 318–19
Kelland, Gilbert 217–18,
 333
Kelly, Peter 325, 334
Kempton, Freda 187–8
Kenrick, Michael 257
Kersey, Lenny 177
Khashoggi, Adnan 310
Khashoggi, Soraya 310
Kidwell, Frank 279
Kiki, Sid (Nathan
 Mercado) 349–50
Kilroy-Silk, Robert x
Kimber, William 15–17,
 19–21, 23, 29, 95
King, George 9, 12
King's Cross Gang 43, 65
Knight, David 329–30
Knight, James 376
Knight, Johnny 329–39,
 334, 376
Knight, Ronnie 284–5,
 329–34, 376, 394
Knowles, Roderic 431
Krays xvi, 32, 34, 52, 54–5,
 70, 72n, 73, 77, 78n, 89,
 102, 104, 110, 112, 120n,
 170–72, 183, 230, 257n,
 260, 298, 328, 345, 353,
 357, 367, 376, 388n, 394,
 421–2, 426, 427, 430
Kray, Charles 132–3, 165–7,
 262–3, 267, 345, 376
Kray, Charles Snr. 133
Kray, Dolly ('Dolly

Gray') 262–3
Kray, Frances (née Shea)
    151–2, 157
Kray, Reggie x, 82, 84, 94,
    131–67, 176n, 261, 263,
    329, 345
Kray, Ronnie 5, 32, 82, 84,
    94, 123, 131–67, 176n, 261,
    329, 345, 377n
Kray, Violet 133, 139

Lacroix, George Edward
    (Marcel Vernon) 192–3
La Grange, Jean 117, 119
Lambrianou brothers 160,
    162
Lambrianou, Tony 160–61,
    163, 353
Lambton, Anthony 354
Laming, James 423–4
Lane, John (John
    Gobba) 424
Lang, Fookie 403
Lang, Tanya 429
Lansky, Meyer 72–3, 430
Lashley, David 418–19
Latif, Parvez 382–3
Lawless, Terry 181
Lawson, Judge 289, 397
Lawton, Mr Justice
    Charles 89–90, 95, 127,
    226, 279
Leatherslade Farm 247–9,
    252, 326n
Lee, Supt. Bob 236
Leeson, Det. Sgt. B. 3
Legal & General

murders 356–7, 361
Legge, Det. Insp. 218–19
Lemmie, Paul 411
Leroy (Norman Smith) 411
Lewis, Abraham 352–3
Lewis, Dai 23
Li Kwok Bun 402–3
Li Mah 404–5
Lipton, Marcus 144
Lissack, Victor 166
Longman, Johnny 111, 114,
    124
'Looneys' 16
Lowe, Charlie 265, 281
Lucas-Tooth, Sir Hugh 307
Lundy, Det. Chief Insp.
    Tony 282, 284–8, 320–22,
    369–71, 297
'Lunies' 16
Lyell, Mr Justice 176
Lyon, Alex 319

McArthur, Gerald 118, 126,
    170, 243–5, 248
McAvoy, Michael 377–8
McCabe, John 281
McCowan, Hew 142,
    148–51
McDonald, Sean 398
MacKenny, Henry 366,
    368–73, 394, 426
McKay, Mrs 179n, 365
MacMillan, John 234
McNaughten, Mr Justice 36
McVicar, John 255, 280
McVitie, Jack 'the Hat' 99,
    160–63, 165, 166–7, 261,

325, 365

Machin, Judge Keith 322
Machin, Michael 177, 180
Machin, Teddy 132, 177, 234
Machin, Victor 181n
Maffia, Arthur 345, 347
Maffia, Tony ('The Magpie', 'The Fox') 340, 342, 344–8
Mafia 13, 73, 153, 331, 351, 416, 427, 430
Maguire, John 84
Mah, Li 404–5
Mahon, Supt. 200–201
Maile, Johnnie (Johnny the Flower) 128n
Mancini, Antonio 'Baby Face' 20, 34–7, 330
Mangion, Anthony 205
Manito, Bobby 133
Manning, Eddie 187n, 188–9
Manson, WPC Elaine 182
Mark, Commissioner Sir Robert 171
Marks, Anne 328n
Marks, Ginger 248n, 326–8, 349, 365
Marks, Philip 328n
Marrinan, Patrick 64, 65, 307–8
Marsh, Bert (Pasqualino Papa) 26–7, 57, 73–4, 204, 429–30
Marshall, Jim 273, 275, 282
Martin, Josephine (French Fifi) 192
Martin, Terry 136
Marwood, Ronald 78, 137
Mason, Eric 140–41
Mason, Jeff 215
Mason, John 215, 217–18
Mason, John James 376
Masters, Doreen 79, 81, 82
Masterson, John 421
Maud, Judge 212–13
Maxwell, David 362–3
Maxwell, Mickey 362
Maxwell, Robert 386
May, Mr Justice 371
Maynard, Bobby ('Fat Bob') 357–61
Maynard, Bobby (Junior) 361
Meason, Donald 181
Meiklejohn, Insp. 313
Mella, Tony xv, 47, 204, 363–5, 429–30
Melvin, Big Alf 364–5
Mendez, Steven 411
Mercado, Nathan see Kiki, Sid
Messina brothers 45, 48, 195–204, 212, 303, 304, 311
Messina, Alfredo 194, 199–201, 203
Messina, Attilio (Raymond Maynard) 194, 199, 201, 203
Messina, Carmelo (Carlos Marino) 194, 198–9, 202–4
Messina, Eugenio 194–203

Messina, Guiseppe 194
Messina, Salvatore 194, 199, 203
Messina, Virginia 194
Meyrick, Kate (Queen of the Night Clubs) 314–15
Micallef, Irene 213n
Micallef, Tony 205, 304
Micallef, Victor 205, 213n
Micheletti, Casimir (the Assassin) 189–93
Michell, Robert 182
Miesel, George 349
Mifsud, 'Big Frank' 204–5, 210–11, 214, 219, 221–3
Miles, Michelle 416
Millen, Commander Ernie 148, 251
Miller, Sir Eric 430
Mills, Freddie 326n
Mills, Jack 242, 247
Millwood, Hubbert 411
Milmo, Mr Justice 368n
Mitchell, Frank ('Mad Axe-Man') 154, 157–60, 166–7, 328–9, 365
Mitchell, Peter 298
Miyakawa, Sess 189
Monte Columbo, Massimino 25–6
Monte Columbo, Nestor 26
Moody, Det. Chief Supt. 214, 217–18, 318
Moody, Jimmy 121, 122–3, 125
Mooney, George 427
Mooney, Det. Chief Insp.

Harry 170
Moriarty, John 288, 358, 423
Morland, Francis 181n
Morris, Peter 373
Morris, Philip 279
Morrison, DC Jim 259
Morrison, Steinie 1, 170, 232
Morton-Thurtle, Paul 368, 371
Moseley, Billy 357–8, 359–60
Moses, Max (Kid McCoy) 4
Mosley, Oswald 38–9
Mottram, Brian 101, 108, 112, 125, 127, 154
Mountbatten Report 254
Mountain Bike Gang 413
Murray, Courtney 411
Mussies, The 85

Narborough, Supt. Fred 53
Napoletano, Jimmy 32
Nash family 76–8, 82, 84, 135, 137–8, 140, 152, 161, 169, 215
Nash, Billy 77, 82–3, 115
Nash, George 77
Nash, Jimmy ('Trunky') 77, 79–81, 82–3
Nash, Johnny 77–8, 102, 105, 140, 161
Nash, Ronnie 77, 78–9
Nash, Roy 77
National Council for Civil Liberties 88, 126

National Hunt
  Committee 42, 71
Natrass, Mark 373
Naylor, Stanley 177–8, 180
Neal, Kenneth 421
Neil, Andrew 226
'Newcastle Fred' 40
Newton, Arthur 301
Nicholls family 175–9
Nicholls, Albert 175–8
Nicholls, Terence 177–8
Nicholson, Major
  Herbert 117
Nielson, Donald 396
Norris, Dave 290, 420
Nott-Bower, Sir John 304,
  306
Noye, Kenneth 378–9

O'Connell, Jacky 277
O'Connor, Mr Justice 174–5
Odessians 3–5
Oliva, Joseph Francis 74–6,
  86–7
O'Mahoney, Bernard 421
O'Mahoney, Maurice (King
  Squealer) xi, 280–82, 321n
O'Neil, Sean 385
O'Nione, Patrick ('Paddy
  Onions') 336–8
Onufrejczyk, case of 365
Operation Carter 288
Operation Countryman 319
Operation Wrecker 392
Operation Yamato 387
Opiola, Allen 375–6
Oreman, Samuel 4

Orsler, Brenda 266n
Osbourne, Colin
  'Duke' 145–6, 230, 394
O'Sullivan, Tim 43

Page, Morris 303–4
Palmer, John 379
Parkhurst Prison Riot
  (1969) 99, 100n, 128
Parsons, Debbie Lee 423
Patience, Beverley 261–2
Patience, Bob 261, 366
Patience, Muriel 261, 263
Patriarco, Raymond 164
Paul, Philip 372
Payne, Leslie 142, 149, 158,
  162–3
Payne, Nicholas 380, 395
Pearson, John 55, 131, 142,
  144
Pedrini, Riccardo 86, 90
Pelly, Roland 284
Penrose, Commander
  Roy 410–11
Pepperhill Mob 413
Perkoff (Bessarabian) 4
Peters, Det. Chief Insp.
  Bill 286, 424
Phillips, Ann 350–51
Piggott, Maxwell Thomas
  (George Bradshaw)
  284–5, 331–4
Pilch, Angela 354
Pinfold, Terence 366,
  370–71
Pitts family 397
Pitts, Charles 398

Police & Criminal Evidence
 Act 1984   359n, 361
Pollard, Gary   182
Pook, Sgt.   377
Porritt family   95–7, 385
Porritt, George   95–6
Posses   407; The Shower
 410; Rankers (New York)
 411; Spangler (Jamaica)
 429
Powell, Dennis   363
Powis, Asst. Commissioner
 David 'Crazy Horse'   289
Prater, Frank   118–19, 126
Price, Walter   283
Prison Officers
 Association   99
Priston, Avril   256, 257–8
Pritchard, Jack   244
Pritchett, Oliver   181
Proetta, Carmen   226
Profumo, John   354

Racecourse Bookmakers &
 Backers Protection
 Association   18–19
Rachman, Peter   138, 141
Raft, George   431
Ramm, Det. Chief Supt.
 Roy   227, 322
Ramsey, Bobby   132, 135–6,
 150
Rasini, Peter   424
Rawlins, Henry
 (Harry)   122–3, 125
Ray, Maurice   249
Read, Leonard 'Nipper'   52,
 70, 93–4, 144–50, 152–3,
 156, 162–6, 169, 206,
 209–10, 235, 241–2, 244–7,
 250, 253, 318, 326n,
 349–50, 353, 428, 430
Reader, Brian   378–9, 396–7
Reader, David   362–3
Reader, Ronnie   362–3
Redden family   385
Redskins   15
Reece, Daniel   418–19
Reed, John   298
Reeder, Robert   350
Rees, Geraint   309–10
Refreshment Houses Act
 1964   206
Reid, Major Pat   342
Relton, Michael   310–11
Reubens, Marks   231–2
Reubens, Morris   231–2
Reynolds, Bruce   237–8,
 240, 246, 247, 253
Rice, Johnny   66
Richardsons   xiii, xvi, 59, 77,
 95, 98, 104–5, 123, 127,
 140, 152–4, 155, 158,
 170–71, 172, 176n, 309,
 328, 357, 422, 430
Richardson, Alan   100
Richardson, Charles   xvii,
 95, 98, 100–120, 124–8,
 153, 297–8
Richardson, Eddie   xi, 101,
 105, 106, 108–10, 115–17,
 120–23, 124, 127, 128, 153,
 426
Richardson, Fay (The Black

Widow) (later Sadler) 48–9, 79, 80–82, 84, 90, 103, 221, 417, 419
Richardson, Supt. Gerald 215, 391–2
Rillington Place enquiry 200
Ritchie, John 65, 99
Roberts, Alan 381
Roberts, G. D. 'Khaki' 58
Roberts, Harry 391
Robertson, Det. Sgt. 303
Robey, Edward 89
Robey, Sir George 89
Robinson, Brian 377–8
Robinson, Stella 274, 276
Robson, Det. Insp. Bernard 317
Roff brothers 105
Rogers, Bertie 'Bandy' xiii
Rooum, Donald 88–9, 91
Roper, William xiii
Rosa family 103–4
Rosa, David 65
Rosa, Jackie 27, 51, 103
Rosa, Ray 123
Rosato, Captain Francisco 331
Rose, James 384
Rose, John du (Four Day Johnny) 89–90, 164, 326n
Ross, Kenny 288
Rossi, Robert 'Battles' 65–6, 99, 348–9
Rubin, Eric 382–3
Russo, Victor ('Scarface Jock') 66–7

Sabinis (the Italian Mob) xv, 7, 13–32, 33–4, 37, 41, 43, 104–5, 193–4, 430
Sabini, Darby (Charles) 13–24, 30–32, 194, 426
Sabini, Fred 13
Sabini, George 13, 31
Sabini, Harryboy 13, 24, 31
Sabini, Johnny 32
Sabini, Joseph 13, 31
Sadler, Fay *see* Richardson, Fay
Saggs, Colin 358–9
Saggs, Sharon 358
Salih, Ygar 416
Salmon, Frank 181–2
Samson, John 328n
Samuel, Darren 413
Saunders, Arthur John 260n
Saward, James Townsend (Jem the Penman) 300, 301
Sayer, Ettie 185
Saxe, Clifford 376
Schack, Bernard ('Sonny the Yank') 61
Scott, John 179–80
Seamarks, Pamela 382
Seaton, Reginald 57–8
Setty, Stanley 199n
Sewell, Freddie 215, 391–2
Sewell, Micky 285, 286
Shaer, Josephine 126
Sharman, Charles 301–2
Sharpe, Chief Insp. 'Nutty' 192

Shepherd, Janie 418
Sherbourne, Monty 174
Sheridan, April 416
Sherrard, Michael 89
Sherwood, Frederick 368, 371
Shing May Wong 403–5
Sillitoe, Sir Percy 427
Silva, Charles de 72
Silver, Bernie 140, 204–5, 210, 212, 213n, 214, 219–21, 222–3, 349
Simon, PC Peter 390–91
Simons, Johnny 80, 81–4
Simpson, Ron 284
Simpson, Sir Joseph 142–3
Sinclair, Det. Insp. Peter 234
Sinfield, Freddie 288
Skelhorne, Sir Norman, D.P.P. 279
Slipper, Jack 278, 281–2, 321n
Smalls, Derek Creighton (Bertie) 229, 255, 260n, 272–82, 290
Smalls, Diane 273, 274, 276, 278–9
Smith family 385
Smith, David 282–4
Smith, Edward ('Witch Doctor') xiii
Smith, John 'Half Hanged' 272n
Smith, Mad 'Scouse' Alan 422
Smith, Paul 416

Smith, Roy (Fuzzy Kaye) 364
Smithson, Fay *See* Richardson, Fay
Smithson, Tommy (Mr Loser, Scarface) 46–51, 79, 204, 220, 221–2
Smithyman, Mick 416
Smythe, Clifford 126
Solomons, Arthur 29
South-Western Gang 236
Spampinato, Victor 221–2
Sparks, Chief Supt. Herbert 340, 343
Spencer, Derek 322
Spencer, Edward ('the Count') 6
Spencer, Paul 384
Spot, Jack ('Benny the Kid' etc.) xv–xvi, 14, 28–30, 33, 37–47, 51–68, 69–70, 73, 74, 99–100, 112, 131–2, 138, 146, 153, 177n, 199, 204, 300, 307–8, 348
Stagg, Det. Chief Supt. 319
Starkey, Greville 424
Stayton, Billy 125, 330
Steggles, Peter 275
Stevenson, Mr Justice Melford 215n, 261–2
Stocker, Harold 210, 222
Street Bookmakers' Federation 97
Streeter family 135–6
Street Offences Act 1959 77
Stringer, Bernard 173
Strutton Ground Mob 5

Sullivan, Frederick 'Slip' 47, 235
Sutcliffe, Judge Edward 266n
Swanwick, Mr Justice 360
Symonds, Det. Sgt. John 317
Syndicate, The 205, 219–21, 223

Taggart, James 118
Tedeschi, Augustus 330
Teresa, Vincent 164
Thompson, Arthur x
Thompson, Leonard 367, 371
Thorogood, Brian 417–18
Thorp, Det. Insp. Arthur 35
Tibbs family 175–81, 367
Tibbs, Georgie 'Bogie' 175
Tibbs, George 176
Tibbs, James (senior) 175–6, 180–81
Tibbs, Jimmy 175, 178, 180–81
Tibbs, Johnny 176
Tibbs, Robert 176, 181
Titanic Mob 7–8
Tobin family 385
Tobin, Billy 269–70, 298, 417
Tooti Nung gang 414–15
Torrance, Rabina Dickson 198–9, 201, 203
Treen, Insp. 370–71
Trenchard, Sir Hugh 315–16
Tresidern (Harding) Gang 10–11
Triads 401–7; 320: 14K 402–3, 405–6; San Yee On 405; Sui Fong 406; Wo On Lok 405; Wo Sing Wo 405–6
Tudor Price, Dai (later Justice) 72, 178

Upton Park Mob 177n

Vassallo, Carmela 196–7
Vaughan, John 30
Vaughan, Paul (Ellis) 5
Vaughan, Sydney 150–51
Vendetta Mob 6–7, 8, 9, 13, 20
Venton, James 335
Vibart, Peter 250
Viccei, Valerio 382–3
Virgo, Commander Wally 214, 217–18, 319
Virgo, Leon (Kenneth Smith/ Barnard) 319
Von Lamm, Herman K. 236

Waddell, Bill 414
Waddington, James ('Jimmy the Wad') 361–3
Waddington, Winifred 363
Wajcenburg, Benny 109–11
Waldeck, Thomas 117–18, 119
Waldron, Commissioner Sir John 171
Walker, Charlie ('One-Eyed Charlie') 6

Walker, Billy 56
Walker, George 56
Walker, William 421
Ward, Buller xv, 345n, 365
Wardle, Donald 352
Warren, Frank 61
Warren, Robert 61–2, 64, 67, 70
Waterman, Francis Square 'Split' 256–8
Waterman, Harry 112
Watkins, Lennie ('Teddy Bear') 392–4
Watney Street Mob 112, 135–6, 152
Watts, Arthur 195
Watts, Ernest 236–8
Watts, Marthe 194–7, 198–9, 200, 202
Webb, Duncan xvi, 53–4, 56, 66, 199
Webb, Lionel 424
Wein, Emmanuel 311
Weinstein (Kikal) 3–4
Welch, Bob 253, 254
Wensley, Frederick 1–3, 9, 12–13, 170, 232
West End Boys 28
West, Sister Joan 266n
Wheater, John 241, 252, 253
Wheatley, Carol 425
White, Jimmy 239, 253, 254
Whitehead, Connie 172
White family (Kings Cross Gang) 25, 28, 29–31, 33–4, 42–4, 105, 138, 388

White, Alf 30, 41–2
White, Harry 41–4, 64–5, 66, 71
White, Tony 377–8, 419
White Slave Trade 185–7, 192–4
Whiting, Nick 379–80
Whitlock, Derek 380
Whitnall, Charles 'Waggy' 350, 352
Whittle, Lesley 396n
Wicks, Jim 26
Wickstead, Commander Bert (Gangbuster, Grey Fox) 48–9, 79, 81, 83, 171–9, 219–23, 235, 260n, 335, 356, 359, 367
Wild Bunch 338
Wilding, Insp. Victor 274–5
Wilkins, Bert 26–7, 429
Wilkins, Joe 223–6, 380, 429
Wilkins, Pearl 225, 226
Williams, Alvan 339
Williams, Billy 336
Williams, Frederick x
Williams, George ('Fat George') 283
Williams, Leroy 281
Williams, Michael St George 409
Williams, Sidney 65
Williamson, Frank (H.M. Inspector of Constabulary for Crime) 317–18
Williamson, Kate 416
Wilson, Brian 362
Wilson, Charlie 117, 238–9,

240–41, 253, 383–4, 426
Wilson, Patricia 383
Wilson, Phil 111, 112–13
Windsor, Barbara 329, 332, 334, 376
Wisbey, Tommy 250, 253, 420
Witney, John 391
Wombwell, DC David 291
Wong Pun Hai 402
Woods, Phoebe 150
Wooler, Stephen 377n
Wright, Sally 198–9
Wyatt (Lewis), Tony 179–80
Wymer, Major 23

Yakuza organisation (Japan) 432
Yardies 401, 407–14, 432; 'Big Man' 409
Yeow, Molly 405
Yiddishers 23–4, 34, 35–6
Young, Billy 286, 288, 319
Young, Michael 173–4

Zomparelli, Alfredo 330–31, 349, 394
Zomparelli, Tony 329, 333–4, 349, 376, 394
Zomparelli, Tony Alberto 333–4

NIPPER

Leonard Read with *James Morton*

Just after 7 pm on the evening of Tuesday 4 March 1969, at the Old Bailey, the jurors filed back into Court 1 to give their verdict on Ronald Kray. The word 'guilty' brought to a triumphant conclusion the months of painstaking work put in by Read and his team in their efforts to bring the infamous Kray brothers to justice.

Now for the first time Leonard Read tells his own story, that of the small Nottingham lad, nicknamed Nipper, who went to join the Metropolitan Police because of their less stringent height requirements – and who rose through the ranks to become part of the team solving the Great Train Robbery.

In 1964 Read was invited to put together a team to 'have a go' at the Kray gang – the seemingly untouchable East End criminals whose reign of terror involved blackmail, protection rackets and finally murder. In an enthralling recreation of the operation, Read and Morton cover the case from the first time Nipper saw Ronald Kray in a pub in the Whitechapel Road – where he turned up flanked by minders – to the brothers' eventual arrest in May 1968 and the nailbiting suspense of their sensational trial.

'A tasty dish . . . a tribute to the author's frankness and his co-author's skill'
Independent

'Vividly described'
Daily Telegraph

BENT COPPERS

James Morton

Since the days of the Bow Street Runners, allegations of brutality, bribery and underhand dealing among police officers have been a constant reminder that criminal activity is not restricted to the criminal fraternity. Given their positions of power, and the diversity inherent in human nature, it is perhaps inevitable that there should be occasions when policemen and women are themselves guilty of the very offences they are trying to prevent.

Bent Coppers is the first study of police corruption in all its forms in the United Kingdom. The author traces the history of criminal activity within the force from its earliest days, thoroughly documenting such cases as the sergeant who ran a string of brothels in Manchester and the infamous Soho porn scandal of the early 1970s, which led to the conviction of several senior officers.

Shocking in its scope and thought-provoking in its implications, *Bent Coppers* offers a sobering antidote to the myth of the guileless British bobby, and an essential insight into some of the problems, both actual and potential, faced by our police force today.

MOBSTER

John Cummings & Ernest Volkman

John Gotti is the man who currently heads the largest
and most powerful criminal organization in the world, the
Gambino branch of the American Mafia. MOBSTER is
his story: the story of a one-time low-level hood who now
controls a Mafia empire worth five billion dollars a year.

In this chilling exposé, MOBSTER probes the real world
of the Mafia: its unique lifestyle, its rigid but unwritten
code of behaviour, the world of Mafia wives and
mistresses, how 'organized' crime is organized – and the
curious relationship between the Mafiosi and the FBI
agents out to destroy them. MOBSTER also examines the
dramatic courtroom battles that have marked Gotti's
criminal career.

Drawing on wiretap records and sources on both sides of
the law, MOBSTER is the fullest portrait we are ever
likely to encounter of John Gotti and his gang.

'Must reading for anyone who wants to understand La
Cosa Nostra'
Publishers Weekly

Other bestselling Warner titles available by mail: